T0335706

SELF-ADAPTIVE SYSTEMS FOR MACHINE INTELLIGENCE

SELF-ADAPTIVE SYSTEMS FOR MACHINE INTELLIGENCE

Haibo He

A JOHN WILEY & SONS, INC., PUBLICATION

Published by John Wiley & Sons, Inc., Hoboken, New Jersey.
Published simultaneously in Canada

Library of Congress Cataloging-in-Publication Data:

He, Haibo, 1976–
Self-adaptive systems for machine intelligence / Haibo He.
p. cm.
Includes bibliographical references and index.
ISBN 978-0-470-34396-8 (hardback)
1. Machine learning. 2. Self-organizing systems. 3. Artificial intelligence. I. Title.
Q325.5.H425 2011
006.3′1–dc22

2010046375

Printed in Singapore

10 9 8 7 6 5 4 3 2 1

CONTENTS

PREFACE

The understanding of natural intelligence and developing self-adaptive systems to potentially replicate such a level of intelligence is still one of the greatest unsolved scientific and engineering challenges. With the recent development of brain research and modern technologies, scientists and engineers will hopefully find solutions to develop general-purpose brain-like intelligent systems that are highly robust, adaptive, scalable, and fault tolerant. Yet, there is still a long way to go to achieve this goal. The biggest challenge is how to understand the fundamental principles and develop integrated complex systems to potentially capture those capabilities and eventually bring such a level of intelligence closer to reality.

The goal of this book is to advance the understanding and development of self-adaptive systems for machine intelligence research, and to present the models and architectures that can adaptively learn information, accumulate knowledge over time, and adjust actions to achieve goals. Machine intelligence research draws on theories and concepts from many disciplines, including neuroscience, artificial intelligence, cognitive science, computational theory, statistics, computer science, engineering design, and many others. Because of the inherent cross-disciplinary nature of the research on this topic, most of the materials presented in this book are motivated by the latest research developments across different fields. I hope the research results presented in this book can provide useful and important insights to understand the essential problems of machine intelligence research, and provide new techniques and solutions across a wide range of application domains.

Recent research results have provided strong evidence that brain-like intelligence is very different when compared to traditional artificial intelligence. For instance, although today's computers can solve very complicated mathematical problems, predict large-scale weather changes, and even win the world chess championship, they use fundamentally different ways of information processing as in the biological brain organism. To this end, this book focuses on the computational foundations and methodologies of machine intelligence toward the "computational thinking" capability for self-adaptive intelligent systems design. Therefore, the research results presented in this book can naturally be grounded as two major parts: *data-driven approaches* and *biologically inspired approaches*.

The data-driven approaches aim to understand how to design self-adaptive systems that can autonomously learn from vast amounts of raw data for information and knowledge representation to support the decision-making processes within uncertain and unstructured environments, and the biologically inspired approaches target to understand the principles of information processing, association, optimization, and prediction within distributed hierarchical neural network structures. All of these are essential capabilities and characteristics to achieve the general-purpose brain-like machine intelligence in the future. In the last chapter of this book, I also provide a comment about the hardware design for machine intelligence research, which could provide useful suggestions about how to build complex and integrated intelligent systems in massive, parallel, and scalable hardware platforms, such as the dedicated very large scale integration (VLSI) systems and reconfigurable field-programmable gate array (FPGA) technology. Emerging technologies such as memristor are also briefly discussed in the last chapter since such technologies might provide us significant new capabilities to mimic the complexity level of neural structures in the human brain. Furthermore, in order to highlight the wide applications of machine intelligence research, at the end of each chapter, I provide a case study to demonstrate the effectiveness of the proposed method across different domains. These examples should provide useful suggestions about the practical applications of the proposed methods.

This book consists of four major sections, organized as follows:

1. Section 1 (Chapter 1) gives a brief introduction of the self-adaptive systems for machine intelligence research. The research significances and the major differences between traditional computation and brain-like intelligence are presented. A brief review of the book organization and suggested usage is also given in this chapter.
2. Section 2 (Chapters 2, 3, and 4) presents the data-driven approaches for machine intelligence research. The focus is to develop adaptive learning methods to transform a large volume of raw data into knowledge and information representation to support the decision-making processes with uncertainty. Specifically, incremental learning, imbalanced learning, and ensemble learning are presented in this section.
3. Section 3 (Chapters 5, 6, and 7) focuses on biologically inspired machine intelligence research. The goal here is to understand the fundamental principles of neural information processing and develop learning, memory, optimization, and prediction architectures to potentially mimic certain levels of such intelligence. Specifically, adaptive dynamic programming (ADP), associative learning, and sequence learning are discussed in detail.
4. Section 4 (Chapter 8) provides a brief discussion regarding the hardware design for machine intelligence. The goal is to provide some suggestions about the critical design considerations, such as power consumption, design density, and memory and speed requirements, to potentially build such complex and integrated system into real hardware.

This book is intended for researchers and practitioners in academia and industry who are interested in machine intelligence research and adaptive systems development. The presented learning principles, architectures, algorithms, and case studies will hopefully not only bring the community new insights of machine intelligence research, but it will also provide potential techniques and solutions to bring such a level of capability closer to reality across a wide range of application domains. Furthermore, all the issues discussed in this book are active research topics and present significant challenges to the research community, making this book a valuable resource for graduate students to motivate their own research projects toward their Ph.D. or master-level research. Finally, as machine intelligence research is continuing to attract more and more attention across different disciplines, I also hope this book will provide interesting ideas and suggestions to stimulate undergraduate students and young researchers with a keen interest in science and technology into this exciting and rewarding field; their participation will be critical for the long-term development of a healthy and promising research community.

ACKNOWLEDGMENTS

I am deeply indebted to many colleagues, friends, reviewers, and students who have greatly helped the research development in this field as well the writing of this book.

I am very grateful to my colleagues and friends at the University of Rhode Island (URI) and Stevens Institute of Technology (SIT) for their tremendous support in the development stage of this book. At the URI, many colleagues in the Department of Electrical, Computer, and Biomedical Engineering (ECBE) and the College of Engineering (COE) have provided enormous support in different forms, and I am especially grateful to G. Faye Boudreaux-Bartels, Raymond Wright, Qing (Ken) Yang, Yan (Lindsay) Sun, He (Helen) Huang, Steven M. Kay, Godi Fischer, Leland B. Jackson, Walter G. Besio, Peter F. Swaszek, Frederick J. Vetter, Resit Sendag, Richard J. Vaccaro, Ying Sun, Harish Sunak, Ramdas Kumaresan, Jien-Chung Lo, William J. Ohley, Shmuel Mardix, and Augustus K. Uht for their support for my research and educational development in this area. At Stevens, many friends and colleagues in the Department of Electrical and Computer Engineering (ECE) and Schaefer School of Engineering & Science have provided enormous support for my research development. I am particularly grateful to Joseph Mitola III, Yu-Dong Yao, George Korfiatis, Michael Bruno, Stuart Tewksbury, Victor Lawrence, Yi Guo, Rajarathnam Chandramouli, Koduvayur Subbalakshmi, Harry Heffes, Hong Man, Hongbin Li, Jennifer Chen, Yan Meng, Cristina Comaniciu, and Bruce McNair for their great support for my research development in this field.

I am also deeply indebted to many students and visiting scholars that I have worked with over all these years. Particularly, I would like to thank Sheng Chen, Yuan Cao, Bo Liu, Qiao Cai, Jin Xu, Jie Li, Jian Fu, Jianlong Qiu, Yi Cao, Zhen Ni, Hao Peng, Edwardo A. Garcia, Xiaochen Li, and Yang Bai for their valuable discussions, comments, and proof-reading of the materials presented in this book. Meanwhile, I would also like to thank the students in several classes that I taught regularly, especially the ELE 594: Computational Intelligence and Adaptive Systems and CpE/EE 695: Applied Machine Learning courses, for their helpful suggestions and discussions for the contents related to this book. Although there is no space to mention all their names, this book could not have been written without their help.

Many friends from other universities, research laboratories, and industrial partners have also provided great support for my research development as well as the writing of this book. Particularly, I would like to express my deep gratitude to

Janusz A. Starzyk for his always great support and help for my research development; many materials presented in this book are inspired by many discussions and joint research efforts. I am also very grateful to Xiaoping Shen for her strong support from mathematical aspect for the machine intelligence research. Furthermore, Venkataraman Swaminathan, Sachi Desai, Shafik Quoraishee, David Grasing, Paul Willson, and many other members at the U. S. Army, Armament Research, Development and Engineering Center (ARDEC), have also provided great support including practical application case studies, real-world data sets, and technical discussions for several research projects over the past several years. I would also like to take this opportunity to thank Charles Clancy, Tim O'Shea, Ray Camisa, and Jeffrey Spinnanger for many stimulating technical discussions at various meetings and their great support for my research development in this field.

I would also like to thank many international experts and scientists who took their precious time to review the materials and provide suggestions for this book. While there is no space to mention all their names, I am particularly grateful to the following experts for their great support: Derong Liu, Jennie Si, Jun Wang, Gary Yen, Robert Kozma, Donald C. Wunsch II, Danil Prokhorov, Marios M. Polycarpou, Mengchu Zhou, Shiejie Cheng, Ping Li, Yaochu Jin, Kang Li, Daniel W Repperger, Wen Yu, Anwar Walid, Tin Kam Ho, Zeng-Guang Hou, Fuchun Sun, Changyin Sun, Robi Polikar, Jinyu Wen, Tiejian Luo, Ying Tan, Xin Xu, Shutao Li, Zhigang Zeng, and many others. Their expertise greatly helped my research development in this area.

I am also very grateful to the support from the U.S. National Science Foundation (NSF) (under grant CAREER ECCS # 1053717), DARPA, and Army ARDEC for their tremendous support for my research development all these years. Their great support has provided me the opportunity to explore all the challenging and exciting research topics in this field.

John Wiley & Sons has provided outstanding support throughout the development stages of this book. I particularly would like to take this opportunity to thank George J. Telecki and Lucy Hitz for their support, valuable suggestions, and encouragement. Without their dedicated help, the writing and production of this book would have taken much longer.

Finally, I would like to extend my deepest gratitude to my family, particularly my wife Yinjiao, for their strong support along the way. I would also like to devote this book to my lovely little one, Eric.

HAIBO HE

CHAPTER 1

Introduction

1.1 THE MACHINE INTELLIGENCE RESEARCH

As the understanding of brain-like intelligence and developing self-adaptive systems to potentially replicate certain levels of natural intelligence remains one of the greatest unsolved scientific and engineering challenges, the brain itself provides strong evidence of learning, memory, prediction, and optimization capabilities within uncertain and unstructured environments to accomplish goals. Although the recent discoveries from neuroscience research have provided many critical insights about the fundamental mechanisms of brain intelligence, and the latest technology developments have enabled the possibility of building complex intelligent systems, there is still no clear picture about how to design truly general-purpose intelligent machines to mimic such a level of intelligence (Werbos, 2004, 2009; Brooks, 1991; Hawkins & Blakeslee, 2004, 2007; Grossberg, 1988; Sutton & Barto, 1998). The challenges of accomplishing this long-term objective arise from many disciplines of science and engineering research, including, but not limited to:

- Understanding the fundamental principles and mechanisms of neural information processing in the biological brain organism.
- Advancement of principled methodologies of learning, memory, prediction, and optimization for general-purpose machine intelligence.
- Development of adaptive models and architectures to transform vast amounts of raw data into knowledge and information representation to support decision-making processes with uncertainty.
- Embodiment of machine intelligence hardware within systems that learn through interaction with the environment for goal-oriented behaviors.
- Design of robust, scalable, and fault-tolerant systems with massively parallel processing hardware for complex, integrated, and networked systems.

To find potential solutions to address all of these challenges, extensive efforts have been devoted to this field from many disciplines, including neuroscience, artificial

Self-Adaptive Systems for Machine Intelligence, First Edition. Haibo He.

intelligence, cognitive science, computational theory, statistics, computer science, and engineering design, among others. For instance, artificial neural networks have played an important role in the efforts of modeling functions of brain-like learning (Grossberg, 1988). Backpropagation theory has provided a powerful methodology for building intelligent systems and has demonstrated great success across many domains, including pattern recognition, adaptive control and modeling, and sensitivity analysis, among others (Werbos, 1988a, 1988b, 1990, 2005). There are many other representative works in this field as well, including the memory-prediction theory (Hawkins & Blakeslee, 2004, 2007), reinforcement learning (RL) (Sutton & Barto, 1998), embodied intelligence (Brooks, 1991, 2002), adaptive dynamic programming (ADP) (Werbos, 1997, 1998, 2004, 2009; Si, Barto, Powell, & Wunsch, 2004; Powell, 2007), the "new artificial intelligence" theory (Pfeifer & Scheier, 1999), and others. For instance, recently, a new theoretical framework based on hierarchical memory organization was proposed for designing intelligent machines (Hawkins & Blakeslee, 2004, 2007). This theoretical framework provides potential new solutions for how to understand memory and the prediction mechanism based on the neocortex. Because biological intelligent systems can learn through active interaction with the external environment, reinforcement learning has attracted much attention in the community and demonstrated great success in a wide range of applications (Sutton & Barto, 1998). The key idea of reinforcement learning is to learn how to map situations to actions to maximize the expected reward signal. One of the essential aspects of reinforcement learning is the value function, which specifies "good" from "bad" to guide the goal-oriented behaviors of the intelligent system. For instance, in biological systems, it could be a way of measuring happiness or pain (Starzyk, Liu, & He, 2006). The ideas for embodied intelligence originate from the observation that biological intelligent systems have biological bodies and are situated in a set of realistic environments (Brooks, 1991, 2002). The major research efforts for embodied intelligence are focused on understanding biological intelligent systems, discovering fundamental principles for intelligent behavior, and designing real intelligent systems, including living machines and humanoid robotics. Recently, it is recognized that *optimization* and *prediction* play a critical role to bring the brain-like general-purpose intelligence closer to reality (Werbos, 2009). For instance, the recently launched Cognitive Optimization and Prediction (COPN) program from the National Science Foundation (NSF) is a good indication to raise the attention to this critical area by bringing cross-disciplinary teams together to address the essential question of how the brain learns to solve complex optimization and resilient control problems (NSF, 2007). While optimization has a long-standing research foundation in control theory, decision theory, risk analysis, and many other fields, it has specific meanings in terms of machine intelligence research: learning to make better choices to maximize some kind of utility function over time to achieve goals. Extensive research efforts have suggested that ADP is the core methodology, or "the only general-purpose way to learn to approximate the optimal strategy of action in the general case" (Werbos, 2004, 2009). Of course, I would also like to note that many of the aforementioned fields are strongly connected with each other. For instance, ADP/RL approaches can be "embodied" (e.g., coupled with sensory-motor coordination with active interaction with the external environment) or built in a hierarchical way for effective goal-oriented multistage learning, prediction, and optimization (Werbos, 2009).

From the practical application point of view, recent technology developments have enabled the growth and availability of raw data to occur at an explosive rate, such as sensor networks, security and defense applications, Internet, geographic information systems, transportation systems, weather prediction, biomedical industry, and financial engineering, to name a few. In many of such applications, the challenge is not the lack of the availability of raw data. Instead, information processing is failing to keep pace with the explosive increase of the collected raw data to transform them to a usable form. Therefore, this has created immense opportunities as well as challenges for the machine intelligence community to develop self-adaptive systems to process such vast amounts of raw data for information representation and knowledge accumulation to support the decision-making processes.

To this end, this book focuses on the computational foundations of machine intelligence research toward the "computational thinking" (Wing, 2006) capability for self-adaptive intelligent systems design. For instance, although the traditional artificial intelligence methods have made significant progresses and demonstrated great success across different specific application tasks, many such techniques lack the robustness, scalability, and adaptability across different knowledge domains. On the other hand, biological intelligent systems are able to adaptively learn and accumulate knowledge for goal-oriented behaviors. For instance, although today's computers can solve very complicated problems, they use fundamentally different ways of information processing than does the human brain (Hawkins & Blakeslee, 2004, 2007; Hedberg, 2007; Sutton & Barto, 1998). That is why a 3-year-old baby can easily watch, listen, learn, and remember various external environment information and adjust his or her behavior, while the most sophisticated computers cannot. In this sense, one may argue that modern computers are just computational machines without intelligence. This raises critical questions such as "What can humans do better than computers, and vice versa?" or, more fundamentally, "What is computable?" from the computational thinking point of view (Wing, 2006). We believe an in-depth understanding of such fundamental problems is critical for machine intelligence research, and ultimately provide practical techniques and solutions to hopefully bring such a level of intelligence closer to reality across different domains.

To give a brief overview of the major differences between traditional computation and brain-like intelligence, Figure 1.1 compares the major characteristics of these two levels of intelligence. One can clearly see that brain-like intelligence is fundamentally different to that of traditional computation in all of these critical tasks. Therefore, from the computational thinking point of view, new understandings, foundations, principles, and methodologies are needed for the development of brain-like intelligence. This book tries to provide the recent advancements in this field to address such critical needs in the community.

Traditional computation	Tasks	Brain-like intelligence
Sequential	Information processing	Parallel
Fixed	Complexity	Scalable
Centralized	Control mechanism	Distributed
Global	Interactions	Local
Programmed	Source of behaviors	Self-organizing/ conceptualizing
Limited	Fault tolerant	High
Custom designed	Architecture	Evolved
Some	Adaptability	High
Problem specific	Application domains	Robust

Figure 1.1: Comparison of traditional computation and brain-like intelligence.

1.2 THE TWO-FOLD OBJECTIVES: DATA-DRIVEN AND BIOLOGICALLY INSPIRED APPROACHES

Figure 1.2 illustrates a high-level view of the machine intelligence framework that we focus on in this book. Here, there are two important components: the intelligent core such as neural network organizations and learning principles, and the interaction between the intelligent core and the external environment through sensorimotor pathways (embodiment). To this end, this book includes

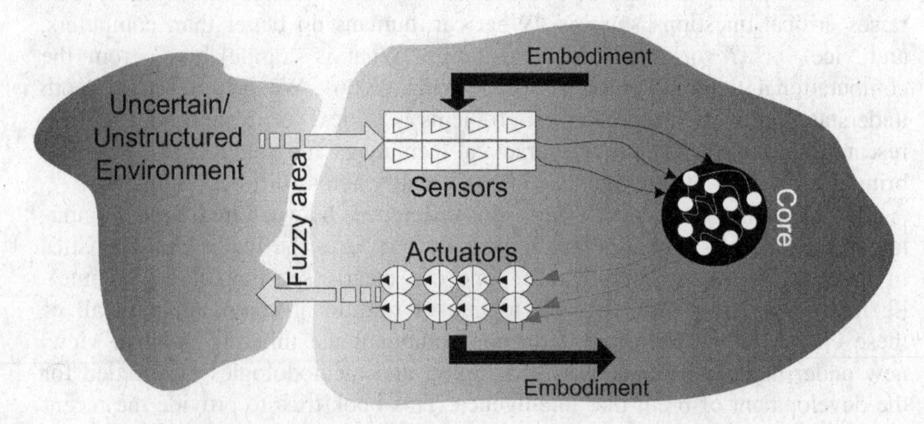

Figure 1.2: A high-level view of machine intelligence.

two major parts to address the two-fold objectives: data-driven approaches and biologically inspired approaches for machine intelligence research. This will not only allow us to understand the foundations and principles of the neural network organizations and learning within the intelligent core, but it also allows us to advance the principled methodologies with a focus on the data processing path (sensing, acquisition, processing, and action). The key is to understand how a brain-like system can adaptively interact with unstructured and uncertain environments to process vast amounts of raw data to develop its internal structures, build associations and predictions, accumulate knowledge over time, and utilize self-control to achieve goals.

The underlying motivation of data-driven approaches is quite straightforward: Data provide the original sources for any kind of information processing, knowledge transformation, and decision-making processes. From the computational intelligence point of view, data are almost involved in every aspect of "intelligence": reasoning, planning, and thinking, among others. Therefore, data can be a vital role for machine intelligence development in different formats, such as sensing, acquisition, processing, transformation, and utilization. You can think about many examples in real-world applications from this perspective, ranging from picking up a pen from your office desk, to driving a car in the metropolitan area of New York City, to scheduling your calendar for the next month. All of these tasks involve data analysis at different levels. If one would like to design an intelligent machine to possibly replicate certain levels of brain-like intelligence, many critical questions are raised from the data computational point of view, such as: What kind of data are necessary to support the decision-making processes? How can an intelligent machine continuously learn from non stationary and noisy data? How do you effectively combine multiple votes from different hypotheses based on different data spaces for optimal decisions?

Specifically, in this book we will discuss the following data-driven approaches for machine intelligence research:

- Incremental Learning. Incremental learning is critical to understand brain-like intelligence and potentially bringing such a level of intelligence closer to reality in at least two aspects. First, intelligent systems should be able to learn information incrementally throughout their lifetimes, accumulate experience, and use such knowledge to benefit future learning and decision-making processes. Second, the raw data that come from the environment with which the intelligent system interacts becomes incrementally available over an indefinitely long (possibly infinite) learning lifetime. Therefore, the learning process in such scenarios is fundamentally different from that of traditional static learning tasks, where a representative data distribution is available during the training time to develop the decision boundaries used to predict future unseen data. Furthermore, how to achieve global generalization through incremental learning is a crucial component in the correct understanding of such problems. Therefore, it is critical to go beyond the conventional "compute–store–retrieve" paradigm for the development of natural intelligent systems for such large-scale and complicated data processing systems.

- Imbalanced Learning. In many real-world applications, an intelligent system needs to learn from skewed data distributions to support decision-making processes. Such skewed distribution with underrepresented data may significantly compromise learning capability and performance. For instance, many of the existing learning algorithms assume or expect balanced data distributions to develop the decision boundary. Therefore, when presented with the imbalanced data, such learning algorithms fail to properly represent the distributive characteristics of the data and resultantly provide worse learning performance. Due to the inherent complex characteristics of imbalanced data and its wide occurrence in many real systems, the imbalanced learning problem has presented a significant new challenge to society with wide-ranging and far-reaching application domains.
- Ensemble Learning. Generally speaking, ensemble learning approaches have the advantage of improved accuracy and robustness compared to the single model–based learning methods. In the ensemble learning scenario, multiple hypotheses are developed and their decisions are combined by a voting method for prediction. Since different hypotheses can provide different views of the target function, the combined decision will hopefully provide more robust and accurate decisions compared to single model–based learning methods. There are two critical aspects related to ensemble learning. First, how can one develop multiple hypotheses given the training data? For instance, to obtain the diversified hypotheses, many techniques such as bootstrap aggregating (bagging), adaptive boosting, random subspace, stacked generalization, mixture of experts, and others have been proposed in the community. Second, how can one effectively integrate multiple hypotheses outputs for improved final decisions? This mainly includes different types of combinational voting strategies, which will also be discussed in this book.

In addition to the data-driven approaches, we have a keen interest to understand and develop biologically inspired approaches for machine intelligence. Recent brain science research has provided strong evidence that the biological brain uses fundamentally different ways in handling various tasks than today's computers (Hawkins & Blakeslee, 2004, 2007; Hedberg, 2007). For instance, although IBM's Deep-Blue can win a chess game against a world champion over a decade ago, it did not tell us too much about the development of general-purpose brain-like intelligent machines as it uses completely different ways of information processing as in the human brain. On the other hand, the evolutionary algorithm has recently showed great potential to develop the self-learning capabilities for a master-level chess program, which could provide us important insights to understanding the essence of machine intelligence (Fogel, Hays, Han, & Quon, 2004). From this perspective, the important question is how to develop biologically inspired system-level models and architectures that are able to mimic certain levels of brain intelligence. In this book we will discuss three major components on this.

- Adaptive Dynamic Programming (ADP). ADP has been widely recognized as the key methodology to understand and replicate general-purpose brain-like intelligence in the community (Werbos, 1994, 1997, 2004, 2009; Si et al., 2004; Powell, 2007). There are two major goals of the ADP research that can contribute to the machine intelligence research: *optimization* and *prediction*. Specifically, optimization in this case can be defined as learning to make better choices to maximize some kind of utility function over time to achieve goals (Werbos, 2009). To this end, the foundation for optimization over time in stochastic processes is the Bellman equation (Bellman, 1957), closely tied with the Cardinal utility function concept by Von Neumann. In addition to optimization, recently strong evidence from neurobiology research suggested that prediction is another equally important component to provide a level of adaptive general-purpose intelligence (Werbos, 2009). Prediction in the ADP design can be considered in a more general way to include much important information, such as the future sensory inputs from observed data as well as modeling and reconstructing of the unobserved state variable, with the objective of facilitating action selection toward optimization (Werbos, 2009). In this book, we propose a hierarchical ADP architecture with multiple-goal representations to effectively integrate optimization and prediction together for machine intelligence research.
- Associative Learning. Associative memory plays a critical role for natural intelligence based on information association and anticipation. Generally speaking, there are two types of associative memories: hetero-associative and auto-associative memory. Hetero-associative memory makes associations between paired patterns, such as words and pictures, while auto-associative memory associates a pattern with itself, recalling stored patterns from fractional parts of the pattern. It is believed that the human brain employs both hetero-associative and auto-associative memory for learning, action planning, and anticipation (Rizzuto & Kahana, 2001; Brown, Dalloz, & Hulme, 1995; Murdock, 1997). The memory evolved in the human brain is self-organized, hierarchically distributed, and data driven. For instance, self-organization is responsible for formation of hierarchically organized structures not only in the human brain but also in the nervous systems of lower vertebrates (Malsburg, 1995). In this book, I will focus on the essential characteristics of associative learning, including self-organization, sparse and local connection, and hierarchical structure.
- Sequence Learning. Sequence learning is widely considered among one of the most important components of human intelligence, as most human behaviors are in the sequential format, including, but not limited to, natural language processing, speech recognition, reasoning and planning, and others. Therefore, the understanding of fundamental problems of sequence learning could provide us critical insights for machine intelligence research.

To this end, we propose a biologically inspired model for sequence learning, storage, and retrieval within distributed hierarchical neural organizations. Prediction capability is an essential element of this sequence learning model.

1.3 HOW TO READ THIS BOOK

This book includes both introductory discussions of machine intelligence backgrounds, as well as the latest advanced theoretical and practical developments in the field. In addition to the presented mathematical foundations, learning principles, models, and algorithms, this book also provides a large number of case studies to demonstrate the applications of such methods to solve real-world problems. All of these could provide a valuable resource for researchers and practitioners interested in the machine intelligence field.

This book can also be used for graduate- and undergraduate-level courses in the area of machine learning, data mining, computational intelligence, and adaptive systems. For courses focused on the data processing perspective, it is suggested students use the materials in Part I of this book (Chapters 2, 3, and 4). For courses focused on biologically inspired learning, students can use the contents in Part II (Chapters 5, 6, and 7). Chapter 8 provides an interesting discussion regarding the hardware design of machine intelligence based on massive, parallel processing architecture, including both the dedicated very large-scale integration (VLSI) systems and reconfigurable field-programmable gate array (FPGA) technology. This chapter could be an interesting resource for anyone who would like to know how existing and emerging technologies (including *memristor*) could potentially change our society by building such complex intelligent systems in hardware. A one-semester course in the computational intelligence topic should be able to cover all the chapters discussed in this book. Furthermore, to improve the readability and flexibility of using this book for course materials at different levels, the chapters have been written to be readable in any sequence to the best effort. However, some interdependence is unavoidable for a coherent and systematic presentation of the materials.

Figure 1.3 shows the organization of the entire book, and a brief review of the chapters is summarized as follows.

1.3.1 Part I: Data-Driven Approaches for Machine Intelligence (Chapters 2, 3, and 4)

Chapter 2 presents basic concepts of incremental learning and its importance for machine intelligence research. The focus is to understand the principles and foundations of adaptive learning over time for knowledge accumulation to support decision-making processes. A specific learning framework is presented and various practical design considerations are given in this chapter. Application case

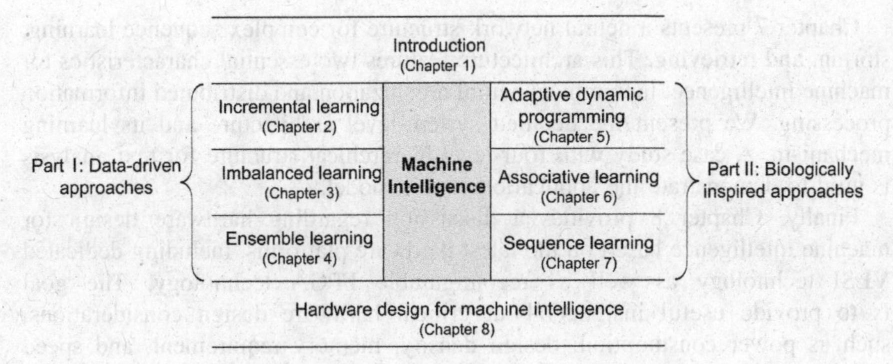

Figure 1.3: The organization of this book.

studies based on video stream data and e-mail data are used to demonstrate the effectiveness of this method.

Chapter 3 covers the imbalanced learning problem. As a relatively new field in the community, the focus for this chapter is to understand the nature of the imbalanced learning problem, and investigate the state-of-the-art techniques to address this problem. Four major categories of methodologies including sampling methods, cost-sensitive methods, kernel-based learning methods, and active learning methods are presented. Assessment metrics used to evaluate learning performance under imbalanced data and the major challenges as well as opportunities on this topic are also discussed in this chapter.

Chapter 4 covers the ensemble learning methods. The focus of this chapter is to discuss techniques used to develop multiple diversified learning hypotheses and to integrate such multiple hypotheses to support the final decision-making processes. Several major approaches including bootstrap aggregating (bagging), adaptive boosting (AdaBoost), and subspace method, among others, are discussed. Numerous combination voting strategies and detailed margin analysis are also presented in this chapter.

1.3.2 Part II: Biologically-Inspired Approaches for Machine Intelligence (Chapters 4, 5, and 6)

Chapter 5 discusses the ADP methods for machine intelligence research. Our focus here is to understand the fundamental principles of ADP design for optimization and prediction. A hierarchical learning architecture with three types of networks is proposed, and a specific learning algorithm based on backpropagation is also presented. We also demonstrate a case study of this architecture to the cart-pole balancing control problem.

Chapter 6 covers self-organizing memory in hierarchical neural network organization. This includes the association learning mechanism, neural network organization, and network operation. Application cases of such memory organization for both hetero-associative and auto-associative learning are also presented.

Chapter 7 presents a neural network structure for complex sequence learning, storing, and retrieving. This architecture features two essential characteristics for machine intelligence: hierarchical neural organization and distributed information processing. We present the detailed system-level architecture and its learning mechanism. A case study with four-level hierarchical structure for text analysis is used to demonstrate the application of this model.

Finally, Chapter 8 provides a discussion regarding hardware design for machine intelligence based on the latest hardware platforms, including dedicated VLSI technology as well as reconfigurable FPGA technology. The goal is to provide useful insights about critical hardware design considerations, such as power consumption, design density, memory requirement, and speed requirement, to potentially build a large-scale, integrated, and complex system into real hardware. We also point to some emerging technologies such as *memristor* for future brain-like intelligent systems design to conclude this book.

1.4 SUMMARY AND FURTHER READING

This book aims to advance the fundamental understanding of general-purpose brain-like intelligence research, and develop principled methodologies and practical techniques to bring such a level of intelligence closer to reality through a wide range of domains. The underlying methodology presented in this book is based on two paths of research: data-driven approaches and biologically inspired approaches for machine intelligence.

Machine intelligence research draws on theories and concepts from many disciplines. For the latest research development in this field, interested readers can find a number of good sources from many international journals, which include, but are not limited to, *IEEE Transactions on Neural Networks*, *Neural Networks*, *Neural Computation*, *IEEE Transactions on Evolutionary Computation*, *IEEE Transactions on Pattern Analysis and Machine Intelligence*, *IEEE Transactions on Knowledge and Data Engineering*, *Artificial Intelligence*, *Cognitive Brain Research*, *Machine Learning*, and others. Meanwhile, there are also a number of conferences that cover different aspects of machine intelligence research, including *International Joint Conference on Neural Networks (IJCNN)*, *National Conference on Artificial Intelligence (AAAI)*, *International Joint Conference on Artificial Intelligence (IJCAI)*, *Neural Information Processing Systems (NIPS)*, *International Conference on Machine Learning (ICML)*, *International Conference on Data Mining (ICDM)*, *Annual Meeting of the Cognitive Science Society (CogSci)*, and others.

REFERENCES

Bellman, R. E. (1957). *Dynamic programming*. Princeton, NJ: Princeton University Press.

Brooks, R. A. (1991). Intelligent without reason. *Proc. Int. Joint Conf. on Artificial Intelligence*, pp. 569–595.

Brooks, R. A. (2002). *Flesh and machines: how robots will change us*. New York: Pantheon.

Brown, G. D. A., Dalloz, P., & Hulme, C. (1995). Mathematical and connectionist models of human memory: a comparison. *Memory*, *3*(2), 113–145.

Fogel, D. B., Hays, T. J., Han, S. L., & Quon, J. (2004). A self-learning evolutionary chess program. *Proc. IEEE*, 92, 1947–1954.

Grossberg, S. (1988). *Neural networks and natural intelligence*. Cambridge, MA: MIT Press.

Hawkins, J., & Blakeslee, S. (2004). *On intelligence*. New York: Times Books.

Hawkins, J., & Blakeslee, S. (2007). Why can't a computer be more like a brain? *IEEE Spectrum*, *44*(4), 20–26.

Hedberg, S. R. (2007). Bridging the gap between neuroscience and AI. *IEEE Intel. Syst.*, *22*(3), 4–7.

Malsburg, C. V. (1995). Self-organization and the brain. In M. Arbib (Ed.), *The Handbook of Brain Theory and Neural Networks* (pp. 840–843). Cambridge, MA: MIT Press.

Murdock, B. B. (1997). Context and mediators in a theory of distributed associative memory (todam2). *Psychological Review*, *104*, 839–862.

NSF. (2007). Emerging frontiers in research and innovation: Cognitive optimization and prediction: From neural systems to neurotechnology (copn). *[online], available: http://www.nsf.gov/pubs/2007/nsf07579/nsf07579.htm.*

Pfeifer, R., & Scheier, C. (1999). *Understanding intelligence*. Cambridge, MA: MIT Press.

Powell, W. B. (2007). *Approximate dynamic programming: Solving the curses of dimensionality*. Hoboken, NJ: Wiley.

Rizzuto, D. S., & Kahana, M. J. (2001). An autoassociative neural network model of paired-associate learning. *Neural Computation*, *13*, 2075–2092.

Si, J., Barto, A., Powell, W. B., & Wunsch, D. (2004). *Handbook of learning and approximate dynamic programming*. Piscataway, NJ: IEEE Press.

Starzyk, J. A., Liu, Y., & He, H. (2006). Challenges of embodied intelligence. *Proc. Int. Conf. on Signals and Electronic Systems*. Lodz, Poland.

Sutton, R. S., & Barto, A. G. (1998). *Reinforcement learning: An introduction*. Cambridge, MA: MIT Press.

Werbos, P. J. (1988a). Backpropagation: Past and future. *Proc. IEEE Int. Conf. Neural Netw.*, I-343–353.

Werbos, P. J. (1988b). Generalization of backpropagation with application to a recurrent gas market model. *Neural Netw.*, *1*, 339–356.

Werbos, P. J. (1990). Backpropagation through time: What it does and how to do it. *Proc. IEEE*, 78, 1550–1560.

Werbos, P. J. (1994). Approximate dynamic programming for real time control and neural modeling. In P. J. White & P. J. Sofge (Eds.), *Handbook of intelligent control* (pp. 493–525). New York: Van Nostrand.

Werbos, P. J. (1997). Brain-like design to learn optimal decision strategies in complex environments. *Proc. Conf. Decision and Control*, pp. 3902–3904.

Werbos, P. J. (1998). A brain-like design to learn optimal decision strategies in complex environments. In M. Karny, K. Warwick, & V. Kurkova (Eds.), *Dealing with complexity: A neural networks approach*. London: Springer.

Werbos, P. J. (2004). ADP: Goals, opportunities and principles. In J. Si, A. G. Barto, W. B. Powell, & D. Wunsch II (Eds.), *Handbook of learning and approximate dynamic programming* (pp. 3–44). Piscataway, NJ: IEEE Press.

Werbos, P. J. (2005). Backwards differentiation in AD and neural nets: Past links and new opportunities. In H. M. Bucker, G. Corliss, P. Hovland, U. Naumann, & B. Norris (Eds.), *Automatic differentiation: Applications, theory and implementations, lecture notes in computational science and engineering* (Vol. 50, pp. 15–34). Berlin, Germany: Springer-Verlag.

Werbos, P. J. (2009). Intelligence in the brain: A theory of how it works and how to build it. *Neural Networks*, *22*, 200–212.

Wing, J. M. (2006). Computational thinking. *Communications of the ACM*, *49*(3), 33–35.

CHAPTER 2

Incremental Learning

2.1 INTRODUCTION

Incremental learning is an important capability for brain-like intelligence as biological systems are able to continuously learn through their lifetimes and accumulate knowledge over time. From the computational point of view, there are three key objectives of incremental learning for machine intelligence research: transforming previously learned knowledge to the currently received data to facilitate learning from new data, accumulating experience over time to support the decision-making process, and achieving global generalization through learning to accomplish goals. This is not only needed for the development of principled learning methodologies to understand how the brain-like system can adaptively process and learn from raw data, but it is also important for many real-world applications involving large volumes of stream data. During the incremental learning situation, raw data that come from the environment with which the intelligent system interacts become incrementally available over an indefinitely long (possibly infinite) learning lifetime. Therefore, the learning process in such scenarios is fundamentally different from that of traditional static learning tasks, where representative data distribution is available during the training time to develop the decision boundaries. In this chapter, we propose an adaptive incremental learning framework to tackle this problem.

2.2 PROBLEM FOUNDATION

Considering the following learning scenario. Let D_{j-1} represent the data chunk received between time t_{j-1} and t_j, and a hypothesis, h_{j-1}, developed on D_{j-1}. The important question is how should the system adaptively learn information when a new chunk of data, D_j, is received? Conventionally, there are two major categories of approaches used to answer this question.

The first category of approaches employ simple data accumulation methods, as illustrated in Figure 2.1(a). In these methods, when a new chunk of

Self-Adaptive Systems for Machine Intelligence, First Edition. Haibo He.

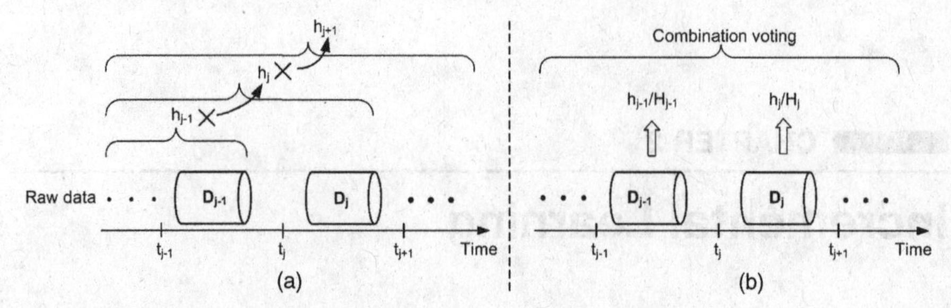

Figure 2.1: The two traditional approaches of incremental learning: (a) data accumulation methodology and (b) ensemble learning methodology.

data, D_j, is received, one simply discards h_{j-1} (denoted by the cross sign) and develops a new hypothesis, h_j, based on all the available data accumulated so far $(\ldots, D_{j-1}; D_j)$. This is a very intuitive approach without consideration of using the existing learned knowledge/experience in h_{j-1} to help learning from new data. In addition, the requirement for storage of all the accumulated data may not be feasible in many real-world applications due to limited memory and computational resources.

The second type of approaches employ ensemble learning ideas, as illustrated in Figure 2.1(b). Briefly speaking, whenever a new chunk of data is available, either a single new hypothesis, h_j, or a set of new hypotheses $H : h_i, i = 1, \ldots, L$, are developed based on the new data. Finally, a voting mechanism can be used to combine all the decisions from different hypotheses to reach the final prediction. The major advantage of this approach is that we do not require storage or access to the previously observed data. Instead, the knowledge has been stored in a series of hypotheses developed along the learning life. However, this approach considers each chunk of the data as separated knowledge representation; therefore, there is no experience accumulation and knowledge transformation from old data to the new data. For instance, the knowledge learned in time period of $[t_{j-1}, t_j]$ cannot be used to benefit the learning process in $[t_j, t_{j+1}]$ though both resulting hypotheses will participate in the final voting. Furthermore, the series of individually developed hypothesis h (or hypotheses set H) along the learning life is still a domain model: There is no guarantee that such a learning scheme will produce a global generalization (or at least a part thereof) from stream data. The only knowledge integration process is in the final voting stage. Therefore, an essential problem of incremental learning for machine intelligence research, that is to say, the accumulation of experience over time and its usage in facilitating the future learning process, is bypassed in this method.

2.3 AN ADAPTIVE INCREMENTAL LEARNING FRAMEWORK

Adaptive boosting (AdaBoost) methods have been studied extensively and have demonstrated great success for machine learning and data mining research

(Freund & Schapire, 1996; 1997; Freund, 2001; Schapire, Freund, Barlett, & Lee, 1998; Oza, 2003, 2004; Dietterich, 2000; Bauer & Kohavi, 1999). It has been theoretically proven that the training error of the final hypothesis for a weak learner drops to zero exponentially fast. In AdaBoost, examples that often tend to be misclassified ("difficult" examples) receive high weights compared to those examples that often tend to be correctly classified ("easy" examples) (Freund & Schapire, 1996; 1997). Therefore, the decision boundary is automatically shifted to pay more attention to difficult examples. This goal is achieved by iteratively updating the weights for the training examples based on the hypothesis evaluation. Under the situation of incremental learning from continuous data, the critical issue is how to update such weights for the received new data based on the previous knowledge. As discussed in section 2.2, many of the existing approaches that adopt the boosting idea for incremental learning are achieved by creating multiple hypotheses based on different subsets of the new training data, then using ensemble learning techniques to obtain the final hypothesis. In this way, the critical part of accumulating knowledge throughout the learning life for future learning and decision-making processes is not addressed. This is not a natural way of using the essential idea of adaptive boosting to accomplish the desired level of incremental learning capability for self-adaptive intelligent systems.

Assume an intelligent system is presented with a data stream over time. At time t, a new set of training data, D_t, is received. The previous knowledge in this case includes the hypothesis h_{t-1}, which was developed at time $t-1$ from the distribution function P_{t-1} applied to the data D_{t-1}. Here the distribution function can be either a sampling probability function or weight distribution for different instances in the data: Difficult examples that are hard to learn will carry higher weight compared to those examples that are easy to learn (Freund & Schapire, 1996; 1997). The objectives here include three aspects: *knowledge transformation from previous data to the currently received data, experience accumulation over time*, and *achieving global generalization*. The system-level framework is illustrated in Figure 2.2, followed by a detailed learning algorithm.

This framework includes three layers of organization and three directions of data flow to accomplish the desired objectives. Layer 1 (D layer) is the stream raw data presented to a learning system, and we represent the data chunk D_t as $(\boldsymbol{x}_i, y_i)(i = 1, \ldots, m)$, where $\boldsymbol{x}_i$ is an instance in the n-dimensional feature space X and $y_i \in Y = \{1, \ldots, C\}$ is the class identity label associated with $\boldsymbol{x}_i$. Layer 2 (P layer) is a distribution function layer to reflect the learnability of the data, which will be used to transform such raw data into knowledge representation on the basis of the accumulation of previous experience. Layer 3 (H layer) then develops multiple hypotheses by integrating the P layer with the data, which will be used to support the final decision-making process. In this way, this architecture implicitly takes into consideration all previous domain data and accumulates knowledge to any future time instance (therefore no "catastrophic forgetting" (Grossberg, 1998, 2003)) without the requirement of access to previously observed data (the dashed-arrow in

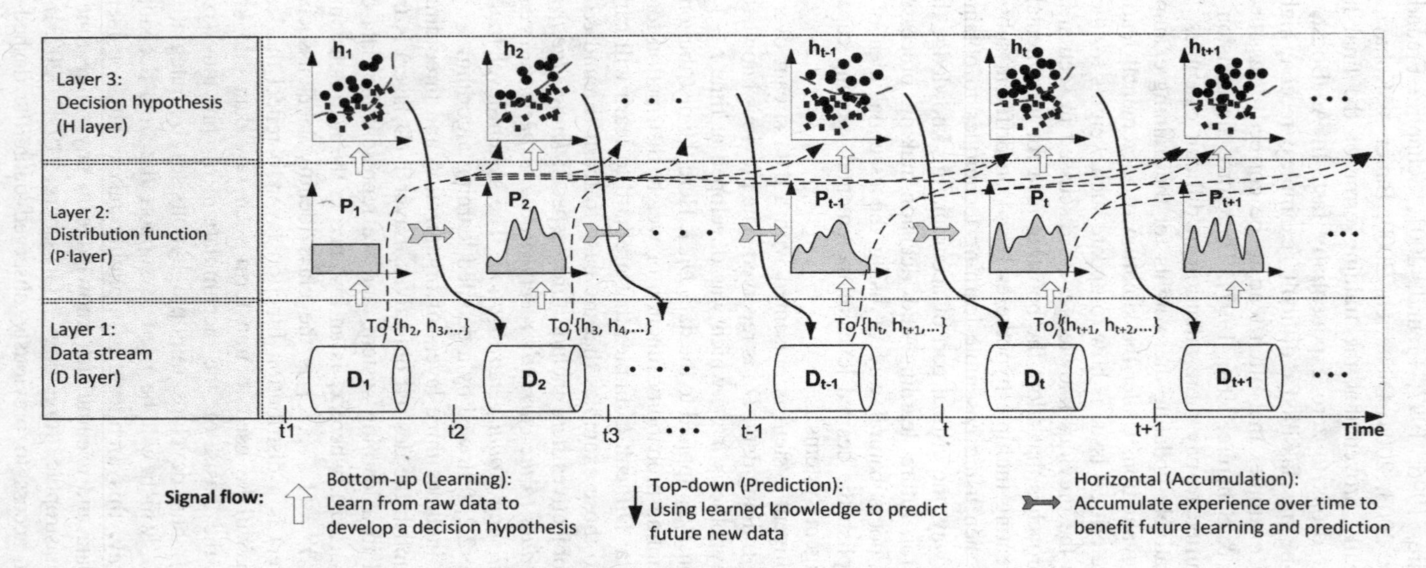

Figure 2.2: Adaptive incremental learning framework.

Figure 2.2). This is fundamentally different from those conventional approaches that are illustrated in Figure 2.1, in which one either needs to explicitly accumulate and store the raw data (Figure 2.1(a)), or considers each chunk of data isolated without knowledge accumulation (Figure 2.1(b)).

[Algorithm 2.1]: Adaptive Incremental Learning

Knowledge at time t:

— Data chunk, D_t, with m instances: $(\boldsymbol{x}_i, y_i)(i = 1, \ldots, m)$, where $\boldsymbol{x}_i$ is an instance in the n-dimensional feature space X and $y_i \in Y = \{1, \ldots, C\}$ is the class identity label associated with $\boldsymbol{x}_i$.

— Distribution function, $\boldsymbol{P}_t$, where $\boldsymbol{P}_t = [w_1^t, w_2^t, \ldots, w_m^t]$ and $\sum_i \boldsymbol{P}_t = 1$.

— A hypothesis, h_t, developed by the data based on D_t with $\boldsymbol{P}_t$.

New input at time $(t+1)$*:*

— A new data chunk, D_{t+1}, with m' may or may not be the same size as m, and can be represented as $(\boldsymbol{x}_j, y_j)(j = 1, \ldots, m')$.

Learning procedure:

(1) Find the relationship between D_t and D_{t+1}:

$$\boldsymbol{Q}_t = \psi(D_t, D_{t+1}), \tag{2.1}$$

where ψ is a predefined mapping function, and $\boldsymbol{Q}_t = [\alpha_1^t, \alpha_2^t, \ldots, \alpha_{m'}^t]$ is a quantitative measurement to reflect the relationship between D_t and D_{t+1}.

(2) Update the initial distribution function for D_{t+1}:

$$\hat{\boldsymbol{P}}_t = \boldsymbol{P}_t \times \boldsymbol{Q}_t \tag{2.2}$$

(3) Apply hypothesis h_t to D_{t+1}, and calculate the pseudo-error of h_t.

$$\varepsilon_t = \sum_{j : h_t(\boldsymbol{x}_j) \neq y_j} \hat{\boldsymbol{P}}_t(j) \tag{2.3}$$

(4) Set $\beta_t = \varepsilon_t / (1 - \varepsilon_t)$.

(5) Refine the distribution function for D_{t+1}:

$$\boldsymbol{P}_{t+1} = \frac{\hat{\boldsymbol{P}}_t}{Z_t} \times \begin{cases} \beta_t & \text{if } h_t(\boldsymbol{x}_j) = y_j \\ 1 & \text{otherwise} \end{cases} \tag{2.4}$$

where Z_t is a normalization constant so that $\boldsymbol{P}_{t+1}$ is a distribution function $(\sum_j \boldsymbol{P}_{t+1} = 1)$, and $\boldsymbol{P}_{t+1}$ can be represented as $\boldsymbol{P}_{t+1} = [w_1^{t+1}, w_2^{t+1}, \ldots, w_{m'}^{t+1}]$.

(6) A hypothesis h_{t+1} is developed by the data based on D_{t+1} with $\boldsymbol{P}_{t+1}$.
(7) Repeat the procedure when the next chunk of new data set is received.

Output: The final hypothesis

$$h_{final}(x) = \arg\max_{y \in Y} \sum_{T:h_T(x)=y} \log\left(\frac{1}{\beta_T}\right) \tag{2.5}$$

where T is the set of incrementally developed hypotheses in the learning life.

The adaptive incremental learning capability is accomplished by the three directions of data processing flow in Figure 2.2, which is also reflected in [Algorithm 2.1]. The bottom-up flow transforms the original raw data to information and knowledge representation: $\boldsymbol{P}_t$ and h_t. Here $\boldsymbol{P}_t$ is a distribution function for the raw data instances in D_t: Difficult instances that are hard to learn will carry higher weights compared to those instances that are easy to learn (Freund & Schapire, 1996, 1997). Based on $\boldsymbol{P}_t$, a learning hypothesis h_t will be developed, in which the decision boundary will be automatically forced to be more focused on the difficult regions. For the first chunk of raw data D_1, the initial distribution function $\boldsymbol{P}_1$ can be set to a uniform distribution because nothing has been learned yet.

After $\boldsymbol{P}_t$ and h_t have been obtained, the system will use such knowledge to facilitate the learning from the next chunk of raw data D_{t+1}. This is achieved by the top-down and horizontal signal flow, as illustrated in Figure 2.2. First, whenever a new chunk of data D_{t+1} is received, a mapping function ψ is used to find the distribution relationship between D_{t+1} and D_t, then an initial estimation of $\boldsymbol{P}_{t+1}$, denoted by $\hat{\boldsymbol{P}}_t$, is calculated based on the mapping function in equation (2.1) and equation (2.2). Then, the $\hat{\boldsymbol{P}}_t$ information is used to assess the learning capability of h_t, which is applied to the new chunk of data D_{t+1}, and the error measurement is accumulated in equation (2.3). Similar to AdaBoost (Freund & Schapire, 1997), β_t is calculated as a function of ε_t. Generally speaking, β_t represents the goodness-of-learning when the previous knowledge h_t is applied to the new raw data D_{t+1}, and is used to refine the distribution function in equation (2.4). In this way, the misclassified instances (difficult instances) in the new data D_{t+1} will receive higher weights, and the learning algorithm will adaptively push the decision boundary over the stream data to focus on those hard instances. Once $\boldsymbol{P}_{t+1}$ is obtained by equation (2.4), a new hypothesis h_{t+1} can be developed, and the entire learning procedure will be repeated for the next chunk of stream data. Finally, a voting method can be used to integrate all the knowledge learned in the incremental learning life for future decision-making processes, as presented in equation (2.5).

In summary, in this incremental learning framework, the horizontal data flow allows the system to accumulate experience and knowledge over time to benefit future learning and prediction, and the top-down process enables the system to use such knowledge to predict and refine its learning capability for stream data received over time. We would like to point out that this framework is a general incremental learning methodology, and therefore different base learning methods, such as decision trees, neural networks, and others, can be integrated into this framework. This provides the flexibility of using this method as a general incremental learning method for machine intelligence research across different application domains.

2.4 DESIGN OF THE MAPPING FUNCTION

One of the key elements of the proposed incremental learning framework in section 2.3 is how to design the mapping function ψ (equation 2.1). The objective of the ψ function is to provide a quantitative representation of the relationship between different data distributions to dynamically update the distribution function across different chunks of stream data. Traditionally, when the boosting idea is applied to static learning problems, the distribution function can be updated iteratively based on the static training data in a sequential format (Freund & Schapire, 1996, 1997). However, in the incremental learning scenario, one can not directly obtain/update such a distribution function when a new chunk of the data is received. In this book, we present three approaches for this purpose: the Euclidean distance approach, the regression learning approach, and the online value system approach.

2.4.1 Mapping Function Based on Euclidean Distance

This approach uses a scaled Euclidean distance to find the relationship between data D_{t+1} and D_t to estimate the initial distribution $\hat{P}_t$, as illustrated in Figure 2.3. To do this, one can first calculate a distance map (DM) function

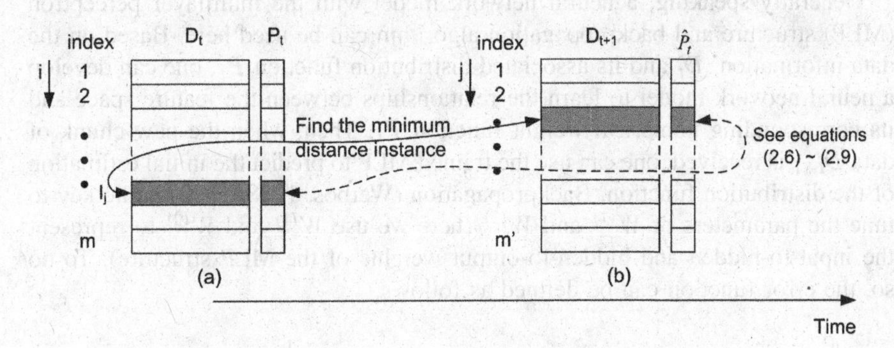

Figure 2.3: Mapping function based on Euclidean distance.

between (D_{t+1}, D_t):

$$\boldsymbol{DM}_{ji} = \sqrt{\sum_{k=1}^{n} (\boldsymbol{x}_{jk} - \boldsymbol{x}_{ik})^2}, \; j = 1, \ldots, m', i = 1, \ldots, m \tag{2.6}$$

$$I_j = \arg \min_{i \in \{1,\ldots,m\}} (\boldsymbol{DM}_{ji}) \tag{2.7}$$

$$\hat{Q}_j = \min(\boldsymbol{DM}_{ji}) \tag{2.8}$$

$\boldsymbol{I} = [I_j] \in \{1, \ldots, m\}$ is the index of the nearest neighbor in D_t for each data instance in D_{t+1}, and $\hat{\boldsymbol{Q}} = [\hat{Q}_j] \in [0, \infty)$ is the corresponding distance value. After the distance $\hat{Q}_j (j = 1, \ldots, m')$ is determined, it is scaled according to:

$$Q_j = \frac{2}{1 + \exp(\hat{Q}_j)} \tag{2.9}$$

where $Q_j \in (0, 1]$. Once Q_j is determined, one can follow equations (2.2) to (2.4) to update the distribution function $\boldsymbol{P}_{t+1}$ for D_{t+1}.

Figure 2.3 visualizes this method, from which one can see that the key idea of using Euclidean distance mapping function is to provide a connection similar to a cluster approach to pass previous knowledge to the new data: For any data instance $\boldsymbol{x}_j$ in D_{t+1}, its associated initial distribution $\hat{\boldsymbol{P}}_t(j)$ is estimated according to the corresponding $\boldsymbol{P}_t$ in previous data D_t with the minimum Euclidean distance.

2.4.2 Mapping Function Based on Regression Learning Model

Regression learning models, such as neural networks, support vector machines, decision tree, and others, can also be integrated into this incremental learning framework to design the mapping function ψ. Figure 2.4 illustrates this idea by using neural network model as an example.

Generally speaking, a neural network model with the multilayer perceptron (MLP) structure and backpropagation algorithm can be used here. Based on the data information, D_t and its associated distribution function $\boldsymbol{P}_t$, one can develop a neural network model to learn the relationships between the feature space and its corresponding numerical weight function $\boldsymbol{P}_t$. Then, when the new chunk of data D_{t+1} is received, one can use the trained MLP to predict the initial estimation of the distribution function. Backpropagation (Werbos, 1988, 1990) is the key to tune the parameters of $W^{(1)}$ and $W^{(2)}$ (here we use $W^{(1)}$ and $W^{(2)}$ to represent the input-to-hidden and hidden-to-output weights of the MLP structure). To do so, the error function can be defined as follows:

$$e(k) = p_{(t)}(k) - o_{(t)}(k); \qquad E(k) = \frac{1}{2}e^2(k), \tag{2.10}$$

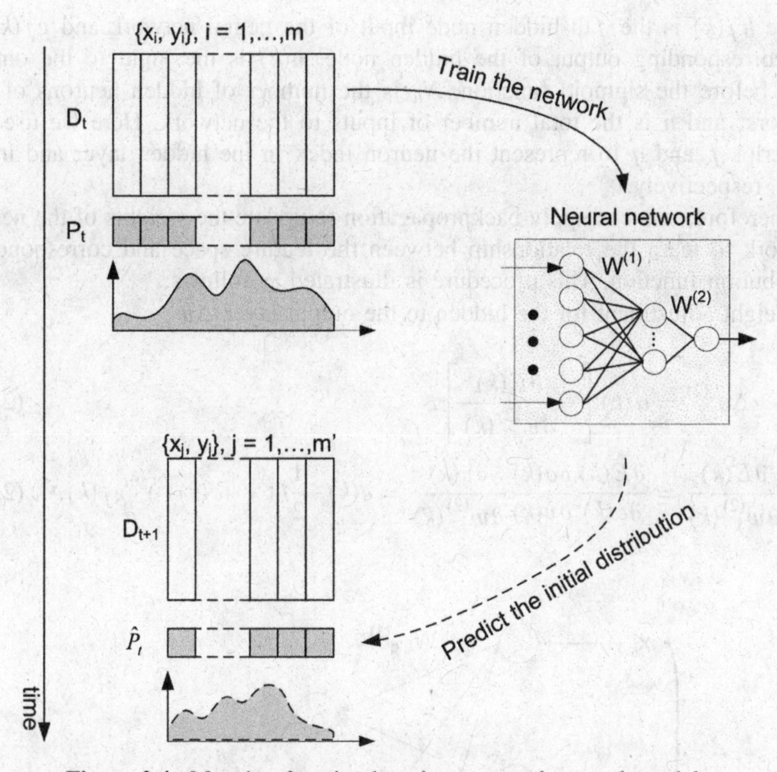

Figure 2.4: Mapping function based on a neural network model.

where k represents the backpropagation training epoch, and $p_t(k)$ and $o_t(k)$ represent the target value and estimated value of the distribution function for data D_t, respectively. For clear presentation, in the following discussion we drop the subscript (t) to derive the update rule of $W^{(1)}$ and $W^{(2)}$.

Assuming sigmoid functions are used at both the hidden and output layers, the associated equations for the MLP network can be defined as follows (see Figure 2.5):

$$o(k) = \frac{1 - \exp^{-v(k)}}{1 + \exp^{-v(k)}}, \tag{2.11}$$

$$v(k) = \sum_{f=1}^{N_h} w_f^{(2)}(k) g_f(k), \tag{2.12}$$

$$g_f(k) = \frac{1 - \exp^{-h_f(k)}}{1 + \exp^{-h_f(k)}}, \quad f = 1, \ldots, N_h, \tag{2.13}$$

$$h_f(k) = \sum_{q=1}^{n} w_{f,\,q}^{(1)}(k) x_{i,q}(k), \quad i = 1, \ldots, N_h, \tag{2.14}$$

where $h_f(k)$ is the fth hidden node input of the neural network and $g_f(k)$ is the corresponding output of the hidden node, $v(k)$ is the input to the output node before the sigmoid function, N_h is the number of hidden neurons of the network, and n is the total number of inputs to the network. Here we use the subscript f and q to represent the neuron index in the hidden layer and input layer, respectively.

Therefore, one can apply backpropagation to update the weights of the neural network to learn the relationship between the feature space and corresponding distribution function. This procedure is illustrated as follows:

Weight adjustment for the hidden to the output layer $\Delta w_f^{(2)}$:

$$\Delta w_f^{(2)} = \alpha(k)\left[-\frac{\partial E(k)}{\partial w_f^{(2)}(k)}\right], \tag{2.15}$$

$$\frac{\partial E(k)}{\partial w_f^{(2)}(k)} = \frac{\partial E(k)}{\partial o(k)}\frac{\partial o(k)}{\partial v(k)}\frac{\partial v(k)}{\partial w_f^{(2)}(k)} = e(k)\cdot\frac{1}{2}(1-(o(k))^2)\cdot g_f(k). \tag{2.16}$$

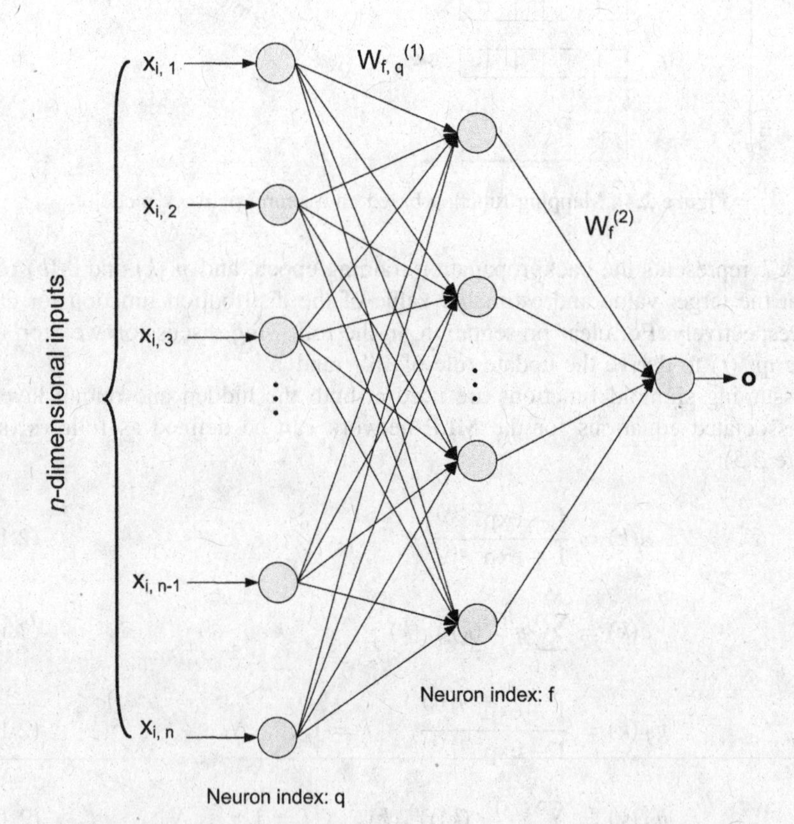

Figure 2.5: MLP with nonlinear neural network with one hidden layer.

Weight adjustments for the input to the hidden layer $\Delta w_{f,q}^{(1)}$:

$$\Delta w_{f,q}^{(1)} = \alpha(k)\left[-\frac{\partial E(k)}{\partial w_{f,q}^{(1)}(k)}\right], \tag{2.17}$$

$$\frac{\partial E(k)}{\partial w_{f,q}^{(1)}(k)} = \frac{\partial E(k)}{\partial o(k)}\frac{\partial o(k)}{\partial v(k)}\frac{\partial v(k)}{\partial g_f(k)}\frac{\partial g_f(k)}{\partial h_f(k)}\frac{\partial h_f(k)}{\partial w_{f,q}^{(1)}(k)} \tag{2.18}$$

$$= e(k)\cdot\frac{1}{2}(1-(o(k))^2)\cdot w_f^{(2)}(k)\cdot\frac{1}{2}(1-g_f^2(k))\cdot x_{i,q}(k),$$

where $\alpha(k)$ is a learning rate. Once $W^{(1)}$ and $W^{(2)}$ are tuned, it can be used to predict the initial distribution function $\hat{P}_{t+1}$ for D_{t+1} (this corresponds to equations (2.1) and (2.2) in [Algorithm 2.1]). This will require only the feedforward propagation in the MLP based on the received new data feature space in D_{t+1}.

2.4.3 Mapping Function Based on Online Value System

In this section, we present a dynamic online value system to design the mapping function ψ for the incremental learning framework. A new concept of the three-curve-fitting technique is introduced to robustly predict the $\hat{\boldsymbol{P}}_t$ value in equation (2.1) and equation (2.2).

2.4.3.1 A Three-Curve Fitting (TCF) Technique Considering dynamic adjustment of the fitting function described by a linear combination of the selected base functions $\varphi_i, i = 1, 2, \ldots, q$, where q is the number of base functions: the objective is to dynamically fit values from the received data samples to minimize the least square error (LSE) of all data $\boldsymbol{x}$ and y as follows:

$$F = a_1 \times \varphi_1 + a_2 \times \varphi_2 + \ldots\ldots + a_q \times \varphi_q \tag{2.19}$$

where F is a general target value to be learned (in this particular case, the initial distribution function value $\hat{\boldsymbol{P}}_t$). The number of base functions can be adjusted according to the accuracy required and the data noise level.

The conventional single-curve fitting approach is illustrated in Figure 2.6(a). In this case, the fitted curve does not reflect the statistical distribution of the input data values in areas $B1$ and $B2$, which will cause poor value estimation in these areas. One could compute a standard deviation (similar to the error bar concept) of the approximated data from the fitted curve, but this would only give a uniform measurement of statistical error that does not reflect the different quality (confidence level) of approximation in different regions of the input space. Increasing the complexity degree of the base functions may provide a "perfect" fitting to such data, but this suffers the over-fitting problem illustrated by the dashed line in Figure 2.6(a).

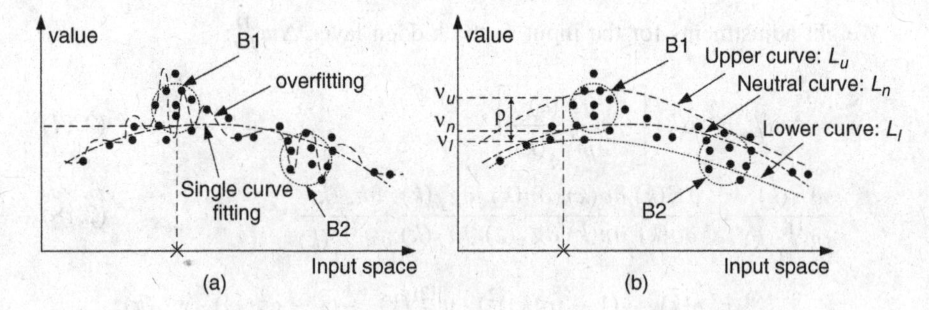

Figure 2.6: Single-curve fitting versus three-curve fitting.

In order to overcome this limitation, a three-curve fitting (TCF) technique is proposed (He & Starzyk, 2007), as illustrated in Figure 2.6(b). This method introduces three curves, named the neutral curve (L_n), upper curve (L_u) and lower curve (L_l), to fit to the data instances in different spaces:

Neutral Curve: fits to all the data instances in the input space, therefore it is the same as the curve in Figure 2.6(a).

Upper Curve: only fits to the data instances that are above the neutral curve.

Lower Curve: only fits to the data instances that are below the neutral curve.

As we can see from Figure 2.6(b), the neutral curve L_n provides a rough estimation of the fitted value, whereas the upper curve L_u and lower curve L_l provide localized statistical distribution information, or the estimation confidence in different input spaces. Therefore, one can locally characterize a statistical deviation of the approximated data from the value estimated by the neutral curve, which can be reflected by the ρ value in Figure 2.6(b). The value of ρ is determined by the v_u and v_l values ($\rho = |v_u - v_l|$), which are the estimated values by the L_u and L_l curve, respectively. In this way, the ρ value reflects the confidence level of the estimated value v_n by the neutral curve compared to its true value: Small values of ρ imply the estimated value v_n is obtained with greater confidence. Therefore, for a value system with k processing elements, in which each of them performs the TCF method for its own input space (see section 2.4.3.2 for details), the voting mechanism is implemented through:

$$v_{vote} = \frac{\sum_{i=1}^{k}(v_{ni} w_i)}{\sum_{i=1}^{k} w_i} \tag{2.20}$$

where the voting weight for each processing element is defined as $w_i = \frac{1}{\rho_i}, i = 1, \ldots, k$.

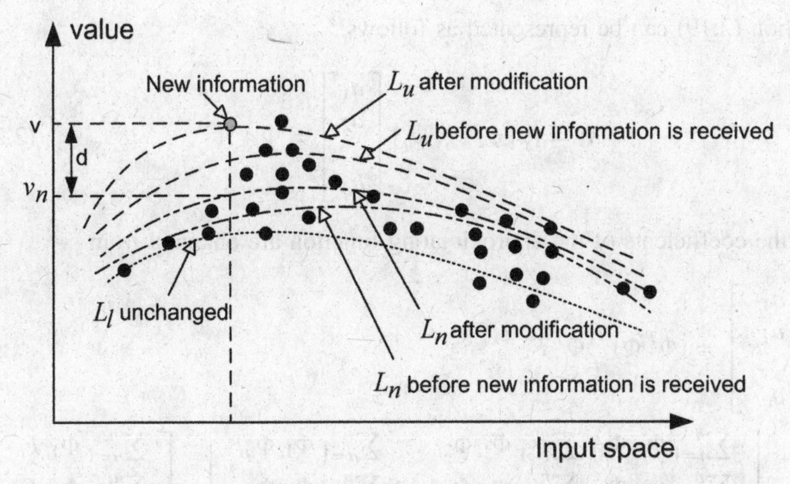

Figure 2.7: An implementation of dynamic learning for TCF.

To facilitate incremental learning, these three curves must be dynamically adjusted to accommodate new data. In this way, any new data instances received over time will only modify the corresponding curves as necessary, and therefore previous knowledge will be preserved. Figure 2.7 and its corresponding [Algorithm 2.2] illustrate a design approach. When the new data sample is presented, L_n is modified first. Then the difference d between the fitted value v_n and the true value v is calculated. If d is less than 0, then L_u is modified and L_l stays unchanged; otherwise, L_l is modified and L_u stays unchanged.

[Algorithm 2.2]: TCF Learning

---

(1) New data is presented;
(2) Modify L_n dynamically;
(3) Calculate $d = v_n - v$;
(4) If $d < 0$
    Modify the upper curve L_u;
    Keep the lower curve L_l unchanged;
Else
    Modify the lower curve L_l;
    Keep the upper curve L_u unchanged;
End

This dynamic learning approach requires online estimation of the coefficients $a_1, \ldots, a_q$ in equation (2.19), therefore, it is necessary to accumulate base function values and their combinations for different input data. To do this, equation (2.19) can be represented as follows:

$$F = [\varphi_1 \, \varphi_2 \ldots \varphi_q] \begin{bmatrix} a_1 \\ a_2 \\ \ldots \\ a_q \end{bmatrix} = \Phi * A \tag{2.21}$$

then the coefficients of the approximating function are obtained from

$$\begin{bmatrix} a_1 \\ a_2 \\ \ldots \\ a_q \end{bmatrix} = (\Phi^T \Phi)^{-1} \Phi^T F$$

$$= \begin{bmatrix} \sum_{i=1}^{n} \Phi_{1i}\Phi_{1i} & \sum_{i=1}^{n} \Phi_{1i}\Phi_{2i} & \ldots & \sum_{i=1}^{n} \Phi_{1i}\Phi_{qi} \\ \sum_{i=1}^{n} \Phi_{2i}\Phi_{1i} & \sum_{i=1}^{n} \Phi_{2i}\Phi_{2i} & \ldots & \sum_{i=1}^{n} \Phi_{2i}\Phi_{qi} \\ \ldots & \ldots & \ldots & \ldots \\ \sum_{i=1}^{n} \Phi_{qi}\Phi_{1i} & \sum_{i=1}^{n} \Phi_{qi}\Phi_{2i} & \ldots & \sum_{i=1}^{n} \Phi_{qi}\Phi_{qi} \end{bmatrix} * \begin{bmatrix} \sum_{i=1}^{n} \Phi_{1i} F_i \\ \sum_{i=1}^{n} \Phi_{2i} F_i \\ \ldots \\ \sum_{i=1}^{n} \Phi_{1i} F_i \end{bmatrix} \tag{2.22}$$

where n is the number of data points. For online implementation, this requires storage of $s = \frac{q(q+1)}{2} + q$ values of a different combination in equation (2.22)

$$\begin{cases} \sum_{i=1}^{n} \Phi_{ki}\Phi_{mi} \\ \sum_{i=1}^{n} \Phi_{ki} F_i \end{cases} \quad where \;\; k, m = 1, \ldots, q \tag{2.23}$$

As new data instances arrive, these s values are updated, and equation (2.22) is solved for new coefficients $a_1, a_2, \ldots a_q$. In general, for q base functions one may need to store s combinations and invert $q \times q$ matrix $(\Phi^T \Phi)$ to update coefficients of the approximating equation.

2.4.3.2 *System-Level Architecture for Online Value Estimation* Based on the TCF method, Figure 2.8 shows the system-level architecture of the proposed value system for the estimation of the $\hat{\boldsymbol{P}}_t$ value in equation (2.1) and equation (2.2). This system has two network structures: a data processing network (DPN) and an information processing network (IPN). The DPN is responsible for the input data space transformation and online dynamic data fitting. The IPN is in charge of the final voting of the results provided by DPN. Each data processing element (DPE) will conduct the three-curve fitting scheme as discussed in section 2.4.3.1, and will output the fitted values of v_{ni}, v_{ui}, and v_{li} for information processing elements (IPE). These values will provide a rough estimation of the true value as well as its statistical distribution information. Based on this information, each IPE will vote on the final value according to equation (2.20).

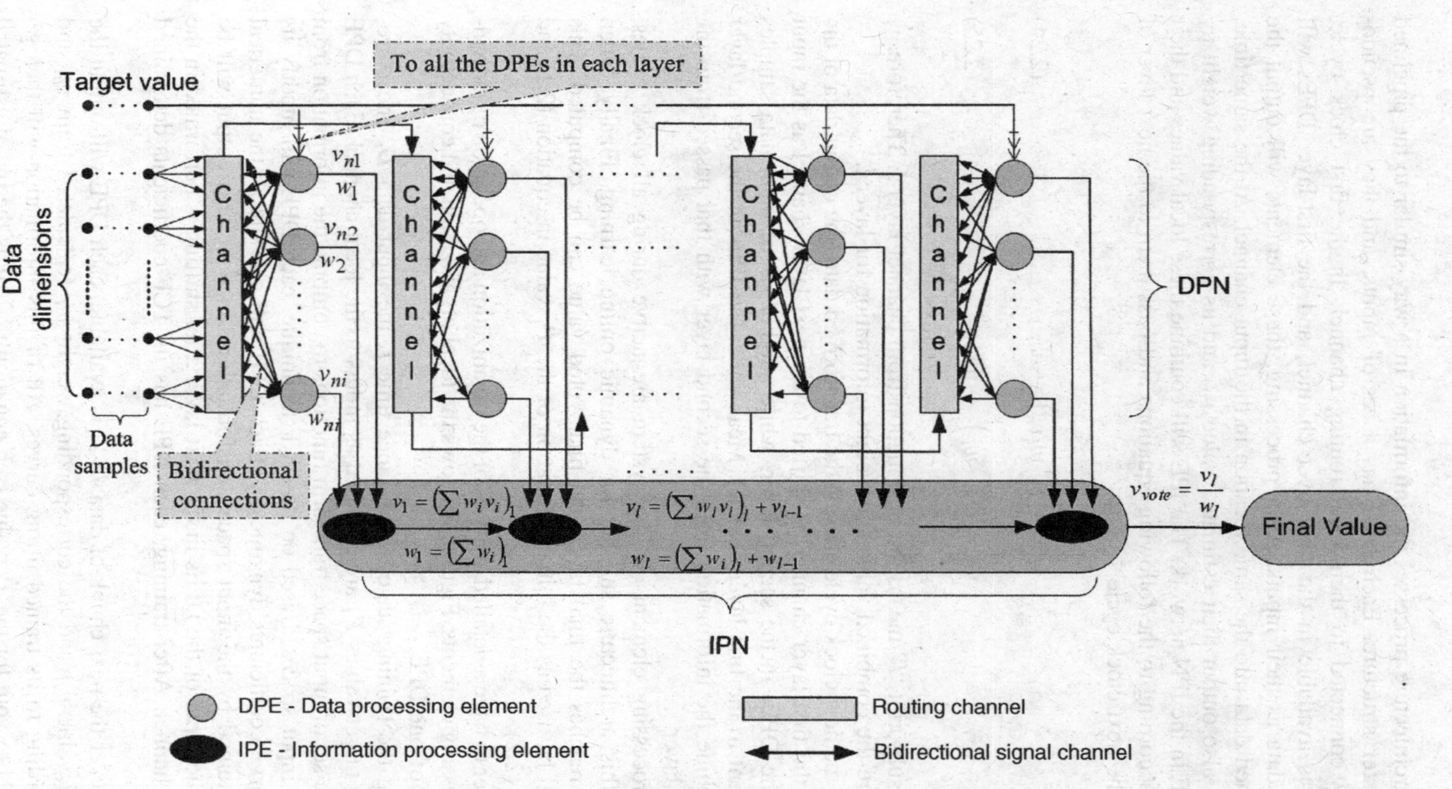

Figure 2.8: Online dynamic value system for incremental learning.

This architecture processes the information in a way similar to the pipelined shift-register structure. Each DPE has a set of inputs, and they are pseudorandomly connected to their local routing channel. In the first clock cycle, the data is available in the first layer channel, and the first-layer DPEs will read the data as their inputs. After processing, these elements will output the transformed data into the same location in the input channel. At the same time, they will also output their estimated value v_{ni} and its corresponding weight w_i to the IPE in the IPN network. The IPE will combine these local values and their weights according to the following equations and pass them to the next layer of IPEs at the next clock cycle.

$$v_l = \left(\sum w_i v_i\right)_l + v_{l-1} \tag{2.24}$$

$$w_l = \left(\sum w_i\right)_l + w_{l-1} \tag{2.25}$$

here the subscript "l" means the information from channel layer l. Therefore, v_l and w_l are the combined value and weight information for layer l.

When the next clock cycle arrives, the transformed data (the output data of the DPEs in the first layer channel) is shifted to the next layer channel as the input data to the DPEs in the second layer, while another set of input data samples can be sent to the first layer channel. Meanwhile, the IPEs in the second layer will combine the information from the second layer with that passed from the previous layer.

All processing elements in the system are active during all clock cycles, making this architecture suitable for dynamic online learning. Finally, when the data reaches the final layer, the final voted value can be computed. This value will be used as the initial estimation of the $\hat{\boldsymbol{P}}_t$ value in equation (2.1) and equation (2.2).

In order to have a detailed analysis of the organization and operation of individual processing elements, Figure 2.9 shows the local organization and connectivity structure of one DPE.

During the training stage, for instance time t, the input data D_t and corresponding target values $\boldsymbol{P}_t$ are provided as inputs to the local channel. Each DPE will use a set of input space transform functions to combine the information from different input spaces. Based on the TCF technique, each DPE will modify its fitting curve coefficients dynamically. Each DPE will also output the numerical value obtained by the input space transformation function. This output will be used as the input of the DPEs in the next layer after shifting is performed in the routing channel. After training, each DPE has its TCF coefficients determined by D_t.

Whenever the next chunk of data D_{t+1} is available, each DPE will output the predicted value v_{ni} and the corresponding weight w_i (calculated from v_{ui} and v_{li}) according to its trained fitting curves. All of this information will then go to the IPN to vote for the $\hat{\boldsymbol{P}}_t$ value (see equation (2.20)) as the initial estimated

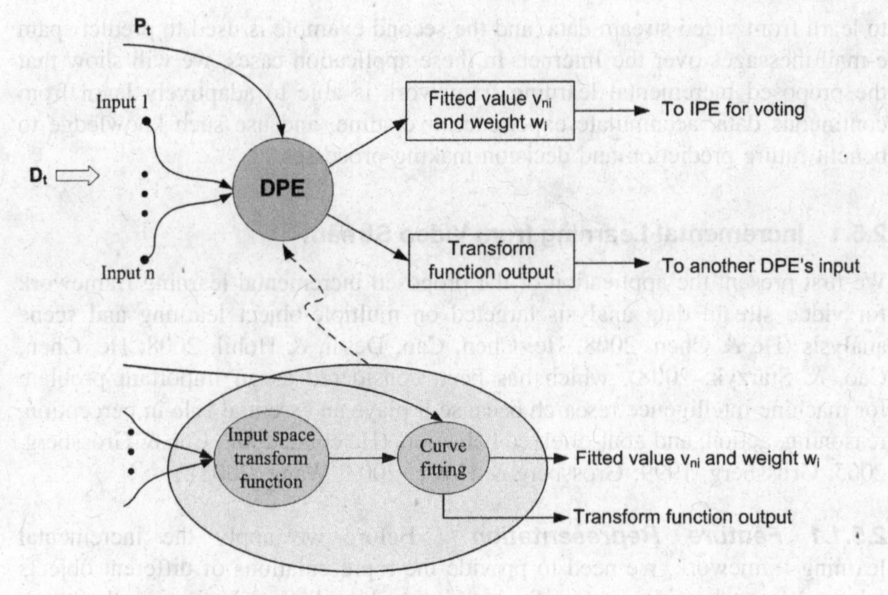

Figure 2.9: A detailed structure of the data processing element.

value of the distribution function for D_{t+1} (this corresponds to equation (2.1) and equation (2.2)).

By comparing the aforementioned three mapping functions in sections 2.4.1, 2.4.2, and 2.4.3, one may expect that the regression model–based mapping function (such as the nonlinear neural network model) and the value system may provide better estimation of the distribution function $\hat{\boldsymbol{P}}_t$ compared to the simple Euclidean distance method. On the other hand, the required computational cost of the regression model and the value system is larger than that of the Euclidean distance mapping. In different application scenarios, one can select these mapping functions according to their specific requirements and trade-off between performance and computational cost. Furthermore, we would like to point out that there are also other methods to design such a mapping function. For instance, the multi dimensional density estimation method might also be used to estimate such a distribution function (Silverman, 1986; Scott, 1992). Generally speaking, the design of an efficient mechanism to estimate the $\boldsymbol{P}$ value (layer 2 in Figure 2.2) is critical for this incremental learning framework, which presents an active research topic to the community. We hope the presented three approaches provide several choices for different application problems.

2.5 CASE STUDY

In this section, we provide two case studies to give a flavor of the applications of the proposed adaptive incremental learning framework. The first example is to learn from video stream data, and the second example is used to predict spam e-mail messages over the Internet. In these application cases, we will show that the proposed incremental learning framework is able to adaptively learn from continuous data, accumulate experience over time, and use such knowledge to benefit future prediction and decision-making processes.

2.5.1 Incremental Learning from Video Stream

We first present the application of the proposed incremental learning framework for video stream data analysis targeted on multiple-object learning and scene analysis (He & Chen, 2008; He, Chen, Cao, Desai, & Hohil, 2008; He, Chen, Cao, & Starzyk, 2008), which has been considered as an important problem for machine intelligence research because it plays an essential role in perception, reasoning, action, and goal-oriented behaviors (He et al., 2008; Can & Grossberg, 2005; Grossberg, 1999; Grossberg & Howe, 2003; Wang, 2005).

2.5.1.1 Feature Representation Before we apply the incremental learning framework, we need to provide the representations of different objects (classes) from the video stream for learning and prediction. Various methods can be adopted for this purpose. For instance, the scale invariant feature transform (SIFT) feature represented by the local key points in an image can be used (Lowe, 1999, 2003; Ke & Sukthankar, 2004; Zickler & Veloso, 2006). Various segmentation methods, such as threshold techniques, edge-based techniques, region-based techniques, and connectivity-preserving relaxation methods can also be used to provide such representations. In this study, the original images are first transformed to gray-scale representations. Then, edge-based segmentation, followed by dilation, morphological stuffing, and grain elimination, is used to identify the corresponding centroid and bounding box of each potential interesting object. A detailed analysis on image segmentation can be found in (Gonzalez & Woods 2002).

Because different objects may have different sizes after the feature representation process, all objects (defined by the bounding box region) are scaled to be the same size to facilitate the training and testing processes. This idea is illustrated in Figure 2.10. In this procedure, one can first find the minimum height H_{min} and width W_{min} of all potential objects based on the training data (H_{min} and W_{min} may or may not be decided by the same object), then scale all representations to the same size (He & Chen, 2008).

$$\frac{H}{H_{min}} = A_H + residual_H \tag{2.26}$$

$$\frac{W}{W_{min}} = A_W + residual_W \tag{2.27}$$

where $residual_H$ and $residual_W$ are the remainders of division. To retain all the information in the scaled representation, one can randomly distribute the number

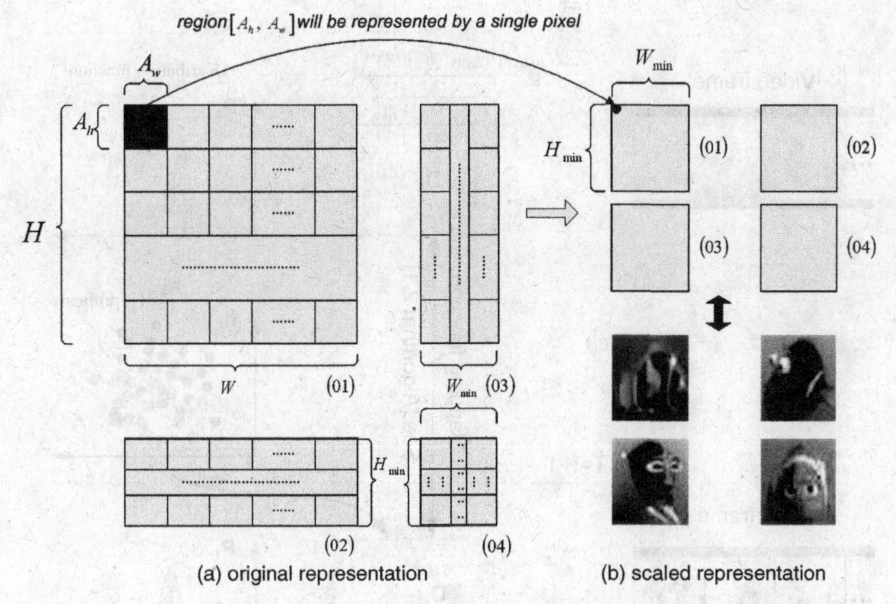

Figure 2.10: Feature representation: (a) original representation and (b) scaled representation.

of residuals across all A_H and A_W:

$$A_h = A_H + rand\,[0\ 1] \tag{2.28}$$

$$A_w = A_W + rand\,[0\ 1] \tag{2.29}$$

In this way, the difference of the number of the containing pixels in all the rectangle areas will be no greater than 1.

2.5.1.2 Experimental Results Different video data from YouTube (*www.youtube.com*, 2009) were used to test the proposed incremental learning framework. The first video clip is "Finding Nemo," with two classes of objects: Dory and Marlin, denoted by "D" and "M," respectively. Based on the data preprocessing method presented in section 2.5.1.1, a total of 4,000 image data examples are extracted. Each data example is represented by a feature vector of 600 dimensions. We randomly select 2,000 examples to train the system and use the remaining 2,000 examples to test the performance. Meanwhile, we assume that the training data will become available incrementally in 100 chunks, each with 20 examples. Figure 2.11 shows the data flow of the incremental learning architecture for this application (He & Chen, 2008).

In this study, a neural network of MLP structure with one hidden layer is used as the base learning algorithm. The number of hidden layer neurons is set to 10, and the input neuron and output neuron are equal to the number of features and the number of classes, respectively. Sigmoid function is used as the

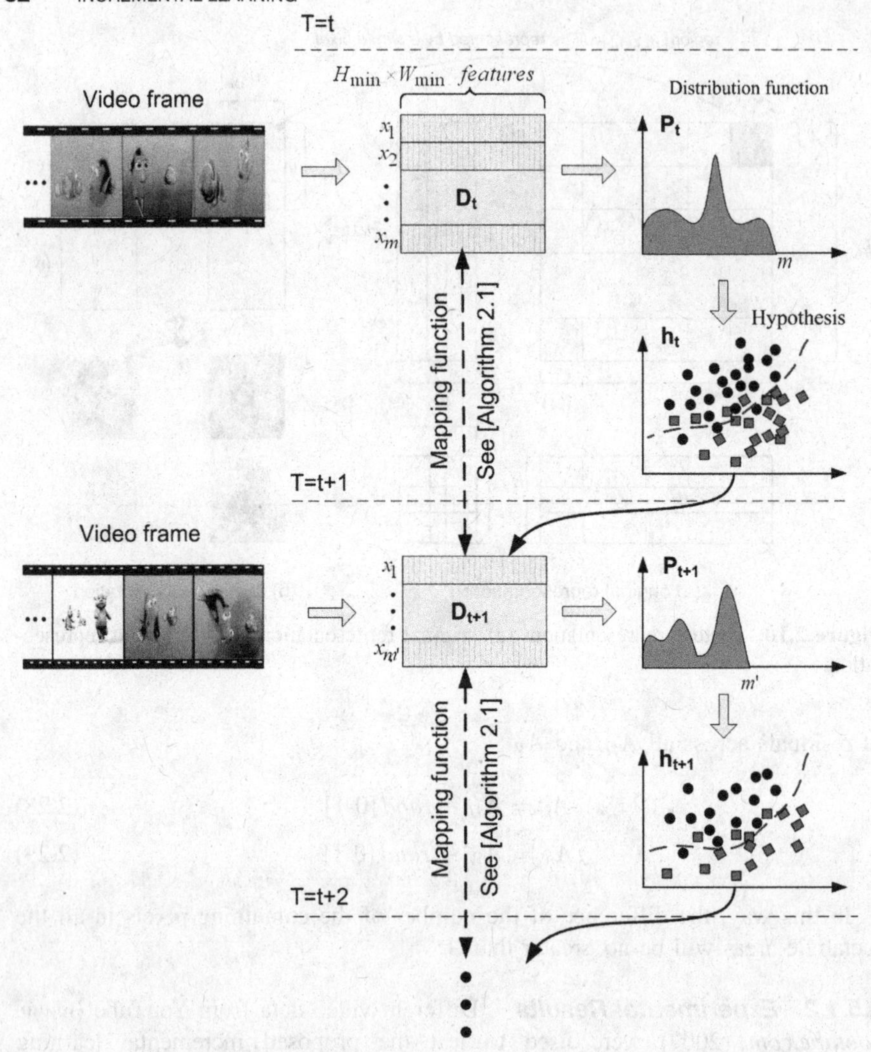

Figure 2.11: Incremental learning for video data analysis.

activation function and backpropagation with 500 iterations is used to train the neural network model. In the current simulation, we use the Euclidean distance–based mapping function as discussed in section 2.4.1.

Figure 2.12 shows the recognition error performance with the learning life based on the average of 20 random runs (He & Chen, 2008). Here, the error rate is measured by the correctly identified instances over all the testing instances at different learning stages. Figure 2.12 also illustrates the error bar information for the 20 runs at different learning stages. The reduction of the spread of the error bar over the learning life indicates that the system can continuously accumulate knowledge to be more stable and robust.

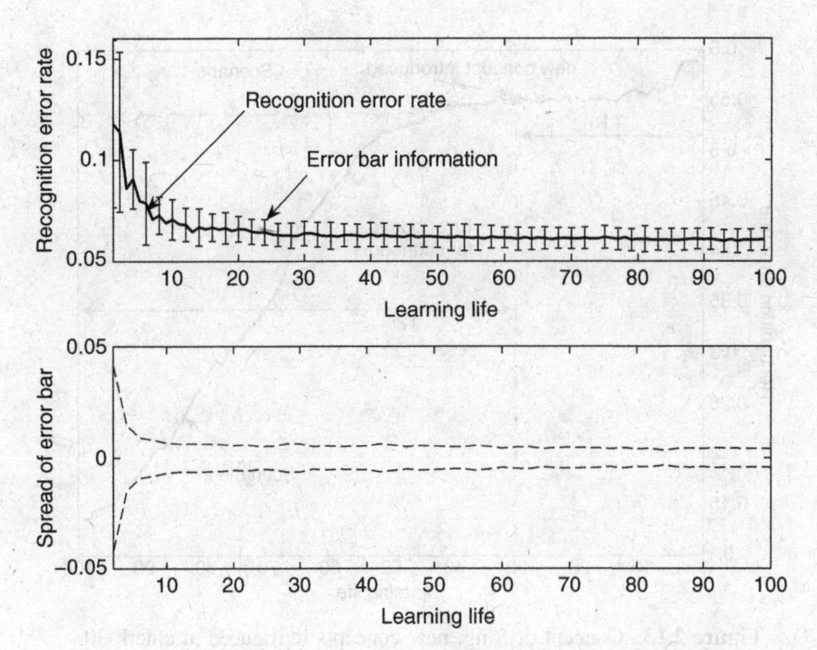

Figure 2.12: The reduction of the recognition error (testing stage).

2.5.1.3 Concept Drifting Issue in Incremental Learning Concept drifting is an important issue in incremental learning. For instance, in multiple-object learning scenarios, it is not uncommon for new interesting objects to be introduced during the learning life. Considering the incremental learning framework presented in section 2.3. Assume at time instance $(t+1)$, the received training data can be represented by $D_t = (D_s, D_n)$, where D_s represents examples from previously observed classes, whereas D_n represents those examples that the learning system has not learned so far (new objects). Under this situation, examples in D_n will all be misclassified by hypothesis h_t. Therefore, the weights for the new class (concept) examples will be increased based on equations (2.3) and (2.4). In this way, the proposed incremental learning framework can automatically assign higher weights to those newly introduced class examples to aggressively learn the new object information.

To test the concept drifting issue, here we combine the video data of "Finding Nemo" with a new video clip, "Baby Shrek." There are three types of objects in "Baby Shrek": Shrek Jr.1, Jr.2, and Jr.3, which are represented by J1, J2, and J3, respectively. Two learning scenarios are considered in this experiment. For scenario 1, only images from "Finding Nemo" are used to train the system throughout the entire learning life. For scenario 2, new objects ("Baby Shrek") are introduced at chunk 30, that is to say, T1 period (from chunk 1 to chunk 29) includes only images from "Finding Nemo" while T2 period (from chunk 30 to chunk 100) includes images from both video data streams. In both scenarios, the testing data are a mixture of half the images from one video clip and half

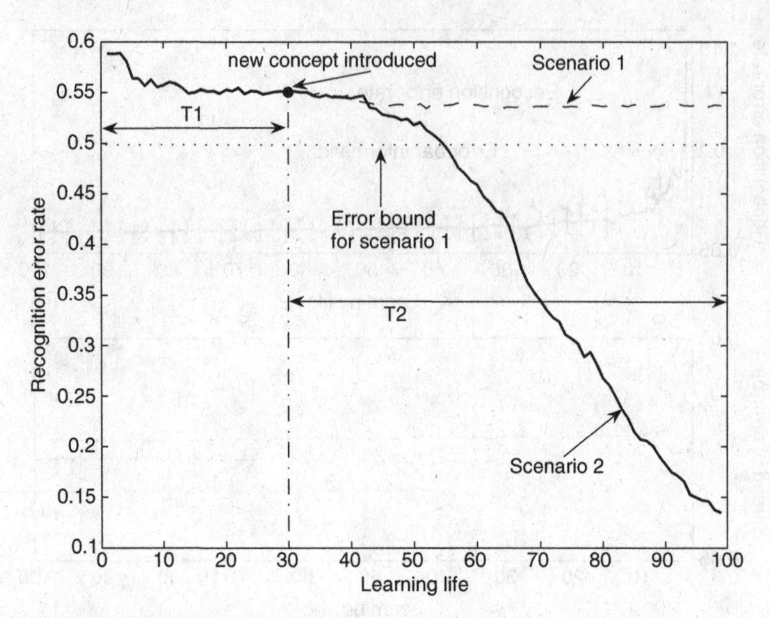

Figure 2.13: Concept drifting: new concepts introduced at chunk 30.

from the other. Figure 2.13 shows the recognition error rate for testing data versus the learning life period, where the solid line represents learning scenario 2 and the dotted line represents scenario 1. Theoretically speaking, the minimum error rate for scenario 1 will be bounded by 50%. This is because none of the "Baby Shrek" objects (half of the testing data) can be correctly recognized by the learning system because it never learned this information during the entire learning life. On the other hand, when the new concepts are introduced at chunk 30 for scenario 2, the error rates begin to gradually decrease again. This improvement is because the incremental learning approach can automatically learn the new object information, and use such knowledge to improve its recognition performance over the testing data.

To observe how the proposed incremental learning framework can adaptively adjust the distribution function for the concept drifting issue, Figure 2.14 shows a detailed view of the change of the weights from time t_{29} to t_{30}, meaning just before and after the new concepts are introduced. From this figure one can see that when the "Baby Shrek" data are introduced at time t_{30}, all these new objects (concepts) tend to receive higher weights compared to those old objects. This clearly indicates that the proposed incremental learning method can adaptively push the system to learn aggressively from those new concepts during the learning life, therefore self-adapt to such new knowledge (He & Chen, 2008).

Another interesting issue for concept drifting during the incremental learning life is how fast the system can self-adjust to the new concept information. From Figure 2.13 one can see that, although at time t_{30} the new concepts have been

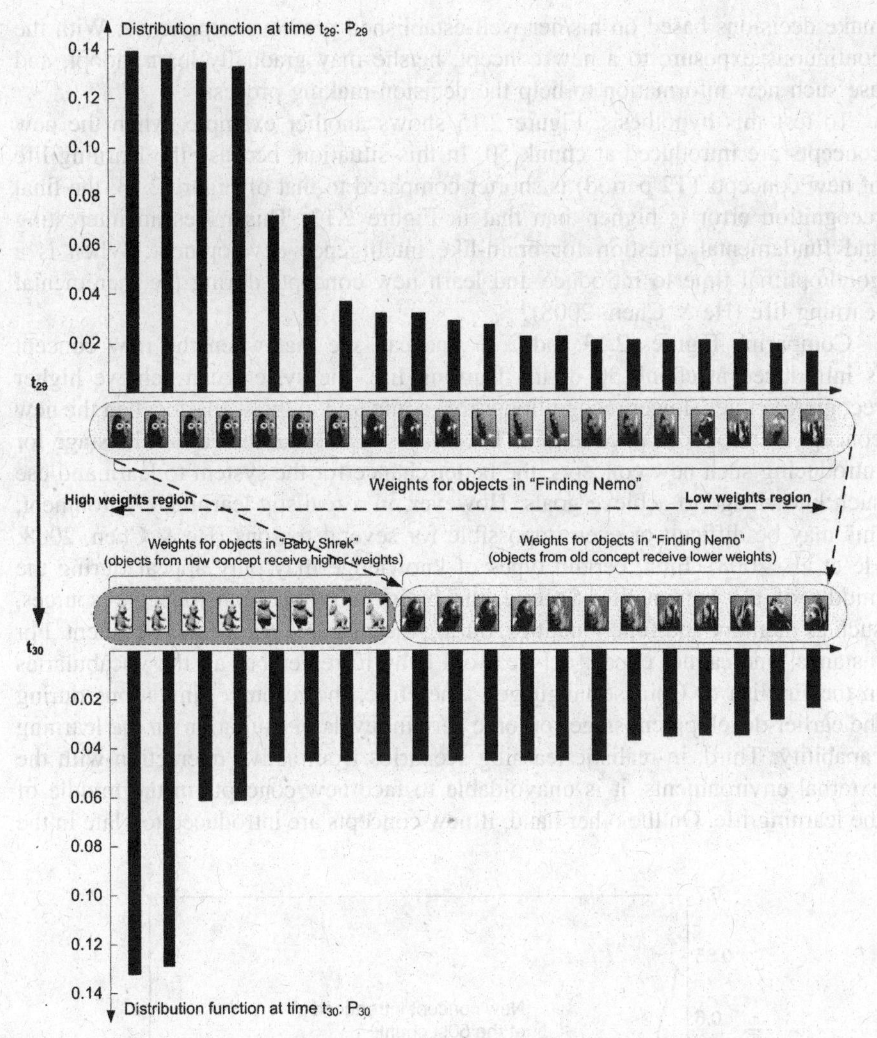

Figure 2.14: Adaptive modification of the distribution function for concept drifting.

introduced, the system cannot dramatically reduce its recognition error at this time instance yet. This is because at this time, the system will make decisions based on the extensive knowledge accumulated over the previous 29 chunks of training data in the T1 period plus the single chunk of new information. With the continuous learning of such new concepts over time in the T2 period, the system will gradually improve recognition performance based on such knowledge. These kinds of characteristics are reflected by the gradual reduction of error rates with the increase of learning life (learning scenario 2). This is similar to high-level intelligence in the human brain: a person with extensive knowledge in one field may initially resist new concept information. Instead, he or she may prefer to make decisions based on his/her well-established previous experience. With the continuous exposure to a new concept, he/she may gradually learn, adopt, and use such new information to help the decision-making process.

To test this hypothesis, Figure 2.15 shows another example, when the new concepts are introduced at chunk 50. In this situation, because the learning life of new concepts (T2 period) is shorter compared to that of Figure 2.13, the final recognition error is higher than that in Figure 2.13. This raises an interesting and fundamental question for brain-like intelligence development: When is a good/optimal time to introduce and learn new concepts during the incremental learning life (He & Chen, 2008)?

Comparing Figures 2.13 and 2.15 one can see that when the new concept is introduced at chunk 30 of the learning life, the system can achieve higher recognition rates (lower recognition error) compared to the scenario when the new concept is introduced at chunk 50. This may suggest that the earlier the stage for introducing such new concepts, the better chance for the system to learn and use such knowledge to achieve goals. However, in a realistic learning environment, this may be difficult or even impossible for several reasons (He & Chen, 2008; He et al., 2008). First, certain types of knowledge may only appear during the middle of the human life. Second, the brain may have constrained resources, such as memory and functionalities, during the earlier stages of development. For instance, one cannot expect a 1-year-old baby to remember all the vocabularies in the English or Chinese languages. Therefore, the resource limitations during the earlier development stages enforce certain levels of limitation on the learning capability. Third, in realistic learning scenarios from active interaction with the external environments, it is unavoidable to face new concepts in the middle of the learning life. On the other hand, if new concepts are introduced too late in the

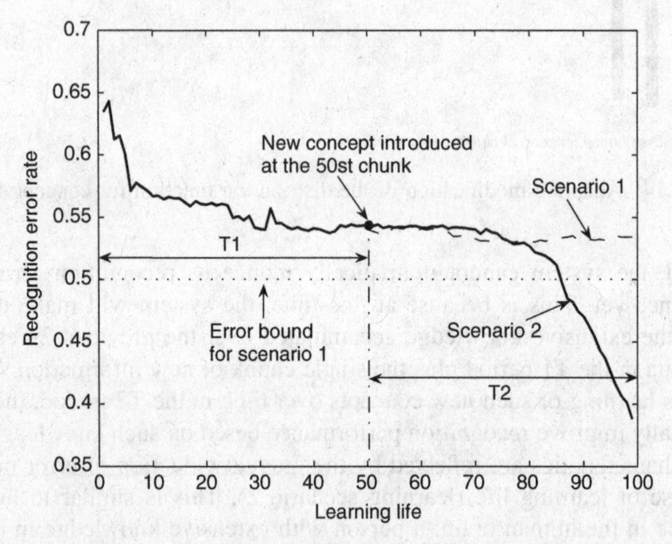

Figure 2.15: Concept drifting: new concepts introduced at chunk 50.

learning life, there may not be enough time (corresponds to a short T2 period) for the intelligent system to explore or fully master such knowledge.

2.5.2 Incremental Learning for Spam E-mail Classification

In this case study, we demonstrate the incremental learning capability of the proposed framework to predict spam e-mails. Recently, growing security issues surrounding e-mail communications and spam detection have attracted significant attention of both the academic and industrial research communities. For instance, based on a survey of 400 network security professionals, spam has now surpassed viruses as the leading unwanted network intrusion (Whitworth & Whitworth, 2004). Furthermore, according to the Global Economic Impact of Spam report (2005) released by Ferris Research, it is estimated that lost productivity and other expenses associated with spam e-mails cost U.S. businesses $17 billion in 2005, up from $10 billion in 2003. Globally, the total cost could reach $50 billion (Ferris Research, 2005). Some of the existing techniques used to classify spam e-mails include the support vector machines (SVMs)–based method (Drucker & Vapnik, 1999), the neural network method (Yang & Elfayoumy, 2007), the particle swarm optimization (PSO) method (Lai & Wu, 2007), the Bayesian belief network (Zhang & Li, 2007), and many others. In this case study, our goal is to demonstrate that the proposed incremental learning framework can adaptively learn from continuous e-mail data, and accumulate knowledge over time to improve the spam detection performance.

2.5.2.1 Data Set Characteristic and System Configuration In our current study, we use the Spam database from the UCI Machine Learning Repository (Asuncion & Newman, 2009). This database includes 4,601 e-mail messages, in which 2,788 are legitimate messages and 1,813 are spam messages. Each message is represented by 57 attributes, of which 48 code the frequency of a particular word (FW), 6 code the frequency of a particular character (FC), and 3 continuous attributes reflect the statistics of the capital letters (SCL) in the e-mails: average length of uninterrupted sequences of capital letters, length of the longest uninterrupted sequence of capital letters, and the total number of capital letters in the e-mail. Table 2.1 summarizes the characteristics of this benchmark.

In our current work, we use both Euclidean distance and the neural network model to design the mapping functions as discussed in sections 2.4.1 and 2.4.2, respectively. For the neural network mapping function design, the number of hidden layer neurons is set to 10, and the number of input neurons and output neurons are 57 (the number of attributes) and 1, respectively. A sigmoid function is used for the activation function and backpropagation is used to train the network. One-thousand training iteration is used with a learning rate of 0.1. For the base classification algorithm, we adopt a decision tree in our current study.

To show the statistical information, all the results presented in this case study are based on 100 random runs. At each run, we randomly select half of the e-mail messages as the training data and the remaining half as the testing data.

Table 2.1: E-mail Data Benchmark Characteristics

Frequency of Word	make	address	all	3d	our	over
(FW): percentage of	remove	Internet	order	mail	receive	will
words in the email	people	report	address	free	business	email
that match a particular	you	credit	your	font	000	money
word	hp	hpl	george	650	lab	labs
	telnet	857	data	415	85	technology
	1999	parts	pm	direct	cs	meeting
	original	project	re	edu	table	conference
Frequency of characteristics (FC): percentage of characters in the e-mail that match a particular character	;	(	[	!	$	#
Statistics of capital letter (SCL)	Average length of uninterrupted sequences of capital letter					
	Length of longest uninterrupted sequences of capital letters					
	Total number of capital letters in the email					

Furthermore, we equally divide the training data to be 20 chunks and assume they become available incrementally over time.

2.5.2.2 Simulation Results Figure 2.16 shows the spam classification error rate versus the learning life for the proposed incremental learning framework. As one can see, classification performance improves with increasing learning life, demonstrating that the proposed method can effectively learn and accumulate experience over time, and use such knowledge to facilitate future learning from new data.

One may also observe that, for this data, the neural network mapping function seems to provide better detection performance than the Euclidean distance function. To have a better understanding of this, we further analyze the result by using a receiver operating characteristic (ROC) graph (Fawcett, 2003, 2006). The ROC graph is a popular evaluation method based on the classifier confusion matrix, which is formed by plotting the True Positive rate (TP rate) versus the False Positive rate (FP rate). In this way, any point in ROC space corresponds to the performance of a single classifier on a given distribution. Generally speaking, for hard-type classifiers that can only output predicted class labels, each of them corresponds to one point (FP rate, TP rate) in ROC space. On the other hand, soft-type classifiers, such as neural networks, which output likelihoods of instances belonging to classes, are represented by curves in the ROC space. Such curves are formulated by adjusting the decision thresholds to generate a series of points. The performance of soft-type classifiers can also be measured by calculating the area under curve (AUC) of their ROC curves. We also want to mention that it is generally very straight forward to make hard-type classifiers provide

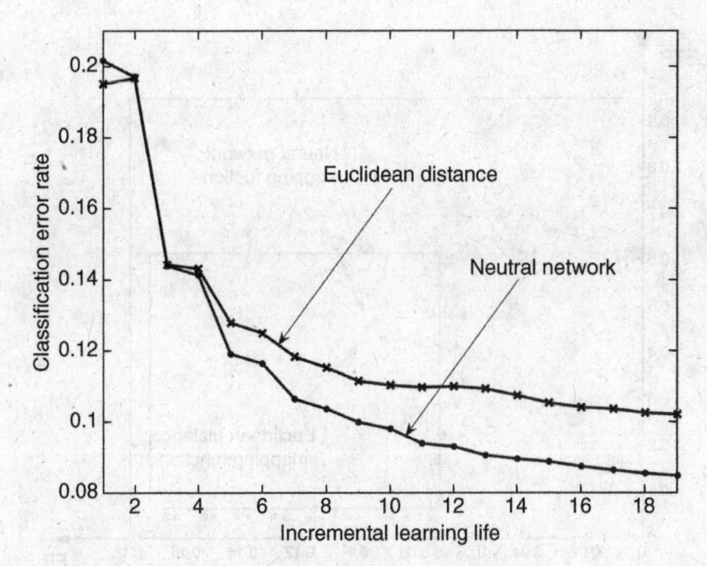

Figure 2.16: Spam e-mail classification error rate versus the incremental learning life (based on Euclidean distance and neural network).

soft-type outputs based on observations of the intrinsic characteristics of those classifiers (Freund & Schapire, 1996).

Figure 2.17 illustrates the ROC analysis of the proposed method for the two types of mapping function designs. We conducted 100 random runs for this experiment and plot the average ROC curve of all these runs. The average is obtained, as discussed in Fawcett (2003), by taking vertical samples of the ROC curves for fixed FP rates and averaging the corresponding TP rates. From Figure 2.17 we can see the ROC curve of the learning method based on the neural network mapping function dominates that based on the Euclidean distance function. This may suggest that, in this case, the nonlinear neural network mapping function provides better classification performance. We also want to note that the neural network mapping function requires more computation time than the Euclidean distance function. Based on our current simulation environment (Intel Core 2 Duo CPU E4400 @ 2.00 GHz, 2.0 GB RAM, and Matlab Version 7.2.0.232(R2006A)), the neural network mapping function takes about 68.7894 second while the Euclidean distance only needs 0.0177 second. These results provide a reference for the selection of the appropriate mapping function according to different application requirements and the trade-off between the accuracy and computational cost.

2.6 SUMMARY

- Incremental learning is critical to understanding brain-like intelligence and potentially bringing such a level of intelligence closer to reality for both

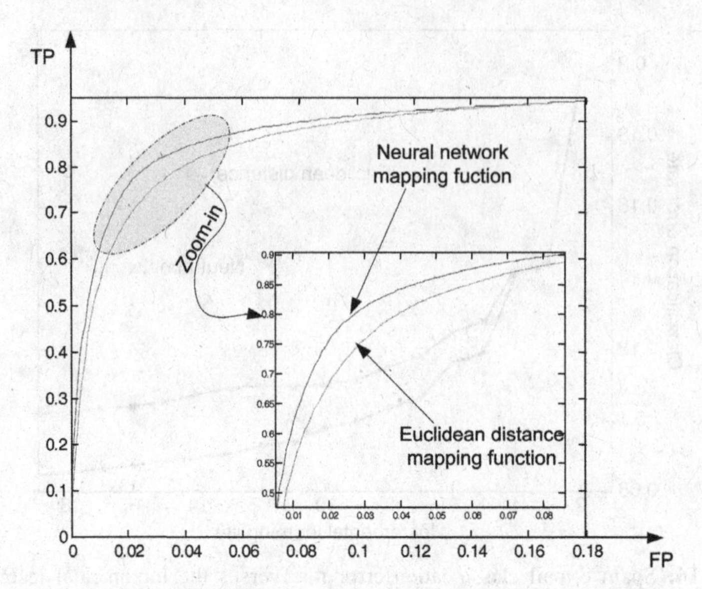

Figure 2.17: ROC analysis of the different mapping functions.

internal and external reasons. Internally, the intelligent system should be able to learn information incrementally throughout its lifetime, accumulate experience over time, and use such knowledge to benefit future learning to achieve its goal. Externally, the raw data that comes from the environment with which the intelligent system interacts becomes incrementally available over an indefinitely long (possibly infinite) learning lifetime. Therefore, the intelligent system should be able to self-adapt and incrementally learn from such continuous data.

- Based on the boosting methodology and adaptive learning principle, a general-purpose incremental learning framework is presented in this chapter. The goals of this learning framework include pass the previously learned knowledge to the current received data to benefit learning from the new information, accumulate experience over time, and achieve global generalization in the learning period.
- Mapping function design is important for the proposed incremental learning framework. Three design approaches are discussed in this chapter: the Euclidean distance approach, the regression learning approach, and the online value system approach.
- Concept drifting is important for understanding the robustness and learning capability during the incremental learning life. For instance, in the scene analysis, new objects may appear in the visual field during the learning period. Therefore, an intelligent system should have the capability to automatically modify its knowledge base to learn new data distributions. Two issues are discussed in this chapter. First, what kind of mechanisms can be

used in the incremental learning framework to enable the intelligent system to adaptively adjust to new concepts? Second, how fast can a learning system shift its decision boundary or knowledge base to accommodate the new concepts?

- Incremental learning has a wide range of applications across different domains. In this work, experimental results based on video stream data and spam e-mail data are presented to demonstrate the effectiveness of this method. These two case studies give a flavor of the application research based on the proposed incremental learning framework, and provide useful suggestions of using this framework to solve practical application problems.

REFERENCES

Asuncion, A., & Newman, D. J. (2009). UCI machine learning repository *[Online]. Available: http://archive.ics.uci.edu/ml/datasets.html*.

Bauer, E., & Kohavi, R. (1999). An empirical comparison of voting classification algorithms: Bagging, boosting, and variants. *Machine Learning*, *36*, 105–142.

Can, Y., & Grossberg, S. (2005). A laminar cortical model of stereopsis and 3d surface perception: Closuer and da vinci stereopsis. *Spatial Vis*., *18*, 515–578.

Dietterich, T. G. (2000). Experimental comparison of three methods for constructing ensembles of decision trees: Bagging, boosting, and randomization. *Machine Learning*, *40*(2), 139–157.

Drucker, W. D. H., & Vapnik, V. N. (1999). Support vector machines for spam categorization. *IEEE Trans. on Neural Netw*., *10*(5), 1048–1054.

Fawcett, T. (2003). ROC Graphs: Notes and practical considerations for data mining researchers. *Technical Report HPL-2003-4*. (HP Lab)

Fawcett, T. (2006). An introduction to ROC analysis. *Pattern Recognition letters*, *27*(8), 861–874.

Ferris Research. (2005). The global economics impact of spam. *[Online], http://www.ferris.com/hidden-pages/reducing-the-50-billion-global-spam-bill/*.

Freund, Y. (2001). An adaptive version of the boost by majority algorithm. *Machine Learning*, *3*, 293–318.

Freund, Y., & Schapire, R. E. (1996). Experiments with a new boosting algorithm. *Proc. Int. Conf. Machine Learning*, pp. 148–165.

Freund, Y., & Schapire, R. E. (1997). Decision-theoretic generalization of on-line learning and application to boosting. *J. Computer and Syst. Sciences*, *55*(1), 119–139.

Gonzalez, R. C., & Woods, R. E. (2002). *Digital image processing* (2nd ed.). Upper Saddle River, NJ: Prentice Hall.

Grossberg, S. (1998). *Neural Substrates of Adaptively Timed Reinforcement, Recognition, and Motor Learning*, in Models of action: Mechanisms for adaptive behavior. In C. D. L. Wynne & J. E. R. Staddon (Eds.), (pp. 29–85). Hillsdale, NJ: Erlbaum Associates.

Grossberg, S. (1999). How does the cerebral cortex work? Learning, attention and grouping by the laminar circuits of visual cortex. *Spatial Vis*., *12*, 163–185.

Grossberg, S. (2003). Adaptive resonance theory. *The Encyclopedia of Cognitive Science*. (Technical Report, CAS/CNS TR-2000-024).

Grossberg, S., & Howe, P. D. (2003). A laminar cortical model of stereopsis and three-dimensional surface perception. *Vis. Res.*, *43*(7), 801–829.

Haykin, S. (1999). *Neural networks: A comprehensive foundation* (2nd ed.). Upper Saddle River, NJ: Prentice Hall.

He, H., & Chen, S. (2008). IMORL: Incremental multi-object recognition and localization. *IEEE Trans. Neural Networks*, *19*(10), 1727–1738.

He, H., Chen, S., Cao, Y., Desai, S., & Hohil, M. E. (2008). Multi-objects recognition for distributed intelligent sensor networks. *Proc. SPIE*, 6963, 69630R–69630R-10.

He, H., Chen, S., Cao, Y., & Starzyk, J. A. (2008). Incremental learning for machine intelligence. *Proc. Int. Conf. on Cognitive and Neural Systems*.

He, H., & Starzyk, J. A. (2007). Online dynamic value system for machine learning. *Lecture Notes in Computer Science*, *4491*, 441–448.

Ke, Y., & Sukthankar, R. (2004). PCA-SIFT: A more distinctive representation for local image descriptors. *Proc. IEEE Comput. Vis. Pattern Recognit*, 2, 506–513.

Lai, C. C., & Wu, C. H. (2007). Particle swarm optimization-aided feature selection for spam email classification. *Proc. Int. Conf. Innovative Computing, Information and Control*, pp. 165.

Lowe, D. G. (1999). Object recognition from local scale-invariant features. *Proc. Int. Conf. Conput. Vis.*, pp. 1150–1157.

Lowe, D. G. (2003). Distinctive image features from scale-invariant keypoints. *Int. J. Comput. Vis.*, *20*.

Oza, N. C. (2003). Boosting with averaged weight vectors. In T. Windeatt & F. Roli (Eds.), *Int. Workshop Multiple Classifier Syst., Lecture Notes in Computer Science* (Vol. 2709, pp. 15–24). Springer.

Oza, N. C. (2004). AveBoost2: Boosting for noisy data. In F. Roli, J. Kittler, & T. Windeatt (Eds.), *Int. Workshop on Multiple Classifier Syst., Lecture Notes in Computer Science* (Vol. 3077, pp. 31–40). Springer.

Qian, N. (1999). On the momentum term in gradient descent learning algorithms. *Neural Networks*, *12*(1), 145–191.

Rumelhart, D. E., & McClelland, J. L. (1986a). *Parallel distributed processing: Explorations in the microstructure of cognition, vol. 1*. Cambridge, MA: MIT Press.

Rumelhart, D. E., & McClelland, J. L. (1986b). *Parallel distributed processing: Explorations in the microstructure of cognition, vol. 2*. Cambridge, MA: MIT Press.

Schapire, R. E., Freund, Y., Barlett, P., & Lee, W. S. (1998). Boosting the margin: A new explanation for the effectiveness of voting methods. *Annals of Statistics*, *26*(5), 1651–1686.

Scott, D. W. (1992). *Multivariate density estimation: Theory, practise, and visualization*. New York: Wiley-Interscience.

Silverman, B. W. (1986). *Density estimation for statistics and data analysis*. Chapman & Hall/CRC.

Wang, D. L. (2005). The time dimension for scene analysis. *IEEE Trans. Neural Networks*, *16*(6), 1401–1426.

Whitworth, B., & Whitworth, E. (2004). Spam and the social technical gap. *IEEE Computer*, *37*(10), 38–45.

Yang, Y., & Elfayoumy, S. (2007). Anti-spam filtering using neural networks and bayesian classifiers. *Proc. IEEE Int. Symposium on Computational Intelligence in Robotics and Automation*, pp. 272–278.

Zhang, H., & Li, D. (2007). Naïve bayes text classifier. *Proc. Int. Conf. Granular Computing*, pp. 708–708.

Zickler, S., & Veloso, M. (2006). Detection and localization of multiple objects. *Proc. Humanoids*, pp. 20–25.

CHAPTER 3

Imbalanced Learning

3.1 INTRODUCTION

In recent years, the imbalanced learning problem has drawn a significant amount of interest from academia and industry. Briefly speaking, the imbalanced learning problem is concerned with the performance of learning algorithms in the presence of underrepresented data and skewed class distributions (He & Garcia, 2009). Due to the inherent complex characteristics of imbalanced data sets, learning from such data requires new understandings, principles, algorithms, and tools to transform vast amounts of raw data efficiently into information and knowledge representation. When translated to real-world domains, the imbalanced learning issue represents a recurring problem of high importance with wide-ranging implications, warranting increasing exploration. This increased interest is reflected in the recent installment of several major workshops, conferences, and special issues including the Association for the Advancement of Artificial Intelligence workshop on Learning from Imbalanced Data Sets (AAAI'00), the International Conference on Machine Learning workshop on Learning from Imbalanced Data Sets (ICML'03) (Chawla, Japkowicz, & Kołcz, 2003), and the Association for Computing Machinery Special Interest Group on Knowledge Discovery and Data Mining Explorations (ACM SIGKDD Explorations '04) (Chawla, Japkowicz, & Kołcz, 2004). In this chapter, we seek to provide a systematic discussion of the nature of the imbalanced problem, and the state-of-the-art solutions created to address this problem (He & Garcia, 2009).

3.2 THE NATURE OF IMBALANCED LEARNING

Before discussing the techniques to address the imbalanced learning problem, let us start with a particular example from biomedical application to understand the nature of imbalanced learning. Consider the "Mammography Data Set," a collection of images acquired from a series of mammography exams performed on a set of distinct patients, which has been widely used in the analysis of

Self-Adaptive Systems for Machine Intelligence, First Edition. Haibo He.

algorithms addressing the imbalanced learning problem (Chawla, Bowyer, Hall, & Kegelmeyer, 2002; Guo & Viktor, 2004b; Woods et al., 1993). Analyzing the images in a binary sense, the natural classes (labels) that arise are "positive" or "negative" for an image representative of a "cancerous" or "healthy" patient, respectively. From experience, one would expect the number of noncancerous patients to exceed greatly the number of cancerous patients; indeed, this data set contains 10,923 "negative" (majority class) samples and 260 "positive" (minority class) samples. Preferably, we require a classifier that provides a balanced degree of predictive accuracy (ideally 100 percent) for both the minority and majority classes on the data set. In reality, we find that classifiers tend to provide a severely imbalanced degree of accuracy, with the majority class having close to 100 percent accuracy and the minority class having accuracies of 0–10 percent, for instance (Chawla et al., 2002; Woods et al., 1993). Suppose a classifier achieves 10 percent accuracy on the minority class of the mammography data set. Analytically, this would suggest that 234 minority samples are misclassified as majority samples. The consequence of this is equivalent to 234 cancerous patients classified (diagnosed) as noncancerous. In the medical industry, the ramifications of such a consequence can be overwhelmingly costly, more so than classifying a noncancerous patient as cancerous (Rao, Krishnan, & Niculescu, 2006). Therefore, it is evident that for this domain, we require a classifier that will provide high accuracy for the minority class without severely jeopardizing the accuracy of the majority class. Furthermore, this also suggests that the conventional evaluation practice of using singular assessment criteria, such as the overall accuracy or error rate, does not provide adequate information in the case of imbalanced learning. Therefore, more informative assessment metrics are necessary for conclusive evaluations of performance in the presence of imbalanced data. These topics will be discussed in detail in section 3.4 of this chapter. In addition to biomedical applications, further speculation will yield similar consequences for domains such as fraud detection, network intrusion, and oil-spill detection, to name a few (Kubat, Holte, & Matwin, 1998; Rao et al., 2006; Chan, Fan, Prodromidis, & Stolfo, 1999; Clifton, Damminda, & Vincent, 2004; Chan & Stolfo, 1998).

Technically speaking, any data set that exhibits an unequal distribution between its classes can be considered imbalanced. However, the common understanding in the community is that imbalanced data correspond to data sets exhibiting significant, and in some cases extreme, imbalances. Specifically, this form of imbalance is referred to as a *between-class imbalance*; not uncommon are between-class imbalances on the order of 100:1, 1,000:1, and 10,000:1, where in each case, one class severely outrepresents another (He & Shen, 2007; Kubat et al., 1998; Pearson, Goney, & Shwaber, 2003). Although this description would seem to imply that all between-class imbalances are innately binary (or two-class), we note that there are multiclass data in which imbalances exist between the various classes (Sun, Kamel, & Wang, 2006; Abe, Zadrozny, & Langford, 2004; Chen, Lu, & Kwok, 2006; Zhou & Liu, 2006; Liu & Zhou, 2006b; Tan, Gilbert, & Deville, 2003).

Imbalances of the aforementioned biomedical example are commonly referred to as *intrinsic*, i.e., the imbalance is a direct result of the nature of the dataspace. However, imbalanced data are not solely restricted to the intrinsic variety. Variable factors such as time and storage also give rise to data sets that are imbalanced. Imbalances of this type are considered *extrinsic*, i.e., the imbalance is not directly related to the nature of the dataspace. Extrinsic imbalances are equally as interesting as their intrinsic counterparts since it may very well occur that the dataspace from which an extrinsic imbalanced data set is attained may not be imbalanced at all. For instance, suppose a data set is procured from a continuous data stream of balanced data over a specific interval of time, and if during this interval, the transmission has sporadic interruptions where data are not transmitted, then it is possible that the acquired data set can be imbalanced, in which case the data set would be an extrinsic imbalanced data set attained from a balanced dataspace (He & Garcia, 2009).

In addition to intrinsic and extrinsic imbalance, it is important to understand the difference between *relative imbalance* and *imbalance due to rare instances* (or "absolute rarity") (Weiss, 2004, 2005). Consider a mammography data set with 100,000 examples and a 100:1 between-class imbalance. We would expect this data set to contain 1,000 minority class examples; clearly, the majority class dominates the minority class. Suppose we then double the sample space by testing more patients, and suppose further that the distribution does not change, i.e., the minority class now contains 2,000 examples. Clearly, the minority class is still outnumbered; however, with 2,000 examples, the minority class is not necessarily rare in its own right but rather relative to the majority class. This example is representative of a relative imbalance. Relative imbalances arise frequently in real-world applications and are often the focus of existing efforts. Some studies have shown that for certain relative imbalanced data sets, the minority concept is accurately learned with little disturbance from the imbalance (Batista, Prati, & Monard, 2004; Japkowicz & Stephen, 2002; Weiss & Provost, 2003). These results are particularly suggestive because they show that the degree of imbalance is not the only factor that hinders learning. As it turns out, data set complexity is the primary determining factor of classification deterioration, which, in turn, is amplified by the addition of a relative imbalance.

Data complexity is a broad term that comprises issues such as overlapping, lack of representative data, small disjuncts, and others (He & Garcia, 2009). In a simple example, consider the depicted distributions in Figure 3.1. In this figure, the stars and circles represent the minority and majority classes, respectively. By inspection, we see that both distributions in Figures 3.1(a) and 3.1(b) exhibit relative imbalances. However, notice how Figure 3.1(a) has no overlapping examples between its classes and has only one concept pertaining to each class, whereas Figure 3.1(b) has both multiple concepts and severe overlapping. Also of interest is subconcept C in the distribution of Figure 3.1(b). This concept might go unlearned by some inducers due to its lack of representative data; this issue embodies imbalances due to rare instances, which we proceed to explore.

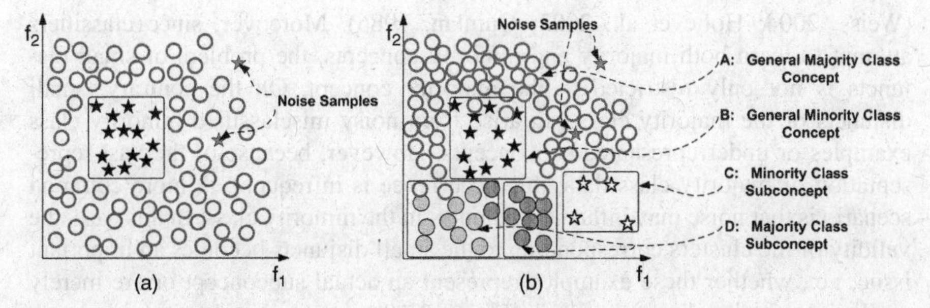

Figure 3.1: The imbalanced learning problem. (a) A data set with a between-class imbalance. (b) A high-complexity data set with both between-class and within-class imbalances, multiple concepts, overlapping, noise, and lack of representative data.

Imbalance due to rare instances is representative of domains where minority class examples are very limited, i.e., where the target concept is rare (He & Garcia, 2009). In this situation, the lack of representative data will make learning difficult regardless of the between-class imbalance (Weiss, 2004). Furthermore, the minority concept may additionally contain a subconcept with limited instances, amounting to diverging degrees of classification difficulty (Holte, Acker, & Porter, 2003; Quinlan, 1986). This, in fact, is the result of another form of imbalance, a *within-class imbalance*, which concerns itself with the distribution of representative data for subconcepts within a class (Jo & Japkowicz, 2004; Japkowicz 2003; Prati, Batista, & Monard, 2004). These ideas are again highlighted in our simplified example in Figure 3.1. In Figure 3.1(b), cluster B represents the dominant minority class concept and cluster C represents a subconcept of the minority class. Cluster D represents two subconcepts of the majority class and cluster A (anything not enclosed) represents the dominant majority class concept. For both classes, the number of examples in the dominant clusters significantly outnumber the examples in their respective subconcept clusters, so that this dataspace exhibits both within-class and between-class imbalances. Moreover, if we completely remove the examples in cluster B, the dataspace would then have a homogeneous minority class concept that is easily identified (cluster C), but can go unlearned due to its severe underrepresentation.

The existence of within-class imbalances is closely intertwined with the problem of small disjuncts, which has been shown to greatly depreciate classification performance (Japkowicz & Stephen, 2002; Jo & Japkowicz, 2004; Japkowicz, 2003; Prati et al., 2004). Briefly, the problem of small disjuncts can be understood as follows: A classifier will attempt to learn a concept by creating multiple disjunct rules that describe the main concept (Weiss, 2004; Holte et al., 2003; Quinlan, 1986). In the case of homogeneous concepts, the classifier will generally create large disjuncts, i.e., rules that cover a large portion (cluster) of examples pertaining to the main concept. However, in the case of heterogeneous concepts, small disjuncts, i.e., rules that cover a small cluster of examples pertaining to the main concept, arise as a direct result of underrepresented subconcepts

(Weiss, 2004; Holte et al., 2003; Quinlan, 1986). Moreover, since classifiers attempt to learn both majority and minority concepts, the problem of small disjuncts is not only restricted to the minority concept. On the contrary, small disjuncts of the majority class can arise from noisy misclassified minority class examples or underrepresented subconcepts. However, because of the vast representation of majority class data, this occurrence is infrequent. A more common scenario is that noise may influence disjuncts in the minority class. In this case, the validity of the clusters corresponding to the small disjuncts becomes an important issue, i.e., whether these examples represent an actual subconcept or are merely attributed to noise. For example, in Figure 3.1(b), suppose a classifier generates disjuncts for each of the two noisy minority samples in cluster A, then these would be illegitimate disjuncts attributed to noise compared to cluster C, for example, which is a legitimate cluster formed from a severely underrepresented subconcept.

The last issue we would like to note is the combination of imbalanced data and the small sample size problem (Raudys & Jain, 1991; Caruana, 2000). In many of today's application domains, it is often unavoidable to have data with high dimensionality and small sample size; some specific examples include face recognition and gene expression data analysis, among others. Traditionally, the small sample size problem has been studied extensively in the pattern recognition community (Raudys & Jain, 1991). Dimensionality reduction methods have been widely adopted to handle this issue, e.g., principal component analysis (PCA) and various extension methods (Yang, Dai, & Yan, 2008). However, when the representative data sets' concepts exhibit imbalances of the forms described earlier, the combination of imbalanced data and small sample size presents a new challenge to the community (Caruana, 2000). In this situation, there are two critical issues that arise simultaneously (Caruana, 2000). First, since the sample size is small, all of the issues related to absolute rarity and within-class imbalances are applicable. Second and more importantly, learning algorithms often fail to generalize inductive rules over the sample space when presented with this form of imbalance. In this case, the combination of small sample size and high dimensionality hinders learning because of difficulty involved in forming conjunctions over the high degree of features with limited samples. If the sample space is sufficiently large enough, a set of general (albeit complex) inductive rules can be defined for the dataspace. However, when samples are limited, the rules formed can become too specific, leading to overfitting. In regards to learning from such data sets, this is a relatively new research topic that requires much needed attention in the community. As a result, we will touch upon this topic again later in our discussions.

3.3 SOLUTIONS FOR IMBALANCED LEARNING

The nature of the imbalanced learning problem discussed in section 3.2 provides the foundation for most of the current research activities to address this challenging problem (He & Garcia, 2009). In particular, the immense hindering effects that these problems have on standard learning algorithms are the focus of most of the existing solutions. When standard learning algorithms are applied to imbalanced data, the induction rules that describe the minority concepts are often fewer and weaker than those of majority concepts, since the minority class is often both outnumbered and underrepresented.

To provide a concrete understanding of the direct effects of the imbalanced learning problem on standard learning algorithms, we observe a case study of the popular decision tree learning algorithm. In this case, imbalanced data sets exploit inadequacies in the splitting criterion at each node of the decision tree (Japkowicz & Stephen, 2002; Weiss & Provost, 2003), (Chawla, 2003). Generally speaking, decision trees use a recursive, top-down greedy search algorithm that uses a feature selection scheme (e.g., information gain) to select the best feature as the split criterion at each node of the tree; a successor (leaf) is then created for each of the possible values corresponding to the split feature (Quinlan, 1986; Mitchell, 1997). As a result, the training set is successively partitioned into smaller subsets that are ultimately used to form disjoint rules pertaining to class concepts. These rules are finally combined so that the final hypothesis minimizes the total error rate across each class. The problem with this procedure in the presence of imbalanced data is two-fold. First, successive partitioning of the dataspace results in fewer and fewer observations of minority class examples resulting in fewer leaves describing minority concepts and successively weaker confidences estimates. Second, concepts that have dependencies on different feature space conjunctions can go unlearned by the sparseness introduced through partitioning. Here, the first issue correlates with the problems of relative and absolute imbalances, while the second issue best correlates with the between-class imbalance and the problem of high dimensionality. In both cases, the effects of imbalanced data on decision tree classification performance are detrimental. In the following sections, we evaluate the solutions proposed to overcome the effects of imbalanced data.

For clear presentation, we establish here some of the notations used in this section. Considering a given training data set S with m examples (i.e., $|S| = m$) we define: $S = \{(\boldsymbol{x}_i, y_i)\}, i = 1, \ldots, m$, where $\boldsymbol{x}_i \in X$ is an instance in the n-dimensional feature space $X = \{f_1, f_2, \ldots, f_n\}$, and $y_i \in Y = \{1, \ldots, C\}$ is a class identity label associated with instance $\boldsymbol{x}_i$. In particular, $C = 2$ represents the two-class classification problem. Furthermore, we define subsets $S_{min} \subset S$ and $S_{maj} \subset S$, where S_{min} is the set of minority class examples in S, and S_{maj} is the set of majority class examples in S, so that $S_{min} \cap S_{maj} = \{\Phi\}$ and $S_{min} \cup S_{maj} = \{S\}$. Lastly, any sets generated from sampling procedures on S are labeled E, with disjoint subsets E_{min} and E_{maj} representing the minority and majority samples of E, respectively, whenever they apply.

3.3.1 Sampling Methods for Imbalanced Learning

Typically, the use of sampling methods in imbalanced learning applications consists of the modification of an imbalanced data set by some mechanisms in order to provide a balanced distribution (He & Garcia, 2009). Studies have shown that for several base classifiers a balanced data set provides improved overall classification performance compared to an imbalanced data set (Weiss & Provost, 2001; Laurikkala, 2001; Estabrooks, Jo, & Japkowicz, 2004). These results justify the use of sampling methods for imbalanced learning. However, they do not imply that classifiers cannot learn from imbalanced data sets; on the contrary, studies have also shown that classifiers induced from certain imbalanced data sets are comparable to classifiers induced from the same data set balanced by sampling techniques (Batista et al., 2004; Japkowicz & Stephen, 2002). This phenomenon has been directly linked to the problem of rare cases and its corresponding consequences as described in section 3.2. Nevertheless, for most imbalanced data sets, the application of sampling techniques does indeed aid in improved classifier accuracy.

3.3.1.1 Random Oversampling and Undersampling The mechanics of *random oversampling* follow naturally from its description by adding a set E sampled from the minority class: for a set of randomly selected minority examples in S_{min}, augment the original set S by replicating the selected examples and adding them to S. In this way, the number of total examples in S_{min} is increased by $|E|$, and the class distribution balance of S is adjusted accordingly. This provides a mechanism for varying the degree of class distribution balance to any desired level. The oversampling method is simple to both understand and visualize, thus we refrain from providing any specific examples of its functionality.

While oversampling appends data to the original data set, *random undersampling* removes data from the original data set. In particular, we randomly select a set of majority class examples in S_{maj}, and remove these samples from S, so that $|S| = |S_{min}| + |S_{maj}| - |E|$. Consequently, undersampling readily gives us a simple method for adjusting the balance of the original data set S.

At first glance, the oversampling and undersampling methods appear to be functionally equivalent since they both alter the size of the original data set and can actually provide the same proportion of balance. However, this commonality is only superficial; each method introduces its own set of problematic consequences that can potentially hinder learning (He & Garcia, 2009; Holte et al., 2003; Mease, Wyner, & Buja, 2007; Drummond & Holte, 2003). In the case of undersampling, the problem is relatively obvious (He & Garcia, 2009): Removing examples from the majority class may cause the classifier to miss important concepts pertaining to the majority class. In regards to oversampling, the problem is a little more opaque: Since oversampling simply appends replicated data to the original data set, multiple instances of certain examples become "tied," leading to overfitting (Mease et al., 2007). In particular, overfitting in oversampling occurs when classifiers produce multiple clauses in a rule for multiple copies of the same example, which causes the rule to become too specific (He & Garcia, 2009); although the training accuracy will be high in this scenario, the classification performance on the unseen testing data is generally far worse (Holte et al., 2003).

3.3.1.2 Informed Undersampling Two examples of informed undersampling that have shown competitive results are presented in Liu, Wu, and Zhou (2006), the *EasyEnsemble* and *BalanceCascade* algorithms. The objective of these two methods is to overcome the deficiency of information loss introduced in the traditional random undersampling method. The implementation of EasyEnsemble is very straightforward: it develops an ensemble learning system by independently sampling several subsets from the majority class and developing multiple classifiers based on the combination of each subset with the minority class data. In this way, EasyEnsemble can be considered as an unsupervised learning algorithm that explores the majority class data by using independent random sampling with replacement. On the other hand, the BalanceCascade algorithm takes a supervised learning approach that develops an ensemble of classifiers to systematically select which majority class examples to undersample. Specifically, for the first hypothesis of the ensemble, $H(1)$, consider a sampled set of majority class examples, E, such that $|E| = |S_{min}|$ and subject the ensemble to set $N = \{E \cup S_{min}\}$ to induce $H(1)$. Observing the results of $H(1)$, identify all $\boldsymbol{x}_i \in N$ that are correctly classified as belonging to S_{maj} and call this collection N^*_{maj}. Then since we already have $H(1)$, it is reasonable to assume that N^*_{maj} is somewhat redundant in S_{maj} given that $H(1)$ is already trained. Based on this, we remove set N^*_{maj} from S_{maj}, and generate a new sampled set of majority class samples, E, with $|E| = |S_{min}|$ and again subject the ensemble to set $N = \{E \cup S_{min}\}$ to derive $H(2)$. This procedure is iterated to a stopping criteria at which point a cascading combination scheme is used to form a final hypothesis (Liu et al., 2006).

Another example of informed undersampling uses the K-nearest neighbor (KNN) classifier to achieve undersampling. Based on the characteristics of the given data distribution, four KNN undersampling methods were proposed in Zhang and Mani (2003), namely NearMiss-1, NearMiss-2, NearMiss-3, and the "most distant" method. The NearMiss-1 method selects those majority examples whose average distance to the three closest minority class examples are the smallest, while the NearMiss-2 method selects the majority class examples whose average distance to the three farthest minority class examples are the smallest. NearMiss-3 selects a given number of the closest majority examples for each minority example to guarantee that every minority example is surrounded by some majority examples. Finally, the "most distance" method selects the majority class examples whose average distance to the three closest minority class examples are the largest. Experimental results suggested that the NearMiss-2 method can provide competitive results for imbalanced learning.

There are also other types of informed undersampling methods. For instance, the one-sided selection (OSS) method (Kubat & Matwin, 1997) selects a representative subset of the majority class, E, and combines it with the set of all minority examples S_{min} to form a preliminary set N, $N = \{E \cup S_{min}\}$. This set N is further refined by using a data cleaning technique. We will return to the discussion of this method in section 3.3.1.5, now turning our attention to synthetic sampling methods.

3.3.1.3 *Synthetic Sampling with Data Generation* In regards to synthetic sampling, the synthetic minority oversampling technique (SMOTE) is a powerful method that has shown a great deal of success in various applications (Chawla et al., 2002). The SMOTE algorithm creates artificial data based on the feature space similarities between existing minority examples. Specifically, for subset $S_{min} \in S$, consider the K-nearest neighbors for each example $\boldsymbol{x}_i \in S_{min}$, for some specified integer K; the K-nearest neighbors are defined as the K elements of S_{min} whose Euclidian distance between itself and the $\boldsymbol{x}_i$ under consideration exhibits the smallest magnitude along the n-dimensions of feature space X. To create a synthetic sample, randomly select one of the K-nearest neighbors, then multiply the corresponding feature vector difference with a random number between [0, 1], and finally add this vector to $\boldsymbol{x}_i$.

$$\boldsymbol{x}_{new} = \boldsymbol{x}_i + (\hat{\boldsymbol{x}}_i - \boldsymbol{x}_i) \times \delta \tag{3.1}$$

Where $\boldsymbol{x}_i \in S_{min}$ is the minority instance under consideration, $\hat{\boldsymbol{x}}_i$ is one of the K-nearest neighbors for $\boldsymbol{x}_i : \hat{\boldsymbol{x}}_i \in S_{min}$, and $\delta \in [0, 1]$ is a random number. Therefore, the resulting synthetic instance according to Equation (3.1) is a point along the line segment joining the $\boldsymbol{x}_i$ under consideration and the randomly selected K-nearest neighbor $\hat{\boldsymbol{x}}_i$.

Figure 3.2 shows an example of the SMOTE procedure. Figure 3.2(a) shows a typical imbalanced data distribution, where the stars and circles represent examples of the minority and majority class, respectively. The number of K-nearest neighbors is set to $K = 6$. Figure 3.2(b) shows a created sample along the line between $\boldsymbol{x}_i$ and $\hat{\boldsymbol{x}}_i$, highlighted by the diamond shape. These synthetic samples help break the ties introduced by simple oversampling and furthermore augment the original data set in a manner that generally significantly improves learning. Though it has shown many promising benefits, the SMOTE algorithm

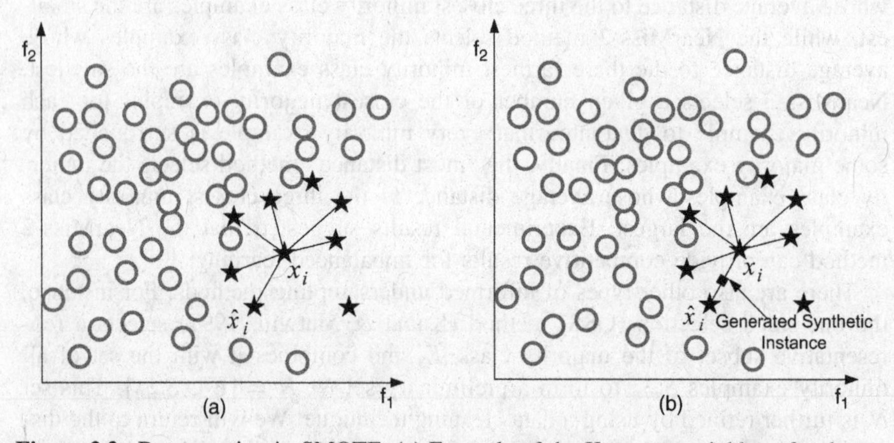

Figure 3.2: Data creation in SMOTE. (a) Example of the K-nearest neighbors for the $\boldsymbol{x}_i$ under consideration ($K = 6$). (b) Data creation based on Euclidian distance.

also has its drawbacks, including over generalization and variance (Wang & Japkowicz, 2004). We will further analyze these limitations in the following discussion.

3.3.1.4 Adaptive Synthetic Sampling In the SMOTE algorithm, the problem of over generalization is largely attributed to the way in which it creates synthetic samples. Specifically, SMOTE generates the same number of synthetic data samples for each original minority example and does so without consideration to neighboring examples, which increases the occurrence of overlapping between classes (Wang & Japkowicz, 2004). To this end, various adaptive sampling methods have been proposed to overcome this limitation; some representative work includes the Borderline-SMOTE (Han, Wang, & Mao, 2005) and Adaptive Synthetic Sampling (ADASYN) (He, Bai, Garcia, & Li, 2008) algorithms.

Of particular interest with these adaptive algorithms are the techniques used to identify minority seed samples. In the case of Borderline-SMOTE this is achieved as follows. First, determine the set of nearest neighbors for each $\boldsymbol{x}_i \in S_{min}$; call this set $S_{i:m-NN}$, $S_{i:m-NN} \subset S$. Next, for each $\boldsymbol{x}_i$ identify the number of nearest neighbors that belongs to the majority class, i.e., $|S_{i:m-NN} \cap S_{maj}|$. Finally, select those $\boldsymbol{x}_i$ that satisfy:

$$\frac{m}{2} \leq |S_{i:m-NN} \cap S_{maj}| < m \tag{3.2}$$

Equation (3.2) suggests that only those $\boldsymbol{x}_i$ that have more majority class neighbors than minority class neighbors are selected to form the set "DANGER" (Han et al., 2005). Therefore, the examples in DANGER represent the borderline minority class examples (the examples that are most likely to be misclassified). The DANGER set is then fed to the SMOTE algorithm to generate synthetic minority samples in the neighborhood of the borders. Figure 3.3 illustrates an example of the Borderline-SMOTE procedure. One should note that if $|S_{i:m-NN} \cap S_{maj}| = m$, i.e., if all of the m nearest neighbors of $\boldsymbol{x}_i$ are majority examples, such as instance C in Figure 3.3, then this $\boldsymbol{x}_i$ is considered as noise and no synthetic examples are generated for it. Comparing Figure 3.3 and Figure 3.2, we see that the major difference between Borderline-SMOTE and SMOTE is that SMOTE generates synthetic instances for each minority instance, while Borderline-SMOTE only generates synthetic instances for those minority examples "closer" to the border.

ADASYN, on the other hand, uses a systematic method to adaptively create different amounts of synthetic data according to their distributions (He et al., 2008). This is achieved as follows. First, calculate the number of synthetic data examples that need to be generated for the entire minority class:

$$G = \left(|S_{maj}| - |S_{min}|\right) \times \beta \tag{3.3}$$

where $\beta \in [0, 1]$ is a parameter used to specify the desired balance level after the synthetic data generation process. Next, for each example $\boldsymbol{x}_i \in S_{min}$, find the

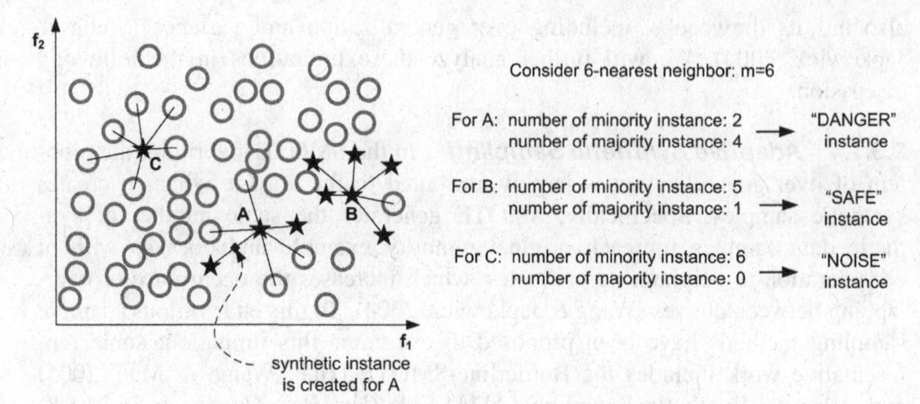

Figure 3.3: Data creation based on Borderline instance.

K-nearest neighbors according to the Euclidean distance, and calculate the ratio Γ_i defined as:

$$\Gamma_i = \frac{\Delta_i / K}{Z}, \quad i = 1, \ldots, |S_{min}| \tag{3.4}$$

where Δ_i is the number of examples in the K-nearest neighbors of $\boldsymbol{x}_i$ that belong to S_{maj}, and Z is a normalization constant so that Γ_i is a distribution function ($\sum \Gamma_i = 1$). Then determine the number of synthetic data samples that need to be generated for each $\boldsymbol{x}_i \in S_{min}$:

$$g_i = \Gamma_i \times G \tag{3.5}$$

Finally, for each $\boldsymbol{x}_i \in S_{min}$, generate g_i synthetic data samples according to equation (3.1). The key idea of the ADASYN algorithm is to use a density distribution Γ as a criterion to automatically decide the number of synthetic samples that need to be generated for each minority example by adaptively changing the weights of different minority examples to compensate for the skewed distributions. In this way, ADASYN can adaptively and systematically generate the synthetic data samples according to the data distribution, which has demonstrated many successful applications across a wide range of data sets (He et al., 2008). One should also note that the nearest neighbor calculation in SMOTE only considers the minority examples, while in the ADASYN and Borderline-SMOTE methods, both minority and majority examples are considered (see Figures 3.3 and 3.2).

Figure 3.4 shows the classification error performance for different β coefficients for a two-class imbalanced data set based on the ADASYN method (He et al., 2008). The training data set includes 50 minority class examples and 200 majority class examples, and the testing data set includes 200 examples. All data examples are generated by multidimensional Gaussian distributions with different mean and covariance matrix parameters. These results are based on the average

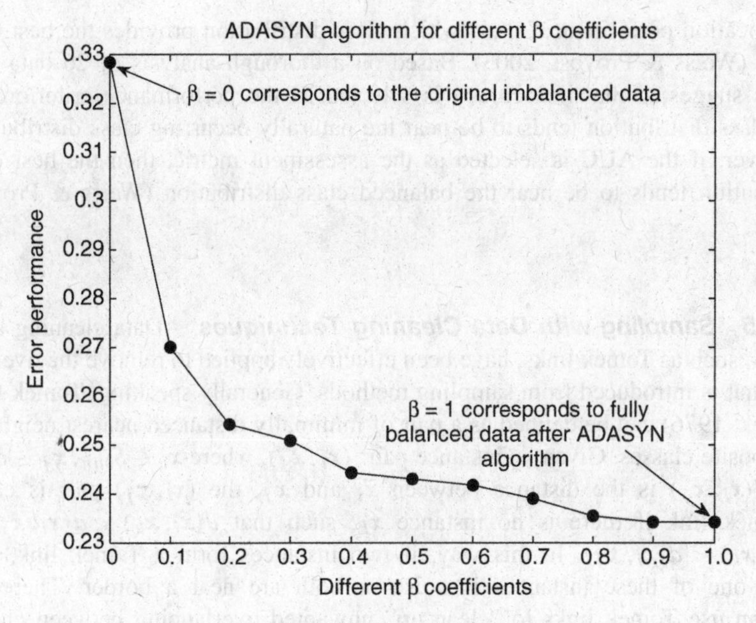

Figure 3.4: ADASYN for imbalanced learning.

of 100 runs with a decision tree as the base classifier. In Figure 3.4, $\beta = 0$ corresponds to the classification error based on the original imbalanced data set, while $\beta = 1$ represents a fully balanced data set generated by the ADASYN algorithm. Figure 3.4 shows that the ADASYN algorithm can improve the classification performance by reducing the bias introduced in the original imbalanced data sets. Furthermore, it also demonstrates the tendency in error reduction as balance level is increased by ADASYN. However, this does not mean in the general case that learning performance will always be increased with the increased balanced level of the data distribution. In fact, there exist many works discussing the "optimal" or "desired" degree of balance ratio for learning from imbalanced data (Weiss & Provost, 2003; Estabrooks et al., 2004). For instance, the rate of oversampling and undersampling was discussed in Estabrooks et al. (2004) as a possible aid for imbalanced learning. Generally speaking, though the resampling paradigm has demonstrated many successful cases in the community, tuning these algorithms effectively is a challenging task. To alleviate this challenge, Estabrooks et al. suggested that a combination of different expressions of resampling methods may be an effective solution to the tuning problem (Estabrooks et al., 2004). Weiss and Provost (2003) have analyzed, for a fixed training set size, the relationship between the class distribution of training data (expressed as the percentage of minority class examples) and classifier performance in terms of accuracy and AUC (area under the receiver operating characteristic [ROC] curve, which will be discussed in detail in section 3.4.2). This work provided important suggestions regarding "how do different training data class distributions affect classification performance" and "which class distribution provides the best classifier" (Weiss & Provost, 2003). Based on a thorough analysis of 26 data sets, it was suggested that if accuracy is selected as the performance criterion, the best class distribution tends to be near the naturally occurring class distribution. However, if the AUC is selected as the assessment metric, then the best class distribution tends to be near the balanced class distribution (Weiss & Provost, 2003).

3.3.1.5 Sampling with Data Cleaning Techniques Data cleaning techniques, such as Tomek links, have been effectively applied to remove the overlapping that is introduced from sampling methods. Generally speaking, Tomek links (Tomek, 1976) can be defined as a pair of minimally distanced nearest neighbors of opposite classes. Given an instance pair: $(\boldsymbol{x}_i, \boldsymbol{x}_j)$, where $\boldsymbol{x}_i \in S_{min}, \boldsymbol{x}_j \in S_{maj}$, and $d(\boldsymbol{x}_i, \boldsymbol{x}_j)$ is the distance between $\boldsymbol{x}_i$ and $\boldsymbol{x}_j$, the $(\boldsymbol{x}_i, \boldsymbol{x}_j)$ pair is called a Tomek link if there is no instance $\boldsymbol{x}_k$, such that $d(\boldsymbol{x}_i, \boldsymbol{x}_k) < d(\boldsymbol{x}_i, \boldsymbol{x}_j)$ or $d(\boldsymbol{x}_j, \boldsymbol{x}_k) < d(\boldsymbol{x}_i, \boldsymbol{x}_j)$. In this way, if two instances form a Tomek link, then either one of these instances is noise or both are near a border. Therefore, one can use Tomek links to "clean up" unwanted overlapping between classes after synthetic sampling where all Tomek links are removed until all minimally distanced nearest neighbor pairs are of the same class. By removing overlapping examples one can establish well-defined class clusters in the training set, which can in turn lead to well-defined classification rules for improved classification performance. Some representative work in this area includes the one-side selection (OSS) method (Kubat & Matwin, 1997); the condensed nearest neighbor rule and Tomek links (CNN+Tomek Links) integration method (Batista et al., 2004); the neighborhood cleaning rule (NCL) (Laurikkala, 2001) based on the edited nearest neighbor (ENN) rule, which removes examples that differ from two of its three nearest neighbors; and the integrations of SMOTE with ENN (SMOTE+ENN) and SMOTE with Tomek links (SMOTE+Tomek) (Batista et al., 2004).

Figure 3.5 shows a typical procedure of using SMOTE and Tomek to clean the overlapping data points (He & Garcia, 2009). Figure 3.5(a) shows the original data set distribution for an artificial imbalanced data set; note the inherent overlapping that exists between the minority and majority examples. Figure 3.5(b) shows the data set distribution after synthetic sampling by SMOTE. As we can see, there is an increased amount of overlapping introduced by SMOTE. In Figure 3.5(c) the Tomek links are identified, which are represented by the dashed boxes. Lastly, Figure 3.5(d) shows the data set after cleanup is performed. We can see that the algorithm produces more well-defined class clusters, which potentially contributes to improved classification performance. Furthermore, the idea illustrated in Figure 3.5 is important since it introduces a consideration for class clusters; we further investigate class clusters in the following discussion of the cluster-based sampling algorithm.

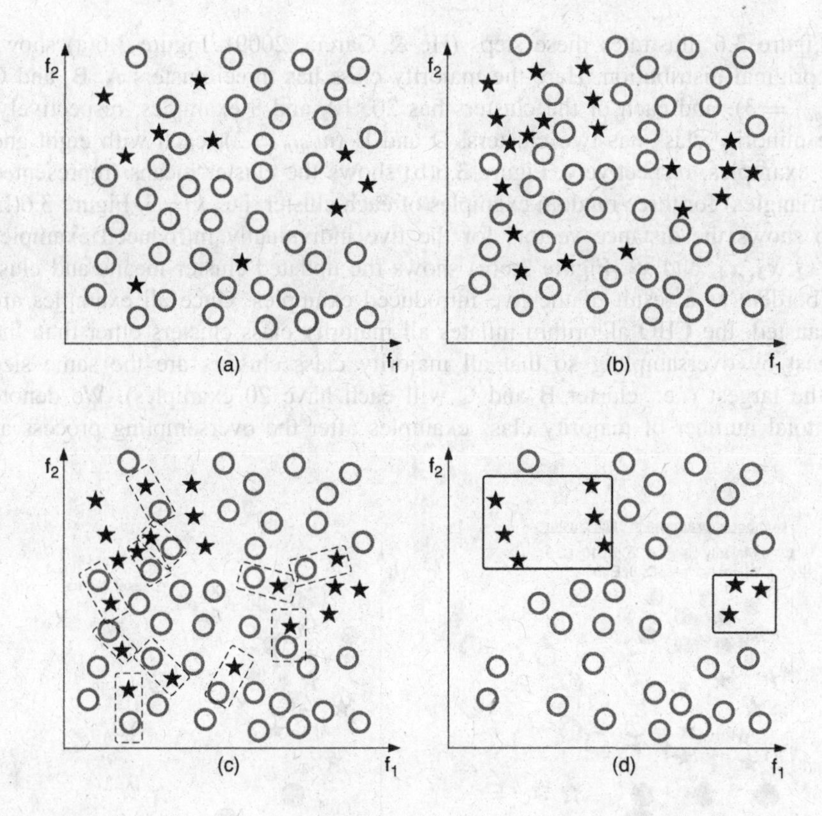

Figure 3.5: Sampling with data cleaning. (a) Original data set distribution. (b) Post-SMOTE data set. (c) The identified Tomek links. (d) The data set after removing Tomek links.

3.3.1.6 Cluster-Based Sampling Method Cluster-based sampling algorithms are particularly interesting because they provide an added element of flexibility that is not available in most simple and synthetic sampling algorithms, and accordingly can be tailored to target very specific problems. For instance, the cluster-based oversampling (CBO) algorithm was proposed in Jo and Japkowicz (2004) to effectively deal with the within-class imbalance problem in tandem with the between-class imbalance problem.

The CBO algorithm makes use of the K-means clustering technique. This procedure takes a random set of K examples from each cluster (for both classes) and computes the mean feature vector of these examples, which is designated as the cluster center. Next, the remaining training examples are presented one at a time and for each example, the Euclidean distance vector between it and each cluster center is computed. Each training example is then assigned to the cluster that exhibits the smallest distance vector magnitude. Lastly, all cluster means are updated and the process is repeated until all examples are exhausted (i.e., only one cluster mean is essentially updated for each example).

Figure 3.6 illustrates these steps (He & Garcia, 2009). Figure 3.6(a) shows the original distribution. Here the majority class has three clusters A, B, and C ($m_{maj} = 3$), and each of the clusters has 20, 10, and 8 examples, respectively. The minority class has two clusters, D and E ($m_{min} = 2$), each with eight and five examples, respectively. Figure 3.6(b) shows the cluster means (represented by triangles) for three random examples of each cluster, i.e., $k = 3$. Figure 3.6(b) also shows the distance vectors for the five individually introduced examples $\boldsymbol{x}_1, \boldsymbol{x}_2, \boldsymbol{x}_3, \boldsymbol{x}_4$, and $\boldsymbol{x}_5$. Figure 3.6(c) shows the updated cluster means and cluster borders as a result of the five introduced examples. Once all examples are exhausted, the CBO algorithm inflates all majority class clusters other than the largest by oversampling so that all majority class clusters are the same size as the largest (i.e., cluster B and C will each have 20 examples). We denote the total number of majority class examples after the oversampling process as

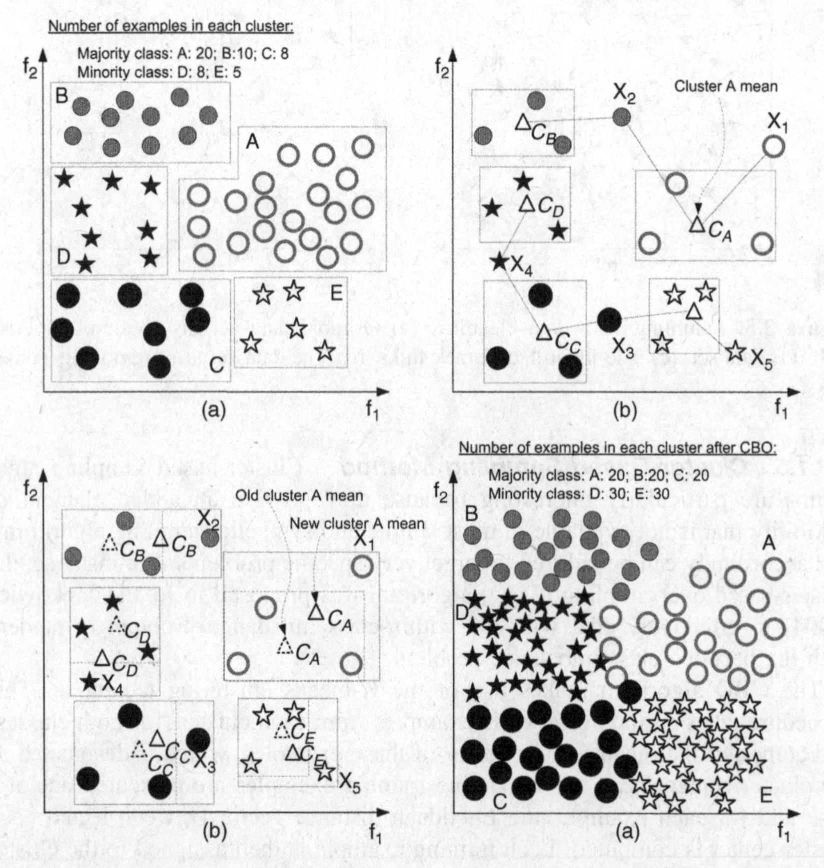

Figure 3.6: Cluster-based oversampling. (a) Original data set distribution. (b) Distance vectors of examples and cluster means. (c) Newly defined cluster means and cluster borders. (d) The data set after the cluster-based oversampling method.

N_{CBO}, $N_{CBO} = |S_{maj}| + |E_{maj}|$ (e.g., $N_{CBO} = 60$ in our example). Then we oversample the minority clusters so that each cluster contains N_{CBO}/m_{min} total examples (i.e., each minority cluster D and E will have a total number of $60/2 = 30$ examples after the oversampling procedure). Figure 3.6(d) shows the final data set after applying the CBO method. Compared to Figure 3.6(a), we can see that the final data set has a stronger representation of rare concepts. We also would like to note that different oversampling methods can be integrated into the CBO algorithm. For instance, Jo and Japkowicz (2004) used the random oversampling method discussed in section 3.3.1.1, while our example in Figure 3.6 uses synthetic sampling. Empirical results of CBO are very suggestive into the nature of the imbalanced learning problem; namely, that targeting *within-class imbalance* in tandem with the *between-class imbalance* is an effective strategy for imbalanced data sets.

3.3.1.7 *Integration of Sampling and Boosting* The integration of sampling strategies with ensemble learning techniques has also been studied in the community. For instance, the SMOTEBoost (Chawla, 2003) algorithm is based on the idea of integrating SMOTE with Adaboost.M2. Specifically, SMOTEBoost introduces synthetic sampling at each boosting iteration. In this way, each successive classifier ensemble focuses more on the minority class. Since each classifier ensemble is built on a different sampling of data, the final voted classifier is expected to have a broadened and well-defined decision region for the minority class.

Another integrated approach, the DataBoost-IM (Guo & Viktor, 2004b) method, combines the data generation techniques introduced in Guo and Viktor (2004a) with AdaBoost.M1 to achieve high predictive accuracy for the minority class without sacrificing accuracy on the majority class. Briefly, DataBoost-IM generates synthetic samples according to the ratio of difficult-to-learn samples between classes. Concretely, for a data set S with corresponding subsets $S_{min} \subset S$ and $S_{maj} \subset S$, and weighted distribution D_t representing the relative difficulty of learning for each example $\boldsymbol{x}_i \in S$, we rank the $\boldsymbol{x}_i$ in descending order according to their respective weight. We then select the top $|S| \times error(t)$ examples to populate set E, $E \subset S$, where $error(t)$ is the error rate of the current learned classifier. Thus E is a collection of the hard-to-learn samples from both classes, and has subsets $E_{min} \subset E$ and $E_{maj} \subset E$. Moreover, since minority class samples are generally more difficult to learn than majority class samples, it is expected that $|E_{maj}| \leq |E_{min}|$.

Once the difficult examples are identified, DataBoost-IM proceeds to create synthetic samples according to a two-tier process: First, identify the "seeds" of E from which synthetic samples are formed, and then generate synthetic data based on these samples. The seed identification procedure is based on the ratio of class representation in E and S. The number of majority class seeds, M_L, is defined as $M_L = min\left(\frac{|S_{maj}|}{|S_{min}|}, |E_{maj}|\right)$, and the number of minority seeds, M_S, is defined as $M_S = min\left(\frac{|S_{maj}| \times M_L}{|S_{min}|}, |E_{min}|\right)$. We then proceed to generate synthetic set

E_{syn}, with subsets $E_{smin} \subset E_{syn}$ and $E_{smaj} \subset E_{syn}$, such that $|E_{smin}| = M_S \times |S_{min}|$ and $|E_{smaj}| = M_L \times |S_{maj}|$. Set S is then augmented by E_{syn} to provide a more balanced class distribution with more new instances of the minority class. Lastly, the weighted distribution D_t is updated with consideration to the newly added synthetic samples.

In order to integrate the advantages of ADASYN and boosting techniques, a recent study proposes a ranked minority oversampling method based on boosting, the RAMOBoost approach (Chen, He, & Garcia, 2010). Briefly, RAMOBoost adaptively ranks minority class instances at each learning iteration according to a sampling probability distribution that is based on the underlying data distribution, and can adaptively shift the decision boundary toward difficult-to-learn minority and majority class instances by using a hypothesis assessment procedure. The objective of RAMOBoost is twofold, to reduce the induction biases introduced from imbalanced data and to adaptively learn information from the data distribution. This is achieved in two respects: First, an adaptive weight adjustment procedure is embedded in RAMOBoost that shifts the decision boundary toward the difficult-to-learn examples from both the minority and majority classes. Second, a ranked sampling probability distribution is used to generate synthetic minority instances to balance the skewed distribution. In this way, RAMOBoost evaluates the potential learning contribution of each minority example and determines their sampling weights accordingly. This is achieved by calculating the distance of any single minority example from the set of nearest neighbors to determine how greatly it will benefit the learning process.

To have an in-depth understanding of this approach, here we provide an example of a data set with 2000 majority examples and 100 minority examples to compare the data generation mechanism of RAMOBoost (Chen et al., 2010) with that of SMOTE (Chawla et al., 2002) and ADASYN (He et al., 2008). Figure 3.7(a) shows the original imbalanced data distribution, and Figure 3.7(b)–(d) shows the post-SMOTE data distribution, post-ADASYN data distribution, and the post-RAMOBoost data distribution, respectively. In all of these figures, the x-marks, plus, and point shapes represent the original majority data, original minority data, and the generated synthetic data, respectively. Furthermore, for each figure, we also illustrate the classification confusion matrix (in terms of instant counts) for performance assessment. Comparing the confusion matrix of each figure, we see that the proposed RAMOBoost method can improve classification performance. Specifically, the improvement of true negative (TN) counts for SMOTE with respect to the original data set changes from 1992 to 1993, while for RAMOBoost it increases from 1992 to 1998. This is because in SMOTE the same numbers of instances are generated for each minority example, while in RAMOBoost the data generation process is adaptive according to the data distribution.

From Figure 3.7(c) we also see that ADASYN seems to be very aggressive in learning from the boundary since it generates synthetic data instances very close to the decision boundary. This may have two effects on the learning performance. It may increase the classification accuracy of the minority data

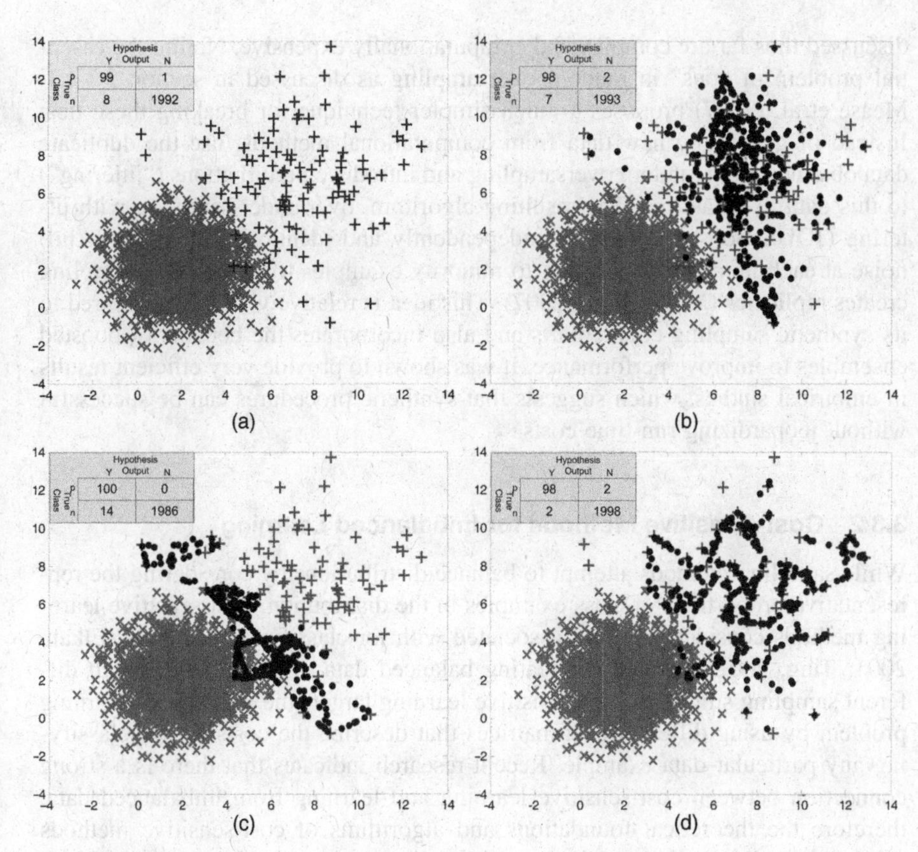

Figure 3.7: Comparison of different synthetic data generation mechanisms: (a) original imbalanced data distribution (2000 majority examples and 100 minority examples); (b) data distribution after SMOTE method; (c) data distribution after ADASYN method; (d) data distribution after RAMOBoost method.

as it provides a good representation of the minority data distribution close to the boundary (therefore improving the *Recall* performance (See section 3.4 for the detailed discussions about the assessment metrics for imbalanced learning)). However, it may also decrease the classification performance of the majority class, which in turn deteriorates the overall classification performance. One can observe from Figure 3.7(c) that although the classification accuracy for minority examples under the ADASYN technique is best among all of these methods (true positive (TP) = 100, therefore *Recall* = 1), the TN counts of ADASYN also decreases significantly (the lowest of all in this case with TN = 1986). To this end, RAMOBoost might be able to take advantage of both SMOTE and ADASYN to improve overall learning performance (Chen et al., 2010).

Evidence that synthetic sampling methods are effective in dealing with learning from imbalanced data is quite strong. However, the data generation methods discussed thus far are complex and computationally expensive. Noting the essential problem of "ties" in random oversampling as discussed in section 3.3.1.1, Mease et al. (2007) proposes a much simpler technique for breaking these ties: Instead of generating new data from computational methods, use the duplicate data obtained from random oversampling and introduce perturbations ("jittering") to this data to break ties. The resulting algorithm, over/under-sampling with jittering (JOUS-Boost), introduces independently and identically distributed (iid) noise at each iteration of boosting to minority examples for which oversampling creates replicates (Mease et al., 2007). This idea is relatively simple compared to its synthetic sampling counterparts and also incorporates the benefits of boosted ensembles to improve performance. It was shown to provide very efficient results in empirical studies, which suggests that synthetic procedures can be successful without jeopardizing run-time costs.

3.3.2 Cost-Sensitive Methods for Imbalanced Learning

While sampling methods attempt to balance distributions by considering the representative proportions of class examples in the distribution, cost-sensitive learning methods consider the costs associated with misclassifying examples (Elkan, 2001; Ting, 2002). Instead of creating balanced data distributions through different sampling strategies, cost-sensitive learning targets the imbalanced learning problem by using different cost-matrices that describe the costs for misclassifying any particular data example. Recent research indicates that there is a strong connection between cost-sensitive learning and learning from imbalanced data, therefore the theoretical foundations and algorithms of cost-sensitive methods can be naturally applied to imbalanced learning problems (Chawla et al., 2004; Weiss, 2004; Maloof, 2003). Moreover, various empirical studies have shown that in some application domains, including certain specific imbalanced learning domains (Liu & Zhou, 2006a, 2006b; McCarthy, Zabar, & Weiss, 2005), cost-sensitive learning is superior to sampling methods. Therefore, cost-sensitive techniques provide a viable alternative to sampling methods for imbalanced learning domains (He & Garcia, 2009).

3.3.2.1 Cost-Sensitive Learning Framework Fundamental to the cost-sensitive learning methodology is the concept of the cost matrix. The cost matrix can be considered as a numerical representation of the penalty of classifying examples from one class to another. For example, in a binary classification scenario we define *C(Min, Maj)* as the cost of misclassifying a majority class example as a minority class example and let *C(Maj, Min)* represent the cost of the contrary case. Typically, there is no cost for correct classification of either class and the cost of misclassifying minority examples is higher than the contrary case, i.e., *C(Maj, Min)* > *C(Min, Maj)*. The objective of cost-sensitive learning then is to develop a hypothesis that minimizes the overall cost on the training data set, which is usually the *Bayes conditional risk*. These concepts are easily extended

Predicted Class i \ True Class j	1	2	...	k
1	*C(1,1)*	*C(1,2)*	...	*C(1,k)*
2	*C(2,1)*	...	...	⋮
⋮	⋮	...	...	⋮
k	*C(k,1)*	...	...	*C(k,k)*

Figure 3.8: Multiclass cost matrix.

to multiclass data by considering $C(i, j)$, which represents the cost of predicting class i when the true class is j, where $i, j \in Y = \{1, \ldots, C\}$. Figure 3.8 shows a typical cost matrix for a multiclass problem. In this case the conditional risk is defined as $R(i|\boldsymbol{x}) = \sum_j P(j|\boldsymbol{x})\, C(i, j)$, where $P(j|\boldsymbol{x})$ represents the probability of each class j for a given example $\boldsymbol{x}$ (Elkan, 2001; Domingos, 1999).

There are many different ways of implementing cost-sensitive learning, but, in general, the majority of techniques fall under three categories (He & Garcia, 2009). The first class of techniques apply misclassification costs to the data set as a form of dataspace weighting; these techniques are essentially cost-sensitive bootstrap sampling approaches where misclassification costs are used to select the best training distribution for induction. The second class applies cost minimizing techniques to the combination schemes of ensemble methods; this class consists of various Meta techniques where standard learning algorithms are integrated with ensemble methods to develop cost-sensitive classifiers. Both of these classes have rich theoretical foundations that justify their approaches, with cost-sensitive dataspace weighting methods building on the *translation theorem* (Zadrozny, Langford, & Abe, 2003), and cost-sensitive Meta techniques building on the *Metacost framework* (Domingos, 1999). In fact, most of the existing research often integrates the Metacost framework with data space weighting and adaptive boosting to achieve stronger classification results. To this end, we consider both of these classes of algorithms as one in the following section. The last class of techniques incorporates cost-sensitive functions or features directly into classification paradigms to essentially "fit" the cost-sensitive framework into these classifiers. Because many of these techniques are specific to a particular paradigm, there is no unifying framework for this class of cost-sensitive learning, but in many cases solutions that work for one paradigm can often be abstracted to work for others. As such, in our discussion of these types of techniques we consider a few methods on a case-specific basis.

3.3.2.2 Cost-Sensitive Data Space Weighting with Adaptive Boosting Motivated by the pioneering work of the AdaBoost algorithms (Freund

& Schapire, 1996, 2002), several cost-sensitive boosting methods for imbalanced learning have been proposed. Three cost-sensitive boosting methods, AdaC1, AdaC2, and AdaC3, were proposed in Sun, Kamel, Wong, and Wang (2007), which introduce cost items into the weight updating strategy of AdaBoost. The key idea of the AdaBoost.M1 method is to iteratively update the distribution function over the training data. In this way, on each iteration $t := 1, \ldots, T$, where T is a preset number of the total number of iterations, the distribution function D_t is updated sequentially and used to train a new hypothesis:

$$D_{t+1}(i) = D_t(i)\exp(-\alpha_t h_t(\boldsymbol{x}_i) y_i)/Z_t \tag{3.6}$$

where $\alpha_t = \frac{1}{2}\ln\left(\frac{1-\varepsilon_t}{\varepsilon_t}\right)$ is the weight updating parameter, $h_t(\boldsymbol{x}_i)$ is the prediction output of hypothesis h_t on the instance $\boldsymbol{x}_i$, ε_t is the error of hypothesis h_t over the training data $\varepsilon_t = \sum_{i:h_t(\boldsymbol{x}_i)\neq y_i} D_t(i)$, and Z_t is a normalization factor so that D_{t+1} is a distribution function, *i.e.*, $\sum_{i=1}^{m} D_{t+1}(i) = 1$. With this description in mind, a cost factor can be applied in three ways: inside of the exponential, outside of the exponential, and both inside and outside the exponential. Analytically this translates to:

$$D_{t+1}(i) = D_t(i)\exp(-\alpha_t C_i h_t(\boldsymbol{x}_i) y_i)/Z_t \tag{3.7}$$

$$D_{t+1}(i) = C_i D_t(i)\exp(-\alpha_t h_t(\boldsymbol{x}_i) y_i)/Z_t \tag{3.8}$$

$$D_{t+1}(i) = C_i D_t(i)\exp(-\alpha_t C_i h_t(\boldsymbol{x}_i) y_i)/Z_t \tag{3.9}$$

Equations (3.7), (3.8), and (3.9) corresponds to the AdaC1, AdaC2, and AdaC3 method, respectively. Here the cost item, C_i, is the associated cost for each $\boldsymbol{x}_i$ and C_i's of higher value correspond to examples with higher misclassification costs. In essence these algorithms increase the probability of sampling a costly example at each iteration, giving the classifier more instances of costly examples for a more targeted approach of induction. In general it was observed that the inclusion of cost factors into the weighting scheme of Adaboost imposes a bias toward the minority concepts and also increases the use of more relevant data samples in each hypothesis, providing for a more robust form of classification.

Another cost-sensitive boosting algorithm that follows a similar methodology is AdaCost (Fan, Stolfo, Zhang, & Chan, 1999). AdaCost, like AdaC1, introduces cost-sensitivity inside the exponent of the weight updating formula of Adaboost. However, instead of applying the cost items directly, AdaCost uses a cost-adjustment function that aggressively increases the weights of costly misclassifications and conservatively decreases the weights of high cost examples that are correctly classified. This modification becomes:

$$D_{t+1}(i) = D_t(i)\exp(-\alpha_t h_t(\boldsymbol{x}_i) y_i \beta_i)/Z_t \tag{3.10}$$

with the cost-adjustment function, β_i, defined as $\beta_i = \beta\,(sign\,(y_i, h_t(\boldsymbol{x}_i)), C_i)$, where $sign(y_i, h_t(\boldsymbol{x}_i))$ is positive for correct classification and negative for misclassification. For clear presentation, one can use β_+ when $sign(y_i, h_t(\boldsymbol{x}_i)) = 1$

and β_- when $sign(y_i, h_t(\mathbf{x}_i)) = -1$. This method also allows some flexibility in the amount of emphasis given to the importance of an example. For instance, Fan et al. (1999) suggest $\beta_+ = -0.5C_i + 0.5$ and $\beta_- = 0.5C_i + 0.5$ for good results in most applications, but these coefficients can be adjusted according to specific needs. An empirical comparison over four imbalanced data sets of AdaC1, AdaC2, AdaC3, and AdaCost and two other similar algorithms, CSB1 and CSB2 (Ting, 2000), was performed in Sun et al. (2007) using decision trees and a rule association system as the base classifiers. It was noted that in all cases, a boosted ensemble performed better than the standalone base classifiers using F-measure (see section 3.4.1) as the evaluation metric, and in nearly all cases the cost-sensitive boosted ensembles performed better than plain boosting.

Though these cost-sensitive algorithms can significantly improve classification performance, they take for granted the availability of a cost matrix and its associated cost items. In many situations an explicit description of misclassification costs is unknown, i.e., only an informal assertion is known, such as *misclassifications on the positive class are more expensive than the negative class* (Maloof, 2003). Moreover, determining a cost representation of a given domain can be particularly challenging and in some cases impossible (Maloof, Langley, Sage, & Binford, 1997). As a result, the techniques discussed in this section are not applicable in these situations and other solutions must be established. This is the prime motivation for the cost-sensitive fitting techniques mentioned earlier. In the following sections we provide an overview of these methods for two popular learning paradigms, namely decision trees and neural networks.

3.3.2.3 Cost-Sensitive Decision Trees In regards to decision trees, cost-sensitive fitting can take three forms: (1) cost-sensitive adjustments can be applied to the decision threshold, (2) cost-sensitive considerations can be given to the split criteria at each node, and (3) cost-sensitive pruning schemes can be applied to the tree.

A decision tree threshold moving scheme for imbalanced data with unknown misclassification costs was observed in Maloof (2003). The relationships between the misclassification costs of each class, the distribution of training examples, and the placement of the decision threshold have been established in Breiman, Friedman, Olshen, and Stone (1984). However, Maloof (2003) notes that the precise definition of these relationships can be task specific, rendering a systematic approach for threshold selection based on these relationships unfeasible. Therefore, instead of relying on the training distribution or exact misclassification costs, the proposed technique uses the ROC evaluation procedure (see section 3.4.2) to plot the range of performance values as the decision threshold is moved from the point where the total misclassifications on the positive class are maximally costly to the point where total misclassifications on the negative class are maximally costly. The decision threshold that yields the most dominant point on the ROC curve is then used as the final decision threshold.

When considering cost-sensitivity in the split criterion, the task at hand is to fit an impurity function that is insensitive to unequal costs. For instance, traditionally accuracy is used as the impurity function for decision trees, which chooses the split with minimal error at each node. However, this metric is sensitive to changes in sample distributions (see section 3.4.1) and thus inherently sensitive to unequal costs. In Drummond and Holte (2000), three specific impurity functions, Gini, Entropy, and DKM, were shown to have improved cost insensitivity compared with the accuracy/error rate baseline. Moreover, these empirical experiments also showed that using the DKM function generally produced smaller unpruned decision trees that at worse provided accuracies comparable to Gini and Entropy. A detailed theoretical basis explaining the conclusions of these empirical results was later established in Elkan (2001), which generalizes the effects of decision tree growth for any choice of spit criteria.

The final case of cost-sensitive decision tree fitting applies to pruning. Pruning is beneficial for decision trees because it improves generalization by removing leaves with class probability estimates below a specified threshold. However, in the presence of imbalanced data, pruning procedures tend to remove leaves describing the minority concept. It has been shown that though pruning trees induced from imbalanced data can hinder performance, using unpruned trees in such cases does not improve performance (Japkowicz & Stephen, 2002). As a result, attention has been given to improving the class probability estimate at each node to develop more representative decision tree structures such that pruning can be applied with positive effects. Some representative works include the Laplace smoothing method of the probability estimate and the Laplace pruning technique (Elkan, 2001).

3.3.2.4 Cost-Sensitive Neural Networks Cost-sensitive neural networks have also been widely studied in the community for imbalanced learning. The neural network is generally represented by a densely interconnected set of simple neurons. Most practical applications of the neural network classifier involve a multilayer structure, such as the popular multilayer perceptron (MLP) model (Haykin, 1999), and learning is facilitated by using the backpropagation algorithm in tandem with the gradient descent rule. Concretely, assume one defines an error function as:

$$E(\boldsymbol{\omega}) = \frac{1}{2}\sum(t_k - o_k)^2 \tag{3.11}$$

where $\boldsymbol{\omega}$ is a set of weights that require training, and t_k and o_k are the target value and network output value for a neuron k, respectively. The gradient descent rule aims to find the steepest descent to modify the weights at each iteration:

$$\Delta\omega_n = -\eta\nabla_\omega E(\omega_n) \tag{3.12}$$

Where η is the specified neural network learning rate and ∇_ω represents the gradient operator with respect to weights ω. Moreover, a probabilistic estimate for the output can be defined by normalizing the output values of all output neurons.

With this framework at hand, cost sensitivity can be introduced to neural networks in four ways (Kubar & Kononenko, 1998): (1) cost-sensitive modifications can be applied to the probabilistic estimate, (2) the neural network outputs (i.e., each o_k) can be made cost-sensitive, (3) cost-sensitive modifications can be applied to the learning rate η, and (4) the error minimization function can be adapted to account for expected costs.

In regards to the probability estimate, Kukar and Kononenko (1998) integrate cost factors into the testing stage of classification to adaptively modify the probability estimate of the neural network output. This has the benefit of maintaining the original structure (and outputs) of the neural network while strengthening the original estimates on the more expensive class through cost consideration. Empirical results in Kubar and Kononenko (1998) showed that this technique improves the performance over the original neural network, although the improvement is not drastic. However, we note that a more significant performance increase can be achieved by applying this estimate to ensemble methods by using cross-validation techniques on a given set; a similar approach is considered in Liu and Zhou (2006b), however using a slightly different estimate.

The second class of neural network cost-sensitive fitting techniques directly changes the outputs of the neural network. In Kubar and Kononenko (1998), the outputs of the neural network are altered during training to bias the neural network to focus more on the expensive class. Empirical results on this method showed an improvement in classification performance on average, but also showed a high degree of variance in the performance measures compared to the least expected cost over the evaluated data sets. We speculate that ensemble methods can be applied to alleviate this problem, but to our knowledge, such experiments have not been performed to date.

The learning rate η can also influence the weight adjustment (see equation (3.12)). As a result, cost-sensitive factors can be applied to the learning rate to change the impact that the modification procedure has on the weights, where costly examples will have a greater impact on weight changes. The key idea of this approach is to put more attention on costly examples during learning by effectively decreasing the learning rate for each corresponding costly example. This also suggests that low cost examples will train at a faster rate than costly examples, so this method also strikes a balance in training time. Experiments on this technique have shown it to be very effective for training neural networks with significant improvements over the base classifier (Kubar & Kononenko, 1998).

The final adaptation of cost-sensitive neural networks replaces the error-minimizing function shown in equation (3.11) by an expected cost-minimization function. This form of cost-sensitive fitting was shown to be the most dominant of the methods discussed in this section (Kubar & Kononenko, 1998). It also is in line with the backpropagation methodology and theoretical foundations established on the transitivity between error-minimizing and cost-minimizing classifiers.

Though we only provide a treatment for decision trees and neural networks, many cost-sensitive fitting techniques exist for other types of learning paradigms as well. For instance, a great deal of work has focused on cost-sensitive Bayesian classifiers (Domingos & Pazzani, 1996; Webb & Pazzani, 1998; Kohavi & Wolpert, 1996; Gama, 2003) and some work exists that integrates cost functions with support vector machines (Fumera & Roli, 2002; Platt, 1999; Kwok, 2003). Interested readers can refer to these works for a broader overview.

3.3.3 Kernel-Based Methods for Imbalanced Learning

Although sampling methods and cost-sensitive learning methods seem to dominate the current research efforts in imbalanced learning, numerous other approaches have also been pursued in the community. In this section, we briefly review kernel-based learning methods. Since kernel-based learning methods provide state-of-the-art techniques for many of today's data engineering applications, the use of kernel-based methods to understand imbalanced learning has naturally attracted growing attention recently (He & Garcia, 2009).

3.3.3.1 Kernel-Based Learning Framework The principles of kernel-based learning are centered on the theories of statistical learning and Vapnik–Chervonenkis (VC) dimensions (Vapnik, 1995). The representative kernel-based learning paradigm, support vector machines (SVMs), can provide relatively robust classification results when applied to imbalanced data sets (Japkowicz & Stephen, 2002). SVMs facilitate learning by using specific examples near concept boundaries (support vectors) to maximize the separation margin (soft-margin maximization) between the support vectors and the hypothesized concept boundary (hyperplane), meanwhile minimizing the total classification error (Vapnik, 1995).

The effects of imbalanced data on SVMs exploit inadequacies of the soft-margin maximization paradigm (Raskutti & Kowalczyk, 2004; Akbani, Kwek, & Japkowicz, 2004). Since SVMs try to minimize total error, they are inherently biased toward the majority concept. In the simplest case, a two-class space is linearly separated by an "ideal" separation line in the neighborhood of the majority concept. In this case it might occur that the support vectors representing the minority concept are "far away" from this "ideal" line and as a result will contribute less to the final hypothesis (Raskutti & Kowalczyk, 2004; Akbani et al., 2004; Wu & Chang, 2003a). Moreover, if there is a lack of data representing the minority concept, there could be an imbalance of representative support vectors that can also degrade performance. These same characteristics are also readily evident in linear non separable spaces. In this case, a kernel function is used to map the linear non separable space into a higher dimensional space where separation is achievable. However, in this case the optimal hyperplane separating the classes will be biased toward the majority class in order to minimize the high error rates of misclassifying the more prevalent majority class. In the worst case, SVMs will learn to classify all examples as pertaining to the majority class—a tactic that, if the imbalance is severe, can provide the minimal error rate across the dataspace.

3.3.3.2 Integration of Kernel Methods with Sampling Methods There have been many works in the community that apply general sampling and ensemble techniques to the SVM framework. Some examples include the SMOTE with Different Costs (SDC) method (Akbani et al., 2004), and the ensembles of over/under-sampled SVMs (Vilarino, Spyridonos, Radeva, & Vitria, 2005; Kang & Cho, 2006; Liu, An, & Huang, 2006; Wang & Japkowicz, 2008). For example, the SDC algorithm uses different error costs (Akbani et al., 2004) for different classes to bias the SVM in order to shift the decision boundary away from positive instances and make positive instances more densely distributed in an attempt to guarantee a more well-defined boundary. Meanwhile, the methods proposed in Kang and Cho (2006) and Liu et al. (2006) develop ensemble systems by modifying the data distributions without modifying the underlying SVM classifier. Lastly, Wang and Japkowicz (2008) proposed to modify the SVMs with asymmetric misclassification costs in order to boost performance. This idea is similar to the AdaBoost.M1 (Freund & Schapire, 1996, 2002) algorithm in that it uses an iterative procedure to effectively modify the weights of the training observations. In this way, one can build a modified version of the training data based on such sequential learning procedures to improve classification performance.

The Granular Support Vector Machines–Repetitive Undersampling algorithm (GSVM-RU) was proposed in Tang and Zhang (2006) to integrate SVM learning with undersampling methods. This method is based on granular support vector machines (GSVMs) which were developed in a series of papers according to the principles from statistical learning theory and granular computing theory (Tang, Jin, & Zhang, 2008; Tang, Jin, Zhang, Fang, & Wang, 2005; Tang, Zhang, Huang, Hu, & Zhao, 2005). The major characteristics of GSVMs are two-fold. First, GSVMs can effectively analyze the inherent data distribution by observing the trade-offs between the local significance of a subset of data and its global correlation. Second, GSVMs improve the computational efficiency of SVMs through use of parallel computation. In the context of imbalanced learning, the GSVM-RU method takes advantage of the GSVM by using an iterative learning procedure that uses the SVM itself for undersampling (Tang & Zhang, 2006). Concretely, since all minority (positive) examples are considered to be informative, a positive information granule is formed from these examples. Then, a linear SVM is developed using the positive granule and the remaining examples in the data set (i.e., S_{maj}); the negative examples that are identified as support vectors by this SVM, the so-called "negative local support vectors" (NLSVs), are formed into a negative information granule and are removed from the original training data to obtain a smaller training data set. Based on this reduced training data set, a new linear SVM is developed, and again the new set of NLSVs are formed into a negative granule and removed from the data set. This procedure is repeated multiple times to obtain multiple negative information granules. Finally, an aggregation operation that considers global correlation is used to select specific sample sets from those iteratively developed negative information granules, which are then combined with all positive samples to develop a final SVM model. In this way, the GSVM-RU method uses the SVM itself as a mechanism for undersampling to sequentially develop multiple information granules with different informative samples, which are later combined to develop a final SVM for classification.

3.3.3.3 Kernel Modification Methods for Imbalanced Learning In addition to the aforementioned sampling and ensemble kernel-based learning methods, another major category of kernel-based learning research efforts focuses more concretely on the mechanics of the SVM itself; this group of methods are often called *kernel modification* methods.

One example of kernel modification is the kernel classifier construction algorithm proposed in Hong, Chen, and Harris (2008) based on orthogonal forward selection (OFS) and the regularized orthogonal weighted least squares (ROWLS) estimator. This algorithm optimizes generalization in the kernel-based learning model by introducing two major components that deal with imbalanced data distributions for two-class data sets. The first component integrates the concepts of leave-one-out (LOO) cross-validation and the area under curve (AUC) evaluation metric (see section 3.4.2) to develop a LOO-AUC objective function as a selection mechanism of the most optimal kernel model. The second component takes advantage of the cost-sensitivity of the parameter estimation cost function in the ROWLS algorithm to assign greater weight to erroneous data examples in the minority class than those in the majority class.

Other examples of kernel modification are the various techniques for adjusting the SVM class boundary. These methods apply boundary alignment techniques to improve SVM classification (Wu & Chang, 2003b, 2004, 2005). For instance, in Wu and Chang (2003b), three algorithmic approaches for adjusting boundary skews were presented: the boundary movement (BM) approach, the biased penalties (BP) approach, and the class-boundary alignment (CBA) approach. Additionally, in Wu and Chang (2004, 2005), the kernel–boundary alignment (KBA) algorithm was proposed, which is based on the idea of modifying the kernel matrix generated by a kernel function according to the imbalanced data distribution. The underlying theoretical foundation of the KBA method builds on the adaptive conformal transformation (ACT) methodology, where the conformal transformation on a kernel function is based on the consideration of the feature–space distance and the class-imbalance ratio (Wu & Chang, 2003b). By generalizing the foundation of ACT, the KBA method tackles the imbalanced learning problem by modifying the kernel matrix in the feature space. Theoretical analyses and empirical studies showed that this method not only provides competitive accuracy, but it can be applied to both vector data and sequence data by modifying the kernel matrix.

In a more integrated approach of kernel based learning, Liu and Chen (2005, 2007) propose the total margin-based adaptive fuzzy SVM kernel method (TAF-SVM) to improve SVM robustness. The major beneficial characteristics of TAF-SVM are three-fold. First, TAF-SVM can handle overfitting by "fuzzifying" the training data, where certain training examples are treated differently according to their relative importance. Second, different cost algorithms are embedded into

TAF-SVM, which allows this algorithm to self-adapt to different data distribution skews. Lastly, the conventional soft-margin maximization paradigm is replaced by the total margin paradigm, which considers both the misclassified and correctly classified data examples in the construction of the optimal separating hyperplane.

A particularly interesting kernel modification method for imbalanced learning is the k-category proximal support vector machine (PSVM) with Newton refinement (Fung & Mangasarian, 2005). This method essentially transforms the soft-margin maximization paradigm into a simple system of k linear equations for either linear or nonlinear classifiers, where k is the number of classes. One of the major advantages of this method is that it can perform the learning procedure very fast because this method requires nothing more sophisticated than solving this simple system of linear equations. Lastly, in the presence of extremely imbalanced data sets, Raskutti and Kowalcyzk (2004) consider both sampling and data space weighting compensation techniques in cases where SVMs completely ignore one of the classes. In this procedure two balancing modes are used in order to balance the data: a *similarity detector* is used to learn a discriminator based predominantly on positive examples, and a *novelty detector* is used to learn a discriminator using primarily negative examples.

Several other kernel modification methods exist in the community, including the support cluster machines (SCMs) for large-scale imbalanced data sets (Yuan, Li, & Zhang, 2006), the kernel neural gas (KNG) algorithm for imbalanced clustering (Qin & Suganthan, 2004), the P2PKNNC algorithm based on the k-nearest neighbors classifier and the P2P communication paradigm (Yu & Yu, 2007), the hybrid kernel machine ensemble (HKME) algorithm including a binary support vector classifier (BSVC) and a one-class support vector classifier ($\nu-SVC$) with Gaussian radial basis kernel function (Li, Chan, & Fang, 2006), and the Adaboost relevance vector machine (RVM) (Tashk, Bayesteh, & Faez, 2007), amongst others. Furthermore, we would like to note that for many kernel-based learning methods there is no strict distinction between the aforementioned two major categories of sections 3.3.3.2 and 3.3.3.3. In many situations learning methods take a hybrid approach where sampling and ensemble techniques are integrated with kernel modification methods for improved performance. For instance, Akbani et al. (2004) and Wu and Chang (2003a) are good examples of hybrid solutions for imbalanced learning. In this section, we categorize kernel-based learning in two subsections for better presentation and organization.

3.3.4 Active Learning Methods for Imbalanced Learning

Active learning methods have also been investigated in the community for imbalanced learning problems (He & Garcia, 2009). Traditionally, active learning methods are used to solve problems related to unlabeled training data. Recently, however, various issues on active learning from imbalanced data sets have been discussed in literature (Abe, 2003; Ertekin, Huang, Bottou, & Giles, 2007a; Ertekin, Huang, & Giles, 2007b; Provost, 2000). Moreover, we point out that active learning approaches for imbalanced learning are often integrated into kernel-based learning methods; as a result, this section is closely intercorrelated with section 3.3.3.

SVM-based active learning aims to select the most informative instances from the unseen training data in order to retrain the kernel-based model (Ertekin et al., 2007b), i.e., those instances that are closest to the current hyperplane. Figure 3.9 illustrates the motivation for the selection procedure for imbalanced data sets (Ertekin et al., 2007a). Assume Figure 3.9 represents the class distribution of an imbalanced data set, where the shaded region corresponds to the class distribution within the margin. In this case, the imbalance ratio of data within the margin is much smaller than the imbalance ratio of the entire data set. Motivated by this observation, Ertekin et al. (2007a, 2007b) proposed an efficient SVM-based active learning method that queries a small pool of data at each iterative step of active learning instead of querying the entire data set. In this procedure an SVM is trained on the given training data, after which the most informative instances are extracted and formed into a new training set according to the developed hyperplane. Finally, the procedure uses this new training set and all unseen training data to actively retrain the SVM using the LASVM on line SVM learning algorithm (Borders, Ertekin, Weston, & Bottou, 2005) to facilitate the active learning procedure.

Ertekin et al. (2007a, 2007b) also point out that the search process for the most informative instances can be computationally expensive because, for each instance of unseen data, the algorithm needs to recalculate the distance between each instance and the current hyperplane. To solve this problem, they proposed a method to effectively select such informative instances from a random set of training populations to reduce the computational cost for large-scale imbalanced data sets (Ertekin et al., 2007a, 2007b). Additionally, early stopping criteria for active learning are also discussed in this work, which can be used to achieve faster convergence of the active learning process as compared to the random sample selection solution.

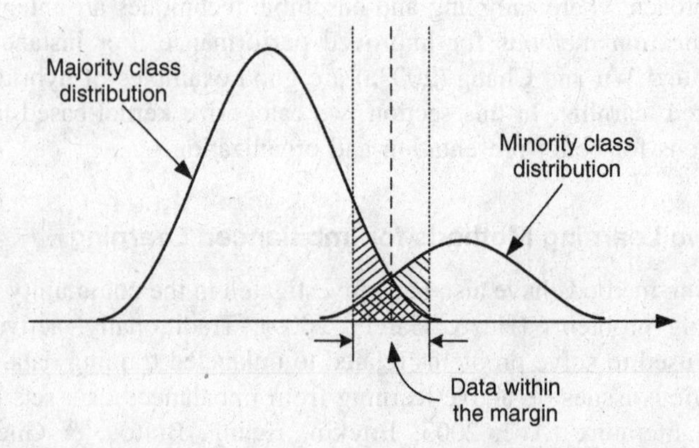

Figure 3.9: Data imbalance ratio within and outside the margin (Ertekin et al., 2007a).

In addition to kernel-based integrations, active learning integrations with sampling techniques have also been investigated in the community. For instance, Zhu and Hovy (2007) analyzed the effect of undersampling and oversampling techniques with active learning for the word sense disambiguation (WSD) imbalanced learning problem. The active learning method studied in this work is based on the uncertainty sampling methodology; here the challenge is how to measure the uncertainty of an unlabeled instance in order to select the maximally uncertain instance to augment the training data. In this case Entropy was used as a metric for determining uncertainty. Additionally, two stopping mechanisms based on maximum confidence and minimal error were investigated in Zhu and Hovy (2007). Simulation results concluded that one can use max-confidence as the upper bound and min-error as the lower bound of the stopping conditions for active learning in this case. Another active learning sampling method is the simple active learning heuristic (SALH) approach proposed in Doucette and Heywood (2008). The key idea of this method is to provide a generic model for the evolution of genetic programming (GP) classifiers by integrating the stochastic sub-sampling method and a modified Wilcoxon–Mann–Whitney (WMW) cost function (Doucette & Heywood, 2008). The major advantages of the SALH method include the ability to actively bias the data distribution for learning, the existence of a robust cost function, and the improvement of the computational cost related to the fitness evaluation. Simulation results over six data sets were used to illustrate the effectiveness of this method.

3.3.5 Additional Methods for Imbalanced Learning

In addition to the previously discussed sampling methods, cost-sensitive methods, kernel-based methods, and active learning methods, we would like to note that community solutions to handle the imbalanced learning problem are not solely in the form of these categories. Other efforts from different angles to address the imbalanced learning issue have also been developed in the community. For instance, the *one-class learning* or *novelty detection* methods have also attracted much attention for imbalanced learning (Chawla et al., 2004). Generally speaking, this category of approaches aims to recognize instances of a concept by using mainly, or only, a single class of examples (i.e., recognition-based methodology) rather than differentiating between instances of both positive and negative classes as in the conventional learning approaches (i.e., discrimination-based inductive methodology). Representative works in this area include the one-class SVMs (Raskutti & Kowalczyk, 2004; Scholkopf, Platt, Shawe-Taylor, Smola, & Williamson, 2001; Manevitz & Yousef, 2001; Zhuang & Dai, 2006a, 2006b; Lee & Cho, 2006) and the autoassociator (or autoencoder) method (Japkowicz, 2000, 2001; Manevitz & Yousef, 2007; Japkowicz, Myers, & Gluck, 1995). Specifically, Raskutti and Kowalcyzk (2004) suggested that one-class learning is particularly useful in dealing with extremely imbalanced data sets with high feature–space dimensionality. Additionally, Japkowicz (2001) proposed an approach to train an autoassociator to reconstruct the positive class at the output layer, and it was suggested that under certain conditions, such as in multimodal domains, the one-class learning approach may be superior to the discrimination-based approaches. Meanwhile, Manevitz and Yousef (2001, 2007) presented the successful applications of the one-class learning approach to the document classification domain based on SVMs and autoencoder, respectively. In Japkowicz (2000), a comparison of different sampling methods and the one-class autoassociator method was presented, which provides useful suggestions about the advantages and limitations of both methods. The novelty detection approach based on redundancy compression and non redundancy differentiation techniques were investigated in Japkowicz et al. (1995). Recently, Lee and Cho (2006) suggested that novelty detection methods are particularly useful for extremely imbalanced data sets, while regular discrimination-based inductive classifiers are suitable for a relatively moderate imbalanced data sets.

Recently, the Mahalanobis–Taguchi System (MTS) has also been used for imbalanced learning (Su & Hsiao, 2007). MTS was originally developed as a diagnostic and forecasting technique for multivariate data (Taguchi, Chowdhury, & Wu, 2001; Taguchi & Jugulum, 2002). Unlike most of the classification paradigms, learning in MTS is performed by developing a continuous measurement scale using single class examples instead of the entire training data. Because of its characteristics, it is expected that the MTS model will not be influenced by the skewed data distribution, therefore providing robust classification performance. Motivated by these observations, Su and Hsiao (2007) presented an evaluation of the MTS model for imbalanced learning with comparisons to stepwise discriminate analysis (SDA), backpropagation neural networks, decision trees, and SVMs. This work showed the effectiveness of MTS in the presence of imbalanced data. Moreover, Su and Hsiao (2007) also present a probabilistic thresholding method based on Chebyshev's theorem to systematically determine an appropriate threshold for MTS classification.

Another important example relates to the combination of imbalanced data and the small sample size problem as discussed in section 3.2. Two major approaches were proposed in Caruana (2000) to address this issue. First, rank metrics were proposed as the training and model selection criteria instead of the traditional accuracy metric. Rank metrics helps facilitate learning from imbalanced data with small sample sizes and high dimensionality by placing a greater emphasis on learning to distinguish classes themselves instead of the internal structure (feature space conjunctions) of classes. The second approach is based on the multitask learning methodology. The idea here is to use a shared representation of the data to train extra task models related to the main task, therefore amplifying the effective size of the under represented class by adding extra training information to the data (Caruana, 2000).

Finally, we would also like to note that although the current efforts in the community are focused on two-class imbalanced problems, multiclass imbalanced learning problems exist and are of equal importance. For instance, in Sun et al. (2006), a cost-sensitive boosting algorithm, AdaC2.M1, was proposed to tackle the class imbalance problem with multiple classes. In this paper, a genetic algorithm was used to search the optimum cost setup for each class. In Abe et al. (2004), an iterative method for multiclass cost-sensitive learning was proposed based on three key ideas: iterative cost weighting, data space expansion, and gradient boosting with stochastic ensembles. In Chen et al. (2006), a min-max modular network was proposed to decompose a multiclass imbalanced learning problem into a series of small two-class subproblems. Other works of multiclass imbalanced learning include the rescaling approach for multiclass cost-sensitive neural networks (Zhou & Liu, 2006; Liu & Zhou, 2006b), the ensemble knowledge for imbalance sample sets (eKISS) method (Tan et al., 2003), and others.

As is evident, the range of existing solutions to the imbalanced learning problem is both multifaceted and well associated. Consequently, the assessment techniques used to evaluate these solutions share similar characteristics. We now turn our attention to these techniques.

3.4 ASSESSMENT METRICS FOR IMBALANCED LEARNING

As the research community continues to develop a greater number of intricate and promising imbalanced learning algorithms, it becomes paramount to have standardized evaluation metrics to properly assess the effectiveness of such algorithms. In this section, we provide a critical review of the major assessment metrics for imbalanced learning (He & Garcia, 2009).

3.4.1 Singular Assessment Metrics

Traditionally the most frequently used metrics are *accuracy* and *error rate*. Considering a basic two-class classification problem, let $\{p, n\}$ be the true positive and negative class labels and $\{Y, N\}$ be the predicted positive and negative class labels. Then a representation of classification performance can be formulated by a *confusion matrix* (contingency table) as illustrated in Figure 3.10.

In this chapter, we use the minority class as the positive class and the majority class as the negative class. Following this convention, accuracy and error rate are defined as:

$$Accuracy = \frac{TP + TN}{P_C + N_C}. \tag{3.13}$$

$$Error\ Rate = 1 - accuracy \tag{3.14}$$

These metrics provide a simple way of describing a classifier's performance on a given data set. However, they can be deceiving in certain situations and are highly sensitive to changes in data. In the simplest situation, if a given data set includes 5% of minority class examples and 95% of majority examples, a naive approach of classifying every example to be a majority class example would provide an accuracy of 95%. Taken at face value, 95% accuracy across the entire data set appears superb, however, on the same token this description

		True class p	n
Hypothesis output	Y	TP (True Positives)	FP (False Positives)
	N	FN (False Negatives)	TN (True Negatives)
Column counts:		P_C	N_C

Figure 3.10: Confusion matrix for performance evaluation.

fails to reflect the fact that 0% of minority examples are identified. That is to say, the accuracy metric in this case does not provide adequate information on a classifier's functionality with respect to the type of classification required.

Many representative works on the ineffectiveness of accuracy in the imbalanced learning scenario exist in the community (He & Garcia, 2009; Guo & Viktor, 2004b; Weiss, 2004; Chawla, 2003; Maloof, 2003; Sun et al., 2007; Joshi, Kumar, & Agarwal, 2001; Provost & Fawcett, 1997; Provost, Fawcett, & Kohavi, 1998). The fundamental issue can be explained by evaluating the confusion matrix in Figure 3.10: The left column represents positive instances of the data set and the right column represents the negative instances. Therefore, the proportion of the two columns is representative of the class distribution of the data set, and any metric that uses values from both columns will be inherently sensitive to imbalances. As we can see from equation (3.13), *accuracy* uses both columns' information; therefore, as class distribution varies, measures of the performance will change even though the underlying fundamental performance of the classifier does not. As one can imagine, this can be very problematic when comparing the performance of different learning algorithms over different data sets because of the inconsistency of performance representation. In other words, in the presence of imbalanced data, it becomes difficult to make relative analysis when the evaluation metrics are sensitive to data distributions.

In lieu of accuracy, other evaluation metrics are frequently adopted in the research community to provide comprehensive assessments of imbalanced learning problems, namely *precision, recall, F−measure* and *G−mean*. These metrics are defined as:

$$Precision = \frac{TP}{TP + FP} \tag{3.15}$$

$$Recall = \frac{TP}{TP + FN} \tag{3.16}$$

$$F - Measure = \frac{(1 + \beta)^2 \cdot Recall \cdot Precision}{\beta^2 \cdot Recall + Precision} \tag{3.17}$$

Where β is a coefficient to adjust the relative importance of precision versus recall (usually, $\beta = 1$).

$$G - mean = \sqrt{\frac{TP}{TP + FN} \times \frac{TN}{TN + FP}} \tag{3.18}$$

Intuitively, precision is a measure of exactness (i.e., of the examples labeled as positive, how many are actually labeled correctly), whereas recall is a measure of completeness (i.e., how many examples of the positive class were labeled correctly). These two metrics, much like accuracy and error, share an inverse relationship between each other. However, unlike accuracy and error, precision and recall are not both sensitive to changes in data distributions. A quick inspection on the precision and recall formulae readily yields that precision (3.15) is sensitive to data distributions while recall (3.16) is not. On the other hand, that recall is not distribution dependent is almost superfluous because an assertion based solely on recall is equivocal, since recall provides no insight to how many examples are incorrectly labeled as positive. Similarly, precision cannot assert how many positive examples are labeled incorrectly. Nevertheless, when used properly, precision and recall can effectively evaluate classification performance in imbalanced learning scenarios. Specifically, the F-Measure metric (3.17) combines precision and recall as a measure of the effectiveness of classification in terms of a ratio of the weighted importance on either recall or precision as determined by the β coefficient set by the user. As a result, F-Measure provides more insight into the functionality of a classifier than the accuracy metric, however remaining sensitive to data distributions. Another metric, the G-Mean metric (3.18), evaluates the degree of inductive bias in terms of a ratio of positive accuracy and negative accuracy. Though F-Measure and G-Mean are great improvements over accuracy, they are still ineffective in answering more generic questions about classification evaluations. For instance, *how can we compare the performance of different classifiers over a range sample distributions?*

3.4.2 Receiver Operating Characteristics (ROC) Curves

In order to overcome such issues, the ROC assessment technique (Fawcett, 2003, 2006) makes use of the proportion of two single-column-based evaluation metrics, namely true positives rate (*TP_rate*) and false positives rate (*FP_rate*), which are defined as:

$$TP\_rate = \frac{TP}{P_C}; \quad FP\_rate = \frac{FP}{N_C} \tag{3.19}$$

The ROC graph is formed by plotting TP_rate over FP_rate, and any point in ROC space corresponds to the performance of a single classifier on a given distribution. The ROC curve is useful because it provides a visual representation of the relative trade-offs between the benefits (reflected by true positives) and costs (reflected by false positives) of classification in regards to data distributions.

For hard-type classifiers that output only discrete class labels, each classifier will produce a (*TP_rate*, *FP_rate*) pair that corresponds to a single point in the ROC space. Figure 3.11 illustrates a typical ROC graph with points A, B, C, D, E, F and G representing ROC points and curves $L1$ and $L2$ representing ROC curves (He & Garcia, 2009). According to the structure of the ROC graph, point A (0, 1) represents a perfect classification. Generally speaking, one classifier is better than another if its corresponding point in ROC space is closer to point A (upper-left hand in the ROC space) than the other. Any classifier whose corresponding ROC point is located on the diagonal, such as point E in Figure 3.11, is representative of a classifier that will provide a random guess of the class labels (i.e., a random classifier). Therefore, any classifier that appears in the lower right triangle of ROC space performs worse than random guessing, such as the classifier associated with point F in the shaded area in Figure 3.11. Nevertheless, a classifier that performs worse than random guessing does not mean that the classifier cannot provide useful information. On the contrary, the classifier is informative; however, the information is incorrectly applied. For instance, if one negates the classification results of classifier F, i.e., reverse its classification decision on each instance, then this will produce point G in Figure 3.11, the symmetric classification point of F.

In the case of soft-type classifiers, i.e., classifiers that output a continuous numeric value to represent the confidence of an instance belonging to the predicted class, a threshold can be used to produce a series of points in ROC space.

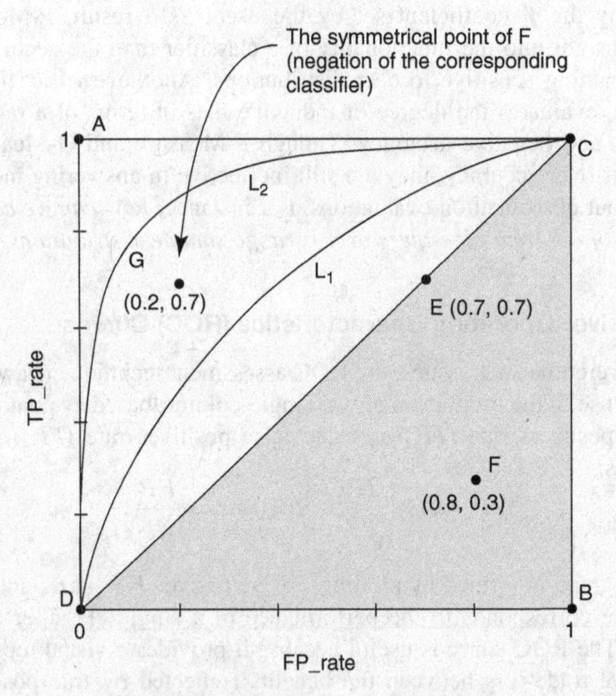

Figure 3.11: ROC curve representation.

This technique can generate an ROC curve instead of a single ROC point, as illustrated by curves L1 and L2 in Figure 3.11. In order to assess different classifiers' performance in this case, one generally uses the area under the curve (AUC) as an evaluation criterion (Fawcett, 2003, 2006). For instance, in Figure 3.11, the $L2$ ROC curve provides a larger AUC measure compared to that of $L1$; therefore, the corresponding classifier associated with curve $L2$ can provide better average performance compared to the classifier associated with curve $L1$. Of course, one should also note that it is possible for a high AUC classifier to perform worse in a specific region in ROC space than a low AUC classifier (Fawcett, 2003, 2006). We additionally note that it is generally very straight forward to make hard-type classifiers provide soft-type outputs based on the observations of the intrinsic characteristics of those classifiers (Domingos, 1999; Freund & Schapire, 1996; Provost & Domingos, 2000; Fawcett, 2001).

3.4.3 Precision-Recall (PR) Curves

Although ROC curves provide powerful methods to visualize performance evaluation, they also have their own limitations. In the case of highly skewed data sets, it is observed that the ROC curve may provide an overly optimistic view of an algorithm's performance. Under such situations, the PR curves can provide a more informative representation of performance assessment (Davis & Goadrich, 2006).

Given a confusion matrix as in Figure 3.10 and the definition of precision (3.15) and recall (3.16), the PR curve is defined by plotting precision rate over the recall rate. PR curves exhibit a strong correspondence to ROC curves: A curve dominates in ROC space *if and only if* it dominates in PR space (Davis & Goadrich, 2006). However, an algorithm that optimizes the AUC in the ROC space is not guaranteed to optimize the AUC in PR space (Davis & Goadrich, 2006). Moreover, while the objective of ROC curves is to be in the upper-left hand of the ROC space, a dominant PR curve resides in the upper-right hand of the PR space. PR space also characterizes curves analogous to the convex hull in the ROC space, namely the achievable PR curve (Davis & Goadrich, 2006). Hence, PR space has all the analogous benefits of ROC space, making it an effective evaluation technique.

To see why the PR curve can provide more informative representations of performance assessment under highly imbalanced data, we consider a distribution where negative examples significantly exceed the number of positive examples (i.e., $N_c >> P_c$). In this case, if a classifier's performance has a large change in the number of false positives, it will not significantly change the FP rate since the denominator (N_c) is very large (see equation (3.19)). Hence the ROC graph will fail to capture this phenomenon. The precision metric, on the other hand, considers the ratio of TP with respect to TP + FP (see Figure 3.10 and equation (3.15), hence it can correctly capture the classifier's performance when the number of false positives drastically changes (Davis & Goadrich, 2006). Hence as evident by this example, the PR curve is an advantageous technique for performance assessment in the presence of highly skewed data. As a result, many of the current research work in the community use PR curves for performance evaluations and comparisons (Bunescu et al., 2005; Davis et al., 2005; Singla & Domingos, 2005; Landgrebe, Paclik, Duin, & Bradley, 2006).

3.4.4 Cost Curves

Another shortcoming of ROC curves is that they lack the ability to provide confidence intervals on a classifier's performance and are unable to infer the statistical significance of different classifiers' performance (Holte & Drummond, 2005, 2006). They also have difficulties providing insights on a classifier's performance over varying class probabilities or misclassification costs (Holte & Drummond, 2005, 2006). In order to provide a more comprehensive evaluation metric to address these issues, cost curves were proposed in Holte and Drummond (2000, 2005, 2006). A cost curve is a cost-sensitive evaluation technique that provides the ability to explicitly express a classifier's performance over varying misclassification costs and class distributions in a visual format. Thus, the cost curve method retains the attractive visual representation features of ROC analysis and further provides a technique that yields a broadened range of information regarding classification performance.

Generally speaking, the cost curve method plots performance (i.e., normalized expected cost) over operation points, which are represented by a probability cost function that is based on the probability of correctly classifying a positive sample. The cost space exhibits a duality with ROC space where each point in ROC space is represented by a line in cost space, and vice versa (Holte & Drummond, 2006). Any (FP, TP) classification pair in ROC space is related to a line in cost space by:

$$E[C] = (1 - TP - FP)PCF(+) + FP \tag{3.20}$$

where E[C] is the expected cost and PCF (+) is the probability of an example being from the positive class. Figure 3.12 provides an example of cost space; here we highlight the correspondence between the ROC points of Figure 3.11 and their lines in cost space. For instance, the bottom axis represents perfect classification while the top axis represents the contrary case; these lines correspond to ROC points A and B, respectively.

With a collection of cost lines at hand, a cost curve is then created by selecting a classification line for each possible operation point. For example, a cost curve can be created that minimizes the normalized expected cost across all possible operation points. In particular, this technique allows for a clearer visual representation of classification performance compared to ROC curves, and allows for more direct assessments between classifiers as they range over operation points.

3.4.5 Assessment Metrics for Multiclass Imbalanced Learning

While all of the assessment metrics discussed so far in this section are appropriate for two-class imbalanced learning problems, some of them can be modified to

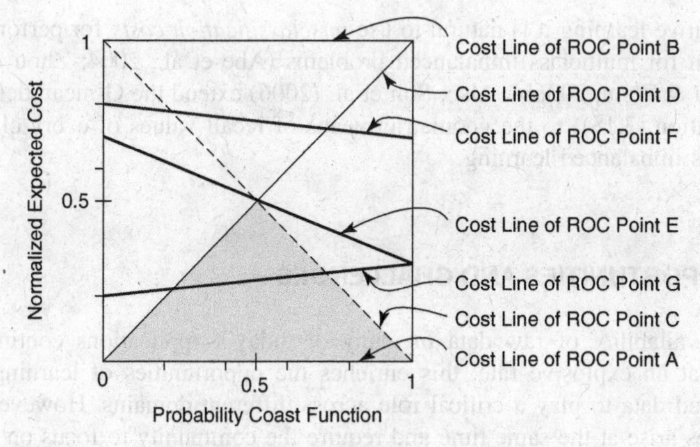

Figure 3.12: Cost curve representation.

accommodate multiclass imbalanced learning problems. For instance, Fawcett (2003, 2006) discussed multiclass ROC graphs. For an n classes problem, the confusion matrix presented in Figure 3.10 becomes an $n \times n$ matrix, with n correct classifications (the major diagonal elements) and $n^2 - n$ errors (the off-diagonal elements). Therefore, instead of representing the trade-offs between a single benefit (TP) and cost (FP), we have to manage n benefits and $n^2 - n$ costs. A straightforward way of doing this is to generate n different ROC graphs, one for each class Fawcett (2003, 2006). For instance, considering a problem with a total of W classes, the ROC graph i, ROC_i, plots classification performance using class w_i as the positive class and all other classes as the negative class. However, this approach compromises one of the major advantages of using ROC analysis for imbalanced learning problems: It becomes sensitive to the class skew because the negative class in this situation is the combination of $n - 1$ classes (see sections 3.4.1 and 3.4.2).

Similarly, under the multiclass imbalanced learning scenario, the AUC values for two-class problems become multiple pair-wise discriminability values (Hand & Till, 2001). To calculate such multiclass AUCs, Provost and Domingos proposed a probability estimation-based approach. First, the ROC curve for each reference class w_i is generated and their respective AUCs are measured. Second, all of the AUCs are combined by a weight coefficient according to the reference class's prevalence in the data. Although this approach is quite simple in calculation, it is sensitive to the class skews for the same reason as mentioned before. To eliminate this constraint, Hand and Till (2001) proposed the *M measure*, a generalization approach that aggregates all pairs of classes based on the inherent characteristics of the AUC. The major advantage of this method is that it is insensitive to class distribution and error costs. Interested readers can refer to (Hand & Till, 2001) for a more detailed overview of this technique.

In addition to multiclass ROC analysis, the community has also adopted other assessment metrics for multiclass imbalanced learning problems. For instance, in cost-sensitive learning it is natural to use *misclassification costs* for performance evaluation for multiclass imbalanced problems (Abe et al., 2004; Zhou & Liu, 2006; Liu & Zhou, 2006b). Also, Sun et al. (2006) extend the G-mean definition (see equation (3.18)) to the geometric means of recall values of every class for multiclass imbalanced learning.

3.5 OPPORTUNITIES AND CHALLENGES

As the availability of raw data in many of today's applications continues to increase at an explosive rate, this enriches the opportunities of learning from imbalanced data to play a critical role across different domains. However, new challenges arise at the same time and require the community to focus on understanding the foundations and develop principled methodologies to handle this problem. In this section, we provide a brief summary of the major opportunities and challenges for imbalanced learning. A more detailed discussion on this can be found in He and Garcia (2009).

First, most of the current research efforts in imbalanced learning focus on specific algorithms and/or case studies; only a very limited amount of theoretical understanding on the principles and consequences of this problem have been addressed (He & Garcia, 2009) (Provost, 2000). For example, although almost every algorithm presented in literature claims to be able to improve classification accuracy over certain benchmarks, there exist certain situations in which learning from the original data sets may provide better performance. This raises an important question: *To what extent do imbalanced learning methods help with learning capabilities?* This is a fundamental and critical question in this field for the following reasons (He & Garcia, 2009). First, suppose there are specific (existing or future) techniques or methodologies that significantly outperform others across most (or, ideally, all) applicable domains, then rigorous studies of the underlying effects of such methods would yield fundamental understandings of the problem at hand. Second, as data engineering research methodologies materialize into real-world solutions, questions such as "How will this solution help?" or "Can this solution efficiently handle various types of data?" become the basis on which economic and administrative decisions are made. Thus, the consequences of this critical question have wide-ranging effects in the advancement of this field and data engineering at large (He & Garcia, 2009). This question is also strongly related to an important proposition addressed by Provost in the invited paper for the AAAI 2000 Workshop on Imbalanced Data Sets (Provost, 2000): "[In regards to imbalanced learning,]... isn't the best research strategy to concentrate on how machine learning algorithms can deal most effectively with whatever data they are given?" We believe the understanding of the underlying foundations of imbalanced learning will not only provide fundamental insights to the imbalanced learning issue, but also provide an added level of comparative assessment between existing and future methodologies.

Second, since data resources are critical for research development in the knowledge discovery and data engineering field, we believe a well-organized, publicly available benchmark specifically dedicated to imbalanced learning will significantly benefit the long-term research development of this field. Although there are currently many publicly available benchmarks for assessing the effectiveness of different data engineering algorithms/tools, there are a very limited number of benchmarks, if any, that are solely dedicated to imbalanced learning problems. For instance, many of the existing benchmarks do not clearly identify imbalanced data sets and their suggested evaluation use in an organized manner. Therefore, many data sets require additional manipulation before they can be applied to imbalanced learning scenarios. This limitation can create a bottleneck for the long-term development of research in imbalanced learning because of the lack of a uniform benchmark for standardized performance assessments and the lack of data sharing and data interoperability.

Third, it is necessary for the community to establish, as a standard, the practice of using more informative assessment metrics such as the curve-based evaluation techniques described in section 3.4 for performance evaluation and comparative study in this field. As we have discussed in detail in section 3.4.1, the traditional technique of using a singular evaluation metric such as overall accuracy or error rate is not sufficient when handling imbalanced learning problems. Although most publications use a broad assortment of singular assessment metrics to evaluate the performance and potential trade-offs of their algorithms, without an accompanied curve-based analysis such as those discussed in sections 3.4.2, 3.4.3, and 3.4.4, it becomes very difficult to provide any concrete relative evaluations between different algorithms, or answer the more rigorous questions of functionality. Therefore, we consider a standardized evaluation practice would be important to benefit long-term research development in this field. Not only because each technique provides its own set of answers to different fundamental questions, but also because an analysis in the evaluation space of one technique can be correlated to the evaluation space of another, leading to increased transitivity and a broader understanding of the functional abilities of existing and future works.

Fourth, it is important for the community to study the emerging applications with the imbalanced data. For instance, how to handle the situation of incremental learning with imbalanced data? In this case, how can a machine learning system autonomously adjust the learning algorithm if an imbalance is introduced in the middle of the learning period? How can one handle the situation when newly introduced concepts are also imbalanced (i.e., the imbalanced concept drifting issue)? Another interesting example is the semisupervised learning from imbalanced data. Briefly speaking, the semisupervised learning problem concerns itself with learning when data sets are a combination of labeled and unlabeled data, as opposed to fully supervised learning where all training data are labeled. In this situation, how can one identify whether an unlabeled data example came from a balanced or imbalanced underlying distribution? What are the effective and efficient methods for recovering the unlabeled data examples given an imbalanced training data with labels? We believe that all of these questions are important not only for theoretical research development, but also for many practical application scenarios.

3.6 CASE STUDY

In this section, we present a case study of the imbalanced learning over numerous benchmarks. Specifically, we discuss the simulations of seven aforementioned learning methods, including RAMOBoost, SMOTEBoost, SMOTE, ADASYN, AdaCost, BorderlineSMOTE, and SMOTE-tomek.

3.6.1 Nonlinear Normalization

Data normalization is an important pre-processing step for many learning algorithms. For instance, the mismatch conditions during different data acquisition periods, such as training and testing data, may degrade classifiers' performance severely. Viikki, Bye, and Laurila (1998) presented that the varying noise conditions during collection of acoustic data for the training and testing period would significantly influence the performance of the speech recognition system. Furthermore, the normalization method can also accelerate the parameter estimation process for a neural network–based classifier (Viikki et al., 1998). Traditional linear normalization methods assume both training and testing data are available at the learning stage, and associate training and testing feature sets together to search for the maximum and minimum values before normalization. However, in many practical application scenarios, it is a common phenomenon that the testing data may not be available during training time. In this section, we present a nonlinear normalization method based on the data distribution, the distribution distance mapping (DDM) method. During the training stage, for each feature, we first sort all the training data and assign a nondecreasing value from a uniformly divided interval $[LB, UB]$ according to its position in the sorted array. Here LB and UB represent the user-defined lower bound (LB) and upper bound (UB) to specify the data range after the normalization procedure, such as [0, 1] in our current simulation. In this way, a monotonic sequence value is created as the result of the scaling of the training data. During the testing stage, we find the region in the corresponding training data that each testing instance falls in, and then use a local linear fitting function to obtain the scaled value for each testing data points. The complete pseudo-code of the DDM method is presented in Figure 3.13.

Example: To better illustrate the idea of the DDM nonlinear normalization method, Figure 3.14 gives a simple example to illustrate its operation procedure. For the multiple dimension data, the DDM method needs to normalize each feature correspondingly according to the pseudo-code in Figure 3.13. For clear presentation, here we consider six data instances and take a single feature as

[*Algorithm* : DDM - Training Feature]

Input :

- Training feature set with m examples in n dimensional feature space: $f = \langle f_1, f_2, \ldots, f_n \rangle$, where f_i $(i = 1, 2, \ldots n)$ is the ith feature vector: $f_i \in R^{m \cdot 1}$.
- LB: the lower boundary of the nonlinear normalization
- UB: the upper boundary of the nonlinear normalization

Do for $i = 1, 2, \ldots, n$

-1. The range $[LB, UB]$ is evenly divided into $m+1$ intervals. The width of each interval, Δ, is calculated as:

$$\Delta = \frac{UB - LB}{m+1}$$

-2. Sort f_i in ascending order, and get back the sorted vector f_i' and the sorted index I such that:

$$f_i' = f_i(I)$$

-3. Set $g(1) = LB + \Delta$, then:

Do for $j = 2, 3, \ldots, m$

-3-1. If $f_i'(j) = f_i'(j-1)$, then:

$$g(j) = g(j-1)$$

-3-2. Else:

$$g(j) = LB + (j-1) \times \Delta$$

End Loop

-4. Set $\hat{f}_i(I) = g$

End Loop

Output : The nonlinear normalization for training feature set:

$$\hat{f} = \langle \hat{f}_1, \hat{f}_2, \ldots \hat{f}_n \rangle$$

(a)

[*Algortithm* : DDM - Testing Feature]

Input :

- Original training feature set: $f = \langle f_1, f_2, \ldots, f_n \rangle$
- Normalized training feature set: $\hat{f} = \langle \hat{f}_1, \hat{f}_2, \ldots, \hat{f}_n \rangle$
- Testing feature set with l instances in n dimensional feature space: $T = \langle T_1, T_2, \ldots, T_n \rangle$, where T_i $(i = 1, 2, \ldots n)$ is the ith feature vector: $T_i \in R^{l \cdot 1}$

Do for $i = 1, 2, \ldots, n$

-1. Sort f_i in ascending order, and get back the sorted vector f_i'.

-2. Sort $\hat{f}_i$ in ascending order, and get back the sorted vector $\hat{f}_i'$.

-3. **Do** for $j = 1, 2, \ldots, l$

-3-1. If $T_i(j) < f_i'(1)$, then:

$$\hat{T}_i(j) = \hat{f}_i'(1)$$

-3-2. Else if $T_i(j) > f_i'(m)$, then:

$$\hat{T}_i(j) = \hat{f}_i'(m)$$

-3-3. Else: search the neighbor index k_1 and k_2 of j that:

$$\begin{cases} f_i'(k_1) \le T_i(j) < f_i'(k_2) \\ k_2 - k_1 = 1 \end{cases}$$

then:

$$\hat{T}_i(j) = \hat{f}_i'(k_1) + \left(f_i'(k_2) - T_i(j)\right) \times \frac{\left(\hat{f}_i'(k_2) - \hat{f}_i'(k_1)\right)}{\left(f_i'(k_2) - f_i'(k_1)\right)}$$

End Loop

End Loop

Output : The nonlinear normalization for testing feature set:

$$\hat{T} = \langle \hat{T}_1, \hat{T}_2, \ldots \hat{T}_n \rangle$$

(b)

Figure 3.13: The nonlinear normalization method: the DDM algorithm (a) for training data and (b) for testing data.

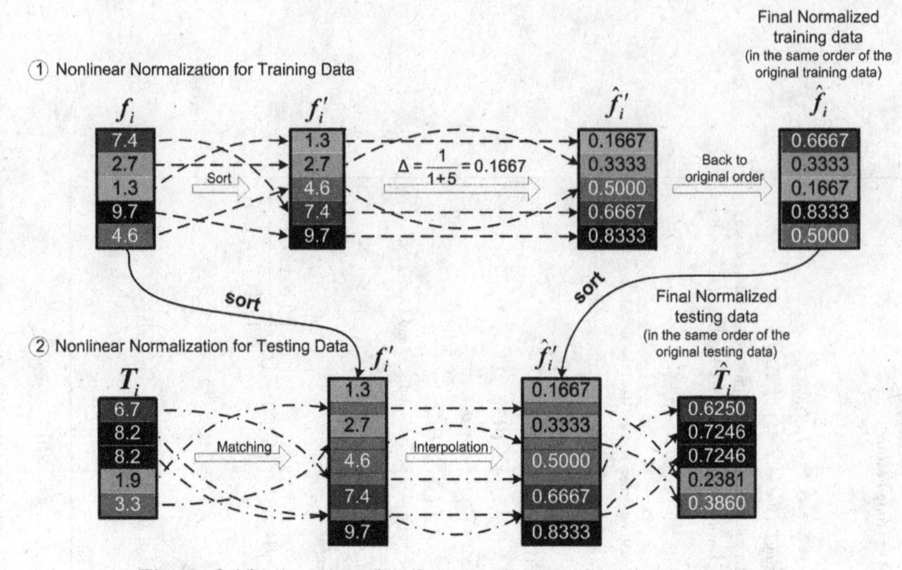

Figure 3.14: An example of the nonlinear normalization method.

an example. Assume the normalized data range is [0, 1] ($LB = 0$ and $UB = 1$). During the training stage, the feature value 1.3 is the first data in the sorted training data vector and thus its normalized value is equal to 0.1667. Once the training data is properly mapped, we can calculate the normalized value for each testing data according to its position in the sorted sequence of training data. For instance, the testing data 6.7 is found to be located between the training data 4.6 and 7.4. Therefore by applying the interpolation equation shown in Figure 3.13(b), the normalized value of 6.7 will be:

$$T = 0.5 + (6.7 - 4.6) \times \frac{0.6667 - 0.5}{7.4 - 4.6} = 0.6250 \tag{3.21}$$

Figure 3.15 visualizes the mapping curve of the nonlinear normalization procedure for one feature vector of a real data set, where the x-axis represents the original feature values and the y-axis represents the normalized feature values. Figure 3.15(a) displays the mapping curve for the training feature vector and Figure 3.15(b) displays part of the mapping curve for the testing feature vector. Here we plot both the training and testing data in Figure 3.15(b) for clear presentation, where the circle and the plus shapes represent the training and testing data, respectively.

Similar to the concept of histogram equalization used in image processing to improve the image contrast to amplify image details (Gonzalez & Woods, 2002), this nonlinear normalization method can also balance the bias distribution of the data sets to facilitate learning. In contrast, the traditional linear normalization methods have no such capability. To observe the data distribution

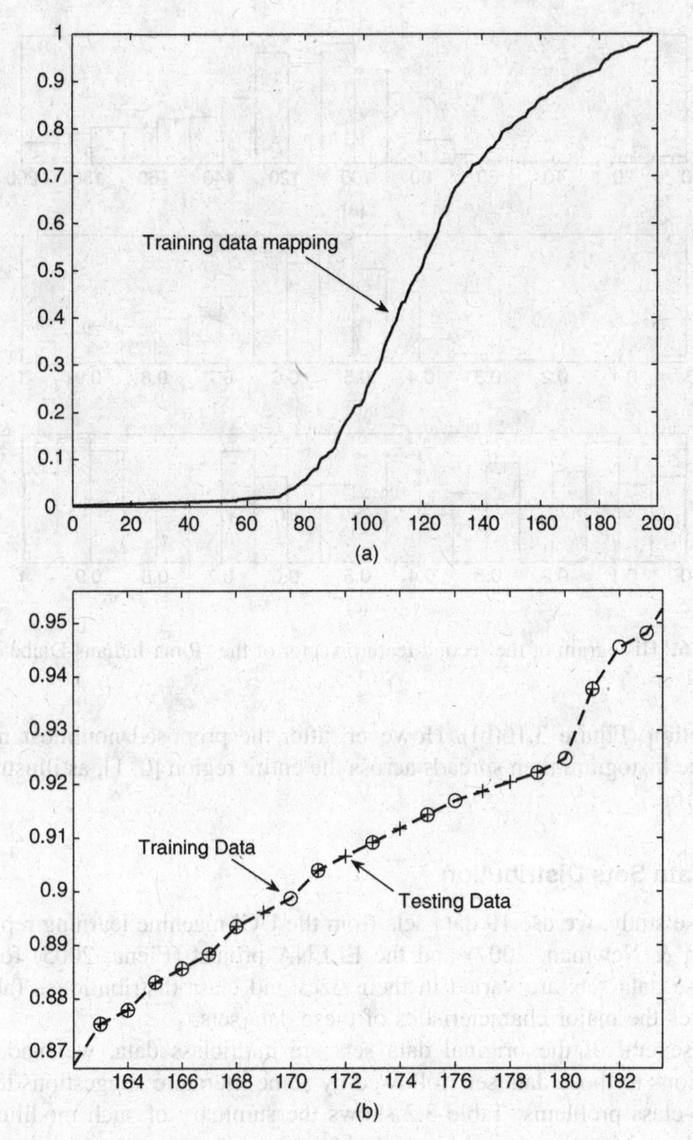

Figure 3.15: Nonlinear normalization for the second feature vector of the "Pima-Indians-Diabetes" data set: (a) training data normalization and (b) testing data normalization.

characteristics after the normalization method, Figure 3.16(a) shows the histogram of one testing feature vector before normalization, while Figure 3.16(b) and (c) represent the histogram after the traditional linear normalization and the proposed DDM method, respectively. From Figure 3.16(a) one can see the histogram of the original testing feature vector is mainly located in the range [80, 200], and such biased distribution remains unvaried after traditional linear

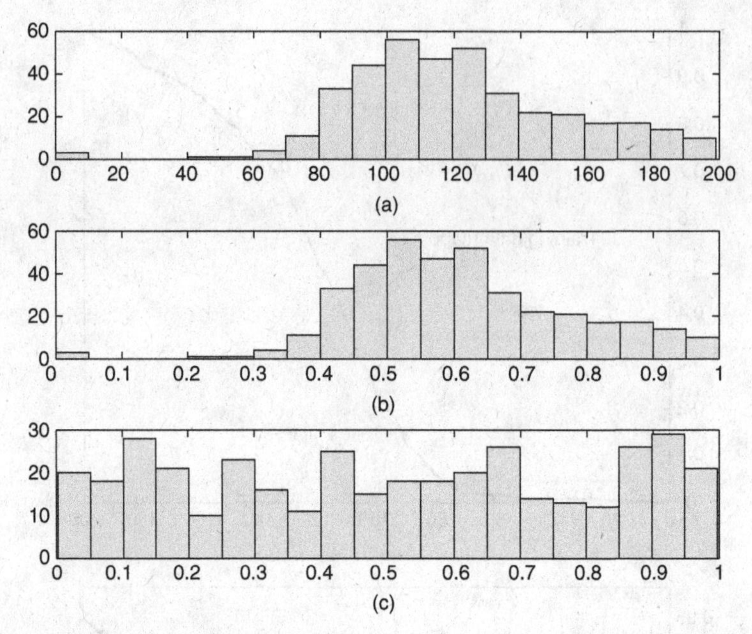

Figure 3.16: Histogram of the second feature vector of the "Pima-Indians-Diabetes" data set.

normalization (Figure 3.16(b)). However, after the proposed nonlinear normalization, the histogram then spreads across the entire region [0, 1], as illustrated in Figure 3.16(c).

3.6.2 Data Sets Distribution

In this case study, we use 19 data sets from the UCI machine learning repository (Asuncion & Newman, 2007) and the ELENA project (Elena, 2005) for analysis. These data sets are varied in their sizes and class distributions. Table 3.1 summarizes the major characteristics of these data sets.

Since several of the original data sets are multiclass data, we made some modifications to those data sets followed by some literature suggestions to make them two-class problems. Table 3.2 shows the summary of such modifications, followed by a brief discussion for each data set.

- Sonar: The original data set is used to train a classifier to discriminate between sonar signals bounced off a metal cylinder and those bounced off a roughly cylinder rock. There are two distinct class labels, "R" (if the instance is a rock) and "M" (if the instance is a metal cylinder). The class "R" is set to be the minority class and the class "M" is set to be the majority class.
- Spambase: The original data set is used to classify between spam e-mails and legitimate emails. This database includes 4601 e-mail messages, in which 2788 are legitimate messages and 1813 are spam messages. Each message

Table 3.1: Summary of the Data Sets Characteristics (sorted in the degree of class skew)

Data set	# Feature	# Data	# Minority instances	# Majority instances	Skewness ratio
Sonar	60	208	97	111	0.47 : 0.53
Spambase	57	4601	1813	2788	0.39 : 0.61
Ionosphere	34	351	126	225	0.36 : 0.64
Pima-Indians-Diabetes	8	768	268	500	0.35 : 0.65
Wine	13	178	59	119	0.33 : 0.67
German	24	1000	300	700	0.30 : 0.70
Phoneme	5	5404	1586	3818	0.29 : 0.71
Vehicle	18	846	199	647	0.24 : 0.76
Texture	40	5500	1000	4500	0.18 : 0.82
Segment	18	2310	330	1980	0.14 : 0.86
Page_Blocks	10	5473	560	4913	0.10 : 0.90
Satimage	36	6435	626	5809	0.10 : 0.90
Mf_Zernike	47	2000	200	1800	0.10 : 0.90
Vowel	10	990	90	900	0.09 : 0.91
Abalone	7	731	42	689	0.06 : 0.94
Glass	9	214	9	205	0.04 : 0.96
Yeast	8	483	20	463	0.04 : 0.96
Letter	16	20000	789	19211	0.04 : 0.96
Shuttle	9	43500	37	43463	0.001 : 0.999

is represented by 57 attributes, including 48 continuous attributes of the frequency of a particular word, six continuous attributes of the frequency of a particular character, and three continuous attributes to reflect the statistics of the capital letters in the e-mails. The spam e-mails and legitimate e-mails are set to be the minority and majority classes, respectively.

- Ionosphere: The original data set has two classes for classifying the quality of radar returns. We choose the "bad radar" instances as the minority class and "good radar" instances as the majority class.
- Pima-Indians-Diabetes: This is a two-class data set used to predict positive diabetes cases. We employ the positive cases to be minority class and negative cases to be majority class.
- Wine: This data set is used to determine the origin of wines based on chemical analysis. The original data set includes three classes: we combine class 2 and 3 to be the majority class and leave class 1 to be the minority class.
- German: This is a two-class classification problem used to classify German customers' credit. We select "customers with good credit" as the majority class and "customers with bad credit" as the minority class.
- Phoneme: The aim of the original data set is to distinguish between nasal (class 0) and oral sounds based on five features. We set class 0 to be the majority class and class 1 to be the minority class.

Table 3.2: Description of Imbalanced Data Sets

Data set	Minority class	Majority class
Sonar	Class "R" (rock instances)	Class "M" (metal cylinder instances)
Spambase	Spam email	Legitimate email
Ionosphere	"Bad radar" class	"Good radar" class
PID	Positive class	Negative class
Wine	Class "1"	Classes "2" and "3"
German	Customers with bad credit	Customers with good credit
Phoneme	Class of "oral sounds (class 1)"	Class of "nasal sounds (class 0)"
Vehicle	Class of "Van"	Classes of "OPEL," "SAAS," and "BUS"
Texture	Classes of "13" and "14"	Classes of "2," "3," "4," "6," "7," "8," "9," "10," and "12"
Segment	Class of "brickface"	Classes of "sky," "foliage," "cement," "window," "path," and "grass"
Page_blocks	Classes of "horizontal line," "graphic," "vertical line," and "picture"	Class of "text"
Satimage	Class of "damp grey soil"	Classes of "red soil," "cotton crop," "grey soil," "soil with vegetation stubble," and "very damp grey soil"
Mf_Zernike	Class of digit "9"	Classes of digits "0," "1," "2,""3,""4,""5,""6,""7," and "8"
Vowel	Class 1	Classes of 2 to 11
Abalone	Class of "18"	Class of "9"
Glass	Class 6 ("tableware")	All other classes
Yeast	Class of "POX"	Class of "CYT"
Letter	Class of letter "Z"	Classes of letters "A"–"Y"
Shuttle	Class of "Fpv Close"	Classes of "Rad Flow," "Fpv Open," "High," "Bypass," "Bpv Close," and "Bpv Open"

- Vehicle: The original data set is used to classify a given silhouette as one of four types of vehicles (OPEL, SAAS, BUS, and VAN). We choose "VAN" as the minority class and combine the remaining three classes as the majority class (Guo & Viktor, 2004b).
- Texture: The data set has been created in order to study the texture discrimination with high-order statistics. There are altogether 11 classes with labels: 2, 3, 4, 6, 7, 8, 9, 10, 12, 13, 14. We combine class 2, 3, 4, 6, 7, 8, 9, 10, and 12 as the majority class and merge the remaining class 13 and 14 to be the minority class.
- Segment: The instances are drawn randomly from a database of seven outdoor images. Thus there were originally seven classes: 1 (brickface), 2 (sky), 3 (foliage), 4 (cement), 5 (window), 6 (path), and 7 (grass). Because the third features of all instances are the same, we abandon this feature in our

simulation. We consider class 1 as the minority class and combine all other classes to be the majority class.

- Page blocks: This data set is used to classify all the blocks of the page layout of a document. There are five classes: text, horizontal line, graphic, vertical line, and picture. We choose class "text" as the majority class and merge the remaining four classes to be the minority class.
- Satimage: The data set is used to classify multispectral values of pixels in 3 by 3 neighbors in a satellite image. Originally, the data set has six classes: 1 (red soil), 2 (cotton crop), 3 (gray soil), 4 (damp gray soil), 5 (soil with vegetation stubble), and 7 (very damp gray soil). We choose class 4 as the minority class and combine the remaining five classes to be the majority class (Guo & Viktor, 2004b).
- Mf_Zernike: The data set was one of the feature sets describing the handwritten digits (0–9) extracted from a collection of Dutch utility maps. According to the suggestion of reference (Liu et al., 2006), examples representing the digit 9 is served as the minority class, while the remaining examples are associated together as the majority class.
- Vowel: This is a speech recognition data set for classification of different vowels. There are 11 classes in original data sets. We set class 1 to be the minority class and combine the remaining classes to be the majority class (Guo & Viktor, 2004b).
- Abalone: The data set is used to predict the age of abalone from physical measurements. There are 29 classes in the original data set. We choose class 18 to be the minority class and class 9 to be the majority class (Guo & Viktor, 2004b). In addition, one symbolic feature ("sex") has been removed from the data set in our current simulation.
- Glass: This data set is used to classify six types of glass according to their oxide content. We select class 6 (tableware) as the minority class and merge the remaining classes as the majority class (Guo & Viktor, 2004b).
- Yeast: The data set was used to classify the localization site of protein. We select class "POX" (peroxisomal) as the minority class and class "CYT" (cytosolic or cytoskeletal) as the majority class (Guo & Viktor, 2004b).
- Letter: The objective of constructing this dataset is to identify each of a large number of black-and-white rectangular pixel displays as one of the 26 capital letters in the English alphabet. We chose to let examples representing letter 'Z' be the minority class and the remaining be the majority class (Liu et al., 2006).
- Shuttle: The motivation for collecting this dataset was the exploration of the U.S. Space Shuttle *Challenger*. Specifically, an investigation ensued into the reliability of the shuttle's propulsion system. There are originally seven classes: 'Rad Flow', 'Fpv Close', 'Fpv Open', 'High', 'Bypass', 'Bpv Close', and 'Bpv Open'. We set class 'Fpv Close' to be the minority class, and associate the remaining classes to be the majority class.

3.6.3 Simulation Results and Discussions

In this case study, all simulation results are based on the average of 10 runs. At each run, we randomly draw half of the data as training data and use the remaining half as the testing data. In our current simulation, a neural network with multilayer perceptron (MLP) is adopted as the base classifier. The detailed configuration is as follows: The number of hidden layer neurons is set to be 4, and the number of input neurons is equal to the number of features for each data set. Similar to most of the existing imbalanced learning methods in the literature, we also only consider two-class imbalanced problems in our current study. Therefore, the number of output neurons is set to be 2 for all the simulations. Sigmoid function is used as the activation function, and the inner training epochs is set to be 100 with a learning rate of 0.1.

In our current simulation, we use 20 boosting iterations as suggested in Opitz and Maclin (1999) for ensemble learning. The number of synthetic data generated at each boosting iteration is set to be 200% of the number of the minority instances (Chawla et al., 2002). For SMOTEBoost, SMOTE, ADASYN, BorderlineSMOTE, and SMOTE-tomek, the number of nearest neighbors is set to be 5. The cost factor C for AdaCost is set to be 3 according to the suggestion of Fan et al. (1999).

Table 3.3 summarizes the performance of the comparative algorithms, in which the best performance of each algorithm across each evaluation criteria is also highlighted in Table 3.3.

The last column of Table 3.3 lists the AUC values for each method; the best performance is also highlighted. In order to demonstrate the ROC curves of all the random runs of each data set for the case study, the vertical averaging approach in Fawcett (2003) is applied to generate the averaged ROC curves. The implementation of this approach can be illustrated in Figure 3.17. Assume one would like to average two ROC curves: l_1 and l_2, each of which is formed by a series of points in the ROC space. The first step is to evenly divide the range of fp_rate into a set of intervals, within each of which the tp_rate values of each ROC curves need to be found and averaged. In Figure 3.17, X_1 and Y_1 are the points from l_1 and l_2 corresponding to the interval fp_rate1. By averaging their tp_rate values, the corresponding point Z_1 on the averaged ROC curve is obtained. In case there exist some ROC curves that do not have corresponding points on certain intervals, one can use the linear interpolation method to obtain the point on the averaged ROC curve. For instance, in Figure 3.17, the point $\overline{X}$ (corresponding to fp_rate2) is calculated on the basis of the linear interpolation of the two neighbor points of X_2 and X_3. Once $\overline{X}$ is obtained, it can be averaged with Y_2 to get the corresponding Z_2 point on the averaged ROC curve. On the basis of this approach, Figure 3.18 shows several snapshots of the averaged ROC curves for the data set "Ionosphere" (Figure 3.18(a)), "Phoneme" (Figure 3.18(b)), "Satimage" (Figure 3.18(c)), and "Abalone" (Figure 3.18(d)).

From the simulation results shown by Table 3.3, one can infer that there seems to be no single imbalanced learning algorithm that can universally outperform all

Table 3.3: Evaluation Metrics and Performance Comparison

Data set	Methods	OA	Precision	Recall	F-measure	G-mean	AUC
Sonar	RAMOBoost	**0.7798**	**0.7566**	0.7813	**0.7672**	**0.7796**	**0.86343**
	SMOTEBoost	0.7702	0.7459	0.7748	0.7579	0.7697	0.86176
	SMOTE	0.7606	0.7330	0.7687	0.7485	0.7605	0.84311
	ADASYN	0.5712	0.5184	**0.9815**	0.6780	0.4624	0.82382
	AdaCost	0.7721	0.7559	0.7644	0.7597	0.7711	0.76864
	BorderlineSMOTE	0.7606	0.7364	0.771	0.7494	0.7607	0.84205
	SMOTE-tomek	0.7442	0.7379	0.8073	0.7144	0.7448	0.82378
Spambase	RAMOBoost	0.9448	**0.9244**	0.9387	**0.9315**	0.9438	0.98379
	SMOTEBoost	0.9435	0.9191	0.9418	0.9302	0.9432	0.98329
	SMOTE	0.9397	0.9194	0.9311	0.9251	0.9382	0.97942
	ADASYN	0.7746	0.6424	**0.9851**	0.7776	0.7904	0.96849
	AdaCost	**0.9472**	0.8974	0.9413	0.8588	**0.9462**	**0.98552**
	BorderlineSMOTE	0.9291	0.9028	0.936	0.8632	0.9302	0.97362
	SMOTE-tomek	0.9376	0.9002	0.9384	0.8611	0.9377	0.97649
Ionosphere	RAMOBoost	**0.8411**	**0.8512**	0.6638	**0.744**	**0.7874**	**0.90138**
	SMOTEBoost	0.8251	0.8244	0.6346	0.7156	0.7662	0.88907
	SMOTE	0.8177	0.8026	0.6425	0.7106	0.7643	0.82093
	ADASYN	0.6749	0.5263	**0.7602**	0.6198	0.6912	0.79778
	AdaCost	0.8337	0.8237	0.6059	0.7352	0.7604	0.88186
	BorderlineSMOTE	0.8206	0.8466	0.6516	0.7078	0.7698	0.81265
	SMOTE-tomek	0.8166	0.8494	0.6539	0.7110	0.7677	0.8265
PID	RAMOBoost	0.724	**0.5766**	0.7467	**0.6497**	**0.729**	0.79608
	SMOTEBoost	0.7229	0.5764	0.74	0.6466	0.7267	0.79825
	SMOTE	0.7214	0.5746	0.7511	0.6496	0.7281	0.80428
	ADASYN	0.5539	0.4357	**0.9709**	0.5994	0.5702	0.8144
	AdaCost	**0.7438**	0.2816	0.61	0.3849	0.7043	**0.81805**
	BorderlineSMOTE	0.7018	0.375	0.7656	0.5029	0.7154	0.7947
	SMOTE-tomek	0.7039	0.3956	0.8102	0.5313	0.7248	0.81186
Wine	RAMOBoost	**0.9798**	**0.9525**	0.9885	**0.9696**	**0.9813**	**0.99940**
	SMOTEBoost	0.9787	0.9492	0.9885	0.9678	0.9805	0.99937
	SMOTE	0.9787	0.9505	0.9885	0.9684	0.9804	0.99908
	ADASYN	0.7933	0.6094	**1.0000**	0.7536	0.8352	0.99607
	AdaCost	0.9764	0.9319	0.9813	0.9648	0.9769	0.99905
	BorderlineSMOTE	0.9753	0.9419	0.9885	0.9681	0.9778	0.99796
	SMOTE-tomek	0.9551	0.9467	0.9853	0.9696	0.9629	0.99753
German	RAMOBoost	0.7262	**0.5602**	0.5270	**0.5409**	**0.6547**	**0.74139**
	SMOTEBoost	0.7072	0.5258	0.5126	0.5176	0.6375	0.73357
	SMOTE	0.6850	0.4878	0.5570	0.5192	0.6420	0.71365
	ADASYN	0.4918	0.3651	**0.8762**	0.5143	0.5282	0.70182
	AdaCost	**0.7482**	0.3963	0.4797	0.5283	0.6446	0.71254
	BorderlineSMOTE	0.6846	0.4522	0.5754	0.5151	0.6492	0.7105
	SMOTE-tomek	0.691	0.4777	0.6296	0.5148	0.6711	0.73469

Table 3.3: (*Continued*)

Data set	Methods	OA	Precision	Recall	F-measure	G-mean	AUC
Phoneme	RAMOBoost	0.7921	0.5914	0.9068	**0.7158**	**0.8222**	**0.90621**
	SMOTEBoost	0.8018	**0.6131**	0.8524	0.7128	0.8159	0.89472
	SMOTE	0.7860	0.5952	0.8248	0.6899	0.7942	0.87186
	ADASYN	0.7260	0.5137	**0.9513**	0.6671	0.7770	0.86497
	AdaCost	**0.8191**	0.2473	0.702	0.3657	0.7797	0.89395
	BorderlineSMOTE	0.7632	0.3308	0.8741	0.4799	0.7918	0.86103
	SMOTE-tomek	0.7884	0.2985	0.8151	0.4369	0.7965	0.87136
Vehicle	RAMOBoost	0.9655	**0.9142**	0.9398	0.926	0.956	0.99487
	SMOTEBoost	**0.9667**	0.9137	0.946	**0.929**	0.9591	0.99446
	SMOTE	0.9589	0.891	0.9373	0.9132	0.9511	0.99314
	ADASYN	0.821	0.5665	**0.9927**	0.7206	0.8737	0.97517
	AdaCost	0.9652	0.9132	0.9575	0.371	0.9623	**0.99511**
	BorderlineSMOTE	0.961	0.9130	0.9652	0.3752	**0.9624**	0.99405
	SMOTE-tomek	0.9482	0.9091	0.9361	0.3679	0.9436	0.98498
Texture	RAMOBoost	**0.9991**	**0.9986**	0.9966	**0.9976**	0.9981	**0.99999**
	SMOTEBoost	0.999	0.9976	**0.997**	0.9973	0.9982	0.99998
	SMOTE	0.9949	0.9853	0.9863	0.9858	0.9916	0.99920
	ADASYN	0.9156	0.6837	0.9950	0.8101	0.9453	0.99487
	AdaCost	0.9987	0.9798	0.9953	0.9946	0.9974	0.99991
	BorderlineSMOTE	0.9928	0.9783	0.9811	0.9917	0.9881	0.99856
	SMOTE-tomek	0.9976	0.9793	0.9913	0.9937	0.9951	0.99967
Segment	RAMOBoost	**0.9966**	**0.9854**	0.9907	**0.9880**	**0.9941**	0.99976
	SMOTEBoost	0.9965	0.9853	0.9900	0.9876	0.9938	**0.99978**
	SMOTE	0.9958	0.9835	0.9863	0.9848	0.9918	0.99959
	ADASYN	0.9254	0.6253	**1.0000**	0.7980	0.9556	0.99903
	AdaCost	0.9965	0.9845	0.9913	0.9843	0.9943	0.99974
	BorderlineSMOTE	0.9954	0.984	0.9869	0.9822	0.9918	0.99950
	SMOTE-tomek	0.9953	0.984	0.9863	0.9820	0.9915	0.99961
Page_Blocks	RAMOBoost	**0.9702**	0.8326	0.8928	**0.8614**	**0.9349**	**0.98899**
	SMOTEBoost	0.9696	**0.8340**	0.8825	0.8573	0.9297	0.98772
	SMOTE	0.9594	0.7781	0.8563	0.8140	0.9118	0.97993
	ADASYN	0.9251	0.5862	0.9414	0.7223	0.9322	0.97621
	AdaCost	0.9704	0.7912	0.8559	0.8469	0.9175	0.98861
	BorderlineSMOTE	0.9463	0.7853	0.8713	0.8171	0.912	0.97063
	SMOTE-tomek	0.9576	0.7832	0.8627	0.8168	0.9139	0.97754
Satimage	RAMOBoost	0.9195	0.5671	0.7127	**0.6312**	0.819	**0.94860**
	SMOTEBoost	**0.923**	**0.5867**	0.6717	0.6276	0.7986	0.94678
	SMOTE	0.8977	0.4791	0.606	0.5327	0.7465	0.89748
	ADASYN	0.8422	0.3645	0.8431	0.5084	**0.8424**	0.92234
	AdaCost	0.9217	0.552	0.5426	0.371	0.7118	0.93255
	BorderlineSMOTE	0.8938	0.685	**0.9652**	0.3752	0.7598	0.90189
	SMOTE-tomek	0.8957	0.701	0.9361	0.3679	0.773	0.90251

(*continued overleaf*)

Table 3.3: (*Continued*)

Data set	Methods	OA	Precision	Recall	F-measure	G-mean	AUC
Mf_Zernike	RAMOBoost	0.8718	0.3608	0.369	0.3645	0.584	0.89452
	SMOTEBoost	0.8701	0.3544	0.364	0.3584	0.5798	0.89537
	SMOTE	0.8838	0.4409	0.592	0.5045	0.7356	0.8922
	ADASYN	0.8634	0.408	**0.809**	**0.5419**	**0.838**	0.90609
	AdaCost	0.8851	0.3604	0.446	0.3935	0.6441	**0.90656**
	BorderlineSMOTE	0.8827	0.3678	0.598	0.4217	0.7377	0.8924
	SMOTE-tomek	**0.8877**	**0.3839**	0.745	0.4518	0.8199	0.90194
Vowel	RAMOBoost	**0.9988**	**0.9934**	**0.9931**	**0.9931**	**0.9962**	**0.99990**
	SMOTEBoost	0.9974	0.9842	0.9867	0.9853	0.9925	0.99988
	SMOTE	0.9794	0.8569	0.9379	0.893	0.9599	0.99615
	ADASYN	0.9101	0.5095	0.9488	0.6623	0.927	0.98512
	AdaCost	0.9913	0.903	0.9696	0.9651	0.9813	0.99906
	BorderlineSMOTE	0.9766	0.8710	0.9222	0.9591	0.9515	0.99552
	SMOTE-tomek	0.9747	0.8890	0.9382	0.9624	0.9576	0.99344
Abalone	RAMOBoost	0.9405	0.4968	0.4889	0.4813	0.6808	**0.97609**
	SMOTEBoost	0.943	0.5181	**0.5348**	0.5173	0.7134	0.92271
	SMOTE	0.9477	**0.5886**	0.5328	0.5412	**0.7166**	0.92291
	ADASYN	0.9101	0.361	0.4838	0.3892	0.6684	0.89179
	AdaCost	**0.9521**	0.241	0.4003	0.455	0.6156	0.92395
	BorderlineSMOTE	0.9493	0.294	0.4855	**0.554**	0.686	0.90322
	SMOTE-tomek	0.9441	0.261	0.4319	0.492	0.6433	0.9039
Glass	RAMOBoost	0.9748	0.6169	0.8464	0.7731	0.8610	0.99478
	SMOTEBoost	0.9748	0.6480	**0.9464**	0.7430	**0.9596**	0.99429
	SMOTE	0.9897	**0.8940**	0.9179	**0.8874**	0.9491	**0.99801**
	ADASYN	0.9421	0.4552	0.7986	0.4970	0.8555	0.97723
	AdaCost	**0.9907**	0.6377	0.9429	0.7722	0.9625	0.99741
	BorderlineSMOTE	0.9907	0.6368	0.9262	0.7040	0.9543	0.99757
	SMOTE-tomek	0.9879	0.6359	0.9119	0.6988	0.9414	0.99736
Yeast	RAMOBoost	0.9581	0.467	0.4341	0.4418	0.6405	0.74512
	SMOTEBoost	0.9585	0.4941	0.4732	0.4687	0.6651	0.74878
	SMOTE	0.9722	**0.7557**	**0.5107**	**0.5761**	0.7030	0.81603
	ADASYN	0.9552	0.5276	0.4891	0.4758	0.6810	0.77902
	AdaCost	0.9718	0.479	0.4524	0.344	0.6593	0.7792
	BorderlineSMOTE	**0.9726**	0.492	0.4882	0.368	0.6812	0.8096
	SMOTE-tomek	0.9768	0.420	0.5107	0.384	**0.7049**	**0.8241**
Letter	RAMOBoost	**0.9982**	**0.9882**	**0.9662**	**0.977**	**0.9827**	**0.99978**
	SMOTEBoost	0.9977	0.983	0.9591	0.9708	0.979	0.99977
	SMOTE	0.9921	0.9122	0.8853	0.8981	0.9391	0.99514
	ADASYN	0.9705	0.5841	0.9122	0.7109	0.942	0.9901
	AdaCost	0.9961	0.9836	0.9261	0.9705	0.9618	0.9989
	BorderlineSMOTE	0.9736	0.9264	0.9003	0.87	0.9375	0.9902
	SMOTE-tomek	0.9925	0.9052	0.8863	0.867	0.9399	0.9943
Shuttle	RAMOBoost	**0.9999**	0.9495	0.9728	**0.9576**	0.9828	**0.9998**
	SMOTEBoost	**0.9999**	0.9442	0.9667	0.9565	0.9828	0.9997
	SMOTE	**0.9999**	**0.9719**	0.9444	0.9538	0.9716	0.9998
	ADASYN	0.9997	0.7984	**1**	0.8855	**0.9999**	0.9995
	AdaCost	**0.9999**	0.9410	0.9667	0.9521	0.9885	0.9998
	BorderlineSMOTE	**0.9999**	0.9400	0.9723	0.9520	0.9857	0.9998
	SMOTE-tomek	**0.9999**	0.9430	0.9333	0.9320	0.9657	0.9998

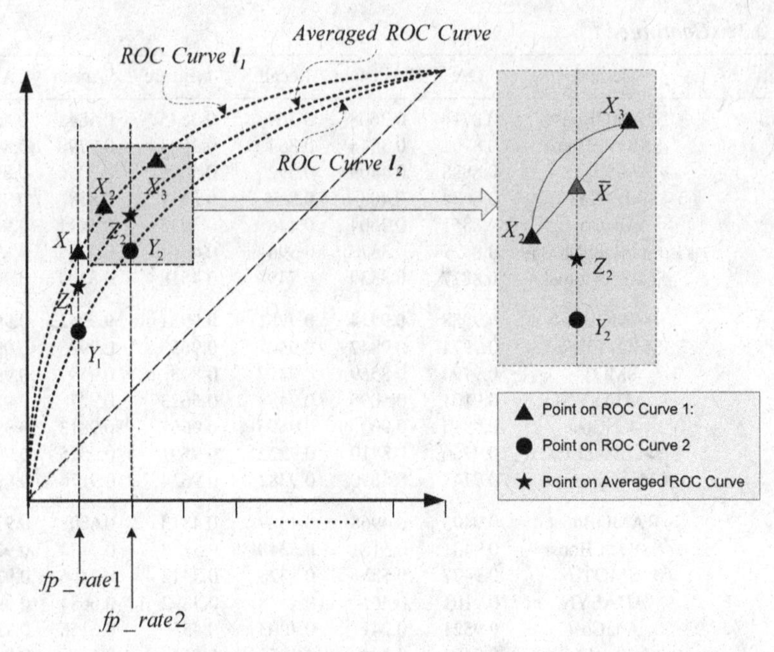

Figure 3.17: Vertical averaging approach of ROC curves (Fawcett, 2003).

other existing approaches in the whatever imbalanced learning scenarios. There are several interesting observations from these results. For instance, except for *Recall* performance, we see that ADASYN seems to provide a better *Recall* rate on most of these data sets. This is because ADASYN can learn very aggressively from the boundary since it generates synthetic data instances very close to the decision boundary (see Figure 3.7(c)). This means that ADASYN may push the algorithm to focus on the minority (positive) class data to improve the *Recall* criteria, while the overall performance may not improve significantly. In other words, if one algorithm classifies all testing data as "positive" (minority class), its "*Recall*" rate will be maximized even if the overall performance is low. These results confirm our discussions in section 3.3.1.7 regarding the different characteristics of these algorithms.

Another interesting experiment is conducted in this study to estimate the robustness of the imbalanced learning algorithm on different skew ratios. In this experiment, we use the "Abalone" data set (28 classes and 4177 examples) as the benchmark. In order to obtain versatile imbalanced ratios, we group different original classes with different policies to form the minority class and the majority class. Table 3.4 summarizes the details of the combination policy and the corresponding skew ratio. The AUC assessment metric is adopted here to evaluate the performance of the imbalanced learning algorithms on the "Abalone" data set with different skew ratio, which is shown in Table 3.5. In this case, although RAMOBoost seems to be able to dominate the performance, there is

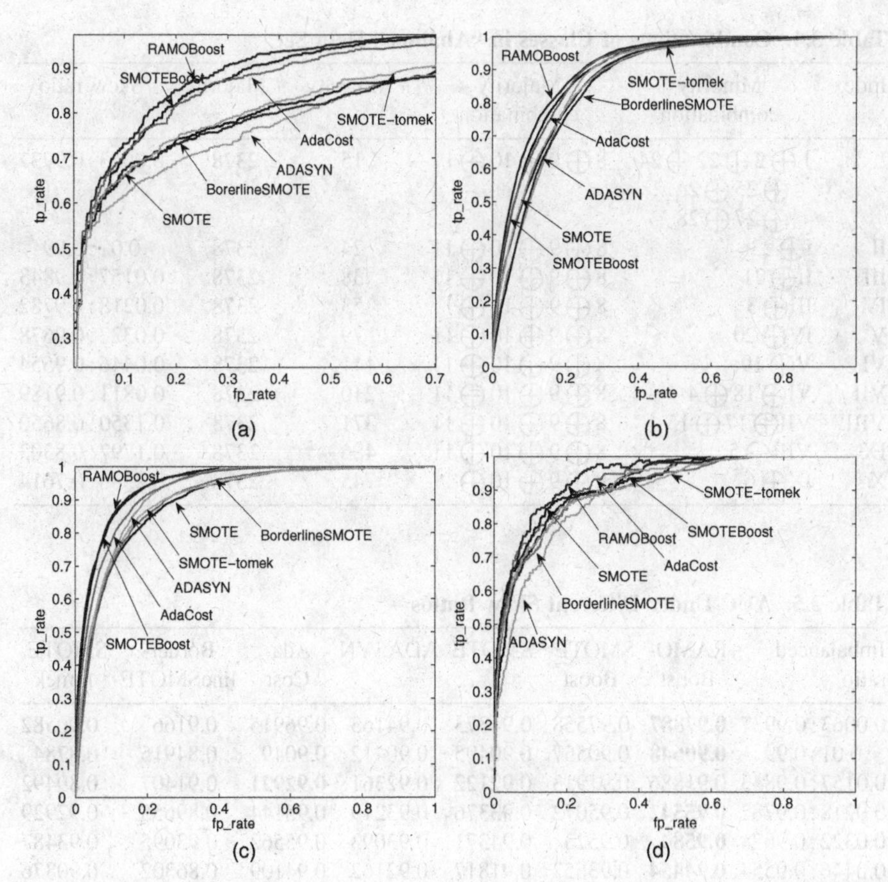

Figure 3.18: The averaged ROC curves for RAMOBoost, SMOTEBoost, SMOTE, ADASYN, AdaCost, BorderlineSMOTE, and SMOTE-tomek methods. (a) Averaged ROC curves for "Ionosphere" data set; (b) Averaged ROC curves for "Phoneme" data set; (c) Averaged ROC curves for "Satimage" data set; (d) Averaged ROC curves for "Abalone" data set.

no single algorithm that can generally perform better than all others even for the same data set of different skew ratio. This result, combined with the previous simulation analysis, confirms that there is no omnipotent algorithm that can handle all imbalanced learning scenarios. Meanwhile, most of the imbalanced learning algorithms are sensitive to parameter configurations. For instance, the iteration number of RAMOBoost and SMOTEBoost, the cost factor of AdaCost, and even how many nearest neighbors of a minority example should be used to create synthetic instances by SMOTE, could all have nontrivial impacts on the performance of these algorithms. To this end, a careful investigation of the imbalanced learning method for different application tasks is necessary to possibly yield an optimum choice of the imbalanced learning algorithm and its right configuration.

Table 3.4: Combinations of Classes in "Abalone" Data Set

Index	Minority combination	Majority combination	# Minority	# Majority	Skew ratio
I	$1 \oplus 2 \oplus 22 \oplus 24 \oplus 25 \oplus 26 \oplus 27 \oplus 28$	$8 \oplus 9 \oplus 10 \oplus 11$	15	2378	0.0063 : 0.9937
II	$\text{I} \oplus 23$	$8 \oplus 9 \oplus 10 \oplus 11$	24	2378	0.01 : 0.99
III	$\text{II} \oplus 21$	$8 \oplus 9 \oplus 10 \oplus 11$	38	2378	0.0157 : 0.9843
IV	$\text{III} \oplus 3$	$8 \oplus 9 \oplus 10 \oplus 11$	53	2378	0.0218 : 0.9782
V	$\text{IV} \oplus 20$	$8 \oplus 9 \oplus 10 \oplus 11$	79	2378	0.0322 : 0.9678
VI	$\text{V} \oplus 19$	$8 \oplus 9 \oplus 10 \oplus 11$	111	2378	0.0446 : 0.9554
VII	$\text{VI} \oplus 18 \oplus 4$	$8 \oplus 9 \oplus 10 \oplus 11$	210	2378	0.0811 : 0.9189
VIII	$\text{VII} \oplus 17 \oplus 15$	$8 \oplus 9 \oplus 10 \oplus 11$	371	2378	0.1350 : 0.8650
IX	$\text{VIII} \oplus 5$	$8 \oplus 9 \oplus 10 \oplus 11$	486	2378	0.1797 : 0.8303
X	$\text{IX} \oplus 6$	$8 \oplus 9 \oplus 10 \oplus 11$	745	2378	0.2386 : 0.7614

Table 3.5: AUC Under Different Skew Ratios

Imbalanced ratio	RAMO-Boost	SMOTE-Boost	SMOTE	ADASYN	Ada-Cost	Border-lineSMOTE	SMOTE-tomek
0.0063 : 0.9937	**0.97887**	0.97558	0.94373	0.94163	0.96915	0.9166	0.90582
0.01 : 0.99	**0.90648**	0.90557	0.90495	0.90412	0.9049	0.84915	0.8784
0.0157 : 0.9843	0.91886	0.91913	0.92122	0.92361	**0.92921**	0.91407	0.89492
0.0218 : 0.9782	**0.95542**	0.95072	0.93376	0.93219	0.95144	0.89655	0.92929
0.0322 : 0.9678	**0.9584**	0.9523	0.94371	0.93093	0.95562	0.93095	0.93487
0.0446 : 0.9554	**0.94454**	0.93652	0.91817	0.92162	0.94109	0.86302	0.90876
0.0811 : 0.9189	0.95025	0.94594	0.93479	0.9348	**0.95068**	0.92926	0.91392
0.1350 : 0.8650	**0.91502**	0.90501	0.89994	0.87255	0.91194	0.89588	0.8867
0.1797 : 0.8303	**0.92274**	0.91745	0.91241	0.90206	0.91994	0.90475	0.90704
0.2386 : 0.7614	**0.89696**	0.884	0.87537	0.87725	0.89389	0.86997	0.86978

3.7 SUMMARY

In this chapter, we discuss the imbalanced learning issue for machine intelligence research. The main points of this chapter include:

- The imbalanced learning problem has become a critical issue and attracted extensively growing attention from both academia and industry. The fundamental problem of imbalanced learning is concerned with the performance of learning algorithms in the presence of underrepresented data and skewed class distributions, and the goal is to develop principled methodologies for improved performance with imbalanced data.

- The nature of the imbalanced learning problem arises from the data complexity of imbalanced distributions; this includes different concepts such as between-class imbalance versus within-class imbalance, intrinsic imbalance versus extrinsic imbalance, relative imbalance versus imbalance due to rare instances (absolute rarity), and others.
- Sampling methods tackle the imbalanced learning problem by modifying imbalanced data sets by certain types of sampling mechanisms to provide a balanced distribution. However, this does not mean base classifiers cannot learn from imbalanced data sets. The representative sampling approaches include random oversampling and undersampling, informed undersampling, synthetic sampling with data generation, adaptive synthetic sampling, sampling with data cleaning techniques, cluster-based sampling, and integration of sampling with boosting.
- Cost-sensitive methods target the imbalanced learning problem by using different cost matrices that describe the cost for misclassifying any particular data example. Therefore, unlike sampling methods which attempt to balance data distributions by considering the representative proportions of class examples, cost-sensitive methods consider the costs associated with misclassifying examples to improve learning performance. The major efforts for cost-sensitive learning methods for imbalanced data include cost-sensitive dataspace weighting such as cost sensitive bootstrap sampling, cost-minimizing techniques such as various meta-techniques, and cost-sensitive fitting techniques such as cost-sensitive decision trees and cost-sensitive neural networks.
- The principles of kernel-based learning are centered on the theory of statistical learning and Vapnik– Chervonenkis (VC) dimensions. Since SVMs try to minimize total error, they are inherently biased toward the majority concept. The major kernel-based approaches tackling imbalanced learning include integration of kernel methods with sampling techniques and kernel modification methods.
- Active learning methods have also been investigated in the community for imbalanced learning. Although active learning methods were traditionally introduced to solve problems related to unlabeled training data, more and more results on active learning from imbalanced data sets have been discussed in the community. For instance, SVM-based active learning aims to select the most informative instances from the unseen training data in order to retrain the kernel-based model (i.e., those instances that are closest to the current hyperplane). Active learning integrations with sampling techniques have also been investigated in the community.
- Assessment metrics for imbalanced learning are critical for the research development in this field. Traditional criteria such as overall accuracy and error rate are highly sensitive to changes in data distribution, therefore they can be deceiving in imbalanced learning situations. To this end, more informative assessment metrics such as ROC curves, PR curves, cost curves,

and others have been proposed and adopted in the community for imbalanced learning.

- Various empirical studies have suggested that there is no universal "best" imbalanced learning technique across all data sets. Therefore, for different application domains, it is important to understand the data distribution characteristics and propose/adopt appropriate techniques for different applications. In-depth theoretical understanding of imbalanced learning and principled methodologies to address such problems are continuous challenges for the community.

REFERENCES

Abe, N. (2003). Invited talk: Sampling approaches to learning from imbalanced data sets: Active learning, cost sensitive learning and beyond. *Proc. Int Conf. Machine Learning, Workshop on Learning from Imbalanced Data Sets II*.

Abe, N., Zadrozny, B., & Langford, J. (2004). An iterative method for multiclass cost-sensitive learning. *Proc. ACM SIGKDD Int Conf. Knowledge Discovery and Data Mining*, pp. 3–11.

Akbani, R., Kwek, S., & Japkowicz, N. (2004). Applying support vector machines to imbalanced data sets. *Lecture Notes in Computer Science*, *3201*, 39–50.

Asuncion, A., & Newman, D. (2007). *UCI machine learning repository [online]. Avaiable: http://www.ics.uci.edu/~mlearn/MLRepository.html*.

Batista, G. E., Prati, R. C., & Monard, M. C. (2004). A study of the behavior of several methods for balancing machine learning training data. *ACM SIGKDD Explorations Newsletter*, *6*(1), 20–29.

Borders, Ertekin, S., Weston, J., & Bottou, L. (2005). Fast kernel classifiers with online and active learning. *J. Machine Learning Research*, *6*, 1579–1619.

Breiman, L., Friedman, J., Olshen, R., & Stone, C. (1984). *Classification and regression trees*. Chapman & Hall/CRC Press.

Bunescu, R., Ge, R., Kate, R., Marcotte, E., R. Moonet, A. R., & Wong, Y. (2005). Comparative experiments on learning information extractors for protein and their interactions. *Artificial Intelligence in Medicine*, *33*, 139–155.

Caruana, R. (2000). Learning from imbalanced data: Rank metrics and extra tasks. *Proc. Association for the Advancement of Artificial Intelligence Conf*., pp. 51–57.

Chan, P., & Stolfo, S. (1998). Towards scalable learning with non-uniform class and cost distributions. *Proc. Int Conf. Knowledge Discovery and Data Mining*, pp. 164–168.

Chan, P. K., Fan, W., Prodromidis, A. L., & Stolfo, S. J. (1999). Distributed data mining in credit card fraud detection. *IEEE Intelligent Systems*, *14*(6), 67–74.

Chawla, N., Japkowicz, N., & Kołcz, A. (2004). Editorial: Special issue on learning from imbalanced data sets. *ACM SIGKDD Explorations Newsletter* (1), 1–6.

Chawla, N. V. (2003). C4.5 and imbalanced data sets: Investigating the effect of sampling method, probabilistic estimate, and decision tree strcuture. *Proc. Int Conf. Machine Learning, Workshop on Learning from Imbalanced Data Sets II*.

Chawla, N. V., Bowyer, K. W., Hall, L. O., & Kegelmeyer, W. P. (2002). SMOTE: Synthetic minority over-sampling technique. *J. Artificial Intelligence Research*, *16*, 321–357.

Chawla, N. V., Japkowicz, N., & Kołcz, A. (2003). Workshop on learning from imbalanced data sets II. *Proc. Int. Conf. Machine Learning*.

Chen, K., Lu, B. L., & Kwok, J. (2006). Efficient classification of multilabel and imbalanced data using min-max modular classifiers. *Proc. World Congress on Computation Intelligence - Int Joint Conf. Neural Networks*, pp. 1770–1775.

Chen, S., He, H., & Garcia, E. A. (2010). RAMOBoost: Ranked Minority Oversampling in Boosting. *IEEE Trans. Neural Networks*, *21*, 1624–1642.

Clifton, P., Damminda, A., & Vincent, L. (2004). Minority report in fraud detection: Classification of skewed data. *ACM SIGKDD Explorations Newsletter*, *6*(1), 50–59.

Davis, J., Burnside, E., Dutra, I., Page, D., Ramakrishnan, R., Costa, V. S., & Shavlik, J. (2005). View learning for statistical relational learning: With an application to mammography. *Proc. Int Joint Conf. Artificial Intelligence*, pp. 677–683.

Davis, J., & Goadrich, M. (2006). The relationship between precision-recall and ROC curves. *Proc. Int Conf. Machine Learning*, pp. 233–240.

Domingos, P. (1999). MetaCost: A general method for making classifiers cost-sensitive. *Proc. Int Conf. Knowledge Discoery and Data Mining*, pp. 155–164.

Domingos, P., & Pazzani, M. (1996). Beyond independence: Conditions for the optimality of the simple bayesian classifier. *Proc. Int. Conf. Machine Learning*, pp. 105–112.

Doucette, J., & Heywood, M. (2008). GP classification under imbalanced data sets: Active sub-sampling AUC approximation. *Lecture Notes in Computer Science*, *4971*, 266–277.

Drummond, C., & Holte, R. C. (2000). Exploiting the cost(in)sensitivity of decision tree splitting criteria. *Proc. Int Conf. Machine Learning*, pp. 239–246.

Drummond, C., & Holte, R. C. (2003). C4.5, class imbalance, and cost sensitivity: Why under sampling beats over-sampling. *Proc. Conf. Machine Learning, Workshop on Learning from Imbalanced Data Sets II*.

Elena Project [Online]. Avaiable: ftp://ftp.dice.ucl.ac.be/pub/neuralnets/elena/databases. (2005).

Elkan, C. (2001). The foundations of cost-sensitive learning. *Proc. Int Joint Conf. Artificial Intelligence*, pp. 973–978.

Ertekin, S., Huang, J., Bottou, L., & Giles, L. (2007a). Learning on the border: Active learning in imbalanced data classification. *Proc. ACM Conf. Information and Knowledge Management*, pp. 127–136.

Ertekin, S., Huang, J., & Giles, C. L. (2007b). Active learning for class imbalance problem. *Proc. Int SIGIR Conf. Research and Development in Information Retrieval*, pp. 823–824.

Estabrooks, A., Jo, T., & Japkowicz, N. (2004). A multiple resampling method for learning from imbalanced data sets. *Computational Intelligence*, *20*, 18–36.

Fan, W., Stolfo, S. J., Zhang, J., & Chan, P. K. (1999). AdaCost: Misclassification cost-sensitive boosting. *Proc. Int Conf. Machine Learning*, pp. 97–105.

Fawcett, T. (2001). Using rule sets to maximize roc performance. *Proc. Int Conf. Data Mining*, pp. 131–138.

Fawcett, T. (2003). ROC graphs: Notes and practical considerations for data mining researchers. *Technical Report HPL-2003-4*. (HP Lab)

Fawcett, T. (2006). An introduction to ROC analysis. *Pattern Recognition Letters*, *27*(8), 861–874.

Freund, Y., & Schapire, R. E. (1996). Experiments with a new boosting algorithm. *Proc. Int Conf. Machine Learning*, pp. 148–156.

Freund, Y., & Schapire, R. (2002). A decision-theoretic generalization of on-line learning and an application to boosting. *J. Computer and System Sciences*, *55*(1), 119–139.

Fumera, G., & Roli, F. (2002). Support vector machines with embedded reject option. *Proc. Int. Conf. Workshop Pattern Recognition with Support Vector Machines*, pp. 68–82.

Fung, G., & Mangasarian, O. L. (2005). Multicategory proximal support vector machine classifiers. *Machine Learning*, *59*(1/2), 77–97.

Gama, J. (2003). Iterative bayes. *Theoretical Computer Science*, *292*(2), 417–430.

Gonzalez, R. C., & Woods, R. E. (2002). Digital image processing. In . (2nd ed.). Upper Saddle River, NJ: Prentice Hall.

Guo, H., & Viktor, H. L. (2004a). Boosting with data generation: Improving the classification of hard to learn examples. *Proc. Int. Conf. Innovations Applied Artificial Intelligence*, pp. 1082–1091.

Guo, H., & Viktor, H. L. (2004b). Learning from imbalanced data sets with boosting and data generation: The databoost IM approach. *ACM SIGKDD Explorations Newsletter*, *6*(1), 30–39.

Han, H., Wang, W. Y., & Mao, B. H. (2005). Borderline-SMOTE: A new over-sampling method in imbalanced data sets learning. *Proc. Int. Intelligent Computing*, pp. 878–887.

Hand, D. J., & Till, R. J. (2001). A simple generalization of the area under the ROC curve to multiple class classification problems. *Machine Learning*, *45*(2), 171–186.

Haykin, S. (1999). *Neural networks: A comprehensive foundation* (2nd ed.). Upper Saddle River, NJ: Prentice-Hall.

He, H., Bai, Y., Garcia, E. A., & Li, S. (2008). ADASYN: Adaptive synthetic sampling approach for imbalanced learning. *Proc Int. Conf. Neural Networks*, pp. 1322–1328.

He, H., & Garcia, E. A. (2009). Learning from imbalanced data. *IEEE Trans. Knowledge and Data Engineering*, *21*(9), 1263–1284.

He, H., & Shen, X. (2007). A ranked subspace learning method for gene expression data classification. *Proc. Int Conf. Artificial Intelligence*, pp. 358–364.

Holte, R., & Drummond, C. (2005). Cost-sensitive classifier evaluation. *Proc. Int. Workshop Utility-Based Data Mining*, pp. 3–9.

Holte, R. C., Acker, L., & Porter, B. W. (2003). Concept learning and the problem of small disjuncts. *Proc. Int J. Conf. Artificial Intelligence*, pp. 315–354.

Holte, R. C., & Drummond, C. (2000). Explicitly representing expected cost: An alternative to roc representation. *Proc. Int. Conf. Knowledge Discovery and Data Mining*, pp. 198–207.

Holte, R. C., & Drummond, C. (2006). Cost curves: An improved method for visulization classifier performance. *Machine Learning*, *65*(1), 95–130.

Hong, X., Chen, S., & Harris, C. J. (2008). A kernel-based two-class classifier for imbalanced data sets. *IEEE Trans. Neural Networks*, *18*(1), 28–41.

Japkowicz, N. (2000). Learning from imbalanced data sets: A comparison of various strategies. *Proc. Association for the Advancement of Artificial Intelligence Workshop Learning from Imbalanced Data Sets*, pp. 10–15. (Technical Report WS-00-05).

Japkowicz, N. (2001). Supervised versus unsupervised binary-learning by feedforward neural networks. *Machine Learning*, *42*, 97–122.

Japkowicz, N. (2003). Class imbalances: Are we focusing on the right issue? *Proc. Int. Conf. Machine Learning. Workshop Learning from Imbalanced Data Sets II*.

Japkowicz, N., Myers, C., & Gluck, M. (1995). A novelty detection approach to classification. *Proc. Joint Conf. Artificial Intelligence*, pp. 518–523.

Japkowicz, N., & Stephen, S. (2002). The class imbalance problem: A systemetic study. *Intelligent Data Analysis*, *6*(5), 429–449.

Jo, T., & Japkowicz, N. (2004). Class imbalances versus small disjuncts. *ACM SIGKDD Explorations Newsletter*, *6*(1), 40–49.

Joshi, M. V., Kumar, V., & Agarwal, R. C. (2001). Evaluating boosting algorithms to classify rare classes: Comparison and improvements. *Proc. Joint Conf. Data Mining*, pp. 257–264.

Kang, P., & Cho, S. (2006). EUS SVMs: Ensemble of under sampled SVMs for data imbalance problems. *Lecture Notes in Computer Science*, *4232*, 873–846.

Kohavi, R., & Wolpert, D. (1996). Bias plus variance decompostion for zero-one loss functions. *Proc. Int. Conf. Machine Learning*.

Kubar, M. Z., & Kononenko, I. (1998). Cost-sensitive learning with neural networks. *Proc. European Conf. Artificial Intelligence*, pp. 445–449.

Kubat, M., Holte, R. C., & Matwin, S. (1998). Machine learning for the detection of oil spills in satellite radar images. *Machine Learning*, *30*(2/3), 195–215.

Kubat, M., & Matwin, S. (1997). Addressing the curse of imbalanced training sets: One-sided selection. *Proc. Int. Conf. Machine Learning*, pp. 179–186.

Kwok, J. T. (2003). Moderating the outputs. *Theoretical Computer Science*, *292*(2), 417–430.

Landgrebe, T., Paclik, P., Duin, R., & Bradley, A. P. (2006). Precision-recall operating characteristic (P-ROC) curves in imprecise environments. *Proc. Int. Conf. Pattern Recognition*, pp. 123–177.

Laurikkala, J. (2001). Improving identifications of difficult small classes by balancing class distribution. *Proc. Conf. AI in Medicine in Europe: Artificial Intelligence Medicine*, pp. 63–66.

Learning from imbalanced data sets. (2000). In N. Japkowicz (ed.), *Proc. Association for the Advancement of Artificial Intelligence Workgroup*. (Technical Report WS-00-05).

Lee, H. J., & Cho, S. (2006). The novelty detection approach for difference degress of class imbalance. *Lecture Notes in Computer Science*, *4233*, 21–30.

Li, P., Chan, K. L., & Fang, W. (2006). Hybrid kernel machine ensemble for imbalanced data sets. *Proc. Int. Conf. Pattern Recognition*, pp. 1108–1111.

Liu, X.-Y., Wu, J., & Zhou, Z.-H. (2006). Exploratory undersampling for class imbalance learning. *Proc. Int. Conf. Data Mining*, pp. 965–969.

Liu, X.-Y., & Zhou, Z.-H. (2006a). The influence of class imbalance on cost-sensitive learning: An empirical study. *Proc. Int. Conf. Data Mining*, pp. 970–974.

Liu, X.-Y., & Zhou, Z.-H. (2006b). Training cost-sensitive neural networks with methods addressing the class imbalance problem. *IEEE Tran. Knowledge and Data Eng.*, *18*(1), 63–77.

Liu, Y., An, A., & Huang, X. (2006). Boosting prediction accuracy on imbalanced data sets with SVM ensembles. *Lecture Notes in Artificial Intelligence*, *3918*, 107–118.

Liu, Y.-H., & Chen, Y.-T. (2005). Total margin-based adaptive fuzzy support vector machines for multiview face recognition. *Proc. Int. Conf. System, Man, and Cybernetics*, pp. 1704–1711.

Liu, Y. H., & Chen, Y. T. (2007). Face recognition using total margin-based adaptive fuzzy support vector machines. *IEEE Trans. Neural Networks*, *18*(1), 178–192.

Maloof, M., Langley, P., Sage, S., & Binford, T. (1997). Learning to detect rooftops in aerial images. *Proc. Image Understanding Workshop*, pp. 835–845.

Maloof, M. A. (2003). Learning when data sets are imbalanced and when costs are unequal and unknown. *Proc. Int. Conf. Machine Learning, Workshop Learning from Imbalanced Data Sets II*.

Manevitz, L., & Yousef, M. (2007). One-class document classification via neural networks. *Neurocomputing*, *70*, 1466–1481.

Manevitz, L. M., & Yousef, M. (2001). One-class SVMs for document classification. *J. Machine Learning Research*, *2*, 139–154.

McCarthy, K., Zabar, B., & Weiss, G. M. (2005). Does cost-sensitive learning best sampling for classifying rare classes. *Proc. Int. Workshop Utility-Based Data Mining*, pp. 69–77.

Mease, D., Wyner, A. J., & Buja, A. (2007). Boosted classification trees and class probability/quantile estimation. *J. Machine Learning Research*, *8*, 409–439.

Mitchell, T. M. (1997). *Machine learning*. New York: McGraw-Hill.

Opitz, D., & Maclin, R. (1999). Popular ensemble methods: An empirical study. *J. Artificial Intelligence Research*, *11*, 169–198.

Pearson, R., Goney, G., & Shwaber, J. (2003). Imbalanced clustering for microarray time-series. *Proc. Int Conf. Machine Learning, Workshop Learning from Imbalanced Data Sets II*.

Platt, J. C. (1999). *Fast Training of Support Vector Machines Using Sequential Minimal Optimization, Advances in Kernel Methods*: Support Vector Learning, pp. 185–208, MIT Press.

Prati, R. C., Batista, G. E. A. P. A., & Monard, M. C. (2004). Class imbalances versus class overlapping: An analysis of a learning system behavior. *Proc. Mexican Int. Conf. Artificial Intelligence*, pp. 312–321.

Provost, F. (2000). Machine learning from imbalanced data sets 101. *Proc. Learning from Imbalanced Data Sets: Association for the Advancement of Artificial Intelligence Workshop*. (Technical Report WS-00-05).

Provost, F., & Domingos, P. (2000). Well-trained pets: Improving probability estimation trees. *CeDER Working Paper*: IS-00-04. New York: Stern School of Business, New York University.

Provost, F. J., & Fawcett, T. (1997). Analysis and visualization of classifier performance: Comparison under imprecise class and cost distributions. *Proc. Int. Conf. Knowledge Discovery and Data Mining*, pp. 43–48.

Provost, F. J., Fawcett, T., & Kohavi, R. (1998). The case against accuracy estimation for comparison induction algorithms. *Proc. Int. Conf. Machine Learning*, pp. 445–453.

Qin, A. K., & Suganthan, P. N. (2004). Kernel neural gas algorithms with application to cluster analysis. *Proc. Int. Conf. Pattern Recognition*.

Quinlan, J. R. (1986). Induction of decision trees. *Machine Learning*, *1* (1).

Rao, R. B., Krishnan, S., & Niculescu, R. S. (2006). Data mining for improved cardiac care. *ACM SIGKDD Explorations Newsletter* (1), 3–10.

Raskutti, B., & Kowalczyk, A. (2004). Extreme re-balancing for SVMs: A case study. *ACM SIGKDD Explorations Newsletter*, *6* (1), 60–69.

Raudys, S. J., & Jain, A. K. (1991). Small sample size effects in statistical pattern recognition: Recommendations for practitioners. *IEEE Trans. Pattern Analysis and Machine Learning*, *13* (3), 252–264.

Scholkopf, B., Platt, J. C., Shawe-Taylor, J., Smola, A. J., & Williamson, R. C. (2001). Estimating the support of a high-dimensional distribution. *Neural Computation*, *13*, 1443–1471.

Singla, P., & Domingos, P. (2005). Discriminative training of markov logic networks. *Proc. Nat. Conf. Artificial Intelligence*, pp. 868–873.

Su, C. T., & Hsiao, Y. H. (2007). An evaluation of the robustness of mts for imbalanced data. *IEEE Trans. Knowledge and Data Eng*., *19* (10), 1321–1332.

Sun, Y., Kamel, M. S., & Wang, Y. (2006). Boosting for learning multiple classes with imbalanced class distribution. *Proc. Int Conf. Data Mining*, pp. 592–602.

Sun, Y., Kamel, M. S., Wong, A. K. C., & Wang, Y. (2007). Cost-sensitive boosting for classification of imbalanced data. *Pattern Recognition*, *40* (12), 3358–3378.

Taguchi, G., Chowdhury, S., & Wu, Y. (2001). *The mahalanobis-taguchi system*. New York: McGraw-Hill.

Taguchi, G., & Jugulum, R. (2002). *The mahalanobis-taguchi strategy*. Hoboken, NJ: Wiley.

Tan, C., Gilbert, D., & Deville, Y. (2003). multiclass protein fold classification using a new ensemble machine learning approach. *Genome Informatics*, *14*, 206–217.

Tang, Y., & Zhang, Y. Q. (2006). Granular SVM with repetitive undersampling for highly imbalanced protein homology rrediction. *Proc. Int. Conf. Granular Computing*, pp. 457–460.

Tang, Y. C., Jin, B., & Zhang, Y.-Q. (2008). Granular support vector machines with association rules mining for protein homology prediction. *Artificial Intelligence in Medicine special issue on computational intelligence techniques in bioinformatics*, *35* (1/2), 121–134.

Tang, Y. C., Jin, B., Zhang, Y.-Q., Fang, H., & Wang, B. (2005). Granular support vector machines using linear decision hyperplanes for fast medical binary classification. *Proc. Int. Conf. Fuzzy Systems*, pp. 138–142.

Tang, Y. C., Zhang, Y. Q., Huang, Z., Hu, X. T., & Zhao, Y. (2005). Granular SVM-REF feature selection algorithm for reliable cancer-related gene subsets extraction on microarray gene expression data. *Proc. IEEE Symp. Bioinformatics and Bioeng*., pp. 290–293.

Tashk, A., Bayesteh, R., & Faez, K. (2007). Boosted baysian kernel classifier method for face detectio. *Proc. Int. Conf. Natural Computation*, pp. 533–537.

Ting, K. M. (2000). A comparative study of cost-sensitive boosting algorithms. *Proc. Int. Conf. Machine Learning*, pp. 983–990.

Ting, K. M. (2002). An instance-weighting method to induce cost-sensitive trees. *IEEE Trans. Knowledge and Data Eng.*, *14*(3), 659–665.

Tomek, I. (1976). Two modifications of CNN. *IEEE Trans. System, Man, Cybernetics*, *6*(11), 769–772.

Vapnik, V. N. (1995). *The nature of statistical learning theory*. Springer.

Viikki, O., Bye, D., & Laurila, K. (1998). A recursive feature vector normalization approach for robust speech recognition in noise. *Proc. IEEE Int. Conf. Acoustics, Speech and Signal Processing*, pp. 733–736.

Vilarino, F., Spyridonos, P., Radeva, P., & Vitria, J. (2005). Experiments with SVM and stratified sampling with an imbalanced problem: Detection of intestinal contractions. *Lecture Notes in Computer Science*, *3687*, 783–791.

Wang, B. X., & Japkowicz, N. (2004). Imbalanced data set learning with synthetic samples. *Proc. IRIS Machine Learning Workshop*.

Wang, B. X., & Japkowicz, N. (2008). Boosting support vector machines for imbalanced data sets. *Lecture Notes in Artificial Intelligence*, *4994*, 38–47.

Webb, G. I., & Pazzani, M. J. (1998). Adjusted probability naive bayesian induction. *Proc. Australian Joint Conf. Artificial Intelligence*, pp. 285–295.

Weiss, G.M. (2005). *Mining Rare Cases, Data Mining and Knowledge Discovery Handbook: A Complete Guide for Practitioners and Researchers*, pp. 765–776, Springer.

Weiss, G. M. (2004). Mining with rarity: A unifying framework. *ACM SIGKDD Explorations Newsletter*, *6*(1), 7–19.

Weiss, G. M., & Provost, F. (2001). The effect of class distribution on classifier learning: An empirical study. *Technical Report ML-TR-43*. New Brunswick, NJ: Department of Computer Science, Rutgers University.

Weiss, G. M., & Provost, F. (2003). Learning when training data are costly: The effect of class distribution on tree induction. *J. Artificial Intelligence Research*, *19*, 315–354.

Woods, K., Doss, C., Bowyer, K., Solka, J., Priebe, C., & Kegelmeyer, W. (1993). Comparative evaluation of pattern recognition techniques for detection of microcalcifications in mammography. *Int J. Pattern Recognition and Artificial Intelligence*, *7*(6), 1417–1436.

Wu, G., & Chang, E. (2003a). Class-boundary alignment for imbalanced data set learning. *Proc. Int. Conf. Data Mining, workshop on Learning from Imbalanced Data Sets II*.

Wu, G., & Chang, E. Y. (2003b). Adaptive feature-space conformal transformation for imbalanced-data learning. *Proc. Int. Conf. Machine Learning*, pp. 816–823.

Wu, G., & Chang, E. (2005). KBA: Kernel boundary alignment considering imbalanced data distribution. *IEEE Trans. Knowledge and Data Eng.*, *17*(6), 786–795.

Wu, G., & Chang, E. Y. (2004). Aligning boundary in kernel space for learning imbalanced data set. *Proc. Int. Conf. Data Mining*, pp. 265–272.

Yang, W. H., Dai, D. Q., & Yan, H. (2008). Feature extraction uncorrelated discriminant analysis for high-dimensional data. *IEEE Trans. Knowledge and Data Eng.*, *20*(5), 601–614.

Yu, X. P., & Yu, X. G. (2007). Novel text classification based on k-nearest neighbor. *Proc. Int. Conf. Machine Learning Cybernetics*, pp. 3425–3430.

Yuan, J., Li, J., & Zhang, B. (2006). Learning concepts from large scale imbalanced data sets using support vector machines. *Proc. Int. Conf. Multimedia*, pp. 441–450.

Zadrozny, B., Langford, J., & Abe, N. (2003). Cost-sensitive learning by cost-proportionate example weighting. *Proc. Int. Conf. Data Mining*, pp. 435–442.

Zhang, J., & Mani, I. (2003). KNN approach to unbalanced data distributions: A case study involving information extraction. *Proc. Int. Conf. Machine Learning, Workshop on Learning from Imbalanced Data Sets*.

Zhou, Z.-H., & Liu, X.-Y. (2006). On multiclass cost-sensitive learning. *Proc. Nat. Conf. Artificial Intelligence*, pp. 567–572.

Zhu, J., & Hovy, E. (2007). Active Learning for Word Sense Disambiguation with Methods for Addressing the Class Imbalance Problem. *Proc. Joint Conf. Empirical Methods in Natural Language Processing and Computational Natural Language Learning*, pp. 783–790.

Zhuang, L., & Dai, H. (2006a). Parameter optimization of kernel-based one-class classifier on imbalance text learning. *Lecture Notes in Artificial Intelligence*, *4099*, 434–443.

Zhuang, L., & Dai, H. (2006b). Parameter estimation of one-class SVM on imbalance text classification. *Lecture Notes in Artificial Intelligence*, *4013*, 538–549.

CHAPTER 4

Ensemble Learning

4.1 INTRODUCTION

Ensemble learning is generally referred as the procedure of *developing* and *integrating* multiple hypotheses (e.g., classifiers, experts, etc.) to support the decision-making processes. Generally speaking, ensemble learning has the advantage of improved accuracy and robustness compared to the single model–based learning methods (Kittler, Hatel, Duin, & Matas, 1998), therefore it has attracted growing attention in the computational intelligence community. There are two critical issues related to ensemble learning. First, how can one develop multiple hypotheses in a principled way? For instance, hypothesis diversity plays a critical role in a successful ensemble learning methodology; therefore, how to systematically develop such diversified hypotheses has become a critical issue. Some popular approaches include bootstrap aggregating (bagging), adaptive boosting (AdaBoost), subspace methods, stacked generalization, and mixture of experts. Second, how can one strategically integrate the outputs of each individual hypothesis for an improved final decision? This problem is normally referred to as the combinational voting methods, such as the geometric average method, arithmetic average method, median value method, and majority voting method, among others. In this chapter, we will focus on discussing these two important issues for ensemble learning.

4.2 HYPOTHESIS DIVERSITY

Hypothesis diversity has been recognized to be a critical characteristic for ensemble learning (Kuncheva & Whitaker, 2003; Krogh & Vedelsby, 1995; Rosen, 1996; Lam, 2000; Littlewood & Miller, 1989). Intuitively speaking, if all hypotheses in an ensemble learning system provide the same decision,

Self-Adaptive Systems for Machine Intelligence, First Edition. Haibo He.

one cannot get any additional benefit from combining all decisions from each individual hypothesis. Therefore, it is important to understand how to measure such diversity for ensemble learning.

Assume an ensemble learning system includes a set of L hypotheses: $\boldsymbol{H} = \{H_1, H_2, \ldots, H_L\}$. $\boldsymbol{U} = \{\boldsymbol{x}_j, y_j\}$, $(j = 1, \ldots, m)$ represents the labeled data set, where $\boldsymbol{x}_j \in \Re^n$ is an instance in the n dimensional feature space $\boldsymbol{X}$, and $y_j \in \boldsymbol{\Omega} = \{1, \ldots, C\}$ is the class identity label associated with $\boldsymbol{x}_j$. In this way, the output of each hypothesis $H_i (i = 1, \ldots, L)$ over this data set can be represented as an n-dimensional vector: $\boldsymbol{v}_i = [v_{1,i}, \ldots, v_{m,i}]$, such that $v_{j,i} = 1$ if H_i correctly predict the class label of $\boldsymbol{x}_j$, and $v_{j,i} = 0$ if the prediction is wrong. Based on this assumption, a matrix (similar to the contingency matrix concept) used to represent the pair-wise relationship between any two hypotheses, H_i and H_k, can be illustrated in Figure 4.1. Here each element of this matrix is used to represent the hypothesis output relationship. For instance, m^{11} represents the number of instances that are correctly classified by both hypotheses, m^{10} represents the number of instances that are correctly classified by H_i but misclassified by H_k, m^{01} represents the number of instances that are correctly classified by H_k but misclassified by H_i, and m^{00} represents the number of instances that are misclassified by both hypotheses ($m = m^{11} + m^{10} + m^{01} + m^{00}$).

Based on the hypothesis pair-wise representation in Figure 4.1, a set of criteria used to assess the hypothesis diversity have been proposed in the community (Kuncheva & Whitaker, 2003).

4.2.1 Q-Statistics

The Q-statistic for two hypotheses H_i and H_k is defined as (Yule, 1900)

$$Q_{i,k} = \frac{m^{11}m^{00} - m^{01}m^{10}}{m^{11}m^{00} + m^{01}m^{10}} \tag{4.1}$$

where $Q_{i,k} \in [-1, 1]$. For statistically independent hypotheses (maximum diversity), the expectation of $Q_{i,k}$ is 0. For a set of L hypotheses, the average Q-statistic

	H_k is correct (represented as "1")	H_k is wrong (represented as "0")
H_i is correct (represented as "1")	$\mathbf{m}^{11}$	$\mathbf{m}^{10}$
H_i is wrong (represented as "0")	$\mathbf{m}^{01}$	$\mathbf{m}^{00}$

Figure 4.1: Pair-wise representation of hypothesis outputs.

over all pairs of hypotheses can be defined as

$$Q_{av} = \frac{2}{L(L-1)} \sum_{i=1}^{L-1} \sum_{k=i+1}^{L} Q_{i,k} \tag{4.2}$$

4.2.2 Correlation Coefficient

In this case, the diversity is measured as the correlation between two hypotheses output:

$$\rho_{i,k} = \frac{m^{11}m^{00} - m^{01}m^{10}}{\sqrt{(m^{11} + m^{10})(m^{01} + m^{00})(m^{11} + m^{01})(m^{10} + m^{00})}} \tag{4.3}$$

Generally speaking, the Q-statistic and correlation coefficient ρ have the same sign and also satisfy $|\rho| \leq |Q|$ (Kuncheva & Whitaker, 2003; Kuncheva, Whitaker, Shipp, & Duin, 2003). Similar to the Q-statistic, maximum diversity is achieved for $\rho = 0$, which means the two hypotheses are uncorrelated.

4.2.3 Disagreement Measure

The disagreement measure is defined as the ratio between the number of instances that the two hypotheses under consideration do not agree with each other with respect to the total number of instances.

$$\zeta_{i,k} = \frac{m^{01} + m^{10}}{m^{11} + m^{10} + m^{01} + m^{00}} \tag{4.4}$$

Intuitively, this is a reflection of the *disagreement* between the two hypotheses and can also be used to measure the diversity. For instance, disagreement measure was used in Skalak (1996) to analyze the diversity between a base classifier and a complementary classifier, and also was used in Ho (1998b) for diversity measurement in the decision forest method.

4.2.4 Double-Fault Measure

The double-fault measure is defined as the ratio between the number of instances that are misclassified by both hypotheses over the total number of instances (Giacinto & Roli, 2001).

$$\gamma_{i,k} = \frac{m^{00}}{m^{11} + m^{10} + m^{01} + m^{00}} \tag{4.5}$$

The double-fault measure was used in various literature to assess the hypotheses diversity for ensemble learning, such as Giacinto and Roli (2001) and Yang, Wang, and He (2007).

4.2.5 Entropy Measure

In addition to the aforementioned pair-wise measures, non-pairwise diversity measures have also been proposed in the community. We first discuss the entropy measure E for this purpose. The assumption here is that the hypotheses diversity is highest if half of the hypotheses are correct while the remaining half are incorrect. Denote δ_j as the number of hypotheses out of the total hypotheses L that correctly classify instance $\boldsymbol{x}_j$, one can define the entropy measurement as:

$$E = \frac{1}{m}\sum_{j=1}^{m}\frac{1}{(L - \lceil L/2 \rceil)}\min(\delta_j, L - \delta_j) \tag{4.6}$$

where $\lceil\cdot\rceil$ is the floor operator. The entropy measure varies between 0 and 1, where 0 indicates no diversity and 1 indicates the highest possible diversity (Kuncheva & Whitaker, 2003).

4.2.6 Kohavi–Wolpert Variance

The Kohavi–Wolpert (KW) variance (Kohavi & Wolpert, 1996) is defined as:

$$KW = \frac{1}{mL^2}\sum_{j=1}^{m}\delta_j(L - \delta_j) \tag{4.7}$$

The *KW* measure of diversity is strongly related to the disagreement measure in equation (4.4). In fact, it can be proved that the *KW* measure is a normalized version of the disagreement measure (Kuncheva & Whitaker, 2003):

$$KW = \frac{L - 1}{2L}\zeta_{av} \tag{4.8}$$

where ζ_{av} is the averaged disagree measure $\zeta_{i,j}$ across all pairs of hypotheses, calculated similar to equation (4.2).

4.2.7 Interrater Agreement

The interrater agreement κ measure is related to the interrater reliability used to assess the level of agreement, the intraclass correlation coefficient, and the significance test of Looney (Kuncheva & Whitaker, 2003; Fleiss, 1981; Looney, 1988; Dietterich, 2000). Specifically, denote $\overline{p}$ as the average individual classification accuracy as:

$$\overline{p} = \frac{1}{mL}\sum_{j=1}^{m}\sum_{i=1}^{L}v_{j,i} \tag{4.9}$$

Then the interrater agreement κ measure is defined as:

$$\kappa = 1 - \frac{(1/L)\sum_{j=1}^{m} \delta_j (L - \delta_j)}{m(L-1)\overline{p}(1-\overline{p})} \tag{4.10}$$

From equations (4.4) and (4.7) one can see, the interrater agreement κ measure is also related to the KW and ζ_{av} (Kuncheva & Whitaker, 2003)

$$\kappa = 1 - \frac{L}{(L-1)\overline{p}(1-\overline{p})} KW = 1 - \frac{1}{2\overline{p}(1-\overline{p})} \zeta_{av} \tag{4.11}$$

4.2.8 Measure of Difficulty

This idea was originally proposed in Hansen and Salamon (1990) for the study of neural network ensembles. In this assessment, we define a random variable $Z(\boldsymbol{x}_j) = \{\frac{0}{L}, \frac{1}{L}, \ldots, \frac{L}{L}\}$ denoting the proportion of hypotheses in $\boldsymbol{H}$ that correctly classify an instance $\boldsymbol{x}_j$ drawn randomly from the distribution of the problem. In this way, the measure of difficulty, θ, is defined as the variance of the random variable Z (Kuncheva & Whitaker, 2003; Hansen & Salamon, 1990; Polikar, 2006):

$$\theta = \frac{1}{L} \sum_{t=1}^{L} (z_t - \overline{z})^2 \tag{4.12}$$

where $\overline{z}$ is the mean of z. The key idea of the θ measure is based on the *distribution of difficulty*. For instance, in the extreme case, if all hypotheses are identical, the distribution of Z will be two singletons (one at 0 and the other one at 1 in the probability mass function space) (Kuncheva & Whitaker, 2003), which results in a large value of θ indicating low diversity. However, if the hypotheses are negatively correlated, i.e., if some instances that are difficult for some hypotheses in $\boldsymbol{H}$ are easy for other hypotheses, then θ will be relatively small, indicating a strong diversity.

4.2.9 Generalized Diversity

This concept was originally proposed by Partridge and Krzanowski (1997). The key is based on the assumption that if two hypotheses are randomly chosen from $\boldsymbol{H}$, maximum diversity occurs when failure of one of these two hypotheses is accompanied by the correct classifying by the other classifier (Kuncheva & Whitaker, 2003; Partridge & Krzanowski, 1997). To this end, let Y be a random variable representing the proportion of hypotheses out of $\boldsymbol{H}$ (a total of L hypotheses) that are incorrect on a randomly drawn $\boldsymbol{x}_j$ instance from the distribution of the problem (i.e., $Y = 1 - Z$ based on section 4.2.8). Therefore, we can define

p_i as the probability that $Y = \frac{i}{L}$, that is to say, the probability that i randomly selected hypotheses will fail on a randomly chosen data instance $\boldsymbol{x}_j$. Therefore, the generalized diversity (GD) is defined as

$$GD = 1 - \frac{\sum_{i=1}^{L} \frac{i(i-1)}{L(L-1)} p_i}{\sum_{i=1}^{L} \frac{i}{L} p_i} \tag{4.13}$$

The value of GD varies between 0 and 1, where $GD = 0$ means minimum diversity while $GD = 1$ means maximum diversity (Partridge & Krzanowski, 1997). A modification of the GD concept, named coincident failure diversity (CFD), was also discussed in Partridge and Krzanowski (1997).

In summary, Table 4.1 highlights the major hypotheses diversity measure as discussed in this section. Here the position "+" and negative "−" sign indicate the relationship between the tendency of the diversity change with respect to the change of the corresponding metric. For instance, with the increase of the

Table 4.1: Summary of the Hypotheses Diversity Measures (Kuncheva & Whitaker, 2003)

Metrics	Symbol	+/−	Pairwise (Yes or No)	Symmetrical (Yes or No)	Reference(s)
Q-statistic	Q	−	Yes	Yes	Yule (1900)
Correlation coefficient	ρ	−	Yes	Yes	Sneath & Sokal (1973)
Disagreement measure	$\zeta_{i,j}$	+	Yes	Yes	Skalak (1996), Ho (1998b)
Double-fault measure	γ	−	Yes	No	Giacinto and Roli (2001)
Entropy agreement	E	+	No	Yes	Cunningham and Carney (2000)
Kohavi–Wolpert variance	KW	+	No	Yes	Kohavi and Wolpert (1996)
Interrater agreement	κ	−	No	Yes	Fleiss (1981), Looney (1988), Dietterich (2000)
Measure of difficulty	θ	−	No	No	Hansen & Salamon (1990)
Generalized diversity/coincident failure diversity	GD/CFD	+	No	No	Partridge & Krzanowski (1997)

corresponding metric in each row, positive "+" sign means the diversity will increase while negative "−" sign means the diversity will decrease.

4.3 DEVELOPING MULTIPLE HYPOTHESES

Developing an ensemble of diversified hypotheses is the first step for ensemble learning. There are various approaches to accomplish this goal. In this chapter, we discuss several of the major methods.

4.3.1 Bootstrap Aggregating

Bootstrap aggregating (bagging) was originally proposed by Breiman (1996). The key idea of bagging is to create multiple hypotheses using bootstrap sampling with replacement in the instance space. In the bagging method, a hypothesis is created by using a uniformly distributed probability sampling function across the entire training instances to acquire a random sample set for induction. A pre-set finite number of hypotheses are then combined using a simple voting scheme to predict the testing instances. Briefly speaking, the bagging algorithm can be summarized as follows (Breiman, 1996).

[Algorithm 4.1]: Bagging

Input:

(a) Training data set $\boldsymbol{U}$ with m instances, which can be represented as $\{\boldsymbol{x}_j, y_j\}$, $(j = 1, \ldots, m)$, where $\boldsymbol{x}_j$ is an instance in the n dimensional feature space $\boldsymbol{X}$, and $y_j \in \boldsymbol{\Omega} = \{1, \ldots, C\}$ is the class identity label associated with $\boldsymbol{x}_j$;
(b) A base learning algorithm: WeakLearn;
(c) Integer T specifying the number of iterations.

Do $t = 1, \ldots, L$:

(1) Obtain bootstrap sample $\boldsymbol{S}_t$ by randomly drawing m instances, with replacement, from the original training set $\boldsymbol{U}$;
(2) Call WeakLearn based on $\boldsymbol{S}_t$ to develop hypothesis h_t.

Testing stage:
Use the majority voting method to combine the output of L hypotheses $\boldsymbol{H} = \{H_1, \ldots, H_L\}$ to predict the final class label for each testing instance.

4.3.2 Adaptive Boosting

In bagging, each instance is treated with the same weight. Therefore, there is no distinction between those instances that are difficult to learn and those that are relatively easy to learn. In order to address this issue, various boosting algorithms have been proposed that can adaptively adjust the weights for different instances according to their distributions and learning difficulties.

The most popular boosting algorithms are variants of the adaptive boosting (AdaBoost) algorithms, AdaBoost.M1 and AdaBoost.M2 (Freund & Schapire, 1996, 1997). The essential idea of AdaBoost is to iteratively update the weights for different training instances according to their learning capabilities (Freund & Schapire, 1996, 1997). AdaBoost trains an ensemble by iteratively applying a booster distribution, D_t, to the training data. Here the distribution D_t can be represented in different formats depending on implementation details. For example, for those base learning algorithms (WeakLearn) that can directly take weighted examples, one can directly apply these weights to the boosting algorithms (reweighting). On the other hand, if the WeakLearn requires unweighted training instances, one can select a set of instances from the training data independently at random (with replacement) according to the booster distribution D_t (resampling). At each iteration, AdaBoost adaptively changes D_t so that the difficult-to-learn instances have greater weights than easy-to-learn examples (Freund & Schapire, 1996, 1997). In this manner, the decision boundary is adaptively shifted to pay more attention to those difficult instances. An extensive theoretical analysis on the error bounds of the boosting algorithms was provided in Freund and Schapire (1997) and empirical studies across different domains have shown great capabilities of this method (Freund & Schapire, 1996; Opitz & Maclin, 1999).

[Algorithm 4.2]: AdaBoost.M1

Input:

(a) Training data set $\boldsymbol{U}$ with m instances, which can be represented as $\{\boldsymbol{x}_j, y_j\}$, $(j = 1, \ldots, m)$, where $\boldsymbol{x}_j$ is an instance in the n dimensional feature space $\boldsymbol{X}$, and $y_j \in \boldsymbol{\Omega} = \{1, \ldots, C\}$ is the class identity label associated with $\boldsymbol{x}_j$;

(b) A base learning algorithm: WeakLearn;

(c) Integer L specifying the number of iterations.

Initialize: $D_1(j) = 1/m$, $j = 1, \ldots, m$.

Do $t = 1, \ldots, L$:

(1) Call WeakLearn based on the distribution D_t, and develop the hypothesis h_t;

(2) Develop the hypothesis $h_t : \boldsymbol{X} \rightarrow \boldsymbol{\Omega}$;

(3) Calculate the error of h_t:

$$\epsilon_t = \sum_{f:h_t(\boldsymbol{x}_j)\neq y_j} D_t(j) \tag{4.14}$$

If $\epsilon_t > 1/2$, set $L = t - 1$ and abort the iteration process;

(4) Set $\beta_t = \frac{\epsilon_t}{1-\epsilon_t}$;

(5) Update the distribution of D_t:

$$D_{t+1}(j) = \frac{D_t(j)}{Z_t} \times \begin{cases} \beta_t, & \textit{if } h_t(\boldsymbol{x}_j) = y_j \\ 1, & \textit{otherwise} \end{cases} \tag{4.15}$$

where Z_t is a normalization constant so that D_{t+1} is a distribution function ($\sum D_{t+1} = 1$).

Output: Final hypothesis:

$$h_{final}(\boldsymbol{x}) = \arg\max_{y \in \Omega} \sum_{t:h_t(\boldsymbol{x})=y} \log \frac{1}{\beta_t} \tag{4.16}$$

Freund and Schapire (1997) presented some important theoretical analysis of the AdaBoost.M1. Specifically, it was theoretically proven that if the WeakLearn can consistently have error only slightly better than 0.5 (for binary cases, this means the WeakLearn just need to be only slightly better than random guessing), then the training error of the final hypothesis h_{final} drops to zero exponentially fast. This was formally expressed in the following way (Freund & Schapire, 1997).

Theorem 1 *(Freund & Schapire, 1997) Suppose AdaBoost.M1 generates a series of hypotheses* h_t, $t = 1, \ldots, L$ *with errors* ϵ_t, $t = 1, \ldots, L$, *and each error* $\epsilon_t \leq 1/2$ *and define* $r_t = 1/2 - \epsilon_t$, *then the following upper bound holds on the error for the final hypothesis* h_{final}:

$$\frac{1}{m}|\{j : h_{final}(\boldsymbol{x}_j) \neq y_j\}| \leq \prod_{t=1}^{L} \sqrt{1 - 4r_t^2} \leq \exp\left(-2\sum_{t=1}^{L} r_t^2\right) \tag{4.17}$$

One limitation of AdaBoost.M1 is that it requires each WeakLearn has error less than 0.5. For multiple class classification problems, this requirements is some kind of strong and may not be met by the base WeakLearn algorithm. To overcome this limitation, Freund and Schapire extended the AdaBoost.M1 algorithm to AdaBoost.M2 to be able to handle this issue. The key idea of AdaBoost.M2 is to use the concept of pseudo-loss for more informative error measure instead of a single-label representation in the AdaBoost.M1 algorithm. Specifically, pseudo-loss is computed with respect to a distribution over the set of all pairs of examples and incorrect labels. In this way, the AdaBoost.M2 not only can focus on hard-to-classify examples, but more important, it can focus on the incorrect labels that are hardest to discriminate (Freund & Schapire, 1997). The following summarizes the AdaBoost.M2 algorithm (Freund & Schapire, 1996, 1997).

[Algorithm 4.3]: AdaBoost.M2

Input:

(a) Training data set $\boldsymbol{U}$ with m instances, which can be represented as $\{\boldsymbol{x}_j, y_j\}$, $(j = 1, \ldots, m)$, where $\boldsymbol{x}_j$ is an instance in the n dimensional feature space $\boldsymbol{X}$, and $y_j \in \boldsymbol{\Omega} = \{1, \ldots, C\}$ is the class identity label associated with $\boldsymbol{x}_j$;
(b) A base learning algorithm: WeakLearn;
(c) Integer L specifying the number of iterations.

Define $\boldsymbol{B}$ as the set of all mislabeled instances:

$$\boldsymbol{B} = \{(j, y) : j \in \{1, \ldots, m\}, y \neq y_j\} \tag{4.18}$$

Initialize: $D_1(j, y) = 1/|\boldsymbol{B}|$ for $(j, y) \in \boldsymbol{B}$, where $|\boldsymbol{B}|$ represents the size of $\boldsymbol{B}$.
Do $t = 1, \ldots, L$:

(1) Call WeakLearn based on the distribution D_t, and develop the hypothesis $h_t - \boldsymbol{X} \times \boldsymbol{\Omega} \to [0, 1]$;
(2) Calculate the pseudo-loss of h_t:

$$\epsilon_t = \frac{1}{2} \sum_{(j,y) \in \boldsymbol{B}} D_t(j, y)(1 - h_t(\boldsymbol{x}_j, y_j) + h_t(\boldsymbol{x}_j, y)) \tag{4.19}$$

(3) Set $\beta_t = \frac{\epsilon_t}{1-\epsilon_t}$;
(4) Update the distribution function D_t:

$$D_{t+1}(j, y) = \frac{D_t(j, y)}{Z_t} \cdot \beta_t^{(1/2)(1+h_t(\boldsymbol{x}_j, y_j) - h_t(\boldsymbol{x}_j, y))} \tag{4.20}$$

where Z_t is a normalization constant so that D_{t+1} is a distribution function $(\sum D_{t+1} = 1)$.

Output: Final hypothesis:

$$h_{final}(\boldsymbol{x}) = \arg\max_{y \in \boldsymbol{\Omega}} \sum_{t:h_t(\boldsymbol{x})=y} (\log \frac{1}{\beta_t}) h_t(\boldsymbol{x}, y) \tag{4.21}$$

Compared to the AdaBoost.M1 algorithm, the important thing of AdaBoost.M2 in terms of implementation is to represent the original data set in the mislabeled representation. Specifically, a *mislabel* is a pair of (j, y) where j is the index of a training instance and y is an incorrect label associated with instance j (see equation (4.18)), and a *mislabel distribution* is a distribution defined over the set $\boldsymbol{B}$ of all mislabels. In each iteration of the boosting process, the WeakLearn is presented with a mislabeled distribution D_t. To give a clear presentation of this, let's observe the following example.

Example: Consider a three-class ($C = 3$) classification problem $\boldsymbol{\Omega} = \{1, 2, 3\}$ with five instances ($m = 5$) and their associated class labels: $(\boldsymbol{x_1}, 1)$, $(\boldsymbol{x_2}, 1)$, $(\boldsymbol{x_3}, 2)$, $(\boldsymbol{x_4}, 3)$, and $(\boldsymbol{x_5}, 3)$. Figure 4.2 shows the D_1 distribution during the initialization process for both the AdaBoost.M1 and AdaBoost.M2 algorithms. From Figure 4.2 one can clearly see the initial distribution D_1 for AdaBoost.M1 and AdaBoost.M2 is set to $\frac{1}{m}$ and $\frac{1}{m(C-1)}$, respectively. Once the initial distribution is set, the boosting process can be followed according to the aforementioned specific algorithms.

The objective of AdaBoost.M2 is to find a weak hypothesis h_t with small pseudo-loss, as defined in equation (4.19). This raises another implementation detail for practical applications of AdaBoost.M2, which requires the base learning algorithm be able to produce probabilistic values for each data instance for the potential class labels: $\boldsymbol{X} \times \boldsymbol{\Omega} \rightarrow [0, 1]$. Therefore, the standard "off-the-shelf"

Original data instances
3-class classification problem (C=3)
5 instances (m=5)

Data instance	Class label
x_1	1
x_2	1
x_3	2
x_4	3
x_5	3

AdaBoost.M1

j	x_j	$D_1(j)$
j=1	x_1	1/5
j=2	x_2	1/5
j=3	x_3	1/5
j=4	x_4	1/5
j=5	x_5	1/5

$D_1(j)=1/m$

AdaBoost.M2

B	(x_j, y)	$D_1(j, y)$
(j=1, y=2)	$(x_1, 2)$	1/10
(j=1, y=3)	$(x_1, 3)$	1/10
(j=2, y=2)	$(x_2, 2)$	1/10
(j=2, y=3)	$(x_2, 3)$	1/10
(j=3, y=1)	$(x_3, 1)$	1/10
(j=3, y=3)	$(x_3, 3)$	1/10
(j=4, y=1)	$(x_4, 1)$	1/10
(j=4, y=2)	$(x_4, 2)$	1/10
(j=5, y=1)	$(x_5, 1)$	1/10
(j=5, y=2)	$(x_5, 2)$	1/10

$D_1(j, y)=1/(m(C-1))$

Figure 4.2: The initialization distribution for AdaBoost.M1 and AdaBoost.M2.

base learning algorithms might need some modification to be used in this manner but such modification is often straightforward (Freund & Schapire, 1996). Similar to the AdaBoost.M1, Freund and Schapire (1997) also presented the theoretical error bounds on the training error for the final hypothesis.

Theorem 2 *(Freund & Schapire, 1997) Suppose AdaBoost.M2 generates a series of hypotheses* h_t, $t = 1, \ldots, L$ *with pseudo-loss* ϵ_t, $t = 1, \ldots, L$, *and define* $r_t = 1/2 - \epsilon_t$, *then the following upper bound holds on the error for the final hypothesis* h_{final}:

$$\frac{1}{m}|\{j : h_{final}(\boldsymbol{x}_j) \neq y_j\}| \leq (C-1)\prod_{t=1}^{L}\sqrt{1-4r_t^2} \leq (C-1)\exp\left(-2\sum_{t=1}^{L}r_t^2\right) \tag{4.22}$$

where C *is the number of class.*

4.3.3 Subspace Learning

Both the bagging and AdaBoost methods develop multiple hypotheses in the *instance space*. Another major category of approaches is based on the *feature space* to develop such multiple hypotheses. In this section, we present the *random subspace* method and *ranked subspace* method.

The key of random subspace methods is to develop multiple hypotheses by randomly selecting subsets of the feature spaces. For instance, in the *decision forest* (Ho, 1998a, 1998b, 1995) or *random forest* (Breiman, 2001), an ensemble of multiple hypotheses are constructed systematically by pseudorandomly selecting subsets of components of the feature space. For instance, Ho discussed that for a given feature space of n dimensions, there are 2^n such selections can be made, of which each selection can be used to contract a decision tree (Ho, 1998b). Furthermore, if the subspace changes within the trees (split on different feature dimensions within a tree), more different trees can be easily constructed. The decision forest is also a parallel learning algorithm, in which the generalization of each decision tree is independent (Ho, 1998b). Many existing works demonstrated such random subspace methods can provide competitive learning performance across different application domains (Ho, 1998a, 1998b, 1995; Breiman, 2001).

In addition to randomly selecting the subspace feature for developing multiple hypotheses, a ranked subspace (RS) method for ensemble learning was proposed in He and Shen (2007). The key of the RS method is to rank and sort all features in a non-ascending order according to a feature score function to facilitate the development of multiple hypotheses. In this way, multiple hypotheses can be developed based on bootstrap sampling of these feature spaces with different weights according to their importance. Compared to the random feature subspace selection procedure in the decision forest and random forest methods, the RS method aims to select the feature subspace in a more informative and systematic way by using a sampling probability function. The RS method is summarized as follows.

[Algorithm 4.4]: Ranked Subspace

Input:

(a) Training data set $\boldsymbol{U}$ with m instances, which can be represented as $\{\boldsymbol{x}_j, y_j\}$, $(j = 1, \ldots, m)$, where $\boldsymbol{x}_j$ is an instance in the n dimensional feature space $\boldsymbol{X}$, and $y_j \in \boldsymbol{\Omega} = \{1, \ldots, C\}$ is the class identity label associated with $\boldsymbol{x}_j$;

(b) A base learning algorithm: WeakLearn;

(c) Integer L specifying the number of iterations.

(1) Define a feature score function $S(\cdot)$, and calculate the feature score for each feature, $S_f(i)$, $i = 1, \ldots, n$;

(2) Rank all features in a non-ascending order according to their feature score $S_f(i) : \{S_f(1), S_f(2), \ldots, S_f(n)\}$ where $S_f(1) \geq S_f(2) \geq \ldots \geq S_f(n)$;

(3) Calculate the feature sampling distribution function $D(i)$ according to their feature score value: $D(i) = \frac{S_f(i)}{Z}$, where Z is a normalization constant so that $D(i)$ is a distribution ($\sum D(i) = 1$);

Do $t = 1, \ldots, L$:

(1) Bootstrap sampling (with replacement) in the feature space with the distribution $D(i)$, denote this feature subspace as $\boldsymbol{F}_t$;

(2) Unique the feature space $\boldsymbol{F}_t$ to be $\boldsymbol{F}_{ut}$;

(3) Call WeakLearn based on D_t with feature subspace $\boldsymbol{F}_{ut}$, and develop the hypothesis $h_t : \boldsymbol{X} \rightarrow \boldsymbol{\Omega}$.

The output of the RS algorithm is a set of multiple hypotheses, which can be combined through different kinds of combination voting methods that will be discussed in section 4.4. One implementation detail for the RS method is that this method requires a feature score function, which can be calculated through different ways according to different applications. For instance, a feature score function related to Fisher's discrimination ratio was used in He and Shen (2007) for the microarray data analysis, and Figure 4.3(a) and (b) show a snapshot of the ranked feature score values and its corresponding histogram.

4.3.4 Stacked Generalization

Stacked generalization is another powerful technique for ensemble learning (Wolpert, 1992). The key idea of stacked generalization is to develop multiple

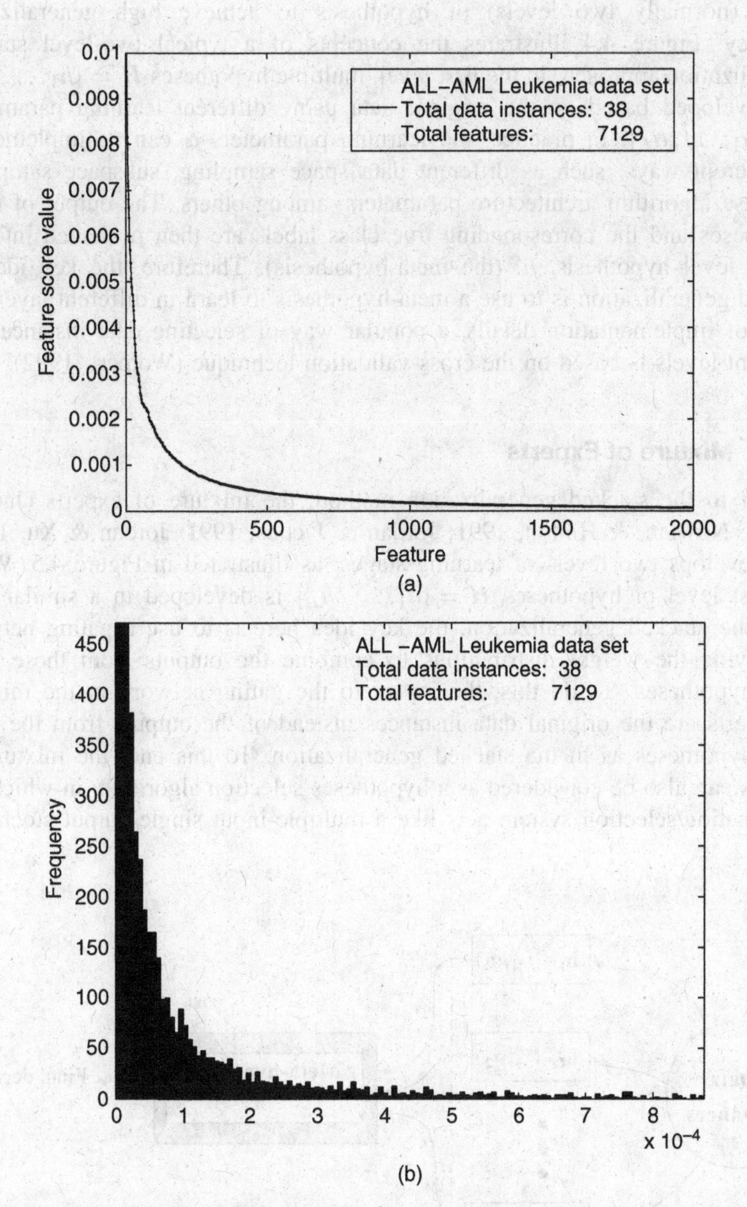

Figure 4.3: Feature score distribution for RS method. (a) A snapshot of the feature score value for a microarray data analysis (zoom-in representation). (b) Histogram of the feature score values.

levels (normally two levels) of hypothesis to achieve high generalization accuracy. Figure 4.4 illustrates the concepts of a typical two-level stacked generalization approach. In the first level, multiple hypotheses $\boldsymbol{H} = \{h_1, \ldots, h_L\}$ are developed based on the original data using different learning parameters $\boldsymbol{\alpha} = \{\alpha_1, \ldots, \alpha_L\}$. In practice, the learning parameters $\boldsymbol{\alpha}$ can be implemented in different ways, such as different data space sampling, subspace sampling, and base algorithm architecture parameters, among others. The output of these hypotheses and the corresponding true class labels are then presented into the second-level hypothesis, h' (the meta-hypothesis). Therefore, the key idea of stacked generalization is to use a meta-hypothesis to learn in different layers. In terms of implementation details, a popular way of selecting data instances for different levels is based on the cross-validation technique (Wolpert, 1992).

4.3.5 Mixture of Experts

Similar to the stacked generalization method, the mixture of experts (Jacobs, Jordan, Nowlan, & Hinton, 1991; Jordan & Jacobs, 1991; Jordan & Xu, 1995) also develops two levels of learning stages, as illustrated in Figure 4.5. While the first level of hypotheses $\boldsymbol{H} = \{h_1, \ldots, h_L\}$ is developed in a similar way as in the stacked generalization, the key idea here is to use a gating network to provide the weight distributions to combine the outputs from these first-level hypotheses. To do this, the inputs to the gating network in the mixture of experts are the original data instances instead of the outputs from the first-level hypotheses as in the stacked generalization. To this end, the mixture of experts can also be considered as a hypotheses selection algorithm, in which the combination/selection system acts like a multiple-input single-output stochastic

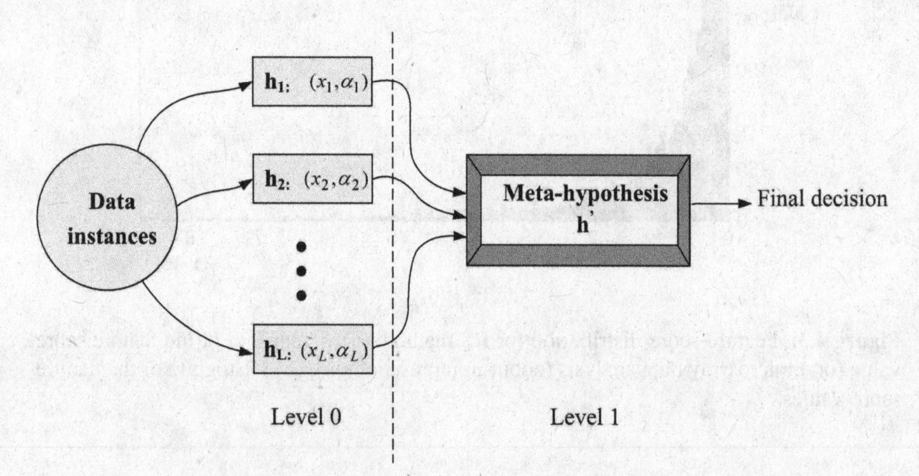

Figure 4.4: Stacked generalization method (a meta learning method).

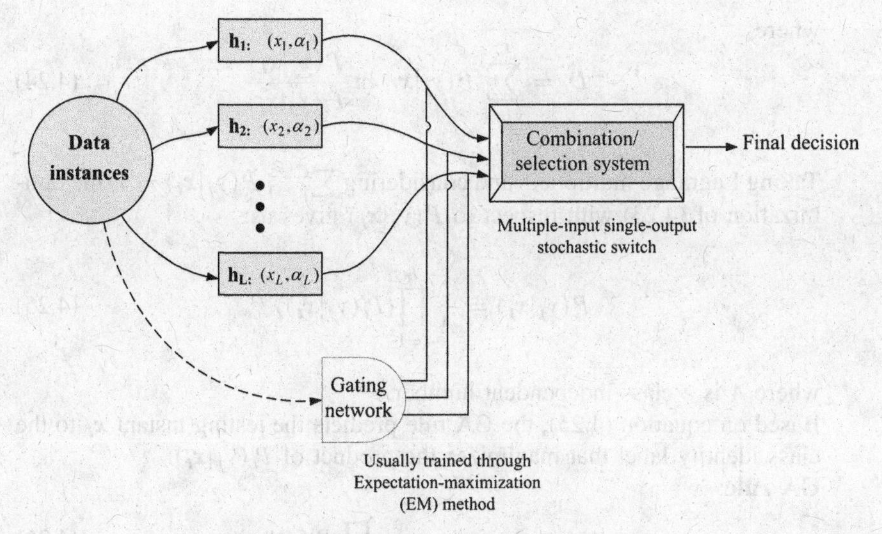

Figure 4.5: Mixture of experts method.

switch to select the most appropriate hypothesis or integrate all these hypotheses together by the weight distributions. Typically, the gating network is trained through expectation-maximization (EM) techniques (Jacobs et al., 1991; Jordan & Jacobs, 1991; Jordan & Xu, 1995).

4.4 INTEGRATING MULTIPLE HYPOTHESES

The second important issue of ensemble learning is to integrate the outputs from multiple hypotheses for the final decision. Assume a set of L hypotheses $\boldsymbol{H} = \{h_1, \ldots, h_L\}$ have been developed in an ensemble learning system. For each testing instant $\boldsymbol{x}_t$, each hypothesis can vote an estimate of the a *posteriori* probability across all the possible class labels y_j, $P_i(y_j|\boldsymbol{x}_t)$, $i = 1, \ldots, L$ and $y_j \in \boldsymbol{\Omega} = \{1, \ldots, C\}$. The objective here is to find an ensemble strategy for an improved estimate of the final *posteriori* probability, $P(y_j|\boldsymbol{x}_t)$, based on the individual $P_i(y_j|\boldsymbol{x}_t)$ from each hypothesis h_i. A detailed discussion regarding various voting methods can be found in Theodoridis and Koutroumbas (2006) and Kittler et al. (1998).

1. Geometric average (GA) rule
   GA rule finds $P(y_j|\boldsymbol{x}_t)$ to minimize the average Kullback–Leibler (KL) distance among probabilities:

$$D_{av} = \frac{1}{L}\sum_{i=1}^{L} D_i \tag{4.23}$$

where

$$D_i = \sum_{y_j=1}^{C} P(y_j|\boldsymbol{x}_t) \ln \frac{P(y_j|\boldsymbol{x}_t)}{P_i(y_j|\boldsymbol{x}_t)} \tag{4.24}$$

Taking Lagrange multipliers and considering $\sum_{y_j=1}^{C} P(y_j|\boldsymbol{x}_t) = 1$, the optimization of (4.23) with respect to $P(y_j|\boldsymbol{x}_t)$ gives us:

$$P(y_j|\boldsymbol{x}_t) = \frac{1}{A} \prod_{i=1}^{L} (P_i(y_j|\boldsymbol{x}_t))^{1/L} \tag{4.25}$$

where A is a class-independent number.
Based on equation (4.25), the GA rule predicts the testing instant $\boldsymbol{x}_t$ to the class identity label that maximizes the product of $P_i(y_j|\boldsymbol{x}_t)$:
GA rule:

$$\boldsymbol{x}_t \rightarrow y_j \textit{ satisfy} \max_{y_j} \prod_{i=1}^{L} P_i(y_j|\boldsymbol{x}_t) \tag{4.26}$$

2. Arithmetic average (AA) rule
Instead of using equation (4.24), one can also define the probability distance by an alternative KL distance as follows

$$D_i = \sum_{y_j=1}^{C} P_i(y_j|\boldsymbol{x}_t) \ln \frac{P_i(y_j|\boldsymbol{x}_t)}{P(y_j|\boldsymbol{x}_t)} \tag{4.27}$$

Substituting equation (4.27) into equation (4.23), one can get

$$P(y_j|\boldsymbol{x}_t) = \frac{1}{L} \sum_{i=1}^{L} P_i(y_j|\boldsymbol{x}_t) \tag{4.28}$$

Therefore, the AA rule can be defined as finding the maximal value of the arithmetic average of $P_i(y_j|\boldsymbol{x}_t)$:
AA rule:

$$\boldsymbol{x}_t \rightarrow y_j \textit{ satisfy} \max_{y_j} \frac{1}{L} \sum_{i=1}^{L} P_i(y_j|\boldsymbol{x}_t) \tag{4.29}$$

3. Median value (MV) rule
In the situation of probability outliers of $P_i(y_j|\boldsymbol{x}_t)$, the AA rule may lead to poor combination performance since the outliers will dominate the voting procedure. In such a case, the MV rule will predict the final class label with the maximum median value:

MV rule:

$$x_t \rightarrow y_j \ satisfy \ \max_{y_j}\{median(P_i(y_j|x_t))\} \tag{4.30}$$

4. Majority voting (MajV) rule
   In addition to the *soft*-type rules such as GA and AA, MajV rule is a *hard*-type ensemble strategy. Based on the training information, assume each hypothesis will predict a class identity label for the testing instant x_t, the MajV rule simply outputs the final predicted label as the one that receives most of the votes across all classes. In case there are multiple class labels that receive the same number of maximum counts, a random class label among them can be selected. The MajV rule can be defined as:
   MajV rule:

$$x_t \rightarrow y_j \ satisfy \ \max_{y_j} \sum_{i=1}^{L} \Delta_i(y_j|x_t) \tag{4.31}$$

where

$$\Delta_i(y_j|x_t) = \begin{cases} 1; & if\ h_i(x_t) = y_j; \\ 0; & otherwise. \end{cases}$$

5. Max rule
   Max rule is based on the information provided by the maximal value of $P_i(y_j|x_t)$ across all potential class labels. Unlike the AA rule which is based on the mean value of $P_i(y_j|x_t)$, Max rule is more like a winner-take-all style of voting:
   Max rule:

$$x_t \rightarrow y_j \ satisfy \ \max_{y_j}\{\max(P_i(y_j|x_t))\} \tag{4.32}$$

6. Min rule
   Similar to the Max rule, the Min rule is based on the idea to vote the final predicted class label based on the maximal of the minimal values of $P_i(y_j|x_t)$ across all potential class labels. Similar to equation (4.32), the Min rule can be defined as:
   Min rule:

$$x_t \rightarrow y_j \ satisfy \ \max_{y_j}\{\min(P_i(y_j|x_t))\} \tag{4.33}$$

7. Borda Count (BC) rule
   The BC rule is based on the ranked order of class labels provided by individual $P_i(y_j|x_t)$. Based on the hypothesis output, each hypothesis ranks all the potential class labels. For a C class problem, the kth-ranked candidate receives $(C - k)$ votes for the final voting systems. Finally, the class label that receives most of the votes will be the final predicted result. The BC rule can be defined as:

BC rule:

$$x_t \rightarrow y_j \; satisfy \; \max_{y_j} \sum_{i=1}^{L} \Omega_i(y_j|\boldsymbol{x}_t) \tag{4.34}$$

where $\Omega_i(y_j|\boldsymbol{x}_t) = C - k$ if hypothesis h_i ranks $\boldsymbol{x}_t$ in the kth position for class label y_j.

8. Weighted rules
In order to reflect different confidence levels from different hypotheses for the final voting results, a weight coefficient can be introduced to each individual hypothesis in several of the above-discussed methods. Here we define two commonly used methods.
Weighted AA rule:

$$\boldsymbol{x}_t \rightarrow y_j \; satisfy \; \max_{y_j} \frac{1}{L} \sum_{i=1}^{L} \omega_i \cdot P_i(y_j|\boldsymbol{x}_t) \tag{4.35}$$

Weighted MajV rule:

$$\boldsymbol{x}_t \rightarrow y_j \; satisfy \; \max_{y_j} \sum_{i=1}^{L} \omega_i \cdot \Delta_i(y_j|\boldsymbol{x}_t) \tag{4.36}$$

where ω_i is a weight coefficient for hypothesis $h_i : \omega_i \geq 0$ and $\sum_{i=1}^{L} \omega_i = 1$. A popular way in determining such weight coefficients is through cross-validation techniques (Theodoridis & Koutroumbas, 2006).

To summarize these methods, Figure 4.6 gives an example of a three-class classification problem ($C = 3$) for all the aforementioned methods. Here we assume the ensemble learning system includes four hypotheses: h_1, h_2, h_3, and h_4. For those weighted methods (weighted AA and weighted MajV rules), the weight coefficients are decided according to the confusion matrix based on the hypothesis performance over the training data sets. From Figure 4.6 one can see that in this particular example the MajV rule and weighted MajV rule vote this testing instant, $\boldsymbol{x}_t$, as a class 2 label. For the MV rule, since the votes for class 1 and 2 are the same, the final predicted label can be randomly selected from these two classes. For the BC rule, the final predicted label can be randomly selected from class 1, 2, and 3. All other methods vote this testing instance as a class 1 label.

4.5 CASE STUDY

In this section, we present a case study of various ensemble learning methods as discussed in this chapter. The goal here is to present the application of ensemble learning to real-world data sets.

Confusion matrix:

h_1

True class label \ Predicted class label	1	2	3
1	0.8	0.1	0.1
2	0.3	0.4	0.3
3	0.2	0.1	0.7

h_2

True class label \ Predicted class label	1	2	3
1	0.7	0.1	0.2
2	0.1	0.7	0.2
3	0.05	0.15	0.8

h_3

True class label \ Predicted class label	1	2	3
1	0.75	0.1	0.15
2	0.1	0.8	0.1
3	0.05	0.1	0.85

h_4

True class label \ Predicted class label	1	2	3
1	0.6	0.3	0.1
2	0.3	0.6	0.1
3	0.3	0.3	0.4

	Hypothesis 1	Hypothesis 2	Hypothesis 3	Hypothesis 4
Hypothesis weights	0.2346	0.2716	0.2963	0.1975

Testing Example: x_t

Class	Hypothesis 1	Hypothesis 2	Hypothesis 3	Hypothesis 4
1	0.25	0.33	0.90	0.32
2	0.46	0.37	0.02	0.28
3	0.29	0.30	0.08	0.40

Voting rules:

	Potential class label			
	Votes for class 1	Votes for class 2	Votes for class 3	Final predicted class label
GA rule:	0.0238	0.0010	0.0028	1
AA rule:	0.45	0.2825	0.2675	1
MV rule:	0.325	0.325	0.295	[1, 2]
MajV rule:	1	2	1	2
Max rule:	0.90	0.46	0.40	1
Min rule:	0.25	0.020	0.080	1
BC rule:	4	4	4	[1, 2, 3]
Weighted AA rule:	0.12	0.067	0.063	1
Weighted MajV rule:	0.30	0.51	0.20	2

Figure 4.6: A summary of the techniques used to integrate multiple hypotheses.

4.5.1 Data Sets and Experiment Configuration

The benchmarks used in our current study include 20 data sets from the UCI Machine Learning Repository (Asuncion & Newman, 2007). Table 4.2 illustrates the data set characteristics.

The neural networks model with multilayer perceptron (MLP) is used as the base learning algorithm, in which the number of input neurons and output neurons are equal to the number of attributes and classes for each data set, respectively. The number of hidden neurons for each data set is shown in Table 4.2, satisfing the condition $N = O(\frac{W}{\epsilon})$ (Haykin, 1999), where N is the size of the training set, $O(\cdot)$ denotes the order of quantity enclosed within, W is the total number of free parameters of the model, and ϵ denotes the expected testing errors that is set to 0.1 in this case study. The sigmoid function is used for the activation functions, and backpropagation is used to train the network. All results presented in this case study are based on the average of 100 random

Table 4.2: Data Set Characteristics Used in This Case Study

Data set name	# Instances	# Classes	# Attributes Cont.	# Attributes Disc.	# Hidden Neuron
ecoli	336	8	7	0	2
german	1000	2	7	13	2
glass	214	7	9	0	2
haberman	306	2	0	3	10
ionosphere	351	2	34	0	2
iris	150	3	4	0	10
letter-recognit	20000	26	16	0	10
musk1	476	2	166	0	2
pima-indians-di	786	2	8	0	10
satimage	6435	6	36	0	10
segmentation	2310	7	19	0	10
shuttle	59000	2	9	0	2
sonar	208	2	60	0	2
soybean-small	47	4	0	35	2
spectf	267	2	44	0	2
vehicle	846	4	18	0	2
vowel	990	11	10	0	2
wdbc	569	2	30	0	2
wine	178	3	13	0	2
yeast	1484	10	8	0	10

runs. At each run, we randomly select half (50%) of the data set as the training set, and use the remaining half (50%) for testing. The bagging method is adopted to create the classifier ensemble system (Breiman, 1996). Opitz and Maclin (1999) suggested for the ensemble learning method that relatively large gains can be observed by using 25 ensemble hypotheses, therefore in our case study, we construct 25 hypotheses through bootstrap sampling in each run.

4.5.2 Simulation Results

Table 4.3 shows the testing error performance for the major combination voting methods as discussed in section 4.4. For each data set, the winning voting strategy is underlined. Furthermore, the total numbers of winning times for each voting strategy across all these data sets are also summarized at the bottom of Table 4.3. One obvious question on this is, "Is there a best approach (or which one is the best approach) for these ensemble combination methods?" There exist many interesting discussions in the community on this question (Kittler et al., 1998; Polikar, 2006; Dietterich, 2000a, 2000b; Breiman, 1998; Bauer & Kohavi, 1999; Quinlan, 1996; Drucker, Cortes, Jackel, LeCun, & Vapnik, 1994; Battiti & Colla, 1994; Kuncheva, 2002; Tax, van Breukelen, Duin, & Kittler, 2000; Jacobs, 1995; Duin & Tax, 2000). In general, the no-free-lunch theorem

Table 4.3: Testing Error Performance

Voting method	GA rule	AA rule	MV rule	MajV rule	Max rule	Min rule	BC rule	Weighted AA rule	Weighted MajV rule
ecoli	19.82	21.07	21.26	21.39	22.94	**17.53**	19.79	21.07	21.39
german	**24.35**	24.44	24.48	24.48	24.47	24.47	24.48	24.43	24.48
glass	**43.37**	43.87	44.88	45.06	44.36	43.48	44.01	43.53	44.66
haberman	25.50	25.61	25.82	25.82	**25.44**	**25.44**	25.82	25.65	25.82
iosphere	13.32	12.99	12.88	12.88	**11.34**	**11.34**	12.88	12.95	12.88
iris	**3.55**	**3.55**	3.63	3.63	3.59	3.57	3.63	3.57	3.63
letter	**38.36**	40.10	42.56	51.26	49.32	39.64	43.00	39.61	48.47
musk1	**23.90**	24.17	25.24	25.24	25.82	25.82	25.24	23.97	25.10
pima-indians-di	32.59	32.65	33.14	33.14	**32.23**	**32.23**	33.14	32.65	33.14
satimage	4.87	6.33	9.09	8.27	6.51	**2.88**	4.04	5.05	6.16
segmentation	**12.29**	13.06	14.24	20.05	16.15	12.32	14.17	12.92	17.65
shuttle	7.23	7.22	7.99	7.89	6.22	**4.07**	8.10	7.22	7.80
sonar	22.23	21.63	**21.51**	**21.51**	25.09	25.09	**21.51**	21.61	**21.51**
soybean-small	1.54	1.42	1.29	1.17	7.25	3.71	1.46	1.33	**1.13**
spectf	21.00	**20.98**	**20.98**	**20.98**	22.48	22.48	**20.98**	**20.98**	**20.98**
vehicle	35.23	36.02	46.11	49.23	38.69	**35.09**	46.55	36.13	49.22
vowel	44.34	45.21	46.11	46.37	46.74	**44.28**	44.96	45.31	46.32
wdbc	13.61	20.42	37.20	37.20	**8.57**	**8.57**	37.20	13.92	34.86
wine	29.47	34.26	47.88	50.04	28.56	**17.66**	48.04	30.89	45.42
yeast	40.02	40.00	40.08	40.09	40.49	40.47	40.05	**40.00**	40.08
Winning times	**6**	**2**	**2**	**2**	**4**	**10**	**2**	**2**	**3**

(Wolpert & Macready, 1997) proves that there is in fact no such best approach. Instead, the best approach for each problem may depend on the particular domain knowledge and data characteristics. To provide more informative discussions on this, in this chapter we proceed with a margin analysis.

4.5.3 Margin Analysis

Margin analysis (Schapire, Freund, Bartlett, & Lee, 1998) provides many important insights and links between the ensemble learning and the state-of-the-art statistical learning methods, such as support vector machines (SVMs) (Vapnik, 1995, 1998). In this section, we provide some theoretical analysis and empirical experiments to investigate the margin analysis for ensemble learning.

4.5.3.1 A Short History of Margin Analysis Generally speaking, large margins will provide high tolerance to the perturbations of the voting noise for the learning system (Schapire et al., 1998). The idea that maximizing the margin can improve the generalization performance of a classifier can be traced back to the classical work of statistical learning theory developed by Vapnik (1995), which provides the foundation for the optimal margin classifiers (Boser, Guyon, & Vapnik, 1992) and SVMs (Cortes & Vapnik, 1995). One of the key ideas of these methods is to transfer a nonlinear classifier from a low-dimensional space to a linear classifier in a high-dimensional space, which is typically accomplished by using the kernel method.

Important links of the boosting methods (Freund & Schapire, 1996, 1997) with maximal margin classifiers in terms of the margin analysis have been developed (Schapire et al., 1998). Both methods aim to find a linear combination of large margins in the high-dimensional spaces. Of course, one should also notice the differences of the mechanisms used to accomplish this goal for these two methods: SVMs use the kernel method for efficient computation in the high-dimensional space, while boosting relies on a base learning classifier to explore the high-dimensional space one coordinant at a time (Schapire et al., 1998). Furthermore, the specific optimization goals of these methods are also different: SVMs target to maximize the minimal margin based on support vectors while boosting aims to minimize an exponential weighting of the instances (Schapire et al., 1998).

There are many interesting works that discuss these margin-based classifiers and analyze their margin characteristics. For instance, shortly after the aforementioned margin discussions for voting methods in Schapire et al. (1998), Breiman (1999) cast serious doubts about that margin explanation, and developed a new upper bound for the generalization error. In that paper, a boosting-type algorithm called arc-gv was developed and the new bound was proven to be sharper than the bound developed in Schapire et al.. However, although the arc-gv method can produce a higher margin distribution than AdaBoost, its performance is worse than AdaBoost. Therefore, Breiman challenges that the margin analysis in Schapire et al. and suggests that the VC-type bounds are misleading in this situation. Recently, Reyzin and Schepire (2006) revisited this issue and obtained more in-depth discovery after a careful investigation of the arc-gv method. The key findings in Reyzin and Schapire are based on the classifier complexity analysis, which explains that the worse performance of arc-gv method is because of the increased complexity of the base classifiers. In this way, Reyzin and Schepire suggested that their new investigation not only explains the doubts by Breiman in, but it is also consistent with the margin theory developed in Schapire et al. Therefore, maximizing the margins is still desirable but not necessary at the expense of base classifier complexity (Reyzin & Schapire, 2006). Most recently, another interesting discussion on this issue was proposed in Wang, Sugiyama, Yang, Zhou, and Feng (2008). In that paper, a bound in terms of a new margin measure named Equilibrium margin (Emargin) was developed and analyzed in detail with respect to the AdaBoost and arc-gv methods.

There are also a lot of other efforts on analyzing the boosting algorithms and providing explanations of the margin analysis. For instance, in Rätsch and Warmuth (2001), a variation of the AdaBoost learning scheme, the marginal boosting algorithm was proposed. This algorithm has been proven to quickly converge to the maximum margin solution. Another margin-based ensemble learning approach, the SoftBoost method, was developed based on the LPBoost algorithm in Warmuth, Glocer, and Rätsch (2008). This method implements the soft margin idea in a practical boosting algorithm and aims to optimize the soft margin. In Rätsch, Mika, Schölkopf, and Müller (2002), it was demonstrated that an SVM algorithm can be translated into a boosting-like algorithm, and vice versa. Based on this relationship, a boosting-like one-class leveraging algorithm was proposed in that paper. Moreover, in Lin and Li (2008), an infinite ensemble learning framework based on SVM was proposed, which also illustrates the relationship between ensemble learning and SVM. An empirical comparison among three margin-based learning methods—SVM, AdaBoost, and feed-forward neuron networks—was presented in (Romero, Carreras, & Marquez, 2004) over a real-world classification application (i.e., the text categorization problem). Other interesting works include the data-dependent margin-based generalization bounds for classification (Antos, Kégl, Linder, & Lugosi, 2002), the new complexity measures and analysis of the upper confidence bounds on the generalization error of complex classifiers (Koltchinskii & Panchanko, 2002, 2005), and the new generalization error bounds based on the thresholded convex combination analysis (Mason, Bartlett, & Golea, 2002), among others.

4.5.3.2 Margin Analysis for Ensemble Learning Consider a two-class classification problem. Suppose all instances in the training data $\boldsymbol{D_{tr}}$ can be represented by $\{\boldsymbol{x}_j, y_j\}$, $j = 1, \ldots, m$, and $y_j \in \{-1, +1\}$ is the class identity label associated with $\boldsymbol{x}_j$. We further assume that $\boldsymbol{h}(\boldsymbol{x})$ is some fixed nonlinear mapping of instances into the high-dimensional spaces. Therefore, the maximal margin classifier can be defined by the vector $\boldsymbol{\sigma}$, which maximizes the following term (Schapire et al., 1998)

$$\min_{(\boldsymbol{x},y)\in \boldsymbol{D_{tr}}} \frac{y(\boldsymbol{\sigma} \cdot \boldsymbol{h}(\boldsymbol{x}))}{\|\boldsymbol{\sigma}\|_2} \tag{4.37}$$

where $\|\boldsymbol{\sigma}\|_2$ is the l_2 norm of the vector $\boldsymbol{\sigma}$. Therefore, the objective of this approach is to find the optimal hyperplane that maximizes the minimal margin in a high-dimensional space. On the other hand, the key idea of the AdaBoost method is to iteratively update the distribution function over the training data set $\boldsymbol{D_{tr}}$. In this way, on each iteration $t := 1, \ldots, L$, where L is a preset number of the total number of iterations, a distribution function D_t is updated sequentially and used to train a new hypothesis:

$$D_{t+1}(j) = \frac{D_t(j)\exp(-y_j\sigma_t h_t(\boldsymbol{x}_j))}{Z_t} \tag{4.38}$$

where $\sigma_t = \frac{1}{2}\ln(\frac{1-\varepsilon_t}{\varepsilon_t})$, $h_t(\boldsymbol{x}_j)$ is the prediction output of hypothesis h_t on the instance $\boldsymbol{x}_j$, ε_t is the error of hypothesis h_t over the training set $\varepsilon_t = \sum_{j:h_t(\boldsymbol{x}_j)\neq y_j} D_t(j)$, and $Z_t = 2\sqrt{\varepsilon_t(1-\varepsilon_t)}$ is a normalization factor so that D_{t+1} is a distribution function, i.e., $\sum_{j=1}^{m} D_{t+1}(j) = 1$ (see section 4.3.2 for more details). In this way, the final combined hypothesis is a weighted majority vote of all these sequentially developed hypotheses (Schapire et al., 1998):

$$f(\boldsymbol{x}) = \frac{\sum_{t=1}^{L} \sigma_t h_t(\boldsymbol{x})}{\sum_{t=1}^{L} \sigma_t}. \tag{4.39}$$

Schapire et al. (1998) illustrated that if one considers the coefficient $\{\sigma_t\}_{t=1}^{L}$ as the coordinates of the vector $\boldsymbol{\sigma} \in \Re^L$ and the hypothesis output $\{h_t(\boldsymbol{x})\}_{t=1}^{L}$ as the coordinates of the vector $\boldsymbol{h}(\boldsymbol{x}) \in \{-1, +1\}^L$, equation (4.39) can be rewritten as

$$f(\boldsymbol{x}) = \frac{\boldsymbol{\sigma} \cdot \boldsymbol{h}(\boldsymbol{x})}{\|\boldsymbol{\sigma}\|_1} \tag{4.40}$$

where $\|\boldsymbol{\sigma}\|_1$ is the l_1 norm of $\boldsymbol{\sigma}$ ($\|\boldsymbol{\sigma}\|_1 = \sum_{t=1}^{L} |\sigma_t|$).

Comparing equations (4.37) and (4.40), one can clearly see the links of the maximal margin classifiers with the boosting methods (Schapire et al., 1998): Both methods aim to find a linear combination of large margin in the high-dimensional spaces. Of course, as we already mentioned in section 4.5.3.1, there are also some differences in terms of specific implementation and computational details. For instance, SVMs target to maximize the minimal margin based on support vectors, whereas boosting aims to minimize an exponential weighting of the instances. In terms of learning mechanisms, SVM relies on the kernel trick for efficient computation in the high-dimensional space, whereas boosting relies on a base learning classifier to explore the high-dimensional space one coordinate at a time.

We now proceed to a formal discussion on the margin analysis for ensemble learning. In this chapter, we adopt the *margin* and *margin distribution graph* terminology used in Schapire et al. (1998).

Definition 1 Consider a classification problem, the classification margin in this instance is defined as the difference between the weight assigned to the correct label and the maximal weight assigned to any single incorrect label, i.e., for an instance $\{\boldsymbol{x}, y\}$,

$$margin(\boldsymbol{x}) = w_{h(\boldsymbol{x})=y} - \max\{w_{h(\boldsymbol{x})\neq y}\} \tag{4.41}$$

Definition 2 Given a data distribution D, the margin distribution graph is defined as the fraction of instances whose margin is at most λ as a function of $\lambda \in [-1, 1]$:

$$F(\lambda) = \frac{|D_\lambda|}{|D|}, \lambda \in [-1, 1] \tag{4.42}$$

where $D_\lambda = \{\boldsymbol{x} : margin(\boldsymbol{x}) \leq \lambda\}$, $|\bullet|$ stands for the size operation and $F(\lambda) \in [0, 1]$.

Based on these definitions, Figure 4.7 shows an example of the margin distribution graphs for the AA rule, MV rule, and AdaBoost.M1 method on the testing

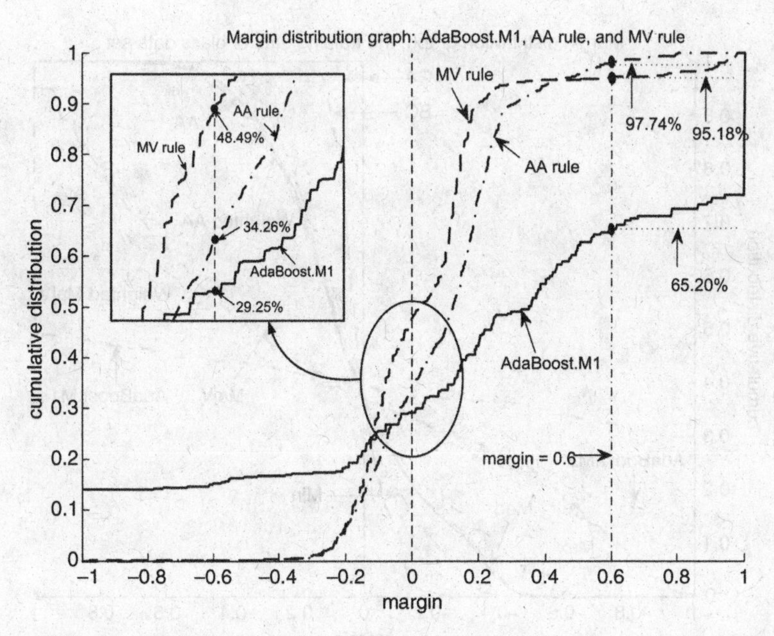

Figure 4.7: Margin distribution graph for the AdaBoost.M1, AA rule, and MV rule.

data of the wine data set from the UCI Machine Learning Repository (Asuncion & Newman, 2007). Here the x-axis is the margin as defined in equation (4.41), and the y-axis is the cumulative distribution based on equation (4.42). From this figure, one can see that AdaBoost.M1 can achieve a high margin in this case. For instance, as illustrated by the solid line, for the AdaBoost.M1 method, there are 65.20% of the testing data with a margin less than 0.6, whereas for the MV rule and AA rule, there are 95.18% and 97.74% of the testing data with a margin less than 0.6, respectively. One should also note in the margin distribution graph that the cumulative distribution value (y-axis) corresponding to the margin value of 0 (the box in Figure 4.7) represents the classification error rate. In the case of Figure 4.7, we highlight that the classification error for the testing data is 29.25%, 34.26%, and 48.49% for the AdaBoost.M1, AA rule, and MV rule, respectively.

To have a more detailed margin analysis for the major ensemble learning methods, we have analyzed the margin distribution graphs for all the data sets for the hypotheses integrating methods presented in section 4.4 and the boosting methods (AdaBoost.M1 and AdaBoost.M2 algorithm). Figure 4.8(a)–(d) give several snapshots of this analysis for the glass and vehicle data sets for both training and testing data. From these figures, it seems that AdaBoost.M1 is particularly aggressive in increasing the margins of the data examples: It significantly pushes the margin distribution graph toward both the positive 1 and negative 1 areas. Our simulation results and observations are also consistent with the discussions in Schapire et al. (1998) regarding this characteristic of the boosting method. As pointed out in Schapire et al., large margins (positive and negative) will provide

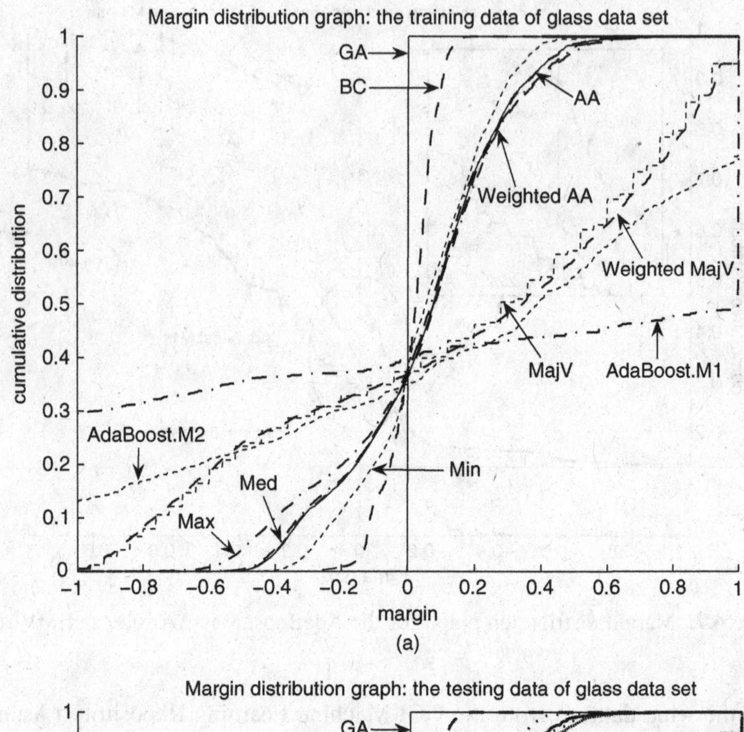

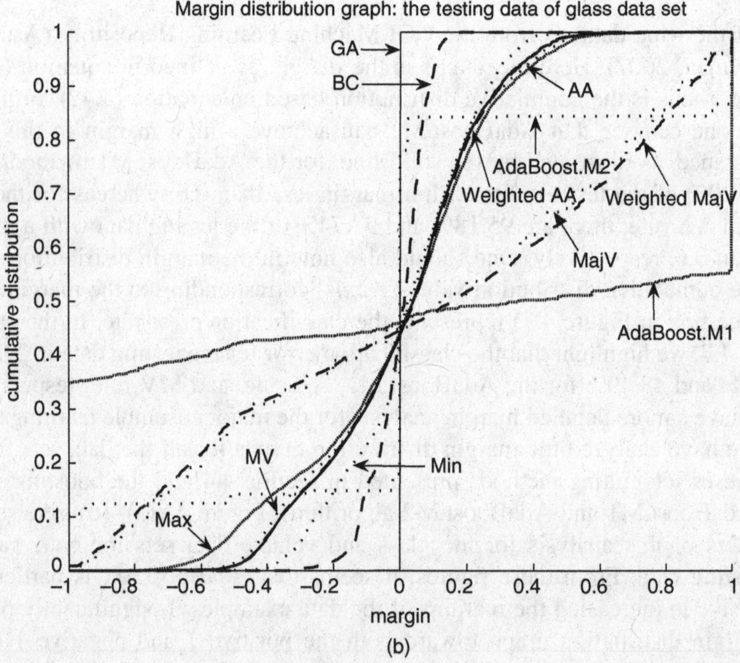

Figure 4.8: Margin distribution graphs: (a) the glass data set (training data); (b) the glass data set (testing data); (c) the vehicle data set (training data); (d) the vehicle data set (testing data).

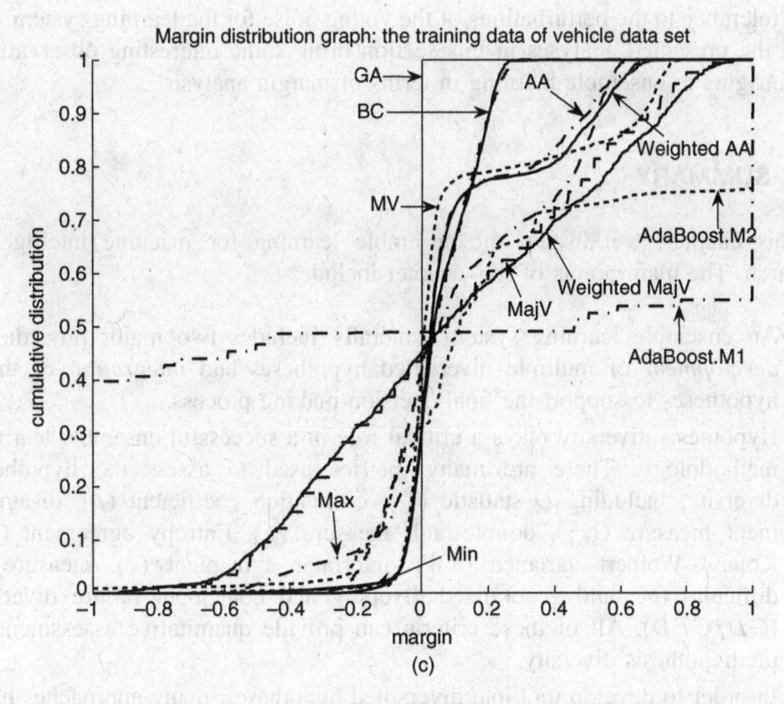

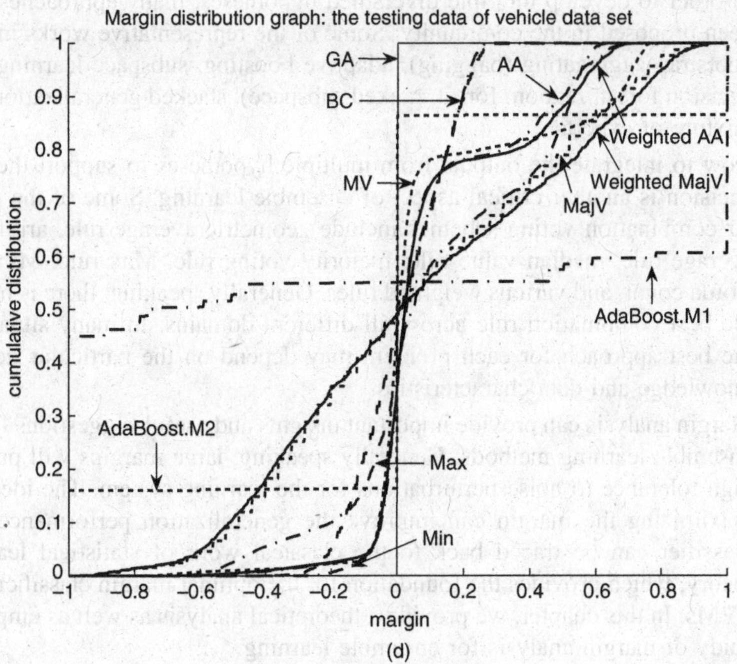

Figure 4.8: *(Continued)*

high tolerance to the perturbations of the voting noise for the learning system. We hope the presented analyses in this section bring some interesting observations and insights to ensemble learning in terms of margin analysis.

4.6 SUMMARY

In this chapter, we discuss the ensemble learning for machine intelligence research. The main points of this chapter include:

- An ensemble learning system generally includes two major procedures: *development* of multiple diversified hypotheses and *integration* of these hypotheses to support the final decision-making process.
- Hypothesis diversity plays a critical role in a successful ensemble learning methodology. There are many metrics used to assess the hypothesis diversity, including Q-statistic (Q), correlation coefficient (ρ), disagreement measure ($\zeta_{i,j}$), double-fault measure (γ), Entropy agreement (E), Kohavi–Wolpert variance (*KW*), interrater agreement (κ), measure of difficulty (θ), and generalized diversity and coincident failure diversity (GD/CFD). All of these criteria can provide quantitative assessment of the hypothesis diversity.
- In order to develop multiple diversified hypotheses, many approaches have been proposed in the community. Some of the representative works include bootstrap aggregating (bagging), adaptive boosting, subspace learning (i.e., decision forest, random forest, ranked subspace), stacked generalization, and mixture of experts.
- How to integrate the outputs from multiple hypotheses to support the final decision is another critical aspect of ensemble learning. Some of the popular combination voting schemes include geometric average rule, arithmetic average rule, median value rule, majority voting rule, Max rule, Min rule, Borda count, and various weighted rules. Generally speaking, there is no single best combination rule across all different domains. In many situations, the best approach for each problem may depend on the particular domain knowledge and data characteristics.
- Margin analysis can provide important insights and useful suggestions for the ensemble learning methods. Generally speaking, large margins will provide high tolerance to noise perturbations for the learning system. The idea that maximizing the margin can improve the generalization performance of a classifier can be traced back to the classical work of statistical learning theory, which provides the foundation for the optimal margin classifiers and SVMs. In this chapter, we provide a theoretical analysis as well as empirical study of margin analysis for ensemble learning.

REFERENCES

Antos, A., Kégl, B., Linder, T., & Lugosi, G. (2002). Data-dependent margin-based generalization bounds for classification. *Journal of Machine Learning Research*, *3*, 73–98.

Asuncion, A., & Newman, D. (2007). *UCI machine learning repository [Online], Available: http://www.ics.uci.edu/~mlearn/MLRepository.html*.

Battiti, R., & Colla, A. M. (1994). Democracy in neural nets: Voting schemes for classification. *Neural Networks*, *7*(4), 691–707.

Bauer, E., & Kohavi, R. (1999). An empiricial comparison of voting classification algorithms: Bagging, boosting and variants. *Machine Learning*, *36*, 105–142.

Boser, B. E., Guyon, I. M., & Vapnik, V. N. (1992). A training algorithm for optimal margin classifiers. *Proc. Annual ACM Workshop on Computational Learning Theory*, pp. 144–152.

Breiman, L. (1996). Bagging predictors. *Machine Learning*, *24*(2), 123–140.

Breiman, L. (1998). Arcing classifiers. *Annals of Statistics*, *26*(3), 801–849.

Breiman, L. (1999). Prediction games and arcing algorithms. *Neural Computation*, *11*, 1493–1517.

Breiman, L. (2001). Random forests. *Machine Learning*, *45*(1), 5–32.

Cortes, C., & Vapnik, V. (1995). Support vector networks. *Machine Learning*, *20*, 273–297.

Cunningham, P., & Carney, J. (2000). Diversity versus quality in classification ensembles based on feature selection. *Technical Report TCD-CS-2000-02*. Department of Computer Science, Trinity College Dublin.

Dietterich, T. (2000a). An experimental comparison of three methods for constructing ensembles of decision trees: Bagging, boosting and randomization. *Information & Software Technology*, *40*(2), 139–157.

Dietterich, T. G. (2000b). Ensemble Methods in Machine Learning. In J. Kittler and F. Roli (Ed.) *First International Workshop on Multiple Classifier Systems, Lecture Notes in Computer Sceince*, vol. 1857 (pp. 1–15). New York: Springer Verlag.

Drucker, H., Cortes, C., Jackel, L. D., LeCun, Y., & Vapnik, V. (1994). Boosting and other ensemble methods. *Neural Computation*, *6*(6), 1289–1301.

Duin, R., & Tax, D. (2000). Int. workshop on multiple classifier systems, lecture notes in computer science. In J. Kittler & F. Roli (Eds.), (Vol. 1857, pp. 16–29). Springer.

Fleiss, J. (1981). *Statistical methods for rates and proportions*. New York: Wiley.

Freund, Y., & Schapire, R. E. (1996). Experiments with a new boosting algorithm. *Proc. Int. Conf. Machine Learning*, pp. 148–156.

Freund, Y., & Schapire, R. E. (1997). A decision-theoretic generalization of on-line learning and application to boosting. *Journal of Computer and System Sciences*, *55*(1), 119–139.

Giacinto, G., & Roli, F. (2001). Design of effective neural network ensembles for image classification processes. *Journal of Image Vision and Computing*, *9*, 699–707.

Hansen, L., & Salamon, P. (1990). Neural network ensembles. *IEEE Trans. Pattern Analysis and Machine Intelligence*, *12*(10), 993–1001.

Haykin, S. (1999). *Neural networks: A comprehensive foundation* (2nd ed.). Upper Saddle River, NJ: Prentice Hall.

He, H., & Shen, X. (2007). A ranked subspace learning method for gene expression data classification. *Proc. Int. Conf. Artificial Intelligence*, pp. 358–364.

Ho, T. K. (1998a). C4.5 decision forests. *Proc. Int. Conf. Pattern Recognition*, pp. 545–549.

Ho, T. K. (1998b). Random subspace method for constructing decision forests. *IEEE Trans. Pattern Analysis and Machine Intelligence*, *20*(8), 832–844.

Ho, T. K. (1995). Random decision forests. *Proc. Int. Conf. Document Analysis and Recognition*, pp. 278–282.

Jacobs, R. A. (1995). Methods for combining experts' probability assessments. *Neural Computation*, *7*(5), 867.

Jacobs, R. A., Jordan, M. I., Nowlan, S. J., & Hinton, G. E. (1991). Adaptive mixtures of local experts. *Neural Computation*, *3*(1), 79–87.

Jordan, M. J., & Jacobs, R. A. (1991). Hierarchical mixtures of experts and the em algorithm. *Neural Computation*, *6*(2), 79–87.

Jordan, M. J., & Xu, L. (1995). Convergence results for the em approach to mixtures of experts architectures. *Neural Networks*, *8*(9), 1409–1431.

Kittler, J., Hatel, M., Duin, R. P. W., & Matas, J. (1998). On combining classifiers. *IEEE Trans. Pattern Analysis and Machine Intelligence*, *20*(3), 226–239.

Kohavi, R., & Wolpert, D. (1996). Machine learning: Proc. 13th international conference. In L. Saitta (ED.), (pp. 275–283). Morgan Kaufmann.

Koltchinskii, V., & Panchanko, D. (2002). Empirical margin distributions and bounding the generalization error of combined classifiers. *Annals of Statistics*, *30*, 1–50.

Koltchinskii, V., & Panchanko, D. (2005). Complexities of convex combinations and bounding the generalization error in classification. *Annals of Statistics*, *33*, 1455–1496.

Krogh, A., & Vedelsby, J. (1995). Advances in neural information processing systems. In G. Tesauro, D. Touretzky, & T. Leen (Eds.), (Vol. 7, pp. 231–238). Cambridge, MA: MIT Press.

Kuncheva, L. I. (2002). Switching between selection and fusion in combining classifiers: An experiment. *IEEE Trans. Systems, Man, and Cybernetics, Part B: Cybernetics*, *32*(2), 146–156.

Kuncheva, L. I., & Whitaker, C. J. (2003). Measures of diversity in classifier ensembles and their relationship with the ensemble accuracy. *Machine Learning*, *51*, 181–207.

Kuncheva, L. I., Whitaker, C., Shipp, C., & Duin, R. (2003). Limits on the majority vote accuracy in classifier fusion. *Pattern Analysis and Applications*, *6*, 22–31.

Lam, L. (2000). Int. workshop on multiple classifier systems, lecture notes in computer science. In J. Kittler & F. Roli (Eds.), (Vol. 1857, pp. 78–86). Springer.

Lin, H.-T., & Li, L. (2008). Support vector machinery for infinite ensemble learning. *Journal of Machine Learning Research*, *9*, 285–312.

Littlewood, B., & Miller, D. (1989). Conceptual modeling of coincident failures in multiversion software. *IEEE Trans. Software Engineering*, *15*(12), 1596–1614.

Looney, S. (1988). A statistical technique for comparing the accuracies of several classifiers. *Pattern Recognition Letters*, *8*, 5–9.

Mason, L., Bartlett, P., & Golea, M. (2002). Generalization error of combined classifiers. *Journal of Computer and System Sciences*, *65*, 415–438.

Opitz, D., & Maclin, R. (1999). Popular ensemble methods: An empirical study. *J. Artificial Intelligence Research*, *11*, 169–198.

Partridge, D., & Krzanowski, W. J. (1997). Software diversity: Practical statistics for its measurement and exploitation. *Information & Software Technology*, *39*, 707–717.

Polikar, R. (2006). Esemble based systems in decision making. *IEEE Circuits and Systems Magazine*, *6*(3), 21–45.

Quinlan, J. R. (1996). Bagging, boosting and c4.5. *Proc. Int. Conf. on Artificial Intelligence*, pp. 725–730.

Rätsch, G., Mika, S., Schölkopf, B., & Müller, K.-R. (2002). Constructing boosting algorithms from svms: an application to one-class classification. *IEEE Trans. Pattern Analysis and Machine Intelligence*, *24*(9), 1184–1199.

Rätsch, G., & Warmuth, M. K. (2001). Marginal boosting. *NeuroCOLT2 Technical Report Series NC2-TR-2001-097*.

Reyzin, L., & Schapire, R. E. (2006). How boosting the margin can also boost classifier complexity. *Proc. Int. Conf. Machine Learning*, 148, 753–760.

Romero, E., Carreras, X., & Marquez, L. (2004). Exploiting diversity of margin-based classifiers. *IEEE International Joint Conference on Neural Networks*, 1, 419–424.

Rosen, B. (1996). Ensemble learning using decorrelated neural networks. *Connection Science*, *8*(3/4), 373–383.

Schapire, R. E., Freund, Y., Bartlett, P., & Lee, W. S. (1998). Boosting the margin: A new explanation for the effectiveness of voting methods. *Annals of Statistics*, *26*(5), 1624–1686.

Skalak, D. (1996). The sources of increased accuracy for two proposed boosting algorithms. *Proc. Association for the Advancement of Artificial Intelligence Conf*.

Sneath, P., & Sokal, R. (1973). *Numerical taxonomy*. New York: W. H. Freeman..

Tax, D. M. J., van Breukelen, M. Duin, R. P. W., & Kittler, J. (2000). Combining multiple classifiers by averaging or by multiplying? *Pattern Rec.*, *33*(9), 1475–1485.

Theodoridis, S., & Koutroumbas, K. (2006). *Pattern recognition* (3rd ed.). New York: Elsevier.

Vapnik, V. N. (1995). *The nature of statistical learning theory*. New York: Springer.

Vapnik, V. N. (1998). *Statistical learning theory*. New York: Wiley-Interscience.

Wang, L., Sugiyama, M., Yang, C., Zhou, Z.-H., & Feng, J. (2008). On the margin explanation of boosting algorithm. *Proc. Annual Conf. Learning Theory*, pp. 479–490.

Warmuth, M. K., Glocer, K., & Rätsch, G. (2008). Boosting algorithms for maximizing the soft margin. *Advances in Neural Information Processing Systems*.

Wolpert, D. H. (1992). Stacked generalization. *Neural Network*, *5*(2), 241–259.

Wolpert, D. H., & Macready, W. (1997). No free lunch theorems for optimization. *IEEE Trans. Evolutionary Computation*, *1*(1), 67–82.

Yang, Y., Wang, G., & He, K. (2007). An approach for selective ensemble feature selection based on rough set theory. *Lecture Notes in Computer Science*, pp. 518–525.

Yule, G. (1900). On the association of attributes in statistics. *Phil. Trans.*, *194*(A), 257–319.

CHAPTER 5

Adaptive Dynamic Programming for Machine Intelligence

5.1 INTRODUCTION

As we have discussed in Chapter 1, strong evidences from brain science research have supported that biological brain uses fundamentally different ways in handling different tasks than today's computers. From the engineering design point of view, if the brain itself is considered as a whole system of an intelligent controller (Werbos, 2002, 2005), the important question is how to develop general-purpose methods that can dynamically learn information, accumulate knowledge, make predictions, and adjust actions to maximize some kind of utility function over time to achieve goals (goal-oriented behaviors) (Werbos, 2004, 2007, 2009a). To this end, it is widely recognized that adaptive dynamic programming (ADP) is the core methodology, or "the only general-purpose way to learn to approximate the optimal strategy of action in the general case" for machine intelligence development (Werbos, 2004, 2007, 2009a). Over the past several decades, ADP has attracted extensive attention in the community ranging from fundamental theoretical research to a wide range of applications (Werbos, 2009b; Si, Barto, Powell, & Wunsch, 2004; Prokhorov & Wunsch, 1997; White & Sofge, 1992; Bertsekas & Tsitsiklis, 1996; Powell, 2007; Liu & Jin, 2009; Wang, Zhang, & Liu 2009; Vamvoudakis & Lewis, 2009; Balakrishnan, Ding, & Lewis, 2008; Al-Tamimi, Abu-Khalaf, & Lewis, 2007; Venayagamoorthy & Harley, 2004; Ray, Venayagamoorthy, Chaudhuri, & Majumder, 2008; Venayagamoorthy, Harley, & Wunsch, 2003). Therefore, in this chapter we provide a discussion of the ADP research with a focus on its learning principles, architectures, and applications for machine intelligence research. Build on the existing community efforts on this topic, we also propose a hierarchical learning ADP architecture with multiple-goal representations to effectively integrate the optimization and prediction together toward general-purpose learning.

Self-Adaptive Systems for Machine Intelligence, First Edition. Haibo He.

5.2 FUNDAMENTAL OBJECTIVES: OPTIMIZATION AND PREDICTION

Among many efforts toward the long-term goal of developing general-purpose brain-like intelligent systems, it is widely recognized that *optimization* and *prediction* are the two essential objectives for goal-oriented behaviors (Werbos, 2009a). For instance, in the reinforcement learning framework (a subset of the ADP problems), the goal of an intelligent system is to take optimal actions through active interaction with the external environment to maximize the expected future reward signal (Sutton & Barto, 1998; Geramifard, Bowling, & Sutton, 2006; Rafols, Ring, Sutton, & Tanner, 2005; Kaelbling, Littman, & Moore, 1996). Therefore, understanding the fundamental problems of *optimization* and *prediction* will help the community to focus on the most critical and promising research topics, and also potentially develop fundamental scientific breakthroughs and engineering techniques and tools to bring such a level of intelligence closer to reality (Werbos, 2009a).

Optimization has a long-standing research foundation in control theory, decision theory, risk analysis, and many other fields. As far as machine intelligence is concerned, optimization can be defined to learn to make better choices to maximize some kind of utility function over time to achieve goals (Werbos, 2009a). To this end, the foundation for optimization over time in stochastic processes is the Bellman equation (Bellman, 1957), closely tied with the Cardinal utility function concept by Von Neumann. Specifically, given a system with performance cost:

$$J[\boldsymbol{x}(i), i] = \sum_{t=i}^{\infty} \gamma^{t-i} U[\boldsymbol{x}(t), u(t), t] \tag{5.1}$$

where $\boldsymbol{x}(t)$ is the state vector of the system, $u(t)$ is the control action, U is the utility function, and γ is a discounted factor. The objective of dynamic programming is to choose control sequence $u(t)$ so the cost function J is minimized:

$$J^{\star}(\boldsymbol{x}(t)) = \min_{u(t)}\{U(\boldsymbol{x}(t), u(t)) + \gamma J^{\star}(\boldsymbol{x}(t+1))\} \tag{5.2}$$

Equation (5.2) provides the foundation for implementing dynamic programming by working backward in time. For instance, universal approximators like neural networks with the backpropagation method are widely used in the community (Werbos, 1983, 1988a, 1988b, 1989, 1991, 1995).

Existing adaptive critic design can be categorized into three major groups (Prokhorov & Wunsch, 1997; Ferrari & Stengel, 2004; Werbos, 1992): heuristic dynamic programming (HDP), dual heuristic dynamic programming (DHP), and globalized dual heuristic dynamic programming (GDHP). These belong to the first-generation models of ADP design (Werbos, 2009a). For instance, HDP (Werbos, 1977, 2009a) was proposed with the objective of using a critic network to critique the action value in order to optimize the future cost function by using temporal differences between two consecutive estimates from the critic network (Si & Wang, 2001). This idea is essentially similar to the temporal-difference (TD) method discussed in the RL literature (Sutton & Barto, 1998). To overcome the limitations of scalability, DHP and GDHP were proposed (Werbos, 1979, 1981), followed by many improvements and demonstrations of such methods (Si et al., 2004; White & Sofge, 1992; Werbos, 2008). The key idea of DHP is to use a critic to approximate the derivatives of the value function with respect to the states, while GDHP takes advantage of both HDP and DHP by using a critic to approximate both the value function and its derivatives. Variations of all of these categories of ADP design have also been investigated in the community, such as the action-dependent (AD) version of the aforementioned methods by taking action values as an additional input to the critic network (Si & Wang, 2001).

Prediction is another critical element to facilitate the development of genera-purpose intelligence (Werbos, 2009a). This is strongly linked to the second generation of ADP design (Werbos, 1987, 1992, 1993, 2009a; Werbos & Pellionisz, 1992). Although the community has looked at the prediction problem for a very long time, particularly from the data mining point of view, the understanding of the general prediction process in the brain is rather limited. For instance, many of the existing solutions of prediction are purely based on the observation of historical data patterns without a principled understanding of how the biological brain can robustly predict information across different domains within the distributed neural organization. On the other hand, evidence from neurobiology suggests that based on the observations of the receptive fields of the ventral posterior medial thalamus (VPM) in adult rats, 73% of neurons showed immediate unmasking of short latency responses (SLRs) in response to stimulation of adjacent regions (Nicolelis, Lin, Woodward, & Chapin, 1993). This may suggest that nearby cells can function as predictors even before the actual input signals have been received (Werbos, 2009a; Nicolelis, Baccala, Lin, & Chapin, 1995). This may support the hypothesis that prediction is another core objective of brain-like general-purpose intelligence, as highlighted in Werbos (2009a). In terms of engineering research and development, much better performance can be achieved when prediction is integrated with optimization. For instance, a significant amount of research results have suggested that the use of recurrent neural networks (RNN), such as cellular simultaneous recurrent neural networks (CSRN) integrated with the extended Kalman filter (EKF) (White & Sofge, 1992; Werbos, 1999, 2004; Ilin, Kozma, & Werbos, 2008) and time-lagged recurrent neural networks (TLRN) (Feldkamp & Prokhorov, 2003; Feldkamp, Prokhorov, Eagen, & Yuan, 1998; Puskorius & Feldkamp, 1994; Sun & Marko, 1998), can effectively integrate prediction and optimization together. This in turn has significantly improved the neural network capabilities in solving complex problems such as control and navigation within complex scenes (Ilin et al., 2008). This concept is also related to the ObjectNet method by mapping complex input field into different types of objects ("inner loop neural networks") (Werbos, 1998a, 2009a), which has demonstrated great potential among different complex problems such as electric power grid control (Qiao, Venayagamoorthy,

& Harley, 2007) and a master-level performance chess program (Fogel, Hays, Han & Quon, 2004).

With these two objectives in mind, we propose a hierarchical learning architecture with multiple-goal representations based on the ADP design to achieve the optimization and prediction goals for machine intelligence research. In addition to the conventional ADP design with the action network and critic network, the key idea of our proposed model is to integrate another type of network, the reference network, to provide multiple levels of internal reinforcement representations (similar to the concept of secondary reinforcement signals) to interact with the operation of the learning system. Such reference networks serve an important role to accomplish the optimization and prediction objectives in the proposed ADP design. In this ADP architecture, instead of using a single binary reinforcement signal as in many of the existing ADP designs, we propose to use two types of reinforcement signals for improved generalization and learning capability: the primary reinforcement signal from the external environment and the secondary reinforcement signals from reference networks. While the primary reinforcement signal could be a binary signal to represent "good" or "bad" or "success" or "failure," the secondary reinforcement signals could be a continuous signal for more informative internal goal representations at different levels for an intelligent system. We now proceed to discuss the proposed architecture, learning and adaptation process, and its practical applications.

5.3 ADP FOR MACHINE INTELLIGENCE

5.3.1 Hierarchical Architecture in ADP Design

Motivated by the recent research developments on ADP (Werbos, 1992, 1998b, 2009a; Si & Wang, 2001; Si et al., 2004; Enns & Si, 2004; Si & Liu, 2004), neurobiological research (Melzack, 1990; Peyron, Laurent, & Garcia-Larrea, 2000; Derbyshire et al., 1997; Hsieh, Tu, & Chen, 2001), as well as hierarchical learning and memory organizations (Starzyk, Liu, & He, 2006), we propose an ADP architecture with multiple levels of goal representation as illustrated in Figure 5.1. The principle of this approach is to develop a hierarchical level of internal reinforcement representation for improved generalization and learning capability. In Figure 5.1, we use multiple levels of reference networks to automatically develop internal reinforcement signals to represent different levels of goals in a hierarchical way. Each higher hierarchical level will provide guidance (like top-down prediction) for the lower hierarchical level learning. The highest hierarchical level will receive the primary reinforcement signal coming from the external environment, which can be considered as the ultimate objective of the learning system. Based on such primary reinforcement signals, multiple internal reinforcement signals will be automatically and adaptively developed to build different levels of goal representations to facilitate the learning process.

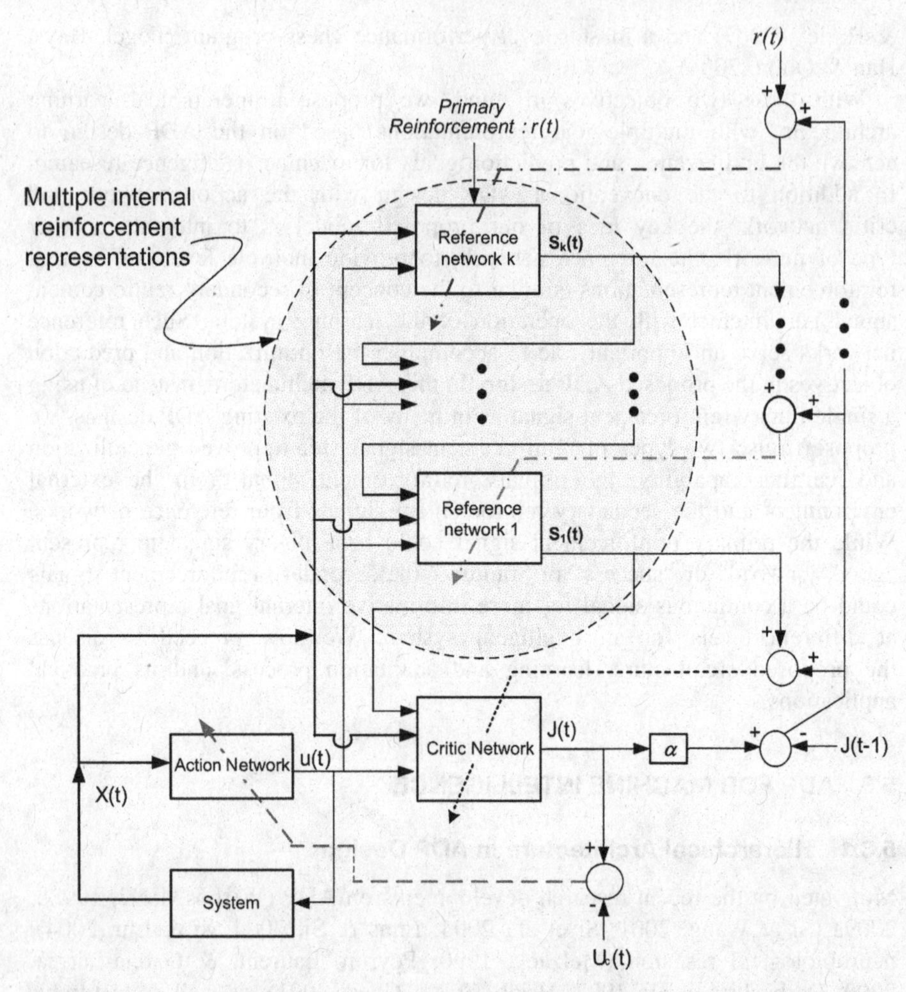

Figure 5.1: Hierarchical learning with multiple-goal representations in ADP design.

Compared to the classic ADP architecture design, an important feature of the proposed architecture is to integrate another type of network, the reference network, to provide multilevel internal reinforcement signals $s(t)$. These internal reinforcement signals are also similar to the "secondary reinforcement signal" as discussed in Werbos (2009a) and Frijda (1987), which serve as an important role to build the interactions between the reference networks and critic network. We would like to note that the use of the reference network is also similar to the idea of the "model network" as discussed in both first-generation and second-generation of ADP design (Werbos, 2009a). For instance, in first-generation ADP design, the model network was designed to learn how to predict the changes of the environment and estimate the objective state of reality (Werbos, 2009a).

In second-generation ADP design, the model network was designed with much more powerful capabilities of prediction, which can be achieved through recurrent networks (this is also called the "two brains in one model" with lower level and upper level adaptive critic systems; Werbos 2009a). In the proposed ADP architecture, the goal of the reference network is well aligned with this objective to bring the prediction capability into the learning and optimization process. To this end, the proposed reference network in this architecture can also be considered as a specific design strategy of the model network as in (Werbos, 2009a).

Since the proposed ADP architecture includes two types of reinforcement signals, it is interesting to observe and analyze how these two types of reinforcement representations can facilitate the learning process. In the traditional ADP designs, the reinforcement signal is normally considered a binary signal, such as using either a 0 or a -1 to represent "success" or "failure" of the system (Si & Liu, 2004). In order to provide more informative reinforcement signals in many complex problems, different ways have been proposed to use non–binary reinforcement signals to improve the learning performance of the ADP design. For instance, in Si and Wang (2001), in addition to the conventional binary reinforcement representation, they also developed a different design strategy by using a three-value reinforcement signal (0, -0.4, and -1) for the pendulum swing up and balancing task. Most recently, a quadratic reinforcement signal was proposed at each sampling time to provide more informative information in ADP design (Enns & Si, 2004):

$$r(t) = -\sum_{i=1}^{n} \left(\frac{(x_i - x_{i,d})}{x_{i,max}} \right)^2 \tag{5.3}$$

where x_i is the ith state of the state vector $\boldsymbol{x}$, $x_{i,d}$ is the desired reference state, and $x_{i,max}$ is the nominal maximum state value. In this way, the ADP architecture showed better generalization and learning performance and was successfully applied to the challenging helicopter flight control application (Enns & Si, 2004).

In our proposed architecture illustrated in Figure 5.1, the internal reinforcement signals $s(t)$ are developed in a more natural and principled way. That is to say, such an internal reinforcement representation is automatically built through different hierarchical levels of the reference networks, which in turn will cooperate with the critic network for optimization and learning. Another support of using such a more informative internal reinforcement representation comes from the psychological study that biological systems are able to develop internal goal representations, which trigger learning and association between the sensory and motor pathways for embodied intelligence. For instance, neurobiological research by using positron emission tomography (PET) and functional magnetic resonance imaging (fMRI) techniques suggest that multiple regions of the brain are involved in the pain system, which form the neomatrix ("pain matrix") for internal intention/value signal representation (Melzack, 1990; Peyron et al., 2000; Derbyshire et al., 1997; Hsieh et al., 2001). Therefore, goal-creation systems (Starzyk et al., 2006) with multiple levels of reinforcement signals in a hierarchical representation could provide important insights of optimization and prediction to understand the brain's capability.

We would also like to discuss how *prediction* is accomplished and integrated into this ADP architecture. Generally speaking, prediction in the ADP design can be considered in a more general way to include much important information, such as the future sensory inputs from observed data as well as modeling and reconstructing of unobserved state variables, with the objective of facilitating action selection toward optimization (Werbos, 2009a). Therefore, in the proposed ADP architecture, the capability of prediction is achieved through the hierarchically organized reference networks to predict the internal reinforcement signals $s(t)$ to provide more informative goal representations for improved optimization performance. The prediction of the $s(t)$ signals can be implemented through nonlinear function approximators such as neural networks (including recurrent networks). We now proceed to discuss the detailed learning and adaptation processes in all three types of networks: action network, critic network, and reference network.

5.3.2 Learning and Adaptation in ADP

To give a clear description of the learning mechanism in this architecture, we use a specific two-level architecture with only one reference network, as illustrated in Figure 5.2, as an example to discuss the learning and adaptation process. From

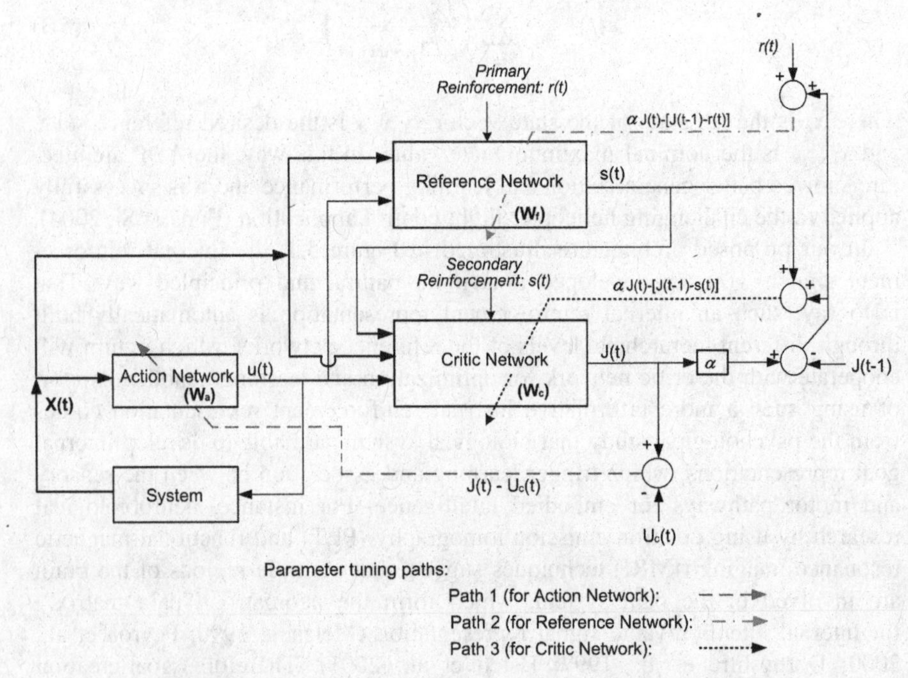

Figure 5.2: The proposed ADP architecture with three networks.

Figure 5.2 one can see, there are three paths to tune the parameters of the three types of networks using the backpropagation rule.

The action network in this architecture is similar to the classic ADP approach to indirectly backpropagate the error between the desired ultimate objective U_c and the J function from the critic network (Si & Wang, 2001)(Si & Liu, 2004). Therefore, the error function $E_a(t)$ used to update the parameters in the action network can be defined as (path 1 in Figure 5.2):

$$e_a(t) = J(t) - U_c(t); \quad E_a(t) = \frac{1}{2}e_a^2(t). \tag{5.4}$$

The key of this architecture relies on the learning and adapting process for the reference network and critic network. As the primary reinforcement signal $r(t)$ is presented to the reference network, the secondary reinforcement signal $s(t)$ is adapted to provide a more informative internal reinforcement representation to the critic network, which in turn is used to provide a better approximation of the $J(t)$. In this way, the primary reinforcement signal $r(t)$ is in a higher hierarchical level and can be a simple binary signal to represent "good" or "bad" (or "success" or "failure"), while the secondary reinforcement signal $s(t)$ can be a more informative continues value for improved learning and generalization performance. Therefore, the error function $E_f(t)$ used to update the parameters in the reference network can be defined as (path 2 in Figure 5.2):

$$e_f(t) = \alpha J(t) - [J(t-1) - r(t)]; \quad E_f(t) = \frac{1}{2}e_f^2(t). \tag{5.5}$$

Once the reference network outputs the $s(t)$ signal, it will be used as an input to the critic network, and also used to define the error function to adjust the parameters of the critic network (path 3 in Figure 5.2).

$$e_c(t) = \alpha J(t) - [J(t-1) - s(t)]; \quad E_c(t) = \frac{1}{2}e_c^2(t). \tag{5.6}$$

From a mathematical point of view, there are two major differences for this framework compared to the traditional critic network design. First, the critic network has one more additional input $s(t)$ from the reference network. Second, the optimization error functions for the reference network and critic network are different: the error function of the reference network is related to the primary reinforcement signal $r(t)$ (equation (5.5)), while for the critic network it is related to the secondary reinforcement signal $s(t)$ (equation (5.6)). The idea is to use such a secondary reinforcement signal to build the internal goal representation through associations and anticipations in the ADP design.

In this architecture, the chain backpropagation rule is the key to training and adaptation of the parameters of all three networks (action network, critic network, and reference network) (Werbos, 1990, 1994). Figure 5.3 shows the three backpropagation paths used to adapt the parameters in the three networks. In this

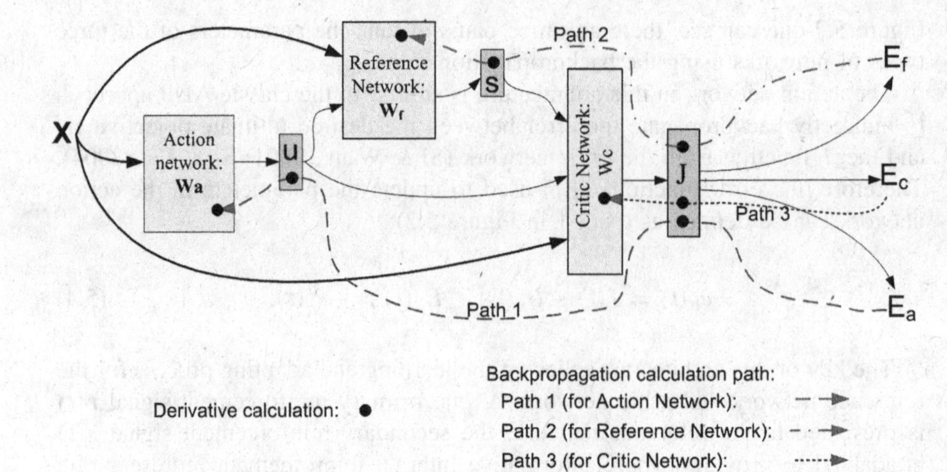

Figure 5.3: Parameters of adaptation and tuning based on backpropagation.

figure, the optimization error functions for the action network E_a, reference network E_f, and critic network E_c are defined in equations (5.4), (5.5), and (5.6), respectively. Therefore, chain backpropagation can be calculated through the three data paths as highlighted in Figure 5.3. Briefly speaking, the high-level conceptual calculation on this can be summarized as follows.

Path 1 For action network:

$$\frac{\partial E_a(t)}{\partial w_a(t)} = \frac{\partial E_a(t)}{\partial J(t)} \frac{\partial J(t)}{\partial u(t)} \frac{\partial u(t)}{\partial w_a(t)} \tag{5.7}$$

Path 2 For reference network:

$$\frac{\partial E_f(t)}{\partial w_f(t)} = \frac{\partial E_f(t)}{\partial J(t)} \frac{\partial J(t)}{\partial s(t)} \frac{\partial s(t)}{\partial w_f(t)} \tag{5.8}$$

Path 3 For critic network:

$$\frac{\partial E_c(t)}{\partial w_c(t)} = \frac{\partial E_c(t)}{\partial J(t)} \frac{\partial J(t)}{\partial w_c(t)} \tag{5.9}$$

We now give detailed discussions of the learning and adaptation process for the three networks in the proposed ADP architecture.

5.3.2.1 The Action Network In order to focus on the learning principle, in this chapter we assume neural networks with a three-layer nonlinear architecture (with one hidden layer) are used in all three networks. We would like to note that the learning principles discussed here can also be generalized to any arbitrary function approximators by properly applying the backpropagation rule.

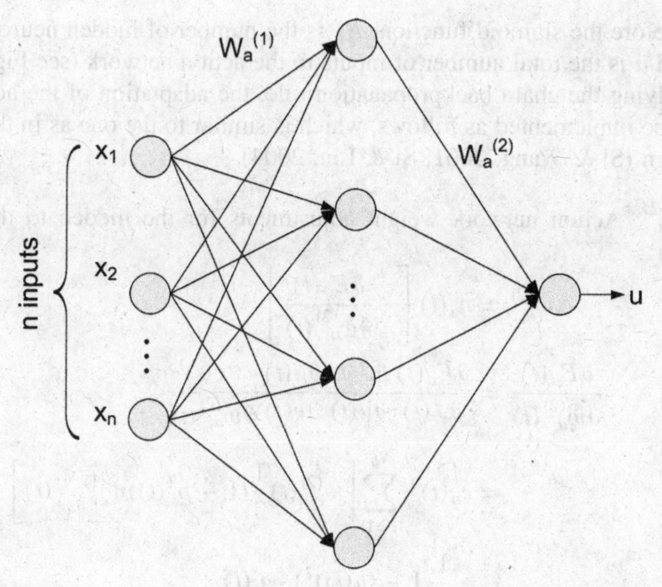

Figure 5.4: Action network with nonlinear neural network with one hidden layer.

Figure 5.4 shows the action network used in this design, which includes n inputs of the system states $\boldsymbol{X}$ and one output of the action value u. The principle in adapting the action network is to indirectly backpropagate the error between the desired ultimate objective $U_c(t)$ and the approximate J function from the critic network. Similar to Si and Wang (2001) and Si & Liu (2004), since we define "0" as the primary reinforcement signal for "success", $U_c(t)$ is set to "0" in our current design in this chapter. As we have discussed in section 5.3.2, the error function $E_a(t)$ used to update the parameters in the action network is defined according to equation (5.4). According to Figure 5.4, the associated equations for the action network are defined as:

$$u(t) = \frac{1 - exp^{-v(t)}}{1 + exp^{-v(t)}}, \tag{5.10}$$

$$v(t) = \sum_{i=1}^{N_h} w_{a_i}^{(2)}(t) g_i(t), \tag{5.11}$$

$$g_i(t) = \frac{1 - exp^{-h_i(t)}}{1 + exp^{-h_i(t)}}, \quad i = 1, \ldots, N_h \tag{5.12}$$

$$h_i(t) = \sum_{j=1}^{n} w_{a_{i,j}}^{(1)}(t) x_j(t), \quad i = 1, \ldots, N_h \tag{5.13}$$

where h_i is the ith hidden node input of the action network and g_i is the corresponding output of the hidden node, v is the input to the output node of the action network before the sigmoid function, N_h is the number of hidden neurons of the action, and n is the total number of inputs to the action network (see Figure 5.4).

By applying the chain backpropagation rule, the adaptation of the action network can be implemented as follows, which is similar to the one as in the classic ADP design (Si & Wang, 2001; Si & Liu, 2004).

1. $\Delta w_a^{(2)}$: Action network weight adjustments for the hidden to the output layer:

$$\Delta w_{a_i}^{(2)} = \eta_a(t)\left[-\frac{\partial E_a(t)}{\partial w_{a_i}^{(2)}(t)}\right] \tag{5.14}$$

$$\begin{aligned}\frac{\partial E_a(t)}{\partial w_{a_i}^{(2)}(t)} &= \frac{\partial E_a(t)}{\partial J(t)}\frac{\partial J(t)}{\partial u(t)}\frac{\partial u(t)}{\partial v(t)}\frac{\partial v(t)}{\partial w_{a_i}^{(2)}(t)} \\ &= e_a(t)\cdot\sum_{i=1}^{N_h}\left[w_{c_i}^{(2)}(t)\frac{1}{2}(1-p_i^2(t))w_{c_{i,\,n+1}}^{(1)}(t)\right] \\ &\quad\cdot\frac{1}{2}(1-(u(t))^2)\cdot g_i(t).\end{aligned} \tag{5.15}$$

2. $\Delta w_a^{(1)}$: Action network weight adjustments for the input to the hidden layer:

$$\Delta w_{a_{i,j}}^{(1)} = \eta_a(t)\left[-\frac{\partial E_a(t)}{\partial w_{a_{i,j}}^{(1)}(t)}\right] \tag{5.16}$$

$$\begin{aligned}\frac{\partial E_a(t)}{\partial w_{a_{i,j}}^{(1)}(t)} &= \frac{\partial E_a(t)}{\partial J(t)}\frac{\partial J(t)}{\partial u(t)}\frac{\partial u(t)}{\partial v(t)}\frac{\partial v(t)}{\partial g_i(t)}\frac{\partial g_i(t)}{\partial h_i(t)}\frac{\partial h_i(t)}{\partial w_{a_{i,j}}^{(1)}(t)} \\ &= e_a(t)\cdot\sum_{i=1}^{N_h}\left[w_{c_i}^{(2)}(t)\frac{1}{2}(1-p_i^2(t))w_{c_{i,n+1}}^{(1)}(t)\right] \\ &\quad\cdot\frac{1}{2}(1-(u(t))^2)\cdot w_{a_i}^{(2)}(t)\cdot\frac{1}{2}(1-g_{g_i}^2(t))\cdot x_j(t).\end{aligned} \tag{5.17}$$

5.3.2.2 *The Reference Network* Figure 5.5 shows the reference network used in this design with a three-layer nonlinear architecture (with one hidden layer). To calculate the backpropagation, we first need to define the reference network output $s(t)$ as follows.

$$s(t) = \frac{1-exp^{-k(t)}}{1+exp^{-k(t)}}. \tag{5.18}$$

$$k(t) = \sum_{i=1}^{N_h} w_{f_i}^{(2)}(t)y_i(t), \tag{5.19}$$

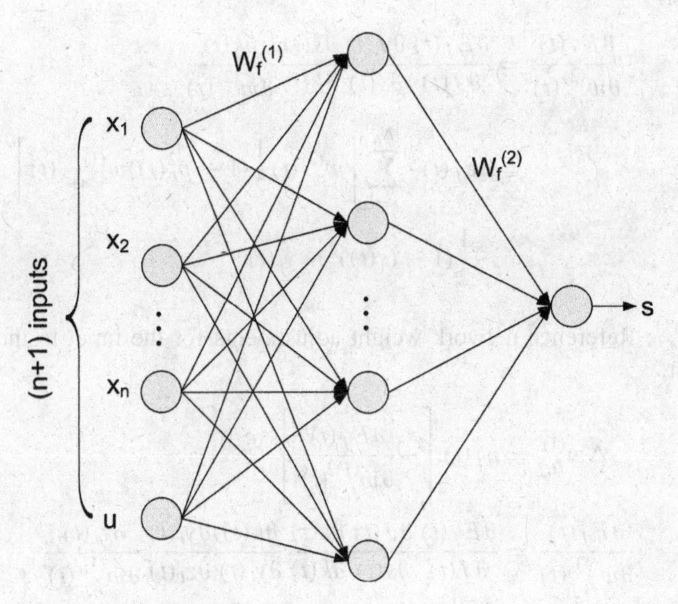

Figure 5.5: Reference network with nonlinear neural network with one hidden layer.

$$y_i(t) = \frac{1 - exp^{-z_i(t)}}{1 + exp^{-z_i(t)}}, \quad i = 1, \ldots, N_h \tag{5.20}$$

$$z_i(t) = \sum_{j=1}^{n+1} w_{f_{i,j}}^{(1)}(t) x_j(t), \quad i = 1, \ldots, N_h \tag{5.21}$$

where z_i is the ith hidden node input of the reference network and y_i is the corresponding output of the hidden node, k is the input to the output node of the reference network before the sigmoid function, N_h is the number of hidden neurons of the reference network, and $(n + 1)$ is the total number of inputs to the reference network, including the action value $u(t)$ from the action network (see Figure 5.4).

To apply the backpropagation rule, one can refer to Figure 5.3 and equations (5.5) and (5.8). Specifically, since the output $s(t)$ is an input to the critic network, backpropagation can be applied here through the chain rule (path 2) to adapt the parameters W_f. This procedure is illustrated as follows.

1. $\Delta w_f^{(2)}$: Reference network weight adjustments for the hidden to the output layer.

$$\Delta w_{f_i}^{(2)} = \eta_f(t) \left[-\frac{\partial E_f(t)}{\partial w_{f_i}^{(2)}(t)} \right] \tag{5.22}$$

$$\frac{\partial E_f(t)}{\partial w_{fi}^{(2)}(t)} = \frac{\partial E_f(t)}{\partial J(t)} \frac{\partial J(t)}{\partial s(t)} \frac{\partial s(t)}{\partial k(t)} \frac{\partial k(t)}{\partial w_{fi}^{(2)}(t)} \tag{5.23}$$

$$= \alpha e_f(t) \cdot \sum_{i=1}^{N_h} \left[w_{c_i}^{(2)}(t) \frac{1}{2}(1 - p_i^2(t)) w_{c_{i,n+2}}^{(1)}(t) \right]$$

$$\cdot \frac{1}{2}(1 - (s(t))^2) \cdot y_i(t)$$

2. $\Delta w_f^{(1)}$: Reference network weight adjustments for the input to the hidden layer.

$$\Delta w_{f_{i,j}}^{(1)} = \eta_f(t) \left[-\frac{\partial E_f(t)}{\partial w_{f_{i,j}}^{(1)}(t)} \right] \tag{5.24}$$

$$\frac{\partial E_f(t)}{\partial w_{f_{i,j}}^{(1)}(t)} = \frac{\partial E_f(t)}{\partial J(t)} \frac{\partial J(t)}{\partial s(t)} \frac{\partial s(t)}{\partial k(t)} \frac{\partial k(t)}{\partial y_i(t)} \frac{\partial y_i(t)}{\partial z_i(t)} \frac{\partial z_i(t)}{\partial w_{f_{i,j}}^{(1)}(t)} \tag{5.25}$$

$$= \alpha e_f(t) \cdot \sum_{i=1}^{N_h} \left[w_{c_i}^{(2)}(t) \frac{1}{2}(1 - p_i^2(t)) w_{c_{i,n+2}}^{(1)}(t) \right]$$

$$\cdot \frac{1}{2}(1 - (s(t))^2) \cdot w_{fi}^{(2)}(t) \cdot \frac{1}{2}(1 - y_i^2(t)) \cdot x_j(t)$$

Once the reference network provides the secondary reinforcement signal $s(t)$ to the critic network, one can adapt the parameters in the critic network.

5.3.2.3 *The Critic Network* Figure 5.6 shows the critic network used in our current design with a three-layer nonlinear architecture (with one hidden layer). To calculate the backpropagation, we first need to define the critic network output $J(t)$ as follows.

$$J(t) = \sum_{i=1}^{N_h} w_{c_i}^{(2)}(t) p_i(t), \tag{5.26}$$

$$p_i(t) = \frac{1 - exp^{-q_i(t)}}{1 + exp^{-q_i(t)}}, \quad i = 1, \ldots, N_h \tag{5.27}$$

$$q_i(t) = \sum_{j=1}^{n+2} w_{c_{i,j}}^{(1)}(t) x_j(t), \quad i = 1, \ldots, N_h \tag{5.28}$$

where q_i and p_i are the input and output of the ith hidden node of the critic network, respectively, and $(n+2)$ is the total number of inputs to the critic network

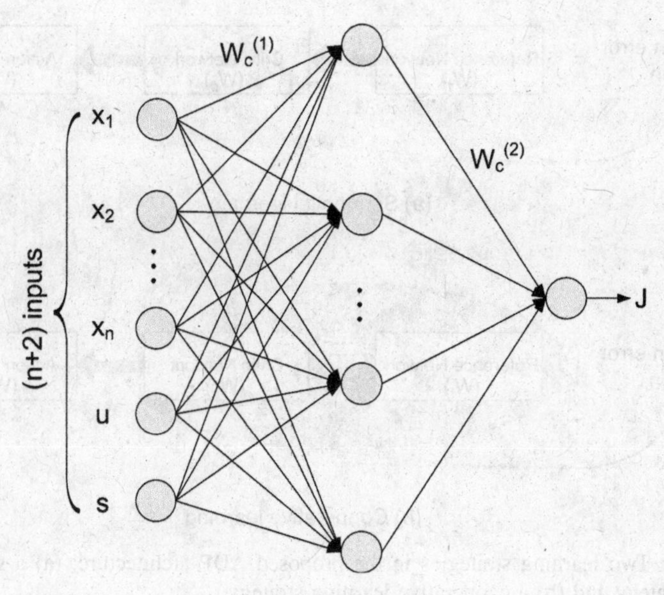

Figure 5.6: Critic network with nonlinear neural network with one hidden layer.

including the action value $u(t)$ from the action network and the secondary reinforcement signal $s(t)$ from the reference network.

By applying the chain backpropagation rule (path 3), the procedure of adapting parameters in the critic network is summarized as follows.

1. $\Delta w_c^{(2)}$: Critic network weight adjustments for the hidden to the output layer.

$$\Delta w_{c_i}^{(2)} = \eta_c(t)\left[-\frac{\partial E_c(t)}{\partial w_{c_i}^{(2)}(t)}\right] \tag{5.29}$$

$$\frac{\partial E_c(t)}{\partial w_{c_i}^{(2)}(t)} = \frac{\partial E_c(t)}{\partial J(t)}\frac{\partial J(t)}{\partial w_{c_i}^{(2)}(t)} = \alpha e_c(t)\cdot p_i(t) \tag{5.30}$$

2. $\Delta w_c^{(1)}$: Critic network weight adjustments for the input to the hidden layer.

$$\Delta w_{c_{i,j}}^{(1)} = \eta_c(t)\left[-\frac{\partial E_c(t)}{\partial w_{c_{i,j}}^{(1)}(t)}\right] \tag{5.31}$$

$$\begin{aligned}\frac{\partial E_c(t)}{\partial w_{c_{i,j}}^{(1)}(t)} &= \frac{\partial E_c(t)}{\partial J(t)}\frac{\partial J(t)}{\partial p_i(t)}\frac{\partial p_i(t)}{\partial q_i(t)}\frac{\partial q_i(t)}{\partial w_{c_{i,j}}^{(1)}(t)} \\ &= \alpha e_c(t)\cdot w_{c_i}^{(2)}(t)\cdot\frac{1}{2}(1-p_i^2(t))\cdot x_j(t)\end{aligned} \tag{5.32}$$

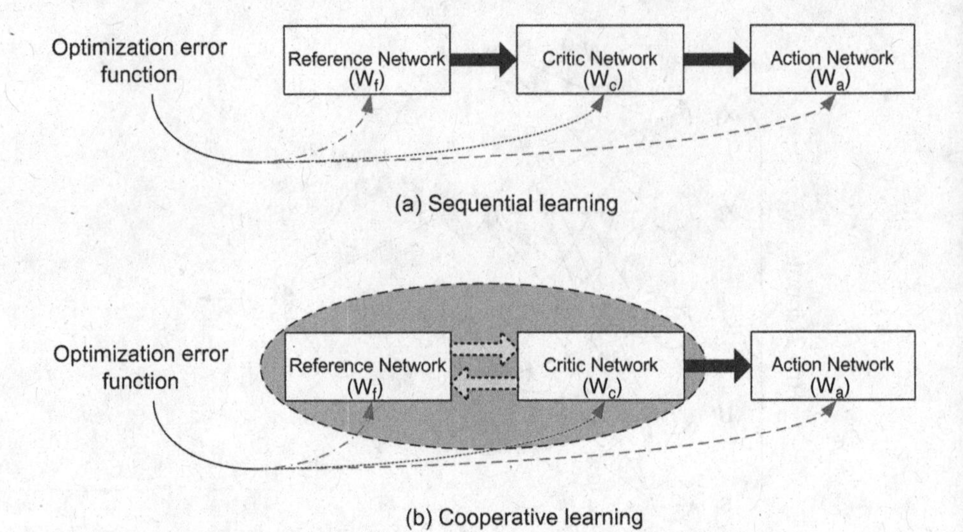

Figure 5.7: Two learning strategies in the proposed ADP architecture: (a) a sequential learning strategy and (b) a cooperative learning strategy.

5.3.3 Learning Strategies: Sequential Learning and Cooperative Learning

By observing Figures 5.2 and 5.3, one can see that, the $s(t)$ signal provides an important link between the reference network and critic network, which makes the chain backpropagation able to adjust the parameters in the reference network and critic network. From this observation, there are two learning strategies that can be implemented in practice.

The first one is a sequential learning procedure, as illustrated in Figure 5.7(a). In this type of learning strategy, one first tunes the weights of the reference network W_f according to equations (5.22) to (5.25). After the adaptation process, the reference network will output the $s(t)$ signal, which is used to adapt the critic network according to equations (5.29) to (5.32), and finally one can adjust the weights for the action network according to equations (5.14) to (5.17).

The second learning strategy is cooperative learning, as shown in Figure 5.7(b), which involves more interactions between the reference network and the critic network. In this learning strategy, at each epoch of the parameter tuning, one can first adapt the reference network W_f based on the primary reinforcement signal $r(t)$ through backpropagation. Then the reference network will output the secondary reinforcement signal $s(t)$, which will be used to tune the parameters in the critic network W_c through backpropagation. Once W_c is tuned in this epoch, the critic network will provide a new $J(t)$ estimation, which in turn can be used to adapt the W_f in the next epoch. In this way, the reference network and critic network are trained in a more collaborative style.

5.4 CASE STUDY

In this section, we present a case study of the proposed ADP architecture for the control of the cart-pole balancing problem, a popular benchmark in the community (Si & Wang, 2001; Si & Liu, 2004; Anderson, 1987, 1989; Barto, Sutton, & Anderson, 1983) (Moriarty & Miikulainen, 1996). In our current study, the cart-pole balancing model we considered is identical to that in Si and Wang (2001), Si & Liu (2004), Barto et al. (1983), which can be described as follows.

$$\frac{d^2\theta}{dt^2} = \frac{g\sin\theta + \cos\theta[-F - ml\dot{\theta}^2\sin\theta + \mu_c \operatorname{sgn}(\dot{x})] - \frac{\mu_p\dot{\theta}}{ml}}{l(\frac{4}{3} - \frac{m\cos^2\theta}{m_c+m})} \tag{5.33}$$

$$\frac{d^2x}{dt^2} = \frac{F + ml[\dot{\theta}^2\sin\theta - \ddot{\theta}\cos\theta] - \mu_c \operatorname{sgn}(\dot{x})}{m_c + m} \tag{5.34}$$

where

g: $9.8 m/s^2$, acceleration due to gravity;
m_c: 1.0 kg, mass of cart;
m: 0.1 kg, mass of pole;
l: 0.5 meter, half-pole length;
μ_c: 0.0005, coefficient of friction of cart on track;
μ_p: 0.000002, coefficient of friction of pole on cart;
F: ± 10 Newtons, force applied to cart center of mass

$$\operatorname{sgn}(x)\text{: here } \operatorname{sgn}(x) = \begin{cases} 1, & if \quad x > 0 \\ 0, & if \quad x = 0 \\ -1, & if \quad x < 0 \end{cases}$$

This system has four state variables: $x(t)$ is the position of the cart on track, $\theta(t)$is the angle of the pole with respect to the vertical position, and $\dot{x}$ and $\dot{\theta}$ are the cart velocity and angular velocity, respectively.

The experiment's setup is also similar to those in Si and Wang (2001). Specifically, a run in our current simulation includes a maximum of 1,000 consecutive trials. A run is considered successful if the last trial (trial number less than 1,000 in this case) of the run lasted 600,000 time steps. Otherwise, if the controller is unable to learn to balance the cart-pole within 1,000 trials, that is to say, none of the 1,000 trials in a run can last over 600,000 time steps, then this run is considered unsuccessful. Each run is initialized to random conditions, and a trial is a complete process from start to fall (we also adopted the same time step of 0.02 as in Si and Wang (2001) in our current study). A pole is considered fallen when the pole is outside the range of $[-12°, 12°]$ or the cart is moving beyond the range of $[-2.4, +2.4]$ meters in reference to the central position on the track. In our current study, for the primary reinforcement signal $r(t)$, we use a simple binary representation as either a 0 or a -1 to represent "success" or "failure," while for the secondary reinforcement signal $s(t)$, the reference network in the proposed

ADP architecture (see Figure 5.2) will automatically build such an internal reinforcement representation to facilitate the learning and optimization process.

For detailed experimental parameters, Table 5.1 summarizes all the parameters used in this chapter. We would like to note that for fair comparison, we adopted the same parameters for the action network and critic network as in Si and Wang (2001). For the action network, critic network, and reference network, their weights w_a, w_c, and w_f are adjusted based on their corresponding internal cycles, N_a, N_c, and N_f, respective. This means within each time step, these weights are updated at most N_a, N_c, and N_f times, respectively, or stopped once their corresponding internal training error threshold T_a, T_c, and T_f have been met. This is also the same configuration as in Si and Wang (2001).

Furthermore, to evaluate the control performance under different noise conditions, we also conducted a series of experiments with noises on both sensor and

Table 5.1: Summary of the Parameters Used in This Chapter

Parameter symbol	Parameter representation	Parameter value
$\eta_c(0)$	Initial learning rate of the critic network	0.3
$\eta_a(0)$	Initial learning rate of the action network	0.3
$\eta_f(0)$	Initial learning rate of the reference network	0.3
$\eta_c(t)$	Learning rate of the critic network at time t	$\eta_c(t)$ is decreased by 0.05 every 5 time steps until it reaches 0.005 and stays at 0.005 thereafter
$\eta_a(t)$	Learning rate of the action network at time t	$\eta_c(t)$ is decreased by 0.05 every 5 time steps until it reaches 0.005 and stays at 0.005 thereafter
$\eta_f(t)$	Learning rate of the reference network at time t	$\eta_f(t)$ is decreased by 0.05 every 5 time steps until it reaches 0.005 and stays at 0.005 thereafter
N_c	Internal back propagation cycle of the critic network	50
N_a	Internal back propagation cycle of the action network	100
N_f	Internal back propagation cycle of the reference network	50
T_c	Internal training error threshold for the critic network	0.05
T_a	Internal training error threshold for the action network	0.005
T_f	Internal training error threshold for the reference network	0.05
N_h	Number of hidden nodes	6

actuator similar to those in Si and Wang (2001). Specifically, actuator noise is added as follows.

$$u(t) = u(t) \times (1 + \rho) \tag{5.35}$$

where ρ is the noise percentage and only uniform noise is considered for actuator. For the sensor noise, we used the following equation to add different levels of noise to θ.

$$\theta = \theta \times (1 + \rho) \tag{5.36}$$

Again, ρ is the noise percentage and here we consider both uniform and Gaussian noise (with zero mean and specific variance).

Table 5.2 shows the simulation results of the proposed ADP architecture with respect to those reported in Si and Wang (2001). All results are based on the average of 100 random runs. The success rate here is calculated as the ratio of the number of successful runs with respect to the total number of runs (in this case, 100 total runs), and the number of trials is calculated as the average number of those trials within all successful runs. Table 5.2 indicates that both methods can achieve a 100% success rate under different noise conditions. By observing the average number of trials that the system needs to learn to balance the cart-pole with both methods (the last two columns of Table 5.2), it suggests that the proposed ADP architecture in this chapter is able to provide better performance. Figure 5.8(a) and Figure 5.8(b) show a snapshot of a typical position trajectory (in meters) and its corresponding histogram for a successful run, and Figure 5.9(a) and 5.9(b) show a snapshot of a typical angle trajectory (in degrees) and its

Table 5.2: Performance Comparison of the Proposed Method with Respect to Those Reported in Si and Wang (2001)

Noise Type	Successful Rate		Number of Trials	
	Reference (Si & Wang, 2001)	Proposed ADP Architecture	Reference (Si & Wang, 2001)	Proposed ADP Architecture
Noise free	100%	100%	6	**5.5**
Uniform 5% actuator	100%	100%	8	**6.86**
Uniform 10% actuator	100%	100%	14	**9.33**
Uniform 5% sensor	100%	100%	32	**11.18**
Uniform 10% sensor	100%	100%	54	**14.14**
Gaussian $\sigma^2 = 0.1$ sensor	100%	100%	164	**44.33**
Gaussian $\sigma^2 = 0.2$ sensor	100%	100%	193	**85.52**

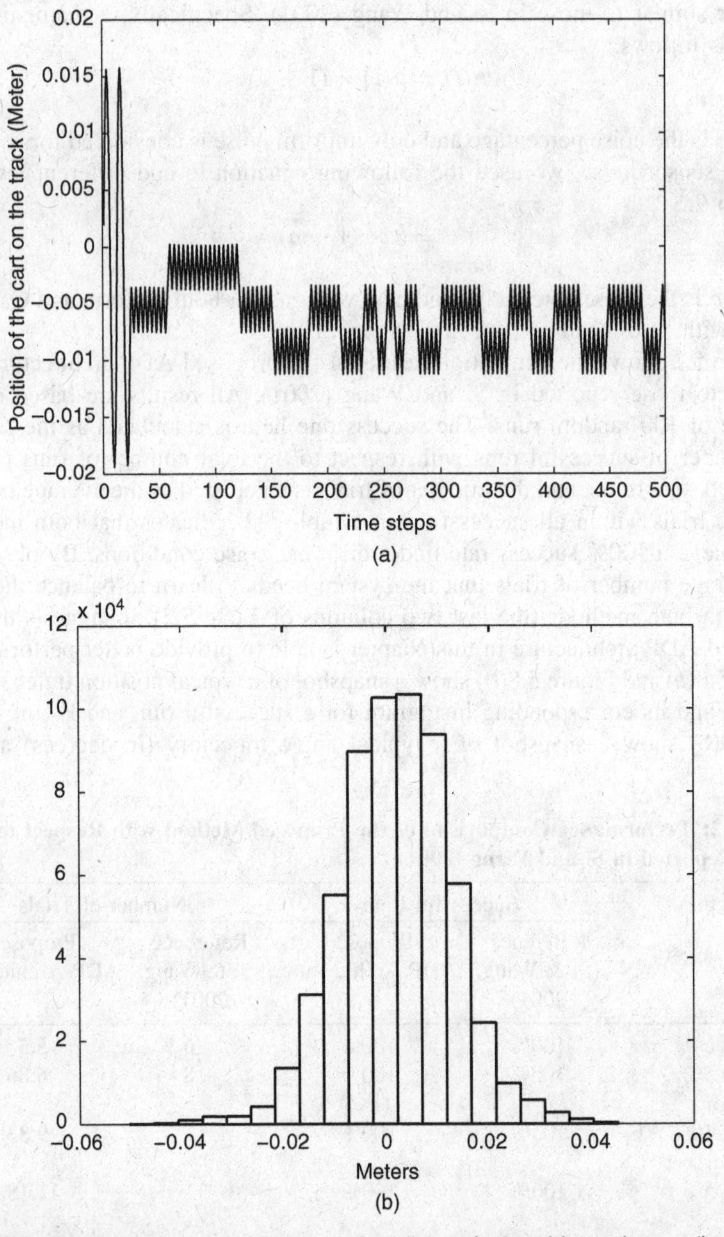

Figure 5.8: Position trajectory of the cart-pole. (a) A typical position trajectory (in meters) in a successful learning trial. (b) Histogram of the position trajectory in a successful learning trial.

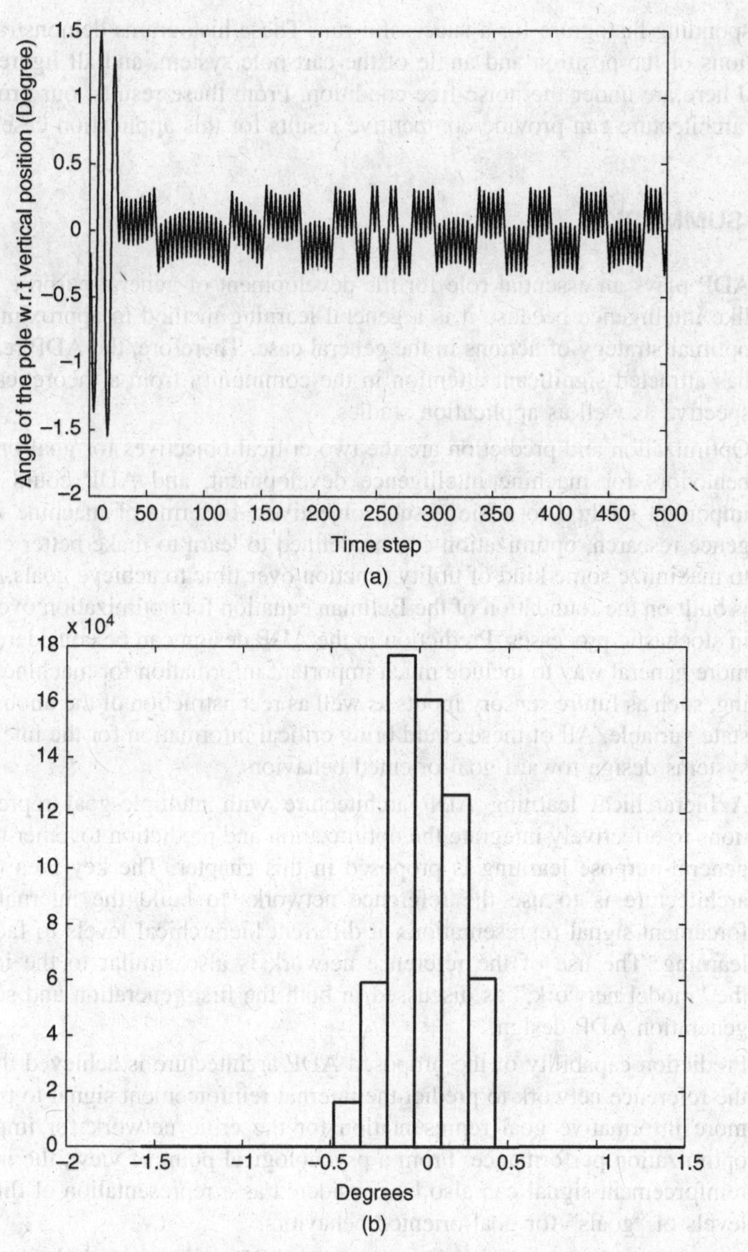

Figure 5.9: Angle trajectory of the cart-pole. (a) A typical angle trajectory (in degrees) in a successful learning trial; (b) Histogram of the angle trajectory in a successful learning trial.

corresponding histogram for a successful run. These histograms demonstrate the variations of the position and angle of the cart-pole system, and all figures presented here are under the noise-free condition. From these results, our proposed ADP architecture can provide competitive results for this application case.

5.5 SUMMARY

- ADP plays an essential role for the development of general-purpose brain-like intelligence because it is a general learning method to approximate an optimal strategy of actions in the general case. Therefore, the ADP research has attracted significant attention in the community from a theoretical perspective as well as application studies.
- Optimization and prediction are the two critical objectives for goal-oriented behaviors for machine intelligence development, and ADP could be an important method to achieve such objectives. In terms of machine intelligence research, optimization can be defined to learn to make better choices to maximize some kind of utility function over time to achieve goals, which is built on the foundation of the Bellman equation for optimization over time in stochastic processes. Prediction in the ADP design can be considered in a more general way to include much important information for machine learning, such as future sensory inputs as well as reconstruction of the unobserved state variable. All of these could bring critical information for the intelligent systems design toward goal-oriented behaviors.
- A hierarchical learning ADP architecture with multiple-goal representations to effectively integrate the optimization and prediction together toward general-purpose learning is proposed in this chapter. The key idea of this architecture is to use the reference networks to build the internal reinforcement signal representations at different hierarchical levels to facilitate learning. The use of the reference network is also similar to the idea of the "model network," as discussed in both the first-generation and second-generation ADP design.
- Prediction capability of the proposed ADP architecture is achieved through the reference network to predict the internal reinforcement signal to provide more informative goal representation for the critic network for improved optimization performance. From a psychological point of view, the internal reinforcement signal can also be considered as a representation of different levels of "goals" for goal-oriented behaviors.
- Learning and adaptation in the proposed ADP architecture is built on the chain backpropagation rule. Two types of learning strategies can be implemented in the proposed ADP architecture: a sequential learning procedure and a cooperative learning strategy.

REFERENCES

Al-Tamimi, A., Abu-Khalaf, M., & Lewis, F. L. (2007). Adaptive critic designs for discrete-time zero-sum games with application to h-infinity control. *IEEE Trans. on Syst. Man, Cybern., Part B*, *37*(1), 240–247.

Anderson, C. (1987). Strategy learning with multi-layer connectionist representation. *Proc. International Workshop on Machine Learning*, pp. 103–114.

Anderson, C. (1989). Learning to control an inverted pendulum using neural networks. *IEEE Control Syst. Mag.*, *9*(3), 31–37.

Balakrishnan, S. N., Ding, J., & Lewis, F. L. (2008). Issues on stability of adp feedback controllers for dynamical systems. *IEEE Trans. on Syst. Man, Cybern., Part B, special issue on ADP/RL, invited survey paper*, *38*(4), 913–917.

Barto, A. G., Sutton, R. S., & Anderson, C. W. (1983). Neuron like adaptive elements that can solve difficult learning control problems. *IEEE Trans. on Syst. Man, Cybern.*, *13*, 834–847.

Bellman, R. E. (1957). *Dynamic programming*. Princeton, NJ: Princeton University Press.

Bertsekas, D. P., & Tsitsiklis, J. (1996). *Neuro-dynamic programming*. Athena Scientific.

Derbyshire, S. W. G., Jones, A. K. P., Gyulai, F., Clark, S., Townsend, D., & Firestone, L. L. (1997). Pain processing during three levels of noxious stimulation produces differential patterns of central activity. *Pain*, *73*(3), 431–445.

Enns, R., & Si, J. (2004). Handbook of learning and approximate dynamic programming. In J. Si, A. G. Barto, W. B. Powell, & D. C. Wunsch (Eds.), *Handbook of learning and approximate dynamic programming* (pp. 535–559). Piscataway, NJ: IEEE Press.

Feldkamp, L., Prokhorov, D., Eagen, C., & Yuan, F. (1998). Nonlinear modeling: Advanced black-box techniques. In J. Suykens & J. Vandewalle (Eds.), (pp. 29–53). Norwell, MA: Kluwer.

Feldkamp, L. A., & Prokhorov, D. V. (2003). Recurrent neural networks for state estimation. In K. Narendra (Ed.), *Proc. Workshop on Adaptive And Learning Systems*. New Haven, CT: Yale University.

Ferrari, S., & Stengel, R. F. (2004). *Handbook of learning and approximate dynamic programming*. Piscataway, NJ: IEEE Press.

Fogel, D. B., Hays, T. J., Han, S. L., & Quon, J. (2004). A self-learning evolutionary chess program. *Proc. of the IEEE*, 92, 1947–1954.

Frijda, N. H. (1987). *The emotions*. Cambridge, UK: Cambridge University Press.

Geramifard, A., Bowling, M., & Sutton, R. S. (2006). Incremental least-squares temporal difference learning. *Proc. Twenty-First National Conf. Artificial Intelligence*, pp. 356–361.

Hsieh, J. C., Tu, C. H., & Chen, F. P. (2001). Activation of the hypothalamus characterizes the acupuncture stimulation at the analgesic point in human: A positron emission tomography study. *Neurosci. Lett.*, *307*, 105–108.

Ilin, R., Kozma, R., & Werbos, P. J. (2008). Beyond feedforward models trained by backpropagation: A practical training tool for a more efficient universal approximator. *IEEE Trans. on Neural Netw.*, *19*(6), 929–937.

Kaelbling, L. P., Littman, M. L., & Moore, A. W. (1996). Reinforcement learning: A survey. *Journal of Artificial Intelligence Research*, *4*, 237–285.

Liu, D., & Jin, N. (2009). Adaptive dynamic programming for discrete-time systems with infinite horizon and epsilon-error bound in the performance cost. *Proc. IEEE Int. Conf. Neural Netw.*

Melzack, R. (1990). Phantom limbs and the concept of a neuromatrix. *Trends Neurosci.*, *13*, 88–92.

Moriarty, D. E., & Miikulainen, R. (1996). Efficient reinforcement learning through symbiotic evolution. *Machine Learning*, *22*, 11–32.

Nicolelis, M. A., Baccala, L. A., Lin, R. C., & Chapin, J. K.. (1995) Sensorimotor encoding by synchronous neural ensemble activity at multiple levels of the somatosensory system. *Science*, *268*(5215), 1353–1358.

Nicolelis, M. A. L., Lin, R. C., Woodward, D. J., & Chapin, J. K. (1993). Induction of immediate spatiotemporal changes in thalamic networks by peripheral block of ascending cutaneous information. *Nature*, *361*(6412), 533–536.

Peyron, R., Laurent, B., & Garcia-Larrea, L. (2000). Functional imaging of brain responses to pain. a review and meta-analysis. *Neurophysiol Clin.*, *30*, 263–288.

Powell, W. B. (2007). *Approximate dynamic programming: Solving the curses of dimensionality*. Hoboken, NJ: Wiley-Interscience.

Prokhorov, D. V., & Wunsch, D. C. (1997). Adaptive critic designs. *IEEE Trans. on Neural Netw.*, *8*(5), 997–1007.

Puskorius, G. V., & Feldkamp, L. A. (1994). Neurocontrol of nonlinear dynamical systems with kalman filter trained recurrent networks. *IEEE Trans. on Neural Netw.*, *5*(2), 279–297.

Qiao, W., Venayagamoorthy, G., & Harley, R. (2007). DHP-based wide-area coordinating control of a power system with a large wind farm and multiple FACTS devices. *Proc. IEEE Int. Conf. Neural Netw.*, pp. 2093–2098.

Rafols, E. J., Ring, M. B., Sutton, R. S., & Tanner, B. (2005). Using predictive representations to improve generalization in reinforcement learning. *Proc. Twenty-First National Conf. Artificial Intelligence*, pp. 835–840.

Ray, S., Venayagamoorthy, G. K., Chaudhuri, B., & Majumder, R. (2008). Comparison of adaptive critics and classical approaches based wide area controllers for a power system. *IEEE Trans. on Syst. Man, Cybern., Part B*, *38*(4), 1002–1007.

Si, J., Barto, A. G., Powell, W. B., & Wunsch, D. C. (2004). *Handbook of learning and approximate dynamic programming*. Piscataway, NJ: IEEE Press.

Si, J., & Liu, D. (2004). Handbook of learning and approximate dynamic programming. In J. Si, A. G. Barto, W. B. Powell, & D. C. Wunsch (Eds.), *Handbook of learning and approximate dynamic programming* (pp. 125–151). Piscataway, NJ: IEEE Press.

Si, J., & Wang, Y. T. (2001). On-line learning control by association and reinforcement. *IEEE Trans. on Neural Netw.*, *12*(2), 264–276.

Starzyk, J. A., Liu, Y., & He, H. (2006). Challenges of embodied intelligence. *Proc. Int. Conf. Signals and Electronic Syst.*, pp. 534–541.

Sun, P., & Marko, K. (1998). Optimal learning rate for training time lagged recurrent neural networks with the extended kalman filter algorithm. *Proc. IEEE Int. Conf. Neural Netw.*, 2, 1287–1292.

Sutton, R. S., & Barto, A. G. (1998). *Reinforcement learning: An introduction*. Cambridge, MA: MIT Press.

Vamvoudakis, K., & Lewis, F. L. (2009). Online actor critic algorithm to solve the continuous-time infinite horizon optimal control problem. *Proc. IEEE Int. Conf. Neural Netw*.

Venayagamoorthy, G. K., & Harley, R. G. (2004). Handbook of learning and approximate dynamic programming. In J. Si, A. G. Barto, W. B. Powell, & D. C. Wunsch (Eds.), *Handbook of learning and approximate dynamic programming* (pp. 479–515). Piscataway, NJ: IEEE Press.

Venayagamoorthy, G. K., Harley, R. G., & Wunsch, D. C. (2003). Dual heuristic programming excitation neurocontrol for generators in a multimachine power system. *IEEE Trans. on Industry Applications*, *39*(2), 382–394.

Wang, F. Y., Zhang, H., & Liu, D. (2009). Adaptive dynamic programming: An introduction. *IEEE Comput. Intel. Mag*., *4*(2), 39–47.

Werbos, P. J. (1977), *Advanced forecasting methods for global crisis warning and models of intelligence*, General System, Yearbook, Vol. 22, 1977.

Werbos, P. J. (1979). Changes in global policy analysis procedures suggested by new methods of optimization. *Policy Analysis and Information Systems*, *3*(1), 27–52.

Werbos, P. J. (1981). *System modeling and optimization*. New York: Springer.

Werbos, P. J. (1983). Solving and optimizing complex systems: lessons from the EIA long-term energy model. In B. Lev (ed.), *Energy Models and Studies*, North Holland, 1983.

Werbos, P. J. (1987). Building and understanding adaptive systems: A statistical/numerical approach to factory automation and brain research. *IEEE Trans. on Syst. Man, Cybern*., *17*(1), 7–20.

Werbos, P. J. (1988a). Backpropagation: Past and future. *Proc. IEEE Int. Conf. Neural Netw*., pp. I-343–I-353.

Werbos, P. J. (1988b). Generalization of backpropagation with application to a recurrent gas market model. *Neural Netw*., *1*, pp. 339–356.

Werbos, P. J. (1989). Backpropagation and neurocontrol: A review and prospectus. *Proc. IEEE Int. Conf. Neural Netw*., *1*, 209–216.

Werbos, P. J. (1990). Backpropagation through time: What it does and how to do it. *Proc. IEEE*, 78, 1550–1560.

Werbos, P. J. (1991). An overview of neural networks for control. *IEEE Control Syst. Mag*., *11*(1), 40–41.

Werbos, P. J. (1992). In D. A. White & D. A. Sofge (Eds.), *Handbook of intelligent control* (pp. 493–525). New York: Van Nostrand.

Werbos, P. J. (1993). Supervised learning: Can it escape its local minimum? *Proceedings WCNN93*, pp. 358–363.

Werbos, P. J. (1994). *The roots of backpropagation: From ordered derivatives to neural networks and political forecasting*. New York: Wiley-Interscience.

Werbos, P. J. (1995). In M. A. Arbib (Ed.), *Handbook of brain theory and neural networks* (pp. 134–139). Cambridge, MA: MIT Press.

Werbos, P. J. (1998a). Dealing with complexity: *A neural networks approach*. Springer.

Werbos, P. J. (1998b). Multiple models for approximate dynamic programming. In K. Narendra (Ed.), *Proc. Yale Conf. on Learning and Adaptive Systems*. New Haven, CT: Yale University.

Werbos, P. J. (1999). *Encyclopedia of electrical and electronics engineering*. New York: Wiley.

Werbos, P. J. (2002). What do neural nets and quantum theory tell us about mind and reality? In K. Yasue, M. Jibu, & T. D. Senta (Eds.), *No matter, never mind: Proceedings of Toward a Science of Consciousness: Fundamental approaches* (pp. 63–87). Springer.

Werbos, P. J. (2004). *Handbook of learning and approximate dynamic programming*. Piscataway, NJ: IEEE Press.

Werbos, P. J. (2005). Automatic differentiation: Applications, theory and implementations, lecture notes in computational science and engineering. In H. M. Bucker, G. Corliss, P. Hovland, U. Naumann, & B. Norris (Eds.), (Vol. 50, pp. 15–34). Springer.

Werbos, P. J. (2007). Using ADP to understand and replicate brain intelligence: the next level design. *IEEE Int. Symposium on Approximate Dynamic Programming and Reinforcement Learning*, pp. 209–216.

Werbos, P. J. (2008). Stable adaptive control using new critic designs *[Online], Available: http://arxiv.org as adap-org/9810001*.

Werbos, P. J. (2009a). Intelligence in the brain: A theory of how it works and how to build it. *Neural Networks*, 200–212.

Werbos, P. J. (2009b). Putting more brain-like intelligence into the electric power grid: What we need and how to do it. *Proc. IEEE Int. Conf. Neural Netw*.

Werbos, P. J., & Pellionisz, A. (1992). Neurocontrol and neurobiology: New developments and connections. *Proc. IEEE Int. Conf. Neural Netw*., 3, 373–378.

White, D. A., & Sofge, D. A. (1992). *Handbook of intelligent control*. New York: Van Nostrand.

CHAPTER 6

Associative Learning

6.1 INTRODUCTION

Biological intelligent systems use a different memory organization than that of digital computers (Hawkins & Blakeslee, 2004, 2007). Their memory is characterized by associations and self-organization within hierarchical structures for distributed information storage, prediction, and recall. Generally speaking, there are two types of associative learning memories: hetero-associative and auto-associative memory. Hetero-associative memory makes associations between paired patterns, such as words and pictures, while auto-associative memory associates a pattern with itself, recalling stored patterns from fractional parts of the pattern. It is believed that the human brain employs both hetero-associative and auto-associative memory for learning, action planning, and anticipation (Rizzuto & Kahana, 2001; Brown, Dalloz, & Hulme, 1995; Murdock, 1997). The memory formed in the human brain is self-organized and data driven. Self-organization is responsible for formation of hierarchically organized structures not only in the human brain but also in the nervous systems of lower vertebrates (Malsburg, 2003). In this chapter, a self-organizing associative memory capable of both hetero-associative and auto-associative learning is designed and analyzed (Starzyk, He, & Li, 2007). This memory model is hierarchically organized with sparse and local connections, self-organizing processing elements, and probabilistic information transmissions.

6.2 ASSOCIATIVE LEARNING MECHANISM

Associative learning memories have been studied extensively in the community for machine intelligence research. For instance, among hetero-associative studies, a bidirectional associative memory (BAM) using feedback neural networks was proposed in Salih, Smith, and Liu (2000). The perceptron training algorithm was used to solve a set of linear inequalities for the BAM neural network design. In Chang and Cho (2003), an adaptive local training rule for the second-order asymmetric bidirectional associative memory design was proposed. Multi-associative neural network (MANN) was studied in Wang (1999), and

Self-Adaptive Systems for Machine Intelligence, First Edition. Haibo He.

was successfully applied to learning and retrieving complex spatio-temporal sequences. Simulation results showed that the proposed MANN model is characterized by fast and accurate learning, and has the ability to store and retrieve a large number of complex sequences of spatial patterns. As far as auto-associative memory is concerned, Hopfield's (1982) paper is a classic reference in this field. Since that paper, many research results have been proposed. For instance, an algorithm for auto-associative memory in sparsely connected networks was proposed in Vogel and Boos (1997). The resulting networks have large information storage capacities relative to the number of synapses per neuron. A lower bound on the storage capacities of two-layer projective networks (P-nets) with binary Hebbian synapses was derived in Vogel and Boos. It is reported that given a 1% tolerance for activation of spurious neurons, the P-net with 1,000 synapses per neuron may store more than 1.5×10^6 training vectors with 20 active neurons per vector. In Wu and Batalama (2000), an efficient learning algorithm for feedforward associative memory was proposed. This memory uses a winner-take-all (WTA) mechanism and involves a two-layer feedforward neural network. Recently, enhanced fuzzy morphological auto-associative memory based on the empirical kernel map was also proposed in Wang and Chen (2005). In this chapter, we focus on the understanding of the associative learning principle within the distributed hierarchical neural network organization.

6.2.1 Structure Individual Processing Elements

The self-organizing associative memory presented in this chapter consists of a multilayer array of processing elements (PE). Figure 6.1 gives the interface model of an individual PE, which consists of two inputs (I_1 and I_2) and one output (O). All the inputs and the output are bidirectional, allowing signals to propagate forward and backward. Each PE stores observed probabilities p_{00}, p_{01}, p_{10}, and p_{11} corresponding to four different combinations of inputs I_1 and I_2 ($\{I_1, I_2\} =$ {00}, {01}, {10}, {11}), respectively. These probabilities specify data distribution in each PE's input space, and are used to make associations.

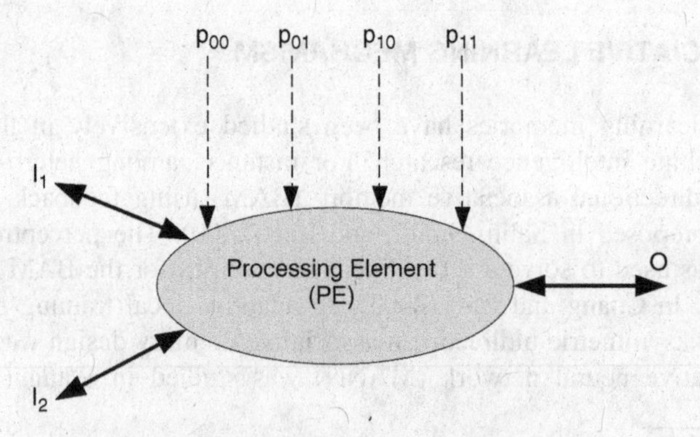

Figure 6.1: Individual PE interface model.

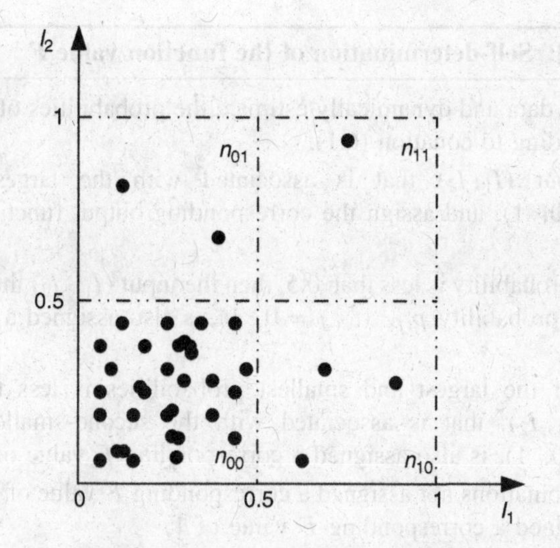

Figure 6.2: An example of input space distribution.

Figure 6.2 gives an example of possible distribution of the observed input data points. Probabilities are estimated as follows.

$$p_{00} = \frac{n_{00}}{n_{tot}}, \; p_{01} = \frac{n_{01}}{n_{tot}}, \; p_{10} = \frac{n_{10}}{n_{tot}}, \; p_{11} = \frac{n_{11}}{n_{tot}} \tag{6.1}$$

where n_{00}, n_{01}, n_{10}, and n_{11} are the number of data points located in $I_1 < 0.5$ & $I_2 < 0.5$, $I_1 < 0.5$ & $I_2 > 0.5$, $I_1 > 0.5$ & $I_2 < 0.5$, and $I_1 > 0.5$ & $I_2 > 0.5$, respectively. The value n_{tot} is the total number of data points defined as $n_{tot} = n_{00} + n_{01} + n_{10} + n_{11}$. An efficient algorithm for dynamic estimation of these probabilities without division on unlimited number of input data can be found in Starzyk and Wang (2004).

6.2.2 Self-Determination of the Function Value

Based on the observed probability distribution p_{00}, p_{01}, p_{10}, and p_{11} of an individual PE as in Figure 6.2, each PE decides its output function value F by specifying its truth table as shown in Table 6.1. The output function values f_{00}, f_{01}, f_{10}, and f_{11} are decided as follows (Starzyk et al., 2007).

Table 6.1: Self-Determination of Function Value *F*

Probability	p_{00}	p_{01}	p_{10}	p_{11}
I_1	0	0	1	1
I_2	0	1	0	1
Function value (F)	f_{00}	f_{01}	f_{10}	f_{11}

[Algorithm 6.1]: Self-determination of the function value F

- Observe input data and dynamically estimate the probabilities of p_{00}, p_{01}, p_{10}, and p_{11} according to equation (6.1);
- Find the input (I_1, I_2) that is associated with the largest probability, p_{ij}, $(i,\ j = 0,\ 1)$, and assign the corresponding output function F value to be 0;
- If the largest probability is less than 0.5, then the input $(I_1,\ I_2)$ that is associated with smallest probability p_{ij}, $(i,\ j = 0,\ 1)$, is also assigned a corresponding F value of 0;
- If the sum of the largest and smallest probabilities is less than 0.5, then the input, (I_1, I_2), that is associated with the second-smallest probability p_{ij}, $(i,\ j = 0,\ 1)$, is also assigned a corresponding F value of 0;
- All input combinations not assigned a corresponding F value of 0 by the above rules are assigned a corresponding F value of 1.

According to [Algorithm 6.1], the probability that the PE is active is no larger than 0.5. This type of assignment is motivated by the sparse activity of biological neurons (Triesch, 2004). In addition to biological motivation, lower activities are also preferable for efficient power consumption. Table 6.2 shows two examples of this self-determination of the function value F.

6.2.3 Signal Strength for Associative Learning

In this associative learning model, external signals are presented to the network in a binary form, while the internal signals have semi-logic values ranging from 0 to 1, where 0 and 1 correspond to logic false (determinate low) and logic true (determinate high), respectively. The signal strength is defined as the absolute value of the distance between the signal level and a specified logic threshold ($Th = 0.5$ in the current model; other threshold values can be used as well, particularly if signals are biased toward 1 or 0):

$$Signal\ strength(SS) = |Signal\ value - logic\ threshold(Th)| \tag{6.2}$$

SS is in the range of $[0,\ 0.5]$. If $SS = 0.5$, the signal is either determinate high (logic true) or determinate low (logic false), corresponding to signal value 1 or

Table 6.2: Two Examples of Setting F Value

p_{00}	p_{01}	p_{10}	p_{11}	F			
0.4	0.2	0.3	0.1	0	1	1	0
0.4	0.05	0.3	0.25	0	0	1	0

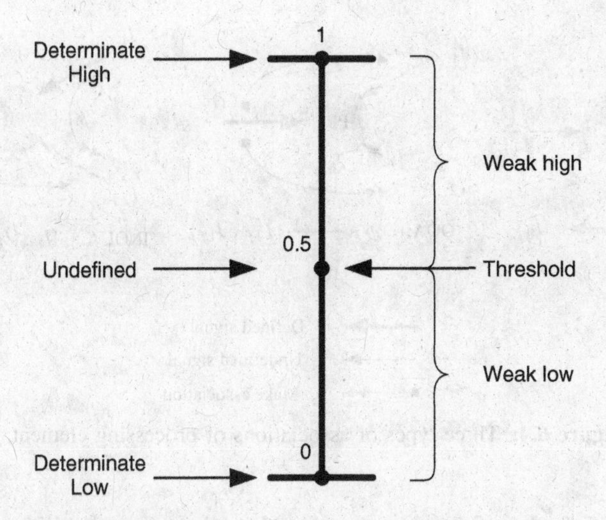

Figure 6.3: Signal strength and its semi-logic value.

0, respectively. If signal value equals Th, it is undefined (inactive) and $SS = 0$. Signals in the range $0 < SS < 0.5$ are intermediate. An intermediate signal is weak low if its value is less than Th or weak high if it is higher than Th.

Figure 6.3 illustrates this definition of the signal strength. In this way, SS provides a coherent mechanism of determining when to trigger an association, and helps to resolve the feedback signal value if more than one feedback signal is presented at the PE's output port (see section 6.3.2.2).

6.2.4 The Associative Learning Principle

During the training stage, each PE counts its input data points in n_{00}, n_{01}, n_{10} and n_{11} and estimates their corresponding probabilities p_{00}, p_{01}, p_{10} and p_{11}. The objective of the training stage for each PE is to discover the potential relationship between its inputs. This relationship is memorized as the corresponding probabilities and is used to make associations during the testing stage.

Figure 6.4 illustrates three types of associations used in the testing stage to infer the undefined signal value.

1. Input-only association (IOA). If, in the testing stage, one input is defined while the other input and the received output feedback signal O_f from other PEs are undefined (for instance, if $I_1 = 0$, $I_2 = 0.5$ and $O_f = 0.5$ as in Figure 6.4(a)), this PE will determine I_2 through association with I_1.
2. Output-only association (OOA). If both inputs, I_1 and I_2, are undefined, a defined feedback signal, O_f, will determine both inputs (Figure 6.4(b)). For instance, let's consider the example in Figure 6.2. This particular PE finds that most of its input data points are distributed in the lower-left corner

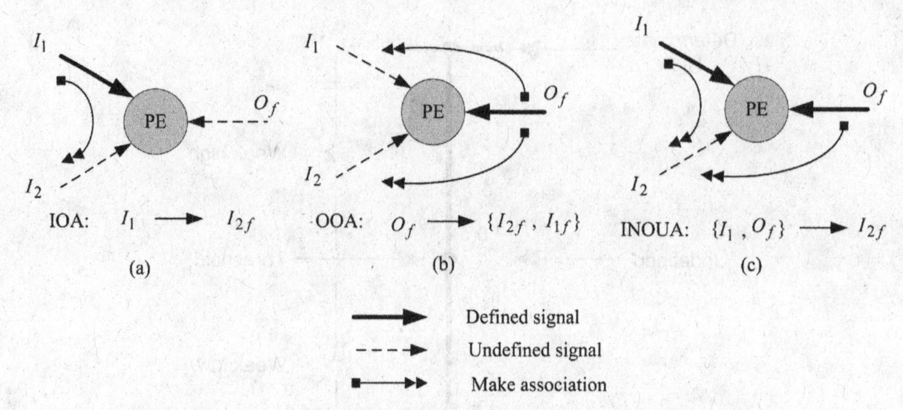

Figure 6.4: Three types of associations of processing element.

$(I_1 < 0.5$ & $I_2 < 0.5)$. Assume that the relevant probabilities are $p_{00} = 0.8$, $p_{01} = 0.07$, $p_{10} = 0.1$ and $p_{11} = 0.03$, resulting in $F = \{0, 1, 1, 1\}$ according to [Algorithm 6.1]. In this case, if $O_f = 0$ and both inputs $I_1 = I_2 = 0.5$, then this PE will infer both inputs, I_1 and I_2 to 0. (Here I_{1f} and I_{2f} are used to denote the feedback signals of inputs 1 and 2 to distinguish them from the corresponding feedforward signals I_1 and I_2.) On the other hand, if the received output feedback signal $O_f = 1$, the input feedback values, I_{1f} and I_{2f}, are intermediate and their values will be estimated according to data distribution probabilities.

3. Input–output association (INOUA). If one input and the output feedback signal, O_f, are defined and the other input is undefined, the PE will infer the other input signal according to its observed probabilities, as shown in Figure 6.4(c).

Now, we will formulate the mathematical foundation of the associative learning mechanism (Starzyk et al., 2007). There are four cases:

Case 1: *Given the semi-logic values of both inputs $V(I_1)$ and V_{I_2}, decide the output value $V(O)$*

Assume one PE received input values $V(I_1) = m$ and $V(I_2) = n$, then

$$V(O) = \frac{p(I_1 = 1,\ I_2 = 1,\ F = 1)}{p(I_1 = 1,\ I_2 = 1)} \cdot V_{11} + \frac{p(I_1 = 0,\ I_2 = 1,\ F = 1)}{p(I_1 = 0,\ I_2 = 1)} \cdot V_{01} + \frac{p(I_1 = 1,\ I_2 = 0,\ F = 1)}{p(I_1 = 1,\ I_2 = 0)} \cdot V_{10} + \frac{p(I_1 = 0,\ I_2 = 0,\ F = 1)}{p(I_1 = 0,\ I_2 = 0)} \cdot V_{00} \tag{6.3}$$

where V_{11}, V_{01}, V_{10}, and V_{00} are defined as:

$$V_{11} = mn, \quad (6.4)$$
$$V_{01} = (1 - m)n,$$
$$V_{10} = m(1 - n),$$
$$V_{00} = (1 - m)(1 - n),$$

and $p(I_1 = 1,\ I_2 = 1,\ F = 1)$, $p(I_1 = 1,\ I_2 = 1)$, etc., are joint probabilities that can be obtained from Table 6.1 using probabilities p_{00}, p_{01}, p_{10}, and p_{11}. For instance, if one PE has $F = \{0,\ 1,\ 1,\ 1\}$, then

$$p(I_1 = 1,\ I_2 = 1,\ F = 1) = p_{11}, \quad (6.5)$$
$$p(I_1 = 0,\ I_2 = 0,\ F = 1) = 0,$$
$$p(I_1 = 0,\ I_2 = 1) = p_{01},$$

This case is required when a signal is propagated forward (during both training and testing stages). In the current model, this input and the output semi-logic values are typically 0, 1, or 0.5. However, these equations are still true if other semi-logic values are used.

Case 2: *Given the values of one input, $V(I_1)$ or $V(I_2)$, and an undefined output $V(O)$, decide the value of the other input.*

This case corresponds to IOA as shown in Figure 6.4(a). Consider the situation that given $V(I_1)$ to decide an unknown $V(I_2)$ as follows:

$$V(I_2) = \frac{p(I_1 = 1,\ I_2 = 1)}{p(I_1 = 1)} \cdot V(I_1) + \frac{p(I_1 = 0,\ I_2 = 1)}{p(I_1 = 0)} \cdot (1 - V(I_1)) \quad (6.6)$$

where

$$p(I_1 = 1) = p_{10} + p_{11}, \quad (6.7)$$
$$p(I_1 = 0) = p_{00} + p_{01},$$

In the case in which $V(I_2)$ is given and determines $V(I_1)$, I_1 and I_2 are switched in equation (6.6). This case is required when a signal is propagated backwards (in testing stage).

Case 3: *Given the value of the output $V(O)$, decide the value of both inputs $V(I_1)$ and $V(I_2)$.*

$$V(I_1) = \frac{p(F = 1,\ I_1 = 1)}{p(F = 1)} \cdot V(O) + \frac{p(F = 0,\ I_1 = 1)}{p(F = 0)} \cdot (1 - V(O)) \quad (6.8)$$

$$V(I_2) = \frac{p(F = 1,\ I_2 = 1)}{p(F = 1)} \cdot V(O) + \frac{p(F = 0,\ I_2 = 1)}{p(F = 0)} \cdot (1 - V(O))$$

This corresponds to OOA, as shown in Figure 6.4(b). $p(F=1)$ and $p(F=0)$ are determined by the probability in Table 6.1 in accordance with the F value. For instance, if $F=\{0\ 1\ 0\ 1\}$, then $p(F=1)=p_{01}+p_{11}$ and $p(F=0)=p_{00}+p_{10}$. This case is required when a signal is propagated backwards.

Case 4: *Given the values of one input, $V(I_1)$ or $V(I_2)$, and the output, $V(O)$,* decide the other input value, $V(I_2)$ or $V(I_1)$;

This case corresponds to the INOUA in Figure 6.4(c). For example, consider the case that given $V(I_1)$ and $V(O)$ to decide $V(I_2)$ as follows:

$$\begin{aligned} V(I_2) = {} & \frac{p(I_1=1,\ F=1,\ I_2=1)}{p(I_1=1,\ F=1)}\cdot\hat{V}_{11} \\ & + \frac{p(I_1=0,\ F=1,\ I_2=1)}{p(I_1=0,\ F=1)}\cdot\hat{V}_{01} \\ & + \frac{p(I_1=1,\ F=0,\ I_2=1)}{p(I_1=1,\ F=0)}\cdot\hat{V}_{10} + \frac{p(I_1=0,\ F=0,\ I_2=1)}{p(I_1=0,\ F=0)}\cdot\hat{V}_{00} \end{aligned} \tag{6.9}$$

where $\hat{V}_{11}$, $\hat{V}_{01}$, $\hat{V}_{10}$, and $\hat{V}_{00}$ are determined in the following way:

$$\hat{V}_{11} = \begin{cases} V(I_1)\bullet V(O) & \begin{cases} X\ X\ 0\ 1 \\ X\ X\ 1\ 0 \end{cases} \\ 0 & X\ X\ 0\ 0 \\ V(I_1) & X\ X\ 1\ 1 \end{cases} \tag{6.10}$$

$$\hat{V}_{10} = \begin{cases} V(I_1)\bullet(1-V(O)) & \begin{cases} X\ X\ 0\ 1 \\ X\ X\ 1\ 0 \end{cases} \\ V(I_1) & X\ X\ 0\ 0 \\ 0 & X\ X\ 1\ 1 \end{cases} \tag{6.11}$$

$$\hat{V}_{01} = \begin{cases} (1-V(I_1))\bullet V(O) & \begin{cases} 0\ 1\ X\ X \\ 1\ 0\ X\ X \end{cases} \\ 0 & 0\ 0\ X\ X \\ (1-V(I_1)) & 1\ 1\ X\ X \end{cases} \tag{6.12}$$

$$\hat{V}_{00} = \begin{cases} (1-V(I_1))\bullet(1-V(O)) & \begin{cases} 0\ 1\ X\ X \\ 1\ 0\ X\ X \end{cases} \\ (1-V(I_1)) & 0\ 0\ X\ X \\ 0 & 1\ 1\ X\ X \end{cases} \tag{6.13}$$

The conditions in equations 6.10–6.13 refer to the value of F in Table 6.1, where "X" is a do not care value, which means its value can be either 0 or 1. For example, if one PE received $V(I_1)=m$ and $V(O)=t$, and the function value of this PE is $F = \{0\ 1\ 1\ 1\}$, we will get the following results:

$$\hat{V}_{11} = m, \tag{6.14}$$
$$\hat{V}_{10} = 0,$$
$$\hat{V}_{01} = (1 - m) \times t,$$
$$\hat{V}_{00} = (1 - m) \times (1 - t),$$

When $V(I_2)$ and $V(O)$ are given one only needs to switch I_1 and I_2 in equations (6.9)–(6.13) to decide $V(I_1)$. This case is required when a signal is propagated backwards.

Before we move to the detailed memory structure and operation process, we will first show a simulation result of this probability inference for associative learning. Assume a PE observed the data distribution with probabilities $p_{00} = 0.4$, $p_{01} = 0.2$, $p_{10} = 0.3$ and $p_{11} = 0.1$. According to [Algorithm 6.1], this PE will self-determine its function F value as: $F = \{0\ 1\ 1\ 0\}$. Using the probability inference methods as presented in the four cases, Figure 6.5 illustrates the corresponding associative signal information.

From Figure 6.5(a) one can see that this PE implements a generalized XOR function. To verify these simulation results, take Figure 6.5(b) as an example. Based on the observed probability distribution of $p_{00} = 0.4$, $p_{01} = 0.2$, $p_{10} = 0.3$, and $p_{11} = 0.1$, one can see that if input I_1 is low, then most likely the other input I_2 will also be low (since $p_{00} > p_{01}$). In a similar way, if we know that I_1 is high, then most likely I_2 will be low (since $p_{10} > p_{11}$). The simulation result in Figure 6.5(b) confirms this observation. In a similar way, one can check that all the other simulation results are consistent with the data distribution probability. Therefore, using this probability inference mechanism, one can discover the relationships of the input data that each PE received, and make correct associations in the testing stage to recover the missing data information.

6.3 ASSOCIATIVE LEARNING IN HIERARCHICAL NEURAL NETWORKS

6.3.1 Network Structure

The overall memory network is a hierarchy of sparsely connected self-organizing processing elements. Each PE in the array can self-organize by dynamically adapting its function in response to the input data. All PEs in the memory network have two inputs, I_1 and I_2, and one output, O. Each port is also associated with a feedback signal for input 1, input 2, and the output denoted by I_{1f}, I_{2f}, and O_f, respectively. All the PEs are identical and function according to their own probability distributions. In the hierarchical structure adopted in this research, each PE connects only to PEs in the next lower and higher layers. Such hierarchical connections are suitable for hardware implementation, time control, and correlate well to the complexity of object representation. The further away a PE is from the sensory input, the more abstract and invariant the representation of objects or their features captured by the PEs. Each PE is more likely to connect to other PEs within a short Euclidean distance, although a small number of distanced connections are also provided. This organization is observed in biological memory where neurons tend to have mostly local connections. Thus, the lateral connection probability is a superposition of a Gaussian and a uniform distribution.

6.3.2 Network Operation

6.3.2.1 Feedforward Operation Feedforward operation is necessary in both the training and testing stages. Figure 6.6 shows a feedforward network structure for associative memory. For simplicity, we will only illustrate four

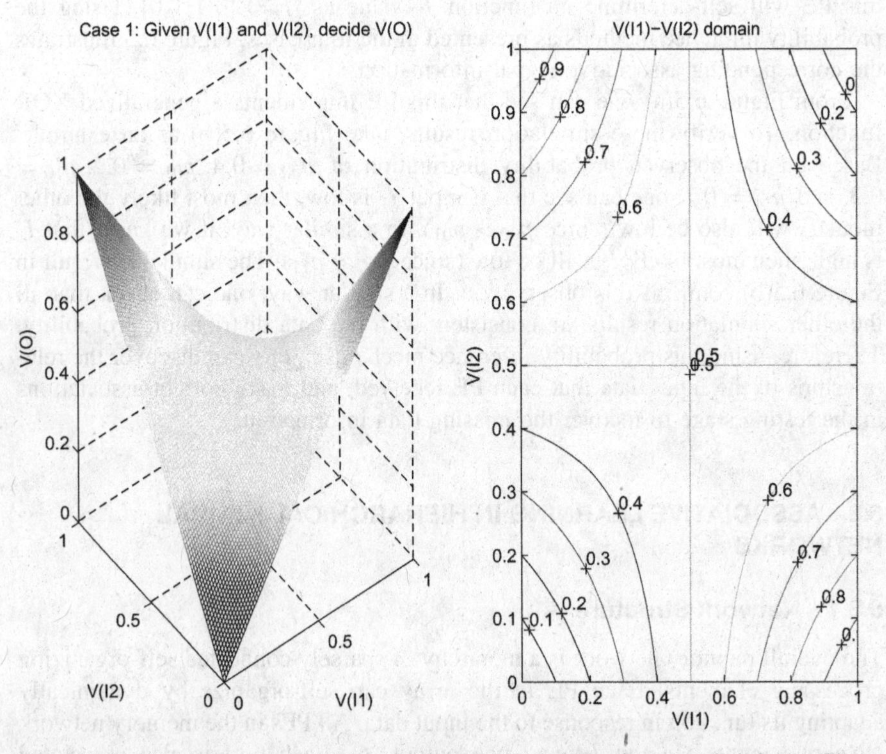

Figure 6.5: Simulation results of the four cases for information association. (a) Given values of both inputs $V(I_1)$ and $V(I_2)$, decide the output value $V(O)$. (b) Given the values of one input, $V(I_1)$ or V_{I_2}, and an undefined output V_O, decide the value of the other input. (c) Given the value of the output $V(O)$, decide the value of both inputs $V(I_1)$ and $V(I_2)$. (d) Given the values of one input, $V(I_1)$ or $V(I_2)$, and the output, $V(O)$, decide the other input value, $V(I_2)$ or $V(I_1)$.

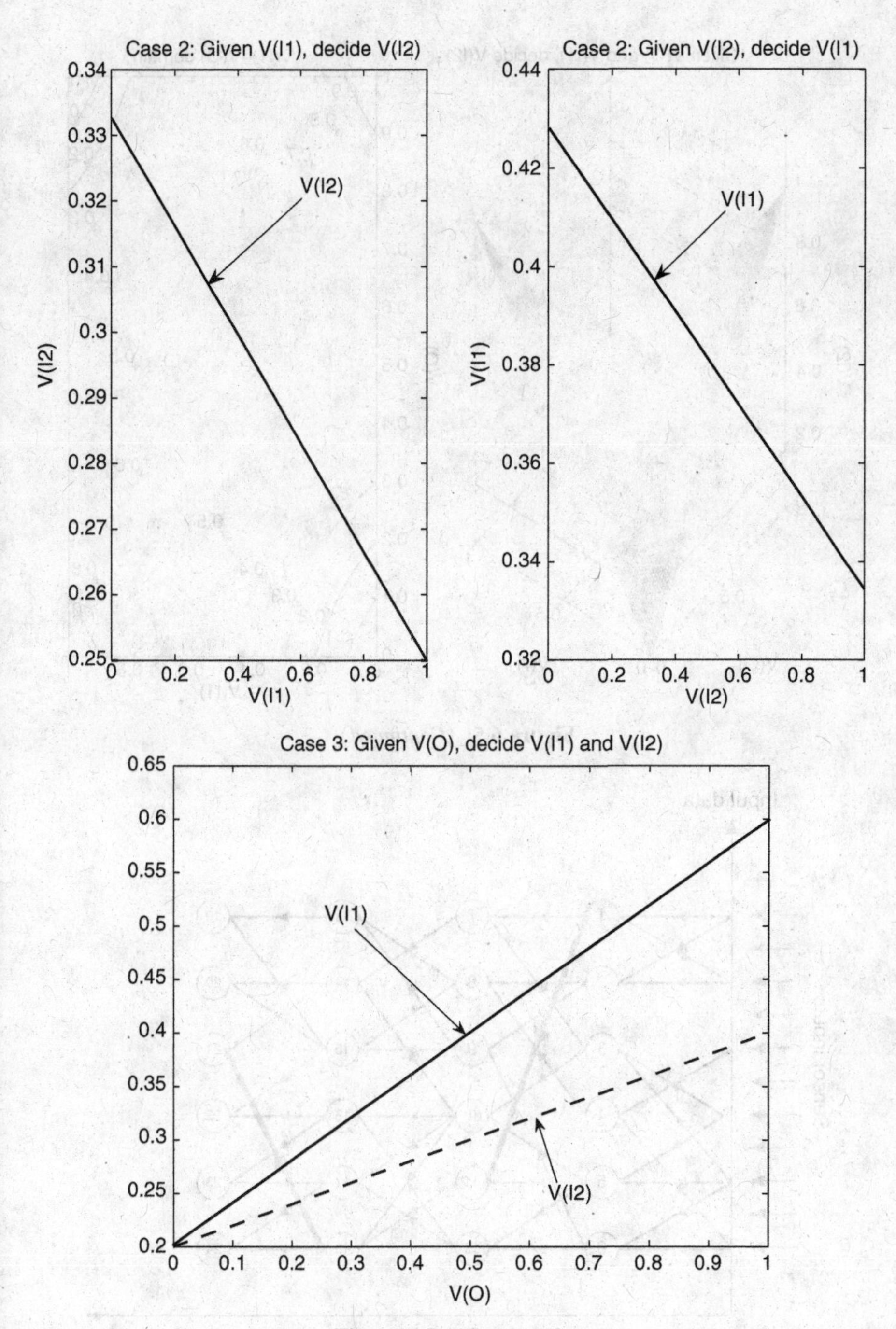

Figure 6.5: (*Continued*)

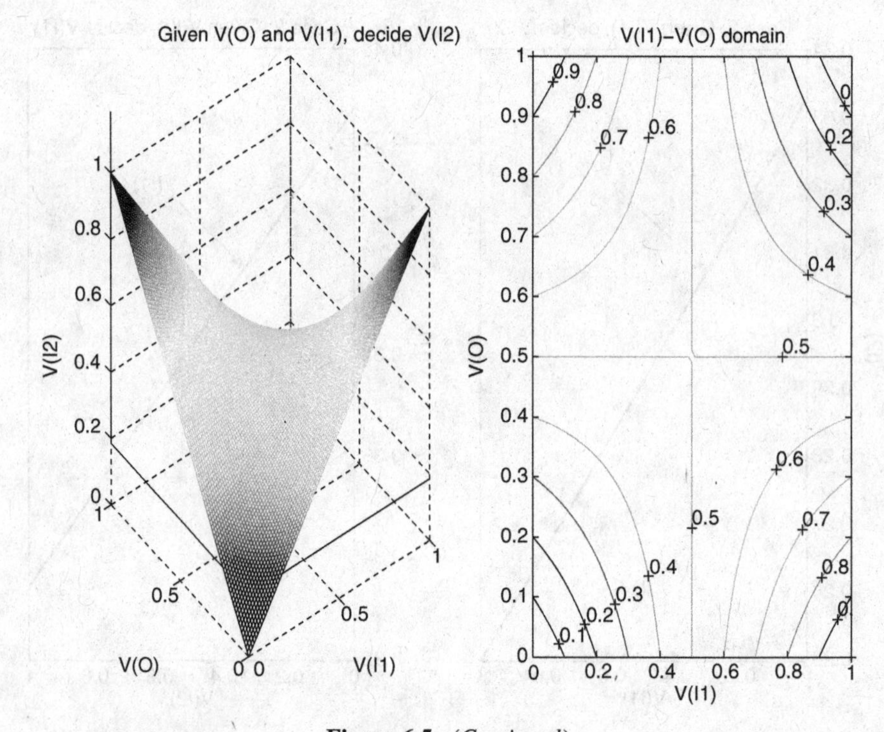

Figure 6.5: (*Continued*)

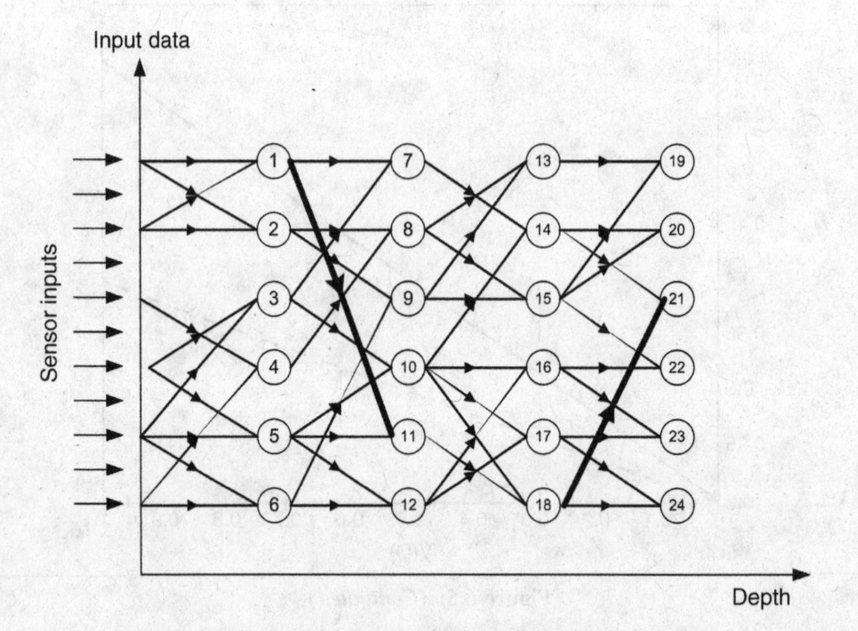

Figure 6.6: An example of feedforward operation network.

layers with six PEs per layer. The bold lines from PE 1 to PE 11 and from PE18 to PE21 are two examples of distant connections.

During the training stage, all external sensor input data is presented to the network. Each PE counts activities on its inputs to estimate the corresponding probabilities, p_{ij}, $(i,\ j = 0, 1)$ and decide its output function as in case 1 of section 6.2.4. During the testing stage, some input values are undefined (the signal value is set to 0.5). Whenever there is an undefined input signal, the output of the PE is undefined; otherwise, it will be decided as in case 1 of section 6.2.4 using the probabilities established during training stage. In fact, the distinction between training and testing is artificial as the network always learns, updating input probabilities of all PEs that receive determinate inputs.

6.3.2.2 Feedback Operation Feedback operation is essential for the network to make correct associations and to recover the missing parts of the input data (Starzyk et al., 2007). Figure 6.7 shows a feedback structure in the testing stage. For consistency, the network connection is the same as shown in Figure 6.6, although some feedforward connections are not shown in order to show feedback signals clearly. In the testing stage, some information is undefined as would be the case in a classification application (all the class identity labels are undefined and only the feature input values are presented to the associative memory

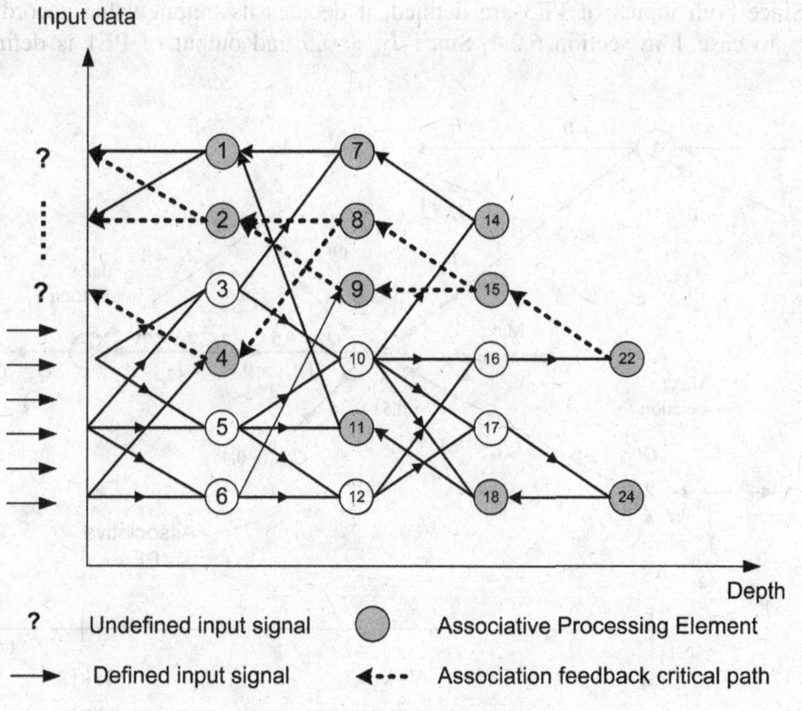

Figure 6.7: Example of feedback structure in the testing stage.

network) or an image recovery application (part of the image could be blocked or undefined). In both cases, the network will use associations to determine the undefined signal values.

In Figure 6.7, the shaded PEs are associative and will use associations to recover the undefined values. All three types of associations presented in section 6.2.4 are used. As illustrated in Figure 6.7, the proposed model has the ability to self-determine the depth of the association used in the feedback structure based on the complexity of the input data. This kind of self-organization provides great flexibility in applications of different complexity.

To illustrate the feedback association mechanism, let us consider part of an associative memory shown in Figure 6.8.

At time $T = k$:

PE1 has two determinate inputs (I_{1_1} is determinate low and I_{2_1} is determinate high, sub-subsripts denote PE number). In this case, PE1 decides its output value according to the probability learning algorithm (case 1) in section 6.2.4. Assume that one gets output $O_1 = 0$. PE2 has two undefined inputs. Accordingly, PE2 outputs an undefined value $O_2 = 0.5$. No associations or feedback values are used.

At time $T = k + 1$:

Since both inputs of PE3 are defined, it decides its output value according to case 1 in section 6.2.4. Since $I_{2_4} = 0.5$ and output of PE1 is defined

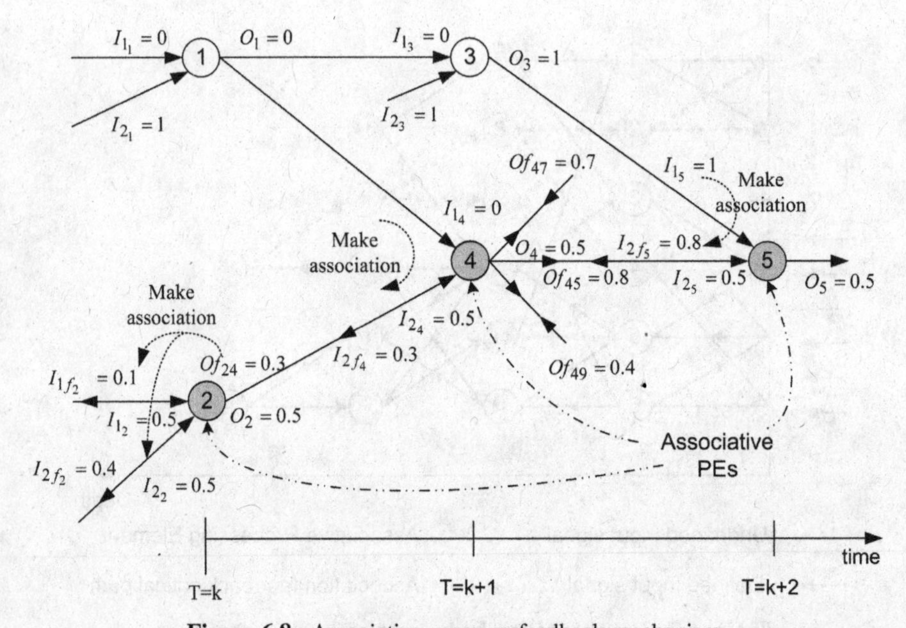

Figure 6.8: Associative memory feedback mechanism.

$(O_1 = 0)$, PE4 makes an IOA to determine the feedback signal I_{2f_4}. Assume that the calculated feedback signal of I_{2f_4} is 0.3. This feedback signal, I_{2f_4}, becomes the output feedback signal of PE2 ($O_{f_{24}} = 0.3$). Here the first and second subscripts indicate the target and source of the feedback (4 onto 2). Since both inputs of PE2 are undefined, $O_{f_{24}}$ triggers the association from output to both inputs (OOA), which corresponds to case 3 in section 6.2.4. Assume that calculation from the training information leads to $I_{1f_2} = 0.1$ and $I_{2f_2} = 0.4$ for PE2. These input feedback signals become the output feedback signals to the targets of PE2 in lower level layers, and may trigger other associations.

At time $T = k + 2$:

Since I_{1_5} is defined ($I_{1_5} = 1$) and I_{2_5} is undefined, the IOA association will decide the input feedback signal of PE5 according to case 2 in section 6.2.4 (assume that the calculated $I_{2f_5} = 0.8$). At the same time, let us assume that PE4 receives three feedback signals from three different PEs (PE 7, PE5, and PE9) with $O_{f_{47}} = 0.7$, $O_{f_{45}} = 0.8$, and $O_{f_{49}} = 0.4$. In this case, the output feedback signal of PE4 is selected as the one with the largest signal strength, which means:

$$O_f = max(SS(O_{f4i})) \tag{6.15}$$

where i represents the PE from which PE4 received the feedback signals. In this case, we have:

$$SS(O_{f47}) = |0.7 - 0.5| = 0.2 \tag{6.16}$$

$$SS(O_{f45}) = |0.8 - 0.5| = 0.3$$

$$SS(O_{f49}) = |0.4 - 0.5| = 0.1$$

Therefore, the feedback signal of PE4 becomes $O_{f_4} = 0.8$. This signal triggers associations in PE4. For PE4, I_{1_4} is defined ($I_{1_4} = 0$), O_{f_4} is defined ($O_{f_4} = 0.8$), and I_{2_4} is undefined. Accordingly, the feedback signal, I_{2f_4}, is based on the input–output association. Assume that, from case 4 in section 6.2.4, one gets $I_{2f_4} = 0.2$. In the previous step, the signal on I_{2f_4} is 0.3. Since there can be only one value in a particular signal line, these two signals need to be resolved. This is achieved by choosing the signal with the largest signal strength. In this case, 0.2 ($SS = 0.3$) is stronger than 0.3 ($SS = 0.2$), so I_{2f_4} is updated to 0.2. Now, updated I_{2f_4} becomes the output feedback signal for PE2, which in turn triggers the associations of PE2 based on case 3 in section 6.2.4.

In summary, the proposed memory makes the necessary associations to trace a signal to previous layers, ultimately deciding the undefined signal values. It should be noted that the updated input feedback signals (I_{1f} and I_{2f}) and the output feedback signal (O_f) must not propagate forward to higher hierarchical layers, since they may cause instability and start oscillations in the network.

6.4 CASE STUDY

In this section, the Iris database from the UCI Machine Learning Repository (Asuncion & Newman, 2007) and two image recovery problems are used to illustrate both the hetero-association and auto-association applications of the self-organizing memory model.

6.4.1 Hetero-Associative Application

The Iris database (Asuncion & Newman, 2007) is used to test the classification performance of the memory model. This database has three classes (Iris Setosa, Iris Versicolour, and Iris Virginica) and four numeric features (sepal length, sepal width, petal length, and petal width).

The N-bits sliding bar coding mechanism is used in this research to code the input data (Starzyk et al., 2007; Starzyk, Zhu, & Li, 2006). Assume that the maximum and minimum values to be coded are V_{max} and V_{min}, respectively. The length of the sliding bar is defined by $N - L = V_{max} - V_{min}$. Assume that the value of the scaled feature to be coded is V. In the coded input, bits numbered from $(V - V_{min}) + 1$ to $(V - V_{min}) + L$ are set to 1's, while the remaining bits are set to 0's. This scheme is illustrated in Figure 6.9.

The class label is coded in a similar way by using M bit code redundancy, as illustrated in Figure 6.10. Since there are three classes in this database, the total number of $M \times 3$ bits are used to code the class label, maximizing their Hamming distance. This is achieved by filling the M bits from position $(C_i - 1) \times M$ to $C_i \times M$ with 1's, while filling the remaining $M \times 2$ bits with 0's. Here $C_i = 1$, 2, and 3 for this three-class Iris database. In this simulation, N is set to 80, L is set to 20, and M is set to 30. Such coding is compatible with a binary neural network in which neurons either fire or do not, and all activation signals are binary.

In the training stage, both the feature code and class label code are presented to associative memory. This information is used to discover the potential relationship in the processing elements' input spaces. In the testing stage, only the feature code is presented to the input layer, and the class label code is filled

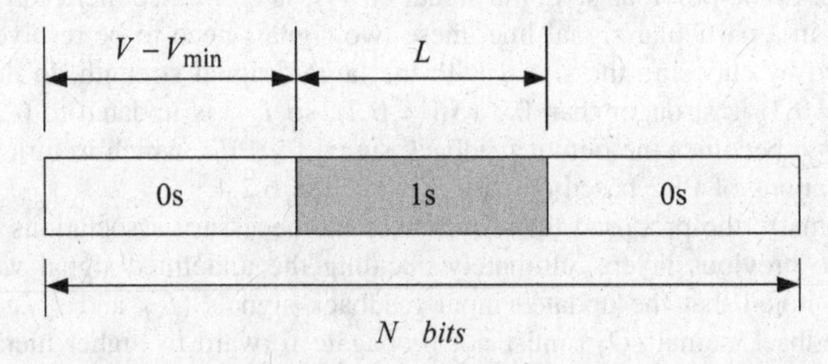

Figure 6.9: The N input bits sliding bar coding mechanism.

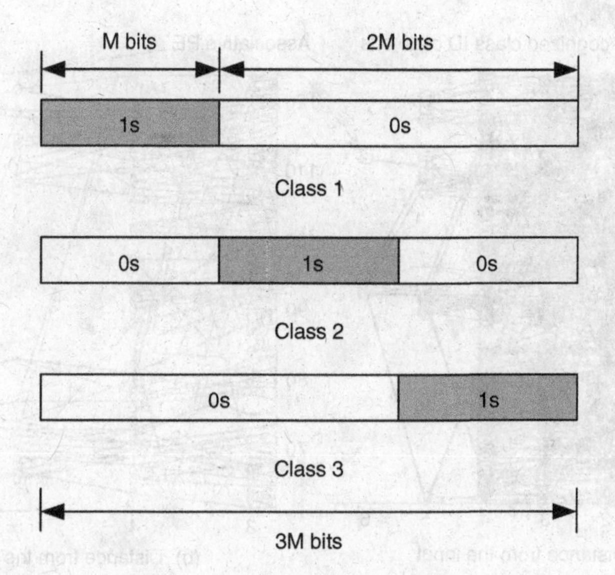

Figure 6.10: The sliding bar code mechanism for class label.

with undefined values. Through the feedback mechanism, the network makes associations and decides the class label code values. After the class label code values are decided, the system votes on the class label of each testing instance according to the minimum Hamming distance to code values of all the possible classes. The classification accuracy is then calculated by the ratio of correctly classified instances over the total number of testing instances.

Since there are only 150 instances in the Iris database, the K-fold cross-validation method is used to handle this small sample data set as used in Hong and Chen (2000), Dasarathy (1980), Quinlan, Compton, Horn, and Lazarus (1987), Lee, Chen, Chen, and Jou (2001), and Chatterjee and Rakshit (2004). In K-fold cross-validation, all instances are randomly divided into K subsets of as nearly equal size as possible. In each trial, one of the K subsets is used as the testing set and the other $K - 1$ subsets are used as training sets. Therefore, totally K trials are necessary in order for each instance to be tested once. The final classification accuracy is calculated by averaging results across all K trials. In this simulation, K is set to 10 (10-fold cross-validation). Figure 6.11(a) shows the associative PEs and their connection structure, and Figure 6.11(b) shows the associative PE firing activity for part of the network. The y-axis represents the input bits, and the x-axis represents the distance from the input (association depth). The associative PEs are represented by circles and their backward propagation paths are marked. The large dots at the input layer represent correctly recognized class label code bits. It may be noted that only six layers are needed for the network to learn the associations in the Iris database.

Table 6.3 shows the classification performance of the proposed associative memory compared with some other classification performances reported in

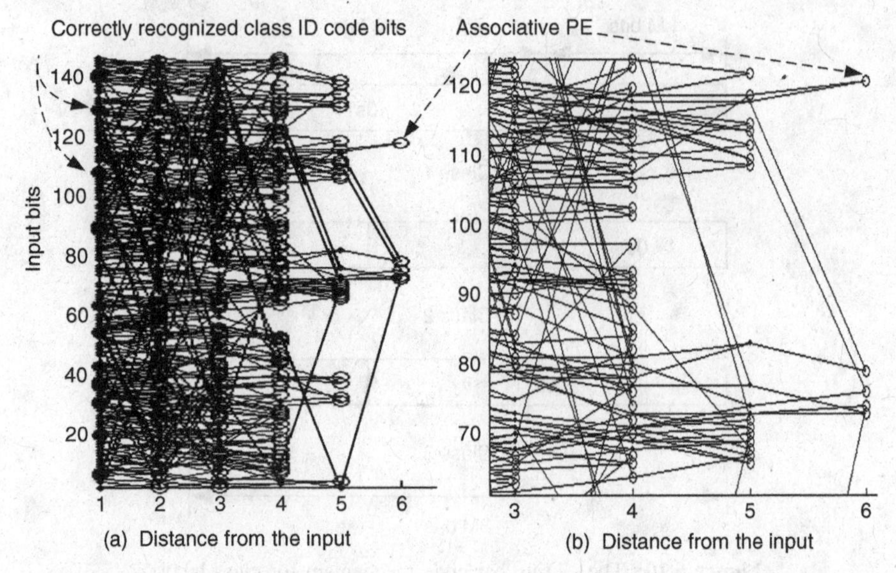

Figure 6.11: Associative processing elements and their interconnection structure.

Table 6.3: Comparison of the Classification Performance on Iris Database

Method	Average classification accuracy
Merging-membership-functions-first (Hong & Chen, 2000)	97.33%
C4 method (Hong & Chen, 2000; Quinlan et al., 1987)	93.87%
Influential rule search schemes (Chatterjee & Rakshit, 2004)	96.00%
Dasarathy's pattern-recognition approach (Hong & Chen, 2000; Dasarathy, 1980)	94.67%
Fuzzy entropy-based fuzzy classifier (Lee et al., 2001)	96.7%
Self-organizing associative memory (the proposed method)	96.00%

literature using the same database. These results indicate that the self-organizing associative memory presented in this chapter shows satisfactory performance in a classification problem, indicating self-organizing learning through associations. Learning through associations is useful if one wants to associate specific behavior in a reinforcement learning value system.

6.4.2 Auto-Associative Application

Image recovery problems can be used to test the effectiveness of the proposed memory for auto-associative applications. This is necessary for applications where only partial images are available without specifying class identities. The proposed memory model can learn features of the training data using unsupervised learning, self-determine the feedback depth, and make associations to recover the original images.

6.4.2.1 *Panda Image Recovery* The 64 × 64 binary panda image used in Djuric, Huang, and Ghirmai (2002) is used in this research. The panda image is represented by a vector $p_i = (x_1, x_2, \ldots, x_n)$, with $x_i = 1$ for a black pixel and $x_i = 0$ for a white pixel. In testing, $r\%$ percentage ($r = 10, 20$, and 30) of the panda image is randomly blocked by setting $n \times (r\%)$ pixels to the undefined value (0.5).

The original panda image and samples of its blocked image are shown in Figure 6.12(a) and (b), respectively. Figure 6.12(c) shows images recovered through the proposed associative memory. As in Djuric et al. (2002), the image recovery performance is evaluated by computing the ratios of the number of incorrectly recovered pixels (both erroneous pixels and pixels remaining undefined

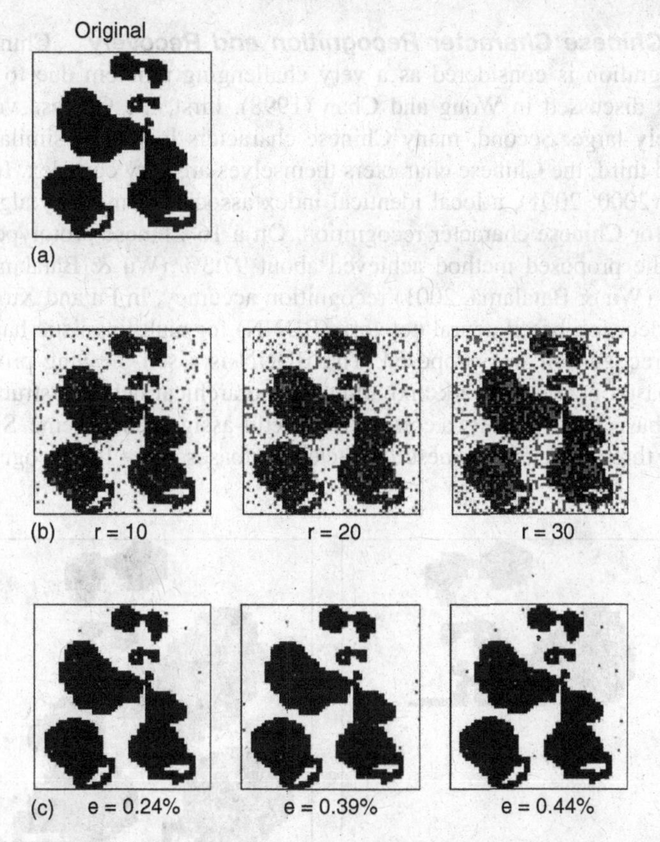

Figure 6.12: The 64 × 64 binary panda image: (a) the original training image; (b) blocked image with $r\%$ of undefined values ($r = 10, 20$, and 30, respectively); (c) recovered image and the recovery error.

Table 6.4: Panda Image Recovery Error Information

Noise/block level	10%	20%	30%
Reference (Djuric et al., 2002)	2.95%	4.83%	6.57%
Self-organizing associative memory (the proposed method)	0.24%	0.39%	0.44%

after recovery) over the total number of pixels. As one can see in Table 6.4, the self-organizing memory model can provide competitive results compared to those in Djuric et al.

While Figure 6.12 tested the capability of the self-organizing associative memory in recovering randomly blocked images, Figure 6.13 shows the recovery performance under the condition of the entire lower half of the panda image being blocked. In this case, the recovery error bits are at the level of 2.42% of the total image.

6.4.2.2 Chinese Character Recognition and Recovery Chinese character recognition is considered as a very challenging problem due to a couple of reasons discussed in Wong and Chan (1998). First, the Chinese vocabulary is extremely large. Second, many Chinese characters look very similar to each other. And third, the Chinese characters themselves are very complex. In Wu and Batalama (2000, 2001), a local identical index associative memory algorithm is proposed for Chinese character recognition. On a 16 Chinese prototype patterns data set, the proposed method achieved about 97.3% (Wu & Batalama, 2000) and 100% (Wu & Batalama, 2001) recognition accuracy. In Fu and Xu (1998), a Bayesian decision-based neural network (BDNN) for multilinguistic handwritten character recognition was proposed. The BDNN is a self-growing probabilistic decision-based neural network and adopts a hierarchical network structure with nonlinear basis functions and a competitive credit-assignment scheme. Simulation results on three different Chinese character databases show the recognition rate

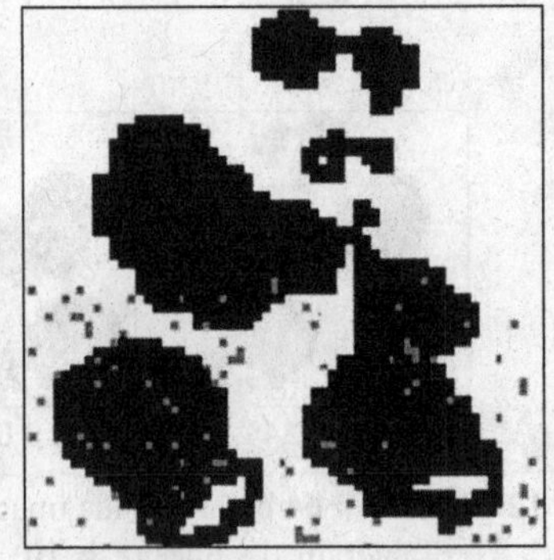

Figure 6.13: Testing image (block half) and recovered image.

around 86–94%. Most of the references in literature solely handle the Chinese character recognition problem. Since the proposed self-organizing associative memory is capable of both classification and image recovery, Chinese character recognition and recovery is illustrated in this section.

Figure 6.14 shows the five black-and-white Chinese characters considered in this research (at the top of each character, we also provided a corresponding English word with similar meaning). As we can see, these five characters are very similar to each other. Each of these patterns is scanned and represented in the vector format (20 × 20 pixel images). Similar to section 6.4.2.1, each pattern is represented by a vector $p_i = (x_1,\ x_2,\ \ldots\ x_n)$, $n = 400$, where $x_i = 1$ if it is a black pixel and $x_i = 0$ if it is a white pixel. In testing, each character is randomly blocked 50%, which means 200 randomly selected pixels are set to the undefined value (0.5). These testing patterns are presented to associative memory for recognition and recovery. Figure 6.15 shows the input testing patterns, corresponding to the training patterns in Figure 6.14.

The performance of the associative memory is evaluated in two ways. The first one is the correct recognition rate, which is similar to what is defined in section 6.4.1. Ten-runs simulation is performed to get the statistical performance, and the memory model achieved an average of 100% correct recognition rate for these similar Chinese characters. The second evaluation step is to observe what the recovered character looks like, and what the ratios of the error bits and missing bits in the recovered pattern are, similar to section 6.4.2.1.

Figure 6.16 shows the recovered patterns corresponding to Figure 6.15, and Table 6.5 is the error bits and missing bits information for each pattern. The gray part in Figure 6.16 shows that there are still some missing pixel values after recovery. From Figure 6.16 one can see that the associative memory can

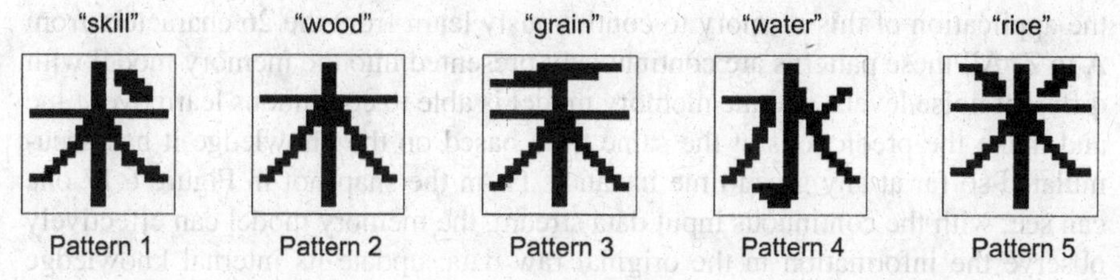

Figure 6.14: Training patterns: Five black-white Chinese characters.

Figure 6.15: Testing patterns with 50% pixels (200 pixels) blocked.

Pattern 1

Pattern 2

Pattern 3

Pattern 4

Pattern 5

Figure 6.16: Recovered Chinese testing pattern.

Table 6.5: Testing Error Bits and Missing Bits Information

Testing pattern	Pattern 1	Pattern 2	Pattern 3	Pattern 4	Pattern 5	Mean
Error bits	12	9	14	13	14	12.4
Error bits percentage	6%	4.5%	7%	6.5%	7%	6.2%
Missing bits	6	5	7	2	4	4.8
Missing bits percentage	3%	2.5%	3.5%	1%	2%	2.4%

correctly recover the original image even if only half of the pattern pixels are presented. Table 6.5 illustrates that the average error bits percentage and missing bits percentage are about 6.2% and 2.4%, respectively.

6.4.2.3 Associative Memory for Online Incremental Learning As we discussed in Chapter 2 of this book, incremental learning is important for developing self-adaptive intelligent systems. The proposed associative memory is also capable of incremental learning. In fact, the distinction between the training and testing stage in the aforementioned examples is artificial for the purpose of clear presentation. All PEs in the memory architecture can continuously learn, accumulate knowledge, and make predictions with stream data. Figure 6.17 illustrates the application of this memory to continuously learn from the 26 characters from A to Z. All these patterns are continuously presented into the memory model with different noise levels, and the memory model is able to continuous learn over time and make the predictions at the same time based on the knowledge it has accumulated so far at any given time instance. From the snapshot in Figure 6.17 one can see, with the continuous input data stream, the memory model can effectively observe the information in the original raw data, update its internal knowledge representation, and build up associations among the distributed network of PEs to support the decision-making and prediction process.

In summary, the simulation results on various application problems presented in this chapter demonstrate competitive performance of the proposed self-organizing associative memory on both hetero- and auto-associations applications. We did not expect these results to be the best among the methods used for comparison, which are optimized for specific problems (e.g., classification with fixed number of classes). The proposed memory model is more robust in terms of the variety of problems it can solve without modification of the network structure. To this end, we consider a flexible structure capable of accumulating knowledge

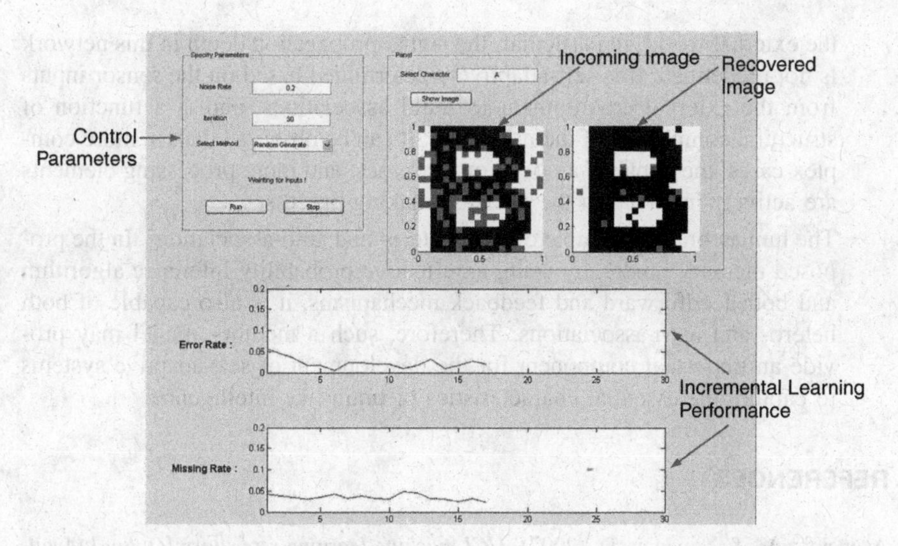

Figure 6.17: A snapshot of the incremental learning capability of associative memory.

and using them to reach higher levels of self-organization and problem solving is more important than specialized and fixed structures for specific applications. The aim of the proposed associative memory is to search for network structures that can be extended toward building real intelligent machines, perhaps toward structures resembling the macrocolumns and minicolumns that have been the objectives of recent biological studies (Mountcastle, 1997; Jones, 2000).

6.5 SUMMARY

This chapter presents a self-organization associative memory for machine intelligence, and investigates its applications to both hetero- and auto-association applications across different domains. The major points of this chapter include:

- Self-organization and association are desirable features of learning structures and evidently play a critical role in development of the brain. Self-organizing structures require no explicit supervision and selectively affect different areas of learning networks, depending on how new data is related to the information stored in the network and how the emergent network behavior is useful to the machine. Self-organization in human memory builds natural associations between different sensors and internal representations of the external world.
- As in the biological intelligent systems, there is no predesignated group of processing elements that represent a specific concept or make a specific association in the proposed self-organizing memory network. These emerge spontaneously from interactions between sensors, processing elements, and

the external world. In particular, the signal propagation depth in this network is not predefined. It is self-adaptively determined based on the sensor inputs from the external environment to build associations, and is a function of structural complexity of the input data. It can be observed that, in more complex cases, the depth of association increases, and more processing elements are actively involved in the decision-making processes.

- The human brain is capable of both hetero- and auto-associations. In the proposed memory model, by using an effective probability inference algorithm and both feedforward and feedback mechanisms, it is also capable of both hetero- and auto-associations. Therefore, such a memory model may provide an important component for the development of self-adaptive systems to capture the essential characteristics of brain-like intelligence.

REFERENCES

Asuncion, A., & Newman, D. (2007). *UCI machine learning repository [Online], Available: http://www.ics.uci.edu/mlearn/MLRepository.html*.

Brown, G. D. A., Dalloz, P., & Hulme, C. (1995). Mathematical and connectionist models of human memory: a comparison. *Memory*, *3*(2), 113–145.

Chang, J. Y., & Cho, C. W. (2003). Second-order asymmetric bam design with a maximal basin of attraction. *IEEE Trans. Systems, Man and Cybernetics, Part A: Systems and Humans*, *33*, 421–428.

Chatterjee, A., & Rakshit, A. (2004). Influential rule search scheme (IRSS)—a new fuzzy pattern classifier. *IEEE Trans. Knowledge and Data Engineering*, *16*(8), 881–893.

Dasarathy, B. V. (1980). Noising around the neighborhood: a new system structure and classification rule for recognition in partially exposed environments. *IEEE Trans. Pattern Analysis and Machine Intelligence*, *2*(1), 67–71.

Djuric, P. M., Huang, Y., & Ghirmai, E. (2002). Perfect sampling: a review and application to signal processing. *IEEE Trans. Signal Processing*, *50*(2), 345–356.

Fu, H. C., & Xu, Y. Y. (1998). Multilinguistic handwritten character recognition by bayesian decision-based neural networks. *IEEE Trans. Signal Processing*, *46*(10), 2781–2789.

Hawkins, J., & Blakeslee, S. (2004). *On intelligence*. New York: Times Books.

Hawkins, J., & Blakeslee, S. (2007). Why can't a computer be more like a brain? *IEEE Spectrum*, *44*(4), 20–26.

Hong, T. P., & Chen, J. B. (2000). Processing individual fuzzy attributes for fuzzy rule organizing learning arrays. *Fuzzy Sets and Systems*, *112*, 127–140.

Hopfield, J. J. (1982). Neural networks and physical systems with emergent collective computational abilities. *Proc. National Academy of Sciences of the USA*, *79*, 2554–2558.

Jones, E. G. (2000). Multicolumns in the cerebral cortex. *Proc. National Academy of Sciences of the USA*, pp. 5019–5021.

Lee, H. M., Chen, C. M., Chen, J. M., & Jou, Y. L. (2001). An efficient fuzzy classifier with feature selection based on fuzzy entropy. *IEEE Trans. Systems, Man and Cybernetics, Part B: Cybernetics*, *31*(3), 426–432.

Malsburg, C. V. (2003). *Handbook of brain theory and neural networks*. Cambridge, MA: MIT Press.

Mountcastle, V. B. (1997). The columnar organization of the neocortex. *Brain*, *120*, 701–722.

Murdock, B. B. (1997). Context and mediators in a theory of distributed associative memory (todam2). *Psychological Review*, *104*, 839–862.

Quinlan, J. R., Compton, P. J., Horn, K. A., & Lazarus, L. (1987). Inductive knowledge acquisition: A case study. *Proc. Australian Conf. Applications of Expert Systems*, pp. 137–156.

Rizzuto, D. S., & Kahana, M. J. (2001). An autoassociative neural network model of paired-associative learning. *Neural Computation*, *13*, 2075–2092.

Salih, I., Smith, S. H., & Liu, D. (2000). Synthesis approach for bidirectional associative memories based on the preceptron training algorithm. *Neuralcomputing*, *35*, 137–148.

Starzyk, J. A., He, H., & Li, Y. (2007). A hierarchical self-organizing associative memory for machine learning. *Lecture Notes in Computer Science*, *4491*, 413–423.

Starzyk, J. A., & Wang, F. (2004). Dynamic probability estimator for machine learning. *IEEE Trans. Neural Networks*, *15*, 298–308.

Starzyk, J. A., Zhu, Z., & Li, Y. (2006). Associative learning in hierarchical self organizing learning arrays. *IEEE Trans. Neural Networks*, *17*(6), 1460–1470.

Triesch, J. (2004). Synergies between intrinsic and synaptic plasticity in individual model neurons. *Advances in Neural Information Processing Systems*, *17*.

Vogel, D., & Boos, W. (1997). Sparsely connected, hebbian networks with strikingly large storage capacities. *Neural Network*, *4*(10), 671–682.

Wang, L. (1999). Multi-associative neural networks and their applications to learning and retrieving complex spatio-temporal sequences. *IEEE Trans. Systems, Man and Cybernetics, Part B: Cybernetics*, *29*, 73–82.

Wang, M., & Chen, S. (2005). Enhanced emam based on empirical kernal map. *IEEE Trans. Neural Networks*, *16*, 557–563.

Wong, P. K., & Chan, C. (1998). Off-line handwritten chinese character recognition as a compound bayes decision problem. *IEEE Trans. Pattern Analysis and Machine Intelligence*, *20*(9), 1016–1023.

Wu, Y., & Batalama, S. N. (2000). An efficient learning algorithm for associative memories. *IEEE Trans. Neural Networks*, *11*(3), 1058–1066.

Wu, Y., & Batalama, S. N. (2001). Improved one-shot learning for feedforward associative memories with application to composite pattern association. *IEEE Trans. Systems, Man and Cybernetics, Part B: Cybernetics*, *31*, 119–125.

CHAPTER 7

Sequence Learning

7.1 INTRODUCTION

Sequence learning is presumably among one of the most important components of human intelligence, as most human behaviors are in the sequential format, including, but not limited to, natural language processing, speech recognition, reasoning and planning, and others (Sun & Giles, 2001; Anderson, 1995; Schneider & Logan, 2006). Over the past decades, models and mechanisms for sequence learning have attracted considerable attention. For instance, the pioneering work by McClelland et al investigated different parallel distributed processing (PDP) models for sequence learning and studied their applications in speech and language processing (McClelland & Rumelhart, 1981; Seidenberg & McClelland, 1989; Plaut, McClelland, Seidenberg, & Patterson, 1996; McClelland & Elman, 1986a, 1986b), such as the interactive activation model (McClelland & Rumelhart, 1981), the TRACE model (McClelland & Elman, 1986a, 1986b), among others. Recently, Sun and Giles (2001) offered an important review of the characteristics, problems, and challenges for sequence learning ranging from recognition and prediction to sequential decision making. In this chapter, we present an anticipation-based hierarchical neural network structure for complex sequence learning, storage, and retrieval (Starzyk & He, 2007).

7.2 FOUNDATIONS FOR SEQUENCE LEARNING

We start this section with a review of the critical foundations for sequence learning. Specifically, we focus on the following important characteristics here: *self-organization*, *hierarchical structure*, *time representation*, and *anticipation and association capabilities*.

Self-organization is critical for the sequence learning model to develop distributed internal information representation and association with the active interaction within unstructured and uncertain environments. Therefore, self-organizing models have been studied extensively for sequence learning. For

Self-Adaptive Systems for Machine Intelligence, First Edition. Haibo He.

instance, a self-organizing connectionist model for bilingual processing was developed in various research (Li & Farkas, 2002a, 2002b, 2002c; Farkas & Li, 2002; Zhao & Li, 2007). For example, in (Li & Farkas, 2002a), a model named SOMBIP was proposed based on two interconnected self-organizing neural networks with recurrent links to compute lexical co-occurrence constrains. The DevLex (and DevLex-II) model, another neural network model based on self-organizing maps, was proposed for language acquisition (Farkas & Li, 2002; Li & Farkas, 2002b, 2002c; Zhao & Li, 2007). The key idea of DevLex is to use two maps, a growing semantic map (GSM) and a phonological map (PMAP), with interconnected associative pathways for the development of lexicon. Evolution algorithms can also be integrated with the self-organizing neural networks to learn sequential decision tasks and language processing (Miikkulainen, 1990, 1992, 1993; Moriarty & Miikkulainen, 1999; James & Miikkulainen, 1995). For example, a natural language processing system named DISCERN was developed at the sub symbolic level (Miikkulainen, 1990, 1993). One of the key characteristics of the DISCERN system is to use the hierarchically organized feature map and modules for information processing. In Moriarty and Miikkulainen (1999), an approach called SANE, the symbiotic, adaptive neuro-evolution model, was proposed based on genetic algorithms and neural networks. The key idea of SANE is to evolve neural networks through genetic algorithms to learn in a wide range of domains with minimal reinforcement. Recent psychology research also provided important suggestions of sequence learning for event perception and temporal processing (Lewkowicz, 2004, 2006; Lewkowicz & Marcovitch, 2006; Lewkowicz & Ghazanfar, 2006). For instance, various experiments were developed to investigate infant perception, learning, and discrimination of serial orders (Lewkowicz, 2004). Perception of complex audiovisual rhythmic patterns for different ages of human infants were studied in Lewkowicz and Marcovitch (2006), which suggests that infants between 4 and 10 months of age can not only perceive and discriminate complex audiovisual temporal patterns, but can also learn the invariant nature of such patterns. Visual short-term memory (VSTM) for multiple sequential arrays was investigated in various studies (Kumar & Jiang, 2005; Liu & Jiang, 2005; Chun & Jiang, 1998; Jiang, Olson, & Chun, 2000). For instance, the research in Jiang et al. (2000) suggested that the organization of the VSTM contains the relational information of individual visual items based on the global spatial configuration, which provides important insights for the development of effective spatio-temporal memory models.

Hierarchical structure has been considered an important characteristic for efficient sequence learning, storage, and retrieval (Starzyk & He, 2007; Schneider & Logan, 2006; Wang & Arbib, 1993; Manning & Witten, 1998; Hawkins & Blakeslee, 2004, 2007; Hawkins & George, 2006; Wang & Yuwono, 1996). For instance, in Schneider and Logan (2006), four experiments was proposed to study the hierarchical control of cognitive process to examine the relationship between sequence- and task-level processing in sequential behaviors. A series of papers by Wang et al. also suggested that sequences could be effectively learned, retrieved, and predicted in a hierarchical organization (Wang & Arbib, 1990, 1993; Wang & Yuwono, 1995, 1996; Wang & Arbib, 1990). For instance, in Wang and Arbib (1990), two special types of neurons were proposed. The first one is the dual neuron, which is used to store a signal for a short period of time. Unlike the traditional binary signal values used in many neural network models, the output of a dual neuron is a graded signal. The second neuron is the sequence-detecting neuron. After learning, this sequence-detecting neuron fires in response to the previous sequence of patterns, not just the previous pattern. It thereby overcomes the limitation of networks that cannot reliably recall sequences that share common patterns. Based on this work, a framework of learning, recognition, and reproduction of complex temporal sequences was proposed in Wang and Arbib. In that model, sequences are acquired by the attention learning rule, which combines Hebbian learning and a normalization rule with sequential system activation. Time intervals between sequence components do not affect recognition. A global inhibitor is proposed to enable the model to learn context lengths required to disambiguate associations in complex sequence reproduction. In order to overcome the capacity limitation of short-term memory (STM), a hierarchical sequence recognition model based on the chunking mechanism was discussed in Wang and Arbib. For instance, in a letter–word–sentence hierarchical structure, a unit for a given word is activated at the end of the presentation of that word, and the model learns the sequence of letters of that word based on the letter units active at that time. Once the word structure has been learned, the same mechanism can be applied to train a higher hierarchical level on the sequence of words. One more issue addressed in Wang and Arbib is interval maintenance, which can be achieved by coding intervals by connection weights from the detector layer to the input layer. Furthermore, a neural network model capable of learning and generating complex temporal patterns by self-organization was proposed (Wang & Yuwono, 1995). This model actively regenerates the next component in a sequence and compares the anticipated component with the next input. A mismatch between what the model anticipates and the actual input triggers one-shot learning. Incremental learning for complex temporal patterns and the catastrophic interference of sequence learning was addressed in Wang and Yuwono (1996). Catastrophic interference in incremental learning for complex sequences is mainly the result of modification of weights representing previously stored patterns. While some interference may be found in human memory (Bower, Thompson-Schill, & Tulving, 1994), catastrophic interference is not. It is showed that the anticipation model proposed in Wang and Yuwono (1995) is capable of incremental learning with retroactive interference but without catastrophic interference. In addition, a chunking mechanism was included in that model to detect repeated subsequences between and within sequences, thereby substantially reducing the amount of retraining in sequential training. In Manning and Witten (1998), a linear-time algorithm called SEQUITUR was proposed for identifying hierarchical structure in sequences. The main idea of this algorithm is that phrases that appear more than once can be replaced by a grammatical rule that generates the phrase, and that this process can be continued recursively, producing a hierarchical representation of the original sequences. The problem of hierarchical structure for temporal sequence learning targets on invariant pattern recognition was discussed in George and Hawkins (2005). It is concluded that the neocortex solves the invariance problem in a hierarchical structure: Each region in the hierarchy learns and recalls sequences of inputs, and temporal sequences at each level of the hierarchy become the spatial inputs to the next higher regions. Recently, Hawkins et al. presented four major reasons to make the hierarchy a critical element for machine intelligence research (Hawkins & Blakeslee, 2004, 2007; Hawkins & George, 2006): generalization and storage efficiency (shared representations), consistency with the spatial and temporal hierarchy of the real world, quick response, and covert attention.

Time representation is another important issue for sequence learning, of which the difficulty is how to represent time in a natural and biologically plausible way (Elman, 1990). To this end, recurrent neural networks (RNNs) have been powerful tools in studying the sequence learning problem (Elman, 1990; Jordan, 1986; Pollack, 1991; Jacobsson, 2005). There are many successful examples of RNNs used for sequence learning, including the sequential behavior learning of arm robots and robotic navigation systems (Tani & Nolfi, 1999; Tani, 2003). However, the traditional RNN network using backpropagation through time (BPTT) is unable to learn sequences with a long time lag (Hochreiter & Schmidhuber, 1997). This is because the backpropagation error signals can be vanished in the BPTT mechanism. To overcome this limitation, Hochreiter and Schmidhuber (1997) proposed a recurrent network architecture in conjunction with the gradient-based learning algorithm, the long short-term memory (LSTM). The idea here is to introduce a memory cell (constant error carousel) in a RNN; therefore, the error signal will not vanish and the system will be able to learn the sequential dynamics in a very long time.

Finally, anticipation and association capabilities are also critical for sequence learning, storage, and retrieval (Starzyk & He, 2007; Wang & Arbib, 1990, 1993 Wang & Yuwono, 1995, 1996). By correct prediction, the intelligent system indicates that it already knows such knowledge, therefore it does not require additional learning. In this way, learning only happens when the prediction is incorrect. For instance, in Wang and Yuwono (1995), an anticipation mechanism was proposed for the system to match the current input with the predicted information, enabling one-shot learning in this model. A neural network model operated in an anticipative fashion for sequence learning was investigated in Ara'ujo and Barreto (2002), and was successfully applied to the robot trajectory planning. Associative learning mechanisms can also be used to learn and predict complex sequences. For instance, Wang (1998, 1999) investigated the usage of associative neural networks with delayed feedback connections for sequence learning and retrieval. Specifically, an associative memory model with three major components—a voting network, a parallel array of hetero-associative neural networks (HANN), and delayed feedback lines from the output of the system to the associative neural network layers—was proposed for spatio-temporal sequence learning (Wang, 1998). The delayed sequence of hetero-associators "votes" on the next output at each time step. After learning, the system can retrieve the entire sequence from a small cue sequence. Since the model in Wang (1998) assumes that each HANN only learns hetero-associations between single spatial patterns and does not learn to associate multiple patterns in groups, that model was further extended to include associations of one pattern with multiple patterns. The proposed model in Wang (1999) has the advantages of short learning time and accurate retrievals, and the ability to store a large number of complex sequences. Recent developments using associative memory for sequential memory include dynamic hetero-associative memory (Chartier & Boukadoum, 2006), a combined model based on context layer and shift-register models (Bose, Furber, & Shapiro, 2005), self-organizing associative memory (Starzyk & He, 2007), and others.

7.3 SEQUENCE LEARNING IN HIERARCHICAL NEURAL STRUCTURE

In this chapter, we will focus on the learning, storage, and retrieval of multiple complex sequences for the development of intelligent systems. Here, we adopt the terminology of sequence definitions introduced by Wang and Arbib (1990, 1993):

$$S : U_1 - U_2 - \ldots - U_k \tag{7.1}$$

U_i, $i = 1, \ldots, k$ is a component or symbol (such as a character, a number, or others) of sequence S, and the length of sequence S is k. Generally speaking, a sequence may include repetitions of the same subsequence in different contexts, such as $S1 : A - B - C - D - B - C - E$. In this way, the prior subsequence required to reproduce the current symbol U_i in S is defined as the context of U_i, and its length is defined as the degree of U_i. For example, the degree of symbol "D" in sequence $S1$ is 3. In this way, one can define the degree of a sequence as the maximum degree of all its components. In this way, a one-degree sequence is called a simple sequence, while others are complex sequences (Wang & Arbib, 1990, 1993). Figure 7.1 shows an example of the hierarchical organization of a three-level sequence representation: the letter–word–sentence representation.

Figure 7.2 illustrates the overall system-level architecture of the proposed model with a hierarchical organization (Starzyk & He, 2007). In this model, the output of one hierarchical level is the input to the next level. At each level, a winner-takes-all (WTA) mechanism is used to select active neurons. In the first layer (level 0), a modified Hebbian learning mechanism is utilized for pattern recognition. Level 1 to level N are identical structures for sequence learning. The key components of each hierarchical level are input register (IR) neuron, time-controlled multiplexer (MUX), prediction neuron (PN), prediction checking neuron (PCN), prediction matching neuron (PMN), learning flag neuron (LFN), multiple winner detection neuron (MWDN), and learning neuron (LN). The IR neuron spatially encodes a sequence of outputs from the next lower level. The sequence may be recently entered or recalled from the sequential memory. The

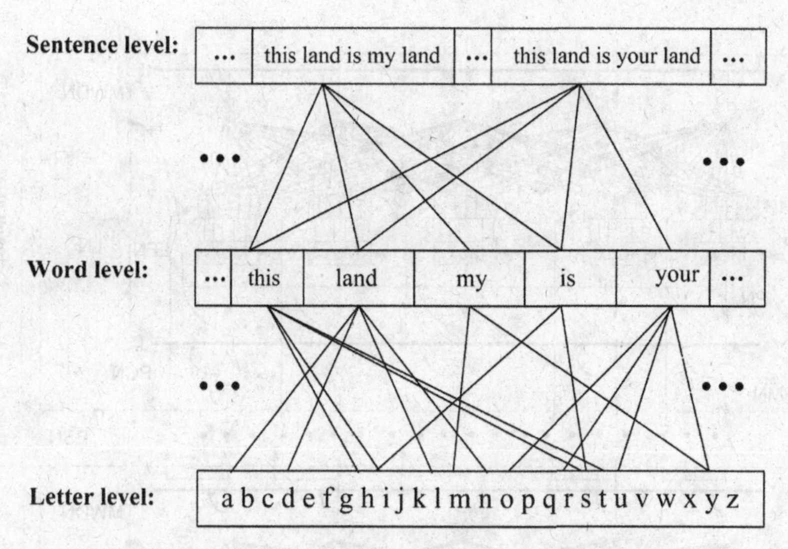

Figure 7.1: Hierarchical organizations of sequences.

MUX calls the contents of the IR sequentially for comparison with a sequence being output by the next lower level. We will show that this organization is efficient for complex sequence learning, storage, and retrieval.

7.4 LEVEL 0: A MODIFIED HEBBIAN LEARNING ARCHITECTURE

A modified Hebbian learning mechanism is used in the first hierarchical layer of the proposed model (level 0 in Figure 7.2). Since biological neurons either fire or do not, it is assumed that each sensory input from the environment is either 0 or 1. In this way, Figure 7.3 illustrates the idea of a both active-0 and active-1 representation of the sensory information. When the sensory input is 1, the left neuron will fire. When the sensory input is 0, this input value is passed through an "inverter" and drives the right neuron to fire. In this way, different neurons firing represent different sensory input values for the binary coded input.

Figure 7.4 shows the detailed structure of the modified Hebbian learning mechanism. For simplification, we only show a three-level hierarchical structure with unsupervised learning. The neurons in the second layer are grouped into several groups. Each neuron of a second layer group is sparsely connected, at random, to the same subset of neurons in the first layer. There is some overlap of the subsets of neurons in the first layer to which second-layer groups project.

Two similar WTA mechanisms are used in this model to improve the learning efficiency of the model as well as to reduce its learning complexity. The first

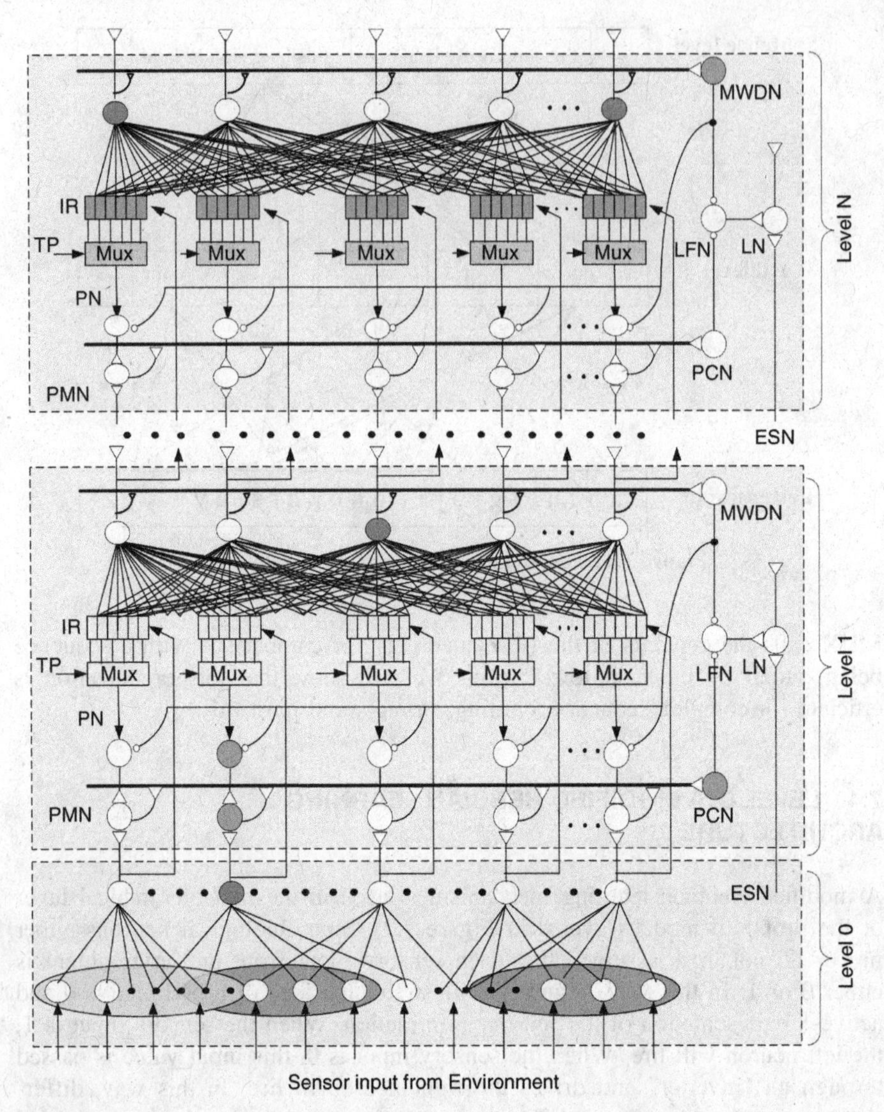

Figure 7.2: System architecture of anticipation-based hierarchical sequence learning model.

one is a stiff WTA (SWTA), which can be achieved by a simple counter. SWTA is used in the second layer. Since the sensory inputs from the environment are either 0 or 1, SWTA simply counts the number of 1's each neuron receives, and selects, as winners, the one neuron from each group that receives the largest number of 1's. In particular, there is no weight adjustment in SWTA.

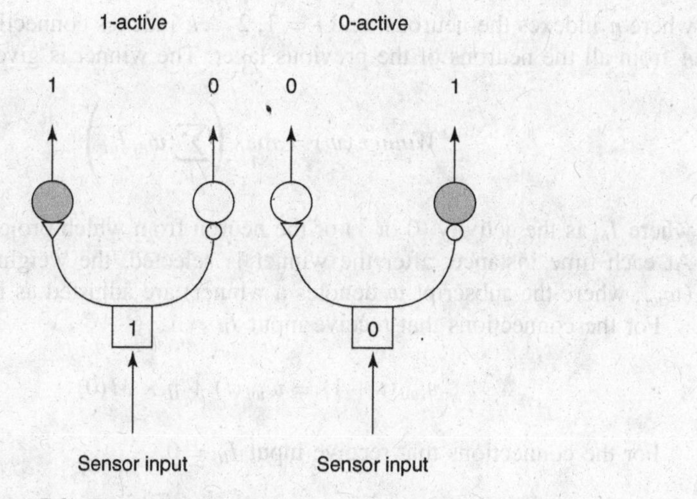

Figure 7.3: The two-active area neuron firing mechanism.

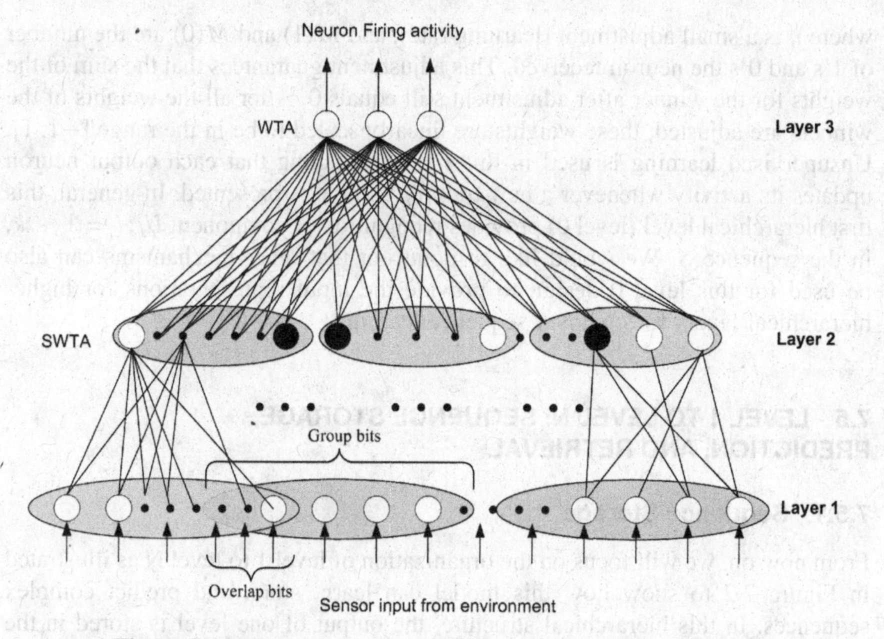

Figure 7.4: Hierarchical structure of modified Hebbian learning.

The second WTA mechanism is used in the output layer (layer 3 in Figure 7.4). Initially, all the weights, w_i, for neurons in the output layer are randomly set with the following conditions:

$$w_{ni} = \pm 1, \text{ and } \sum_i w_{ni} = 0 \tag{7.2}$$

where n indexes the neurons, and $i = 1, 2 \ldots k$ indexes connections onto neuron n from all the neurons of the previous layer. The winner is given by:

$$Winner\,(w) = \max_n \left(\sum_i w_{ni} I_{ni} \right) \tag{7.3}$$

where I_{ni} is the activity (0 or 1) of the neuron from which projection w_{ni} arises. At each time instance, after the winner is selected, the weights of the winner (w_{wi}, where the subscript w denotes a winner) are adjusted as follows:

For the connections that receive input $I_{li} = 1$,

$$w_{wi}(t+1) = w_{wi}(t) + \eta \times M(0) \tag{7.4}$$

For the connections that receive input $I_{li} = 0$,

$$w_{wi}(t+1) = w_{wi}(t) - \eta \times M(1) \tag{7.5}$$

where η is a small adjustment (learning rate), and $M(1)$ and $M(0)$ are the number of 1's and 0's the neuron received. This adjustment guarantees that the sum of the weights for the winner after adjustment still equals 0. After all the weights of the winners are adjusted, these weights are linearly scaled to be in the range $[-1, 1]$. Unsupervised learning is used in this model, meaning that each output neuron updates its activity whenever a new training sample is presented. In general, this first hierarchical level (level 0) provides recognition of component U_i, $i = 1 \ldots k$, in the sequence S. We would like to point out that other mechanisms can also be used for this level 0 design to provide the input representations for higher hierarchical layers for complex sequence learning.

7.5 LEVEL 1 TO LEVEL N: SEQUENCE STORAGE, PREDICTION, AND RETRIEVAL

7.5.1 Sequence Storage

From now on, we will focus on the organization of level 1 to level N as illustrated in Figure 7.2 to show how this model can learn, store, and predict complex sequences. In this hierarchical structure, the output of one level is stored in the input registers of the next higher level. Neurons of the input registers project onto the output neurons of the same level through trainable connections. Initially all output neurons are fully connected to all IRs through untrained links with electrical (resistive) synapses. In the current model, the initial weights for all the output neurons are set to small positive numbers $0.001 < w_i < 0.01$.

Once an input sequence is stored in the input registers, all the output neurons compete and weights of the winning neuron are adjusted. All the weights of projections of active neurons onto a winning neuron in IR are set to 1 (excitatory)

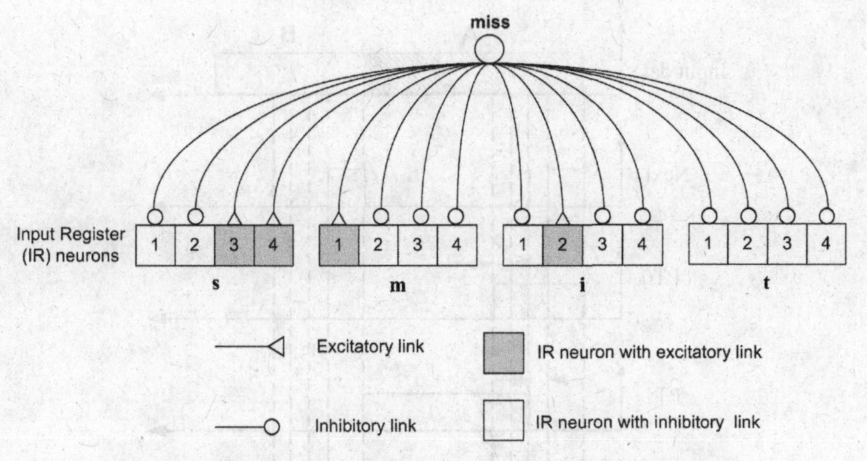

Figure 7.5: Storage of sequence in input register neurons.

and all other weights onto a winning neuron are set to -100 (inhibitory). We employ this strong inhibition to guarantee that once an output neuron is trained to store a sequence, it is excluded from further learning. For instance, consider the IR states as shown in Figure 7.5, where the links with a triangle represent excitatory projections and links with a circle represent inhibitory projections. The locations of the various IRs establish that this neuron stores the letter sequence "miss" (i.e., above the letter "m" there is a excitatory link from the section of the IR neurons representing the first time step). Once an output neuron's links are trained, the neuron responds only to one specific input sequence.

Before discussing the prediction mechanism, we first describe the structure of the IR. In the proposed model, the IR stores the input data selected by WTA in the location indicated by a time pointer, each pattern in a sequence is directed to a different location. The structure of the IR is shown in Figure 7.6, which

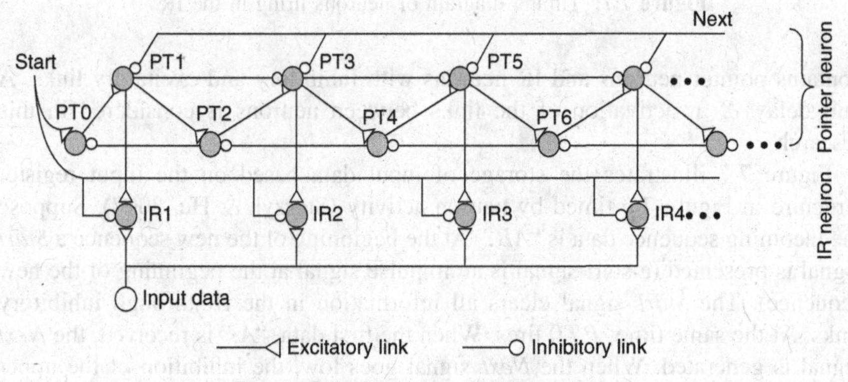

Figure 7.6: Structure of input register.

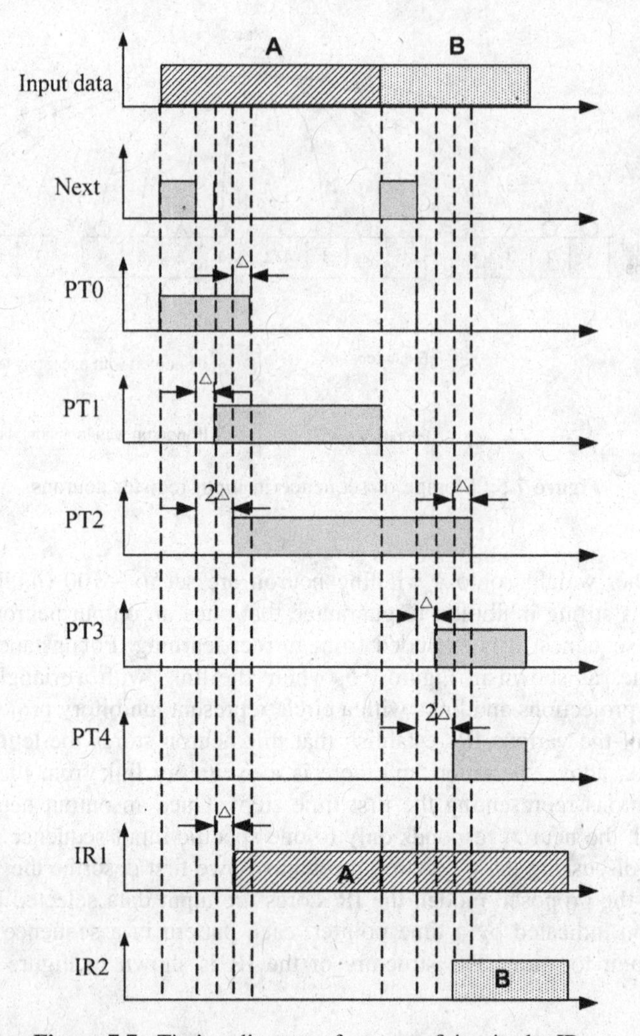

Figure 7.7: Timing diagram of neurons firing in the IR.

contains pointer neurons and IR neurons with inhibitory and excitatory links. A unit delay Δ in activation of the links between neurons is considered in this research.

Figure 7.7 illustrates the storage of input data based on the input register structure in Figure 7.6 timed by neuron activity (Starzyk & He, 2007). Suppose the incoming sequence data is "AB." At the beginning of the new sequence a *Start* signal is presented (a start signal is an impulse signal at the beginning of the new sequence). The *Start* signal clears all information in the IR through inhibitory links. At the same time, $PT0$ fires. When the first data, "*A*," is received, the *Next* signal is generated. When the *Next* signal goes low, the inhibition of the upper pointer neurons is removed. Therefore, after the delay time Δ, $PT1$ will fire.

After one more delay time, the lower pointer neuron $PT2$ fires since it has an excitatory link from $PT1$. At the same time, $PT1$ provides the inhibition to $PT3$. As illustrated in Figure 7.6, since the *Start* signal is low, and both the $PT1$ and the input data neuron are active, input register neuron $IR1$ fires to store the first data in the $IR1$. Assume that after some time, another data "B" is presented, and a pulse signal *Next* is generated. This signal inhibits all the upper pointer neurons $PT1$, $PT3$, $PT5$, and so on. However, $PT2$ continues firing. When the *Next* signal goes low, after the delay time Δ, $PT3$ fires because it is excited by $PT2$. As before, $PT4$ fires after $PT3$ with delay Δ. At the same time, $IR2$ fires because it is excited by $PT3$ and the input data neuron. This will store the data "B" in the second input register, $IR2$. The entire time diagram is illustrated in Figure 7.7.

The process continues until all the input data of the sequence is presented. In this scheme, the lower level pointer neurons provide inhibitory feedback to remove excitation from prior pointer neurons and to excite the next pointer neuron. This approach forms long-term memories (LTM) of the learned sequences. One may make these memories modifiable by allowing training to decay after some specified period of time.

7.5.2 Sequence Prediction

7.5.2.1 Prediction Mechanism Predicting an input sequence is an essential part of sequence learning in this model (Starzyk & He, 2007). By correct prediction, the intelligent system indicates it knows the sequence and does not require additional learning. If there is a single error, the long-term memory is modified to learn the new sequence.

The first stage of prediction is a competition stage. Several sequences stored in LTM compete to determine a unique sequence that may correspond to the input sequence. Once such a sequence is determined, it predicts the consecutive inputs. (Notice that the same mechanism is used if LTM is simply playing back a stored sequence after a high-level node of LTM is triggered by an internal process.) A multiple winner detection neuron (MWDN) is used to detect whether there are multiple winners with trained links. This is achieved by setting the threshold of the MWDN equal to 2. Therefore, it will fire when there are two or more winners in the output layer (this occurs when the sum of the weights of all the winners are the same). The output of the MWDN is connected to the learning flag neuron (LFN) as well as all the prediction neurons (PN) through inhibitory links. This provides a mechanism for setting the proper learning flag signal. The output of the LFN is connected to the learning neuron through an excitatory link. Together with the excitatory links from the end of input sequence neuron (ESN), the whole system provides a proper mechanism for setting the learning signal. It should be noted that each hierarchy level requires its ESN to indicate the end of input sequence for this level. In addition, if an ESN neuron fires in a higher hierarchical level, it automatically generates an ESN signal in all the lower hierarchical levels. Consider an example in which the first level of hierarchy in LTM stores letters, the second level stores words, and the third level stores sentences. The last letter of every word will trigger the activation of the ESN neuron for the second level. The last letter of the last word in every sentence will be followed by the activation of the ESN for the third level, and at the same time, the ESN signal will also be sent to the lower levels (level 2 in this case).

There are three cases of all possible outcomes for the competition stage of the prediction mechanism.

Case 1: *If there is a single winner with trained links in the competition stage, the architecture will either activate the PCN (meaning a correct prediction was made and no learning is needed so far), or activate the LFN (meaning one-shot learning is needed for this new sequence).*

In this case, the MWDN does not fire because it has a threshold of 2. Therefore, PN and LFN are not inhibited. The set of PNs includes one PN corresponding to each output neuron of the next lower level. By a mechanism described in section 7.5.2.3, the LTM acts through the MUX at each time step to activate an excitatory projection onto a PN that represents the prediction of the network for this time step. The time pointer (TP) is incremented with each new symbol (pattern) presented to LTM. As may be seen in Figure 7.2, each PN receives an inhibitory projection from the MWDN, as well as the excitatory projection from the MUX. Since, in this case, the PN is not inhibited by the MWDN, LTM (acting through the MUX) activates the particular PN corresponding to the predicted symbol for the input sequence. Each prediction neuron and its corresponding output neuron from the next lower level form two inputs to a prediction matching neuron (PMN). Firing of a PMN verifies that the predicted symbol corresponds to the input symbol, as shown in Figure 7.8.

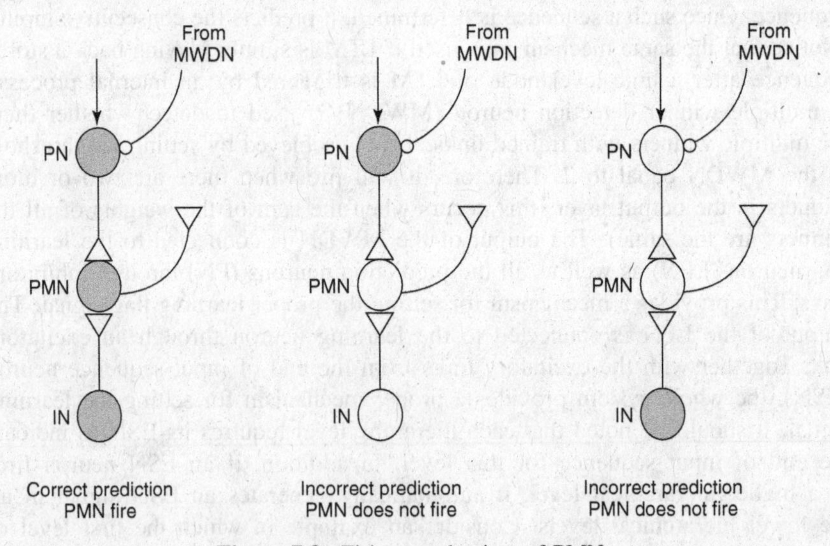

Figure 7.8: Firing mechanism of PMN.

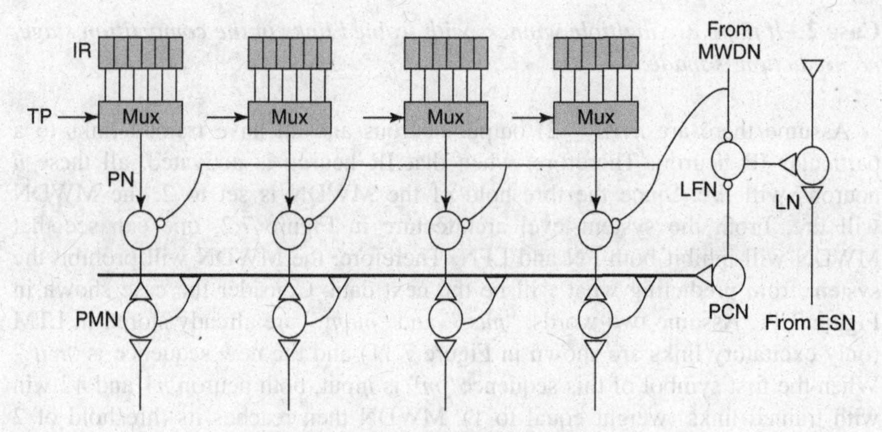

Figure 7.9: Prediction mechanism.

All prediction matching neurons have their outputs connected to the prediction checking neuron (PCN), as shown in Figure 7.9. This neuron fires to indicate there is a correct prediction.

If there is no match, the LFN is set automatically (no inhibition from PCN or MWDN). LFN remains on, and the sequence continues until ESN fires. Thus, the firing of both LFN and ESN triggers the learning neuron, as shown in Figure 7.10(a). If there is a match on the output of the PMN, PCN will fire. Therefore LFN is inhibited. Figure 7.10(b) and (c) show the remaining two conditions for the LN. Figure 7.10(b) indicates that if only the LFN fires (meaning there is no correct prediction), the LN neuron will not fire because the ESN does not fire in this situation. Figure 7.10(c) indicates that if only the ESN fires, the LN will not fire because the LFN does not fire (meaning there is a correct prediction).

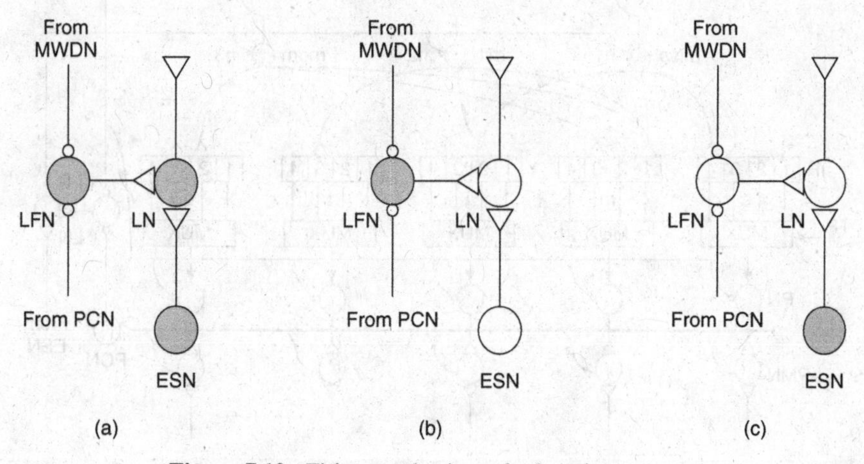

Figure 7.10: Firing mechanism of a learning neuron.

Case 2: *If there are multiple winners with trained links in the competition stage, no prediction is made.*

Assume there are n $(n \geq 2)$ output neurons and all have trained links to a particular IR neuron. Therefore, when that IR neuron is activated, all these n neurons will fire. Since the threshold of the MWDN is set to 2, the MWDN will fire. From the system-level architecture in Figure 7.2, one can see that MWDN will inhibit both PN and LFN. Therefore, the MWDN will prohibit the system from predicting what will be the next data. Consider the case shown in Figure 7.11. Assume two words, "*miss*" and "*mom*," are already stored in LTM (only excitatory links are shown in Figure 7.11) and the new sequence is "*mit*." When the first symbol of this sequence "*m*" is input, both neuron $n1$ and $n3$ win with trained links (weight equal to 1). MWDN then reaches its threshold of 2 and fires. As indicated in Figure 7.11, MWDN inhibits both PN and LFN. Since both neurons are the winners with trained links, it is premature for the network to attempt a prediction (inhibition of all the PNs also reduces energy consumption). When the second symbol "*i*" is presented, neuron $n1$ wins because it receives two excitatory projections from IR, while neuron $n3$ receives an inhibitory projection. In this situation, there is a single winner with trained links (i.e., case 1). MWDN does not fire, removing the inhibition on PN and LFN. With the control of the TP signal through the MUX, $n1$ will predict the next symbol as "*s*," which is not correct in this case. Therefore, PMN will not fire (see Figure 7.8), and PCN does not fire. In this way, LFN will fire because there is no inhibition from PCN. At this time, LN does not fire because ESN does not fire. When the third symbol "*t*" is presented, both $n1$ and $n3$ receive inhibition from IR and neither wins.

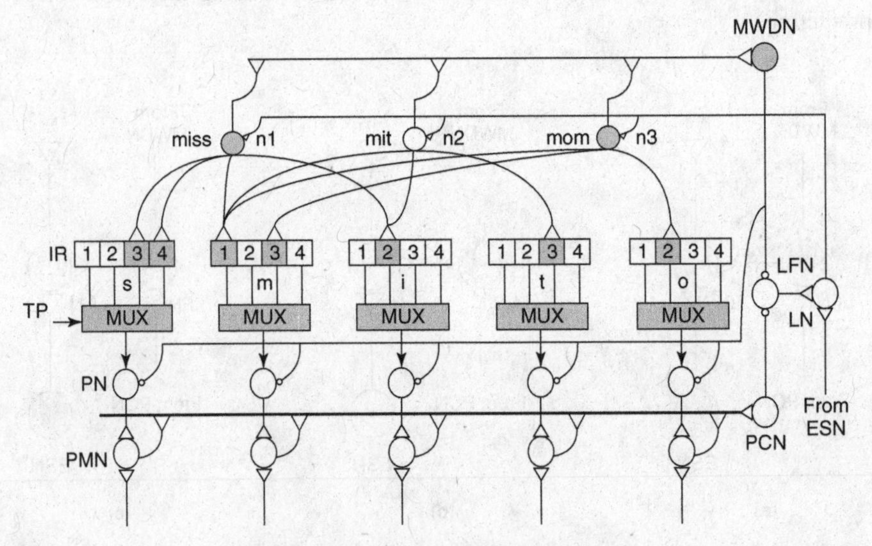

Figure 7.11: LTM and multiple winners.

Assume $n2$ is the winner without lost of generality, this will lead to case 3 in which there is a single winner with untrained links.

Case 3: *If there is a single winner in the output neuron with untrained links, a learning signal will be issued at the end of the sequence, and one-shot learning will be executed to learn this sequence.*

In this situation, the MWDN does not fire, and since the winner has untrained links, PN does not fire. Therefore, the PCN does not fire, allowing the LFN to fire. LFN remains active until ESN fires. The combination of LFN and ESN then causes the LN to fire, and a learning signal activates one-shot learning and adjusts weights according to the previously described rules to learn the sequence "*mit*." Figure 7.11 illustrates the strengthened connections after learning.

From the aforementioned case 1, case 2, and case 3, one can see that under all the conditions of the competition stage, the model can either correctly predict the sequence, or perform one-shot learning at the end of a new sequence to learn such sequence. In the following sections, we will discuss the detailed prediction mechanisms regarding the activation of a prediction neuron and the design of the time-controlled MUX.

7.5.2.2 Activation of Prediction Neuron To perform sequence prediction, each IR neuron is associated with a dual IR neuron. WTA neurons responsible for storing the sequence are linked to dual IR neurons through untrained links. IR neurons connect to their dual neurons through trained links. Thus firing an IR neuron automatically activates its dual neuron. When a sequence is stored in a WTA neuron, connections from the WTA neuron to dual IR neurons corresponding to active IR neurons in the sequence are trained (the bold line in Figure 7.12). When a previously stored sequence is input again, a partially matched sequence may activate the WTA neuron of this sequence. This will activate all dual IR neurons that compose the entire sequence. The structure is shown in Figure 7.12. This structure combined with the time-controlled multiplexer provides the mechanism for the prediction scheme.

7.5.2.3 Time-Controlled Multiplexer The neural network structure of the time-controlled multiplexer is shown in Figure 7.13. The output from WTA activates the dual IR neurons that represent predictions for each time step as discussed in section 7.5.2.2. At a given time step indicated by an active pointer neuron, this dual IR neuron actives the corresponding IR output neuron, and subsequently, the corresponding prediction neuron for the next element of the stored sequence. This predicted data is connected to the PMN, which compares the PN with the actual data and fires if the prediction is correct.

Assume that through the WTA competition, an output neuron that stores "*miss*" is firing. Therefore, this neuron will activate its dual IR neurons. When the time pointer increases to 3, the upper pointer neuron PT5 is firing. In this case, the concurrently active PT5 neuron and the dual IR neuron (that stores the data "*s*")

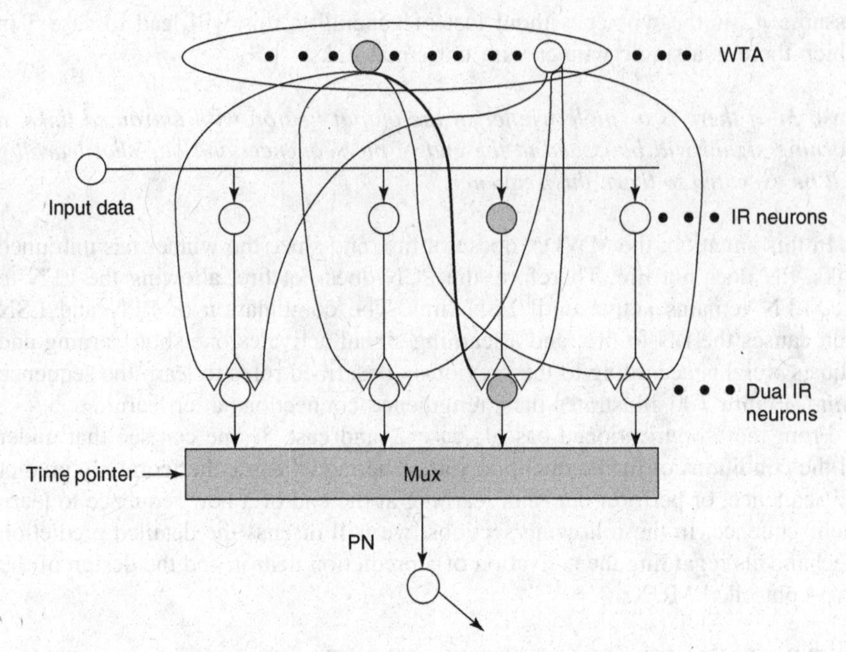

Figure 7.12: Activation of prediction neuron.

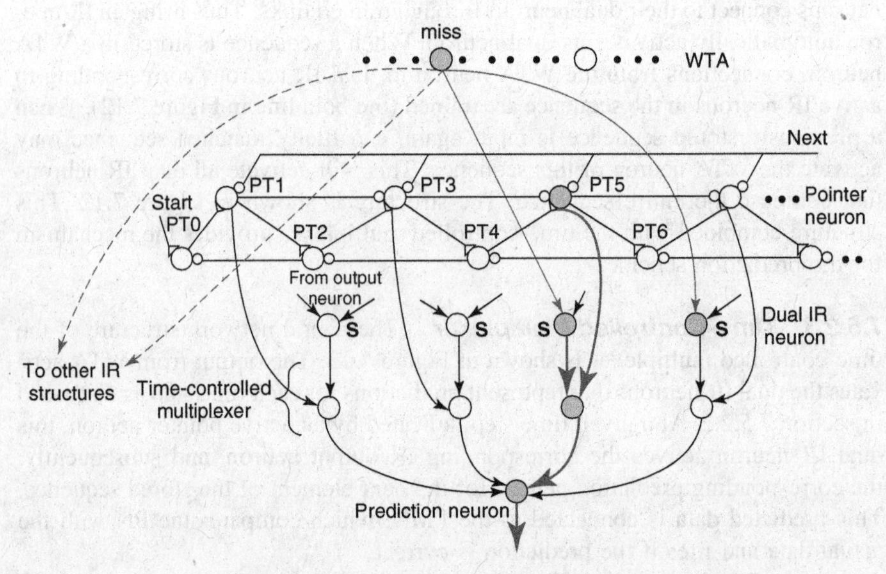

Figure 7.13: Time-controlled multiplexer.

will activate the corresponding time-controlled MUX neuron (active neurons are represented by gray circles in Figure 7.13). This in turn will activate the corresponding PN, and this activation signal will be sent to the PMN to check whether there is a match or mismatch for this predicted data. One should note that Figure 7.13 represents the IR structure that stores letter "*s*" only, while the IR structures for "*m*" and "*i*" are not shown in Figure 7.13.

7.5.3 Sequence Retrieval

Stored spatio-temporal sequences can be retrieved by activating neurons at any hierarchical level through internal processes or by association with a first-level (sensory) input cue. An important element in the process of retrieving the stored sequences is the duration of each element of the sequence. By scaling this time, different speeds of presentation may be achieved. Wang and Arbib (1993) describe a mechanism for storing the presentation time intervals in which timing is related to timing of the input sequences. While it is necessary for applications to reproduce the stored sequence at approximately the pace of the original sequence, it is not necessary in general. For instance, if a person is given a complex task that requires completion of a sequence of operations, timing of the sequence must be determined by the time needed to complete each task, and this timing may be either unknown in advance or may depend on the context in which the task is executed. Biological organisms commonly rely on sensorimotor coordination to provide proper timing for execution of the stored sequences. The speed of retrieval depends on the natural delay and feedback received through sensory inputs, which verifies that a particular element of the sequence was completed. This completion of the sequence element induces presentation of the next element of the stored sequence. Thus the process of retrieval of stored temporal sequences is self-timed and does not depend on any internal clock, but rather on interaction with the environment. This may be a desired feature for many real-world applications where spatio-temporal memories are needed.

7.6 MEMORY REQUIREMENT

Here we give a brief discussion of the memory requirements for this model. Considering the hierarchical level 1 in Figure 7.2, assume that a structure has m_1 input neurons from its lower hierarchical level (i.e., the output neurons form level 0 in Figure 7.2). Therefore, the number of PN and PMN will all be m_1. Assume that in this level, the number of output WTA neurons (that provide the input to the next higher hierarchical level) is m_2, and that the longest sequence that this level can store is of the length l. In this case, the total number of IR neurons, dual IR neurons, and multiplexer neurons will all be equal to $m_1 \times l$. The required number of PT neurons will be $2l$ since such PT neurons can be shared by all the IR neurons. Therefore, in this particular hierarchical level, the total required number of neurons will be $2m_1 + m_2 + 3m_1 \times l + 2l$.

Let us now estimate the required number of interconnection links. From Figure 7.2 one can see that connections between the input of WTA neurons and the dual IR neurons dominate, with the total number of connections equal to $m_1 \times m_2 \times l$. The connections between the PT neurons inside the IR structure will be $4l - 3$ (see Figure 7.6). The other connections include the connections between PMN and the previous hierarchical level output neurons (m_1), PMN and PN(m_1), upper pointer neurons and MUX neurons $(l \times m_1)$, and MUX and PN $(l \times m_1)$. Therefore, the total required connection will be $(m_1 \times m_2 \times l) + (4l - 3) + (2 + 2l) \times m_1$.

Example 7.1: Memory requirements for the model Considering a hierarchical structure of letter–word–sentence structure. Let us assume that we want to store 10,000 words in level 2 and 1,000 sentences in level 3 (see Figure 7.2), and the longest word will have 10 letters while the longest sentence will have 20 words. Therefore, the total required number of neurons in level 2 and level 3 are 1.08×10^4 and 6.21×10^5, respectively, and the required number of interconnections in level 2 and level 3 are 2.6×10^6 and 2.0×10^8, respectively. This estimation provides a rough idea about the memory requirements for the proposed model.

7.7 LEARNING AND ANTICIPATION OF MULTIPLE SEQUENCES

So far, we have shown how the proposed model can correctly and efficiently implement the storage, prediction and retrieval of a complex sequence. we will now give a complete example to demonstrate how this model can learn and predict multiple sequences.

In order to focus on the sequence learning mechanism, we assume that each sensory input from the environment causes a corresponding winning neuron to fire at the output of the first level. Therefore, we will focus on the hierarchical level 1 in Figure 7.2. As in Wang and Yuwono (1995), let "#" be the end-of-sequence marker for this hierarchical level. Assume one needs to store and retrieve the multiple sequences: "*mis#mit#miss#mit#*", as shown in Figure 7.14. Without loss of generality, let this hierarchical level have three output neurons and 27 input neurons (representing the complete alphabet plus the end marker "#"). Each of the output neurons is fully connected to all of the input neurons of the input registers and their initial weights of the synapses are set to $0.001 < w_i < 0.01$.

When the first symbol of the first sequence "m" is activated, the time pointer is set to 1. Since all the weights are initially randomly set, assume neuron 1 $(N1)$ is the winner without loss of generality. Since there is no previous training, there is no prediction at this time. Therefore PCN is not fired, which causes LFN to fire. LFN continues to fire until ESN fires at the end of the first sequence. The combination of LFN and ESN fires LN, which sets the learning signal. One-shot learning is triggered and the weights of the winner are adjusted, as discussed in section 7.5.1 (i.e., the excitatory weights are set to 1 and inhibitory weights are set to -100).

When the first symbol of the second sequence "*m*" is activated, the TP is set to 1. The previously fired neuron ($N1$) becomes the single winner since it receives all the excitatory projections from the first location of the IR. $N1$ predicts the next symbol is "*i*" through the multiplex controlled by the TP signal. In this case the prediction is correct and the corresponding PMN fires, which activates the PCN and inhibits the LFN. When the second symbol "*i*" is presented to the model, TP is incremented to 2. $N1$ is still the only winner since it has two excitatory links and no inhibitory links from the first two locations of the corresponding IRs. The corresponding PN neuron predicts "*s*" as the next input symbol. As this prediction is not true, none of the PMN fires, and the PCN does not fire. Accordingly, LFN is not inhibited and fires. When the third symbol "*t*" is activated, TP is increased to 3. $N1$ is not the winner because it has an inhibitory projection from the IR. Without loss of generality, let us assume $N2$ is the winner. When the end of sequence marker "#" is activated, the ESN fires. When both LFN and ESN fire, LN fires, which sets the learning signal. One-shot learning is triggered and the appropriate weights of the winner ($N2$) are adjusted.

When the first symbol of the third word "*m*" is presented to the model, there will be two winners with trained connections ($N1$ and $N2$). Therefore, MWDN will fire. The firing of MWDN will inhibit all PNs and LFN. The MWDN fires, again, when the second symbol "*i*" is presented. When the third symbol "*s*" is activated, $N1$ is the single winner. MWDN does not fire, and the inhibition of PN and LFN is removed. $N1$ predicts the next symbol is "#", which is not correct. When the fourth symbol "*s*" is activated, both $N1$ and $N2$ are inhibited. Assume $N3$ is the winner without loss of generality. Because $N3$ has no trained link, there is no prediction. Therefore, PCN does not fire and LFN does fire. The procedure continues until the "#" is activated and ESN fires. The combined firing of LFN and ESN sends the learning signal, and one-shot learning is executed, adjusting weights on $N3$.

When the first symbol of the forth sequence "*m*" is activated, there are three winners ($N1$, $N2$ and $N3$). MWDN fires and inhibits the PN and the LFN. When the second symbol "*i*" is activated, these three neurons still are winners. MWDN fires and inhibits PN and LFN. When the third symbol "*t*" is activated, $N2$ is the single winner with trained links. MWDN does not fire, and $N2$ correctly predicts the next symbol, "#". When the last symbol of this sequence "#" is activated, ESN fires. Since LFN does not fire when the prediction is correct, LN does not fire. Therefore, no learning is needed for this last sequence.

Figure 7.14 shows the firing activities of neurons over the course of the above example. The model stored the four sequences in three output neurons (the second and the last sequence being stored in the same neuron: $N2$). One may notice that this anticipation based model does not separate the learning and retrieval processes, which make this model more efficient for sequence learning and retrieval.

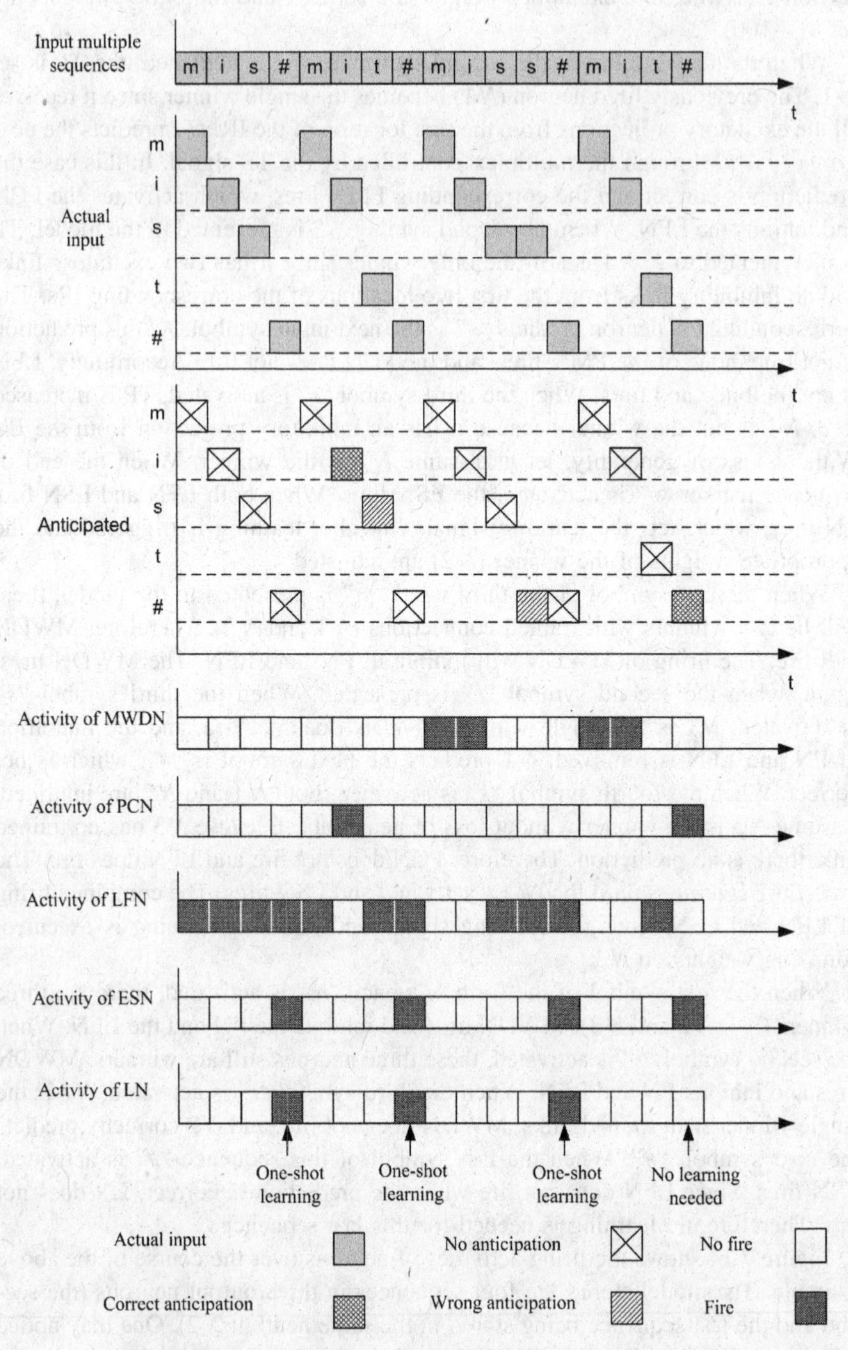

Figure 7.14: Learning and anticipation of multiple sequences.

7.8 CASE STUDY

In this section, a four-level hierarchical structure with letters, words, sentences, and strophes of the popular song "This land is your land" is simulated to illustrate the proposed hierarchical sequence learning model (Starzyk & He, 2007).

The original sensory input data received from the environment contains the scan of 20 × 20 pixel images for the entire alphabet plus three special characters: space, dot, and semicolon for the end of input sequence for word level, sentence level, and strophes level, respectively. There is no distinction between learning and playing back, which means that with each incoming sequence, the model will either correctly predict this sequence, or conduct a one-shot learning at the end of the sequence at a particular level of sequence hierarchy. Figure 7.15 shows the simulation results for this model.

The light text is the input sequence and the bold italic text stands for the correctly predicted elements of the sequence. ① indicates the correct prediction

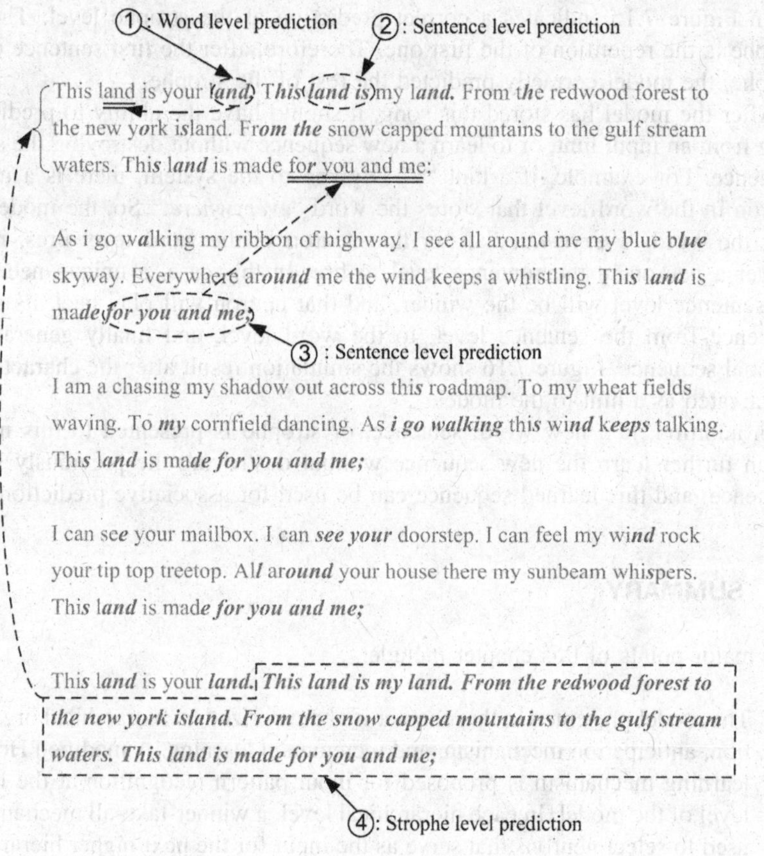

Figure 7.15: Simulation results for the temporal sequence learning model.

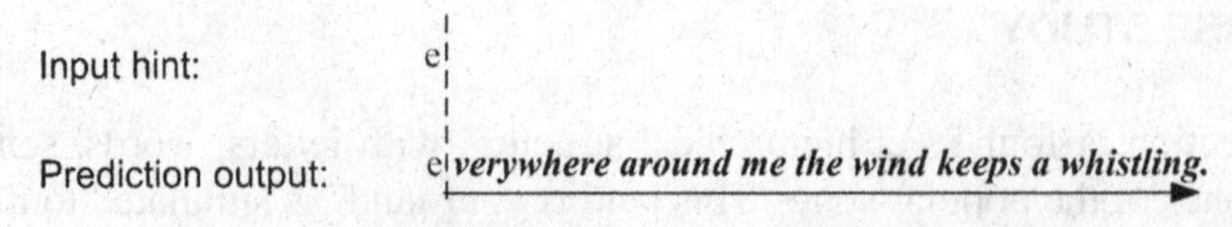

Figure 7.16: Prediction result based on input hint.

at the word level. For instance, when the first letter "*l*" of the second "*land*" is activated, the memory correctly predicted the next symbol, "*a*", because it had already learned the sequence "*land*" when it is presented the first time. ② and ③ in Figure 7.15 indicate correct predictions at the sentence level. "*This land is made for you and me*" is repeated at the end of the second strophe, therefore the words "*for you and me*" were correctly predicted when "This land is made" was presented. The reason "*land is made for you and me*" cannot be predicted after "*This*" as there are other sentences, such as "*This land is your land*" and "*This land is my land*," with the same first three words. Accordingly, the MWDN neuron fired after "*This*" is presented, inhibiting firing of the prediction neuron. ④ in Figure 7.15 indicates a correct prediction at the strophe level. The last strophe is the repetition of the first one. Therefore, after the first sentence of the strophe, the model correctly predicted the rest of the strophe.

After the model has stored this song, it should have the ability to predict the song from an input hint, or to learn a new sequence without destroying the stored sequence. For example, if a hint "*e*" is given to the system, there is a unique neuron in the word level that stores the word "*everywhere*." So, the model will play the word "*everywhere*." After this neuron in the word level fires, it will trigger a neuron in the sentence level to fire. In this case, a unique neuron in the sentence level will be the winner, and that neuron will play back its stored sequence from the sentence level, to the word level, and finally generate the original sequence. Figure 7.16 shows the simulation result after the character "*e*" is activated as a hint to the model.

In addition, if a new word, sentence, or strophe is presented to this model, it can further learn the new sequence without destroying the previously stored sequence, and this learned sequence can be used for associative predictions.

7.9 SUMMARY

The major points of this chapter include:

- The model presented in this chapter is characterized by hierarchical organization, anticipation mechanism, and incremental learning. A modified Hebbian learning mechanism is proposed for input pattern recognition at the lowest level of the model. In each hierarchical level, a winner-take-all mechanism is used to select neurons that serve as the input for the next higher hierarchical level.

- This model can efficiently handle large-scale, multiple, and complex sequence learning, storage, and retrieval. Hierarchical organization and prediction mechanisms are essential components of this model, which enable the system to actively predict the next input at different hierarchical levels. As long as the predicted inputs are correctly verified, no learning is required on any level of the hierarchy. When a mismatch is detected on a given level of the hierarchy, a new sequence on this and all higher levels will be learned by a one-shot learning mechanism.
- The results reported in this chapter suggest that the presented sequence learning model can be an essential element of an intelligent system. The proposed model is hardware oriented and may be of interest for the construction of engineered devices. The use, in this model, of WTA and single neuron representations of symbols flies in the face of the widely held view that biological brains use distributed representations. Furthermore, this model uses memory-like storage of sequential events rather than the shift register structure as used in many literature research. Instead of shifting all inputs as each new element of the sequence is presented to the system, each new element is stored at a specified location in IR in the proposed model.
- The proposed model uses a hierarchical approach that extends the concept of learning by chunking. The entire sequence is learned using only a single presentation of the input data. Any new sequence at any level of the hierarchy is learned by self-organization that allocates the required resources. The proposed approach can store arbitrarily complex sequences so long as the number of distinct subsequences is smaller than the storage capacity expressed by the total number of neurons on various hierarchical levels. We believe that this architecture model is a more natural approach to sequence learning and allows a natural grouping of sequences within the context of learned events.
- In addition to the presented application problem, this hierarchical sequence learning model also has wide application potentials across different domains. For instance, this model can be used for intelligent word processing or speech processing. The model can learn a person's speaking style and later can recognize and predict his or her speech based on some clues. Probably the most important applications of sequence learning are in the embodied intelligence systems, which require constant predictions of incoming information based on observed sequences of events or behaviors.

REFERENCES

Anderson, J. (1995). *Learning and memory*. New York: Wiley.

Ara'ujo, A. F. R., & Barreto, G. A. (2002). Context in temporal sequence processing: A self-organizing approach and its application to robotics. *IEEE Trans. Neural Networks*, *13*(1), 45–57.

Bose, J., Furber, S. B., & Shapiro, J. L. (2005). An associative memory for the on-line recognition and prediction of temporal sequences. *Proc. Int. Joint Conf. Neural Netw.*, pp. 1223–1228.

Bower, G. H., Thompson-Schill, S., & Tulving, E. (1994). Reducing retroactive interference: an interference analysis. *J. Experimental Psychology: Learning, Memory, and Cognition*, 51–66.

Chartier, S., & Boukadoum, M. (2006). A sequential dynamic heteroassociative memory for multistep pattern recognition and one-to-many association. *IEEE Trans. Neural Netw.*, *17*(1), 59–68.

Chun, M. M., & Jiang, Y. (1998). Contextual cueing: Implicit learning and memory of visual context guides spatial attention. *Cognitive Psychology*, *36*, 28–71.

Elman, J. L. (1990). Finding structure in time. *Cognitive Sci.*, *14*, 179–221.

Farkas, I., & Li, P. (2002). DevLex: A self-organizing neural network model of the development of lexicon. In W. D. Grey C. D. Schunn (Eds.), *Proc. Int. Conf. Neural Information Processing*. Singapore: Nanyang Technology University.

George, D., & Hawkins, J. (2005). Invariant pattern recognition using bayesian inference on hierarchical sequences *[Online], Available: http://www.stanford.edu/dil/RNI/DilJeff TechReport.pdf*.

Hawkins, J., & Blakeslee, S. (2004). *On intelligence*. New York: Times Books.

Hawkins, J., & Blakeslee, S. (2007). Why can't a computer be more like a brain. *IEEE Spectrum*, *44*(4), 20–26.

Hawkins, J., & George, D. (2006). Hierarchical temporal memory-concepts, theory, and terminology. *Numenta Inc. [Online], Available: http://www.numenta.com/*.

Hochreiter, S., & Schmidhuber, J. (1997). Long short-term memory. *Neural Computation*, *9*, 1735–1780.

Jacobsson, H. (2005). Rule extraction from recurrent neural networks: A taxonomy and review. *Neural Computation*, *17*(6), 1223–1263.

James, D. L., & Miikkulainen, R. (1995). STARDNET: A self-organizing feature map for sequences. In G. Tesauro, D. S. Touretzky T. K. Leen (Eds.), *Advances in neural information processing systems* (Vol. 7).

Jiang, Y., Olson, I. R., & Chun, M. M. (2000). Organization of visual-short term memory. *J. Experimental Psychology: Learning, Memory and Cognition*, *26*, 683–702.

Jordan, M. I. (1986). Attractor dynamics and parallelism in a connectionist sequential machine. *Proc. Conf. Cognitive Sci. Soc.*, pp. 531–546.

Kumar, A., & Jiang, Y. (2005). Visual short-term memory for sequential arrays. *Memory and Cognition*, *5*(7), 650–658.

Lewkowicz, D. J. (2004). Preception of serial order in infants. *Development Science*, *7*(2), 175–184.

Lewkowicz, D. J. (2006). Learning and discrimination of audiovisual events in human infants: The hierarchical relation between intersensory temporal synchrony and rhythmic pattern cues. *Development Science*, *39*(5), 795–804.

Lewkowicz, D. J., & Ghazanfar, A. A. (2006). The decline of cross-species intersensory perception in human infants. *Proc. National Academy of Sciences*, 103, 6771–6774.

Lewkowicz, D. J., & Marcovitch, S. (2006). Preception of audiovisual rhythm and its invariance in 4- to 10-month-old infants. *Development Science*, *48*, 288–230.

Li, P., & Farkas, I. (2002a). Bilingual sentence processing. In R. Heredial J. Altarriba (Eds.), (pp. 59–85). North Holland: Elsevier Science.

Li, P., & Farkas, I. (2002b). Modeling the development of lexicon with devlex: A self-organizing neural network of lexical acquisition. In W. D. Grey C. D. Schunn (Eds.), *Proc. Annual Conf. Cognitive Science Society*. Mahwah, NJ: Erlbaum.

Li, P., & Farkas, I. (2002c). Modeling the development of lexicon with devlex: A self-organizing neural network of lexical acquisition. *Proc. Annual Conf. Cognitive Science Society*.

Liu, K., & Jiang, Y. (2005). Visual working memory for briefly presented scenes. *J. Vision*, *5*(7), 650–658.

Manning, C. G. N., & Witten, I. H. (1998). Identifying hierarchical structure in sequences: a linear-time algorithm. *Cognitive Psychology*, *36*, 28–71.

McClelland, J. L., & Elman, J. L. (1986a). The trace model for speech preception. *Cognitive Psychology*, *18*, 1–86.

McClelland, J. L., & Elman, J. L. (1986b). Interactive process in speech preception: The TRACE model. In *Parallel distributed processing explorations in the microstructure of cognition. Vol. 2, Psychological and biological models* (pp. 58–121).

McClelland, J. L., & Rumelhart, D. E. (1981). An interactive activation model of context effects in letter preception: Part i – an account of basic findings. *Psychological Review*, *88*, 375–407.

Miikkiulainen, R. (1993). *Subsymbolic: Natural language processing: An integrated model of scripts, lexicon, and memory*. Cambridge, MA: MIT Press.

Miikkulainen, R. (1990). *DISCERN: A distributed artificial neural network model of sScript processing and memory*. Unpublished doctoral dissertation. (Technical Report UCLA-AI-90-05)

Miikkulainen, R. (1992). Trace feature map: A model of episodic associative memory. *Biological Cybernetics*, *66*, 273–282.

Moriarty, D. E., & Miikkulainen, R. (1999). *Advances in the evolutionary synthesis of neural systems*. Cambridge, MA: MIT Press.

Plaut, D. C., McClelland, J. L., Seidenberg, M. S., & Patterson, K. (1996). Understanding normal and impaired word reading: Computational principles in quasi-regular domains. *Psychological Review*, *103*, 56–115.

Pollack, J. B. (1991). The induction of dynamical recognizers. *Machine Learning*, *7*, 227–252.

Schneider, D. W., & Logan, G. D. (2006). Hierarchical control of cognitive processes: Switching tasks in sequences. *J. Experimental Psychology*, *135*(4), 623–640.

Seidenberg, M. S., & McClelland, J. L. (1989). A distributed developmental model of word recognition and naming. *Psychological Review*, *96*, 523–568.

Starzyk, J. A., & He, H. (2007). Anticipation-based temporal sequences learning in hierarchical strcuture. *IEEE Trans. Neural Networks*, *18*, 344–358.

Sun, R., & Giles, C. L. (2001). Sequence learning: From recognition and prediction to sequential decision making. *IEEE Intell. Syst.*, *16*(4), 67–70.

Tani, J. (2003). Learning to generate articulated behavior through the bottom-up and the top-down interaction process. *Neural Networks*, *16*, 11–23.

Tani, J., & Nolfi, S. (1999). Learning to preceive the world as articulated: An approach for hierarchical learning in a sensory-motor systems. *Neural Networks*, *12*, 1131–1141.

Wang, D., & Arbib, M. A. (1990). Complex temporal sequence learning based on short-term memory. *Proc. IEEE*, 78, 1536–1543.

Wang, D., & Arbib, M. A. (1993). Timing and chunking in processing temporal order. *IEEE Trans. Systems, Man, and Cybernetics*, *23*(4), 993–1009.

Wang, D., & Yuwono, B. (1995). Anticipation-based temporal pattern generation. *IEEE Trans. Systems, Man, and Crbernetics*, *25*(4), 615–628.

Wang, D., & Yuwono, B. (1996). Incremental learning of complex temporal patterns. *IEEE Trans. Neural Networks*, *7*(6), 1465–1481.

Wang, L. (1998). Learning and retrieving spatio-temporal sequences with any static associative neural network. *IEEE Trans. Circuits Syst. II, Analog Digit. Signal Process*, *45*(6), 729–739.

Wang, L. (1999). Multi-associative neural networks and their applications to learning and retrieving complex spatio-temporal sequences. *IEEE Trans. Syst., Man, Cybern B, Cybern*, *29*(1), 73–82.

Zhao, X., & Li, P. (2007). Bilingual lexical representation in a self-organizing neural network. In D. S. McNamara J. G. Trafton (Eds.), *Proc. Annual Conf. Cognitive Science Society*.

CHAPTER 8

Hardware Design for Machine Intelligence

8.1 A FINAL COMMENT

As the last chapter of this book, I would like to provide a final comment on the hardware design for self-adaptive intelligent systems. While many of the existing research efforts focus on software development for machine intelligence, recent developments in deep-submicron electronics and nanoelectronics provide the technology platform to design complex and integrated intelligent systems in massive, parallel, and scalable hardware platforms.

Generally speaking, intelligent system models can be simulated in software environments or built in hardware platforms such as very large-scale integration (VLSI) systems and field-programmable gate array (FPGA) technologies. Software implementation may be easier compared to hardware development, however, it has its own inherent limitations. With the existing state of computer technology, it is not practical to develop a network with more than 10,000 neurons in software simulation. This limitation comes from the limited computer speed and their dynamic memory. Therefore, although software-based systems can be used to test some machine learning ideas, they are not sufficient to build the highly integrated and complex intelligent systems. Assuming continuous progress in the computer industry and extrapolating computer efficiency growth into the near future, we can expect computers to be 10 times faster and have 20 times larger random access memory (RAM) in the next 7 years (Arden et al., 2005) (Moore, 2009). This would allow the increase in size of simulated networks to the level of hundreds of thousands of neurons. Yet, as the industry is expected to produce 60 times as many transistors as it produces today (Moore, 2009), the system-level capacity is expected to grow 60 times in the same time period. Thus, the expected capacity of hardware will grow significantly faster than the software speed. In addition, this hardware will operate at increased speed (the same growth rate as the growth rate of computer speed), thus in the next 7 years, the computing capacity of parallel hardware will grow 600 times comparing to 10 times the growth in software speed. This discrepancy between software capacity to

Self-Adaptive Systems for Machine Intelligence, First Edition. Haibo He.

simulate networks of neurons for machine intelligence and hardware capacity to implement them will grow even more in the future. Thus, we need to develop integrated, parallel, and scalable hardware systems, and test their performance in multiple arrays of processors for the development of truly intelligent systems.

Power dissipation is one of the most critical issues for the hardware implementation of such a level of complicated systems. Today, a simple processor running at 3GHz speed dissipates about 100 watts of power. Making a significant array of such processors will be too costly to operate. For comparison, a human brain with the level of 10^{11} neurons dissipates about 10 watts of power. If we consider a neuron to be the elementary processor of intelligent systems, this translates to 10^{-10} watts per neuron. Comparing this to 100 watts dissipated by today's computers, each neuron dissipates on average 10^{12} times less energy. Thus power dissipation could be a key issue for the hardware design of brain-like intelligent systems.

If we look at the dynamic power dissipated by N digital processors working concurrently, we can estimate it to be in proportion to NCV^2f, where C is the total actively switched capacitance of a unit processor, V is the power supply voltage, and f is the frequency of operation. Let us assume that the effective switching capacitance of a unit processor is about $10nF$ (this number corresponds to currently built processors). This capacitance can go down linearly as the feature size will be reduced in the future. Since the feature sizes are reduced at the rate of 2.5 times every 7 years (about 30% reduction every three years (Arden et al., 2005; Maly, 1996), there is not much reduction expected due to this factor. The voltage level is around 1V and will not be significantly reduced in the next 7 years. Thus, if we wish to design a system with 10^{11} processors (not withstanding its cost), its total dynamic power would be:

$$P = 10^{11} \times (10 \times 10^{-9}) \times 1^2 \times f \tag{8.1}$$

Such a system would have to operate at a frequency of $f = 10^{-2}$ Hz to dissipate the same power as the human brain. Since neuron response time is estimated at the order of several milliseconds (let's assume 5 ms here), such a system would be about 20,000 times slower than the human brain while operating on the same power budget. Even if we assume that only 5% of neurons are active at any given time, this would still require the system to operate 1,000 times slower than the brain. Thus, the only viable implementation for a brain-level system in modern VLSI technology is probably in analog VLSI implementation. For instance, many of the pioneering work in analog VLSI circuits for neural network implementation by Mead (1989a, 1989b, Mead & Ismael, 1989) and Vittoz (1985, 1990a, 1990b, 1996, 1998) have provided important insights and design strategies on this. Generally speaking, analog processors are two orders of magnitude smaller (and therefore require to load 100 times smaller capacitance) (Bayraktaroglu, Balkir, & Dundar, 1996; Bayraktaroglu, Ogrenci, Dundar, Balkir, & Alpaydin, 1997), they can also operate at lower voltages. Lowering voltage level to around 40mv in information transformed between neurons (as it is in real neural networks) would lower power requirements over 600 times. This combined with a smaller total capacitance to load would reduce power consumption to levels comparable or lower than those used by the living brain, making hardware implementation of human-level intelligence feasible from an energy point of view.

Handling the power dissipation problem does not guarantee that a system with human-level capacity will be built in the near future. For instance, existing FPGA chips can integrate about 400 picoblaze controllers, this is by no means close to what one would need to design a system with 10^{11} processors. Even if an array of FPGA chips is designed with 10000-chips, it would allow to emulate 4×10^6 processors. Hardware progress in the next 7 years could increase this number to 10^8 processors in a 10,000-chip system (assuming current growth of the number of transistors per chip doubles every 18 months). Even with this capacity, fully parallel implementation will not be comparable to the capacity of the human brain. Thus, a hybrid solution that combines parallel array implementation with software simulation might need to be considered. For instance, if each processor would simulate a cluster of 1,000 neurons, this could bring us closer to the human complexity level. However, 10,000 chips for such a system would carry a high price tag. Assuming a chip cost of, \$1,000 7 years from now, such a system would cost more than \$10 million to build. However, with the current rate of transistor price drop of 1.5 times per year (Moore, 2009), such a system would only cost \$3,000 after 20 years. Power dissipation of such a system would still be on the level of $20KW$, so unless the energy price drops it will be too expensive to operate. This of course will only be true if we learn how to build such large-scale integrated intelligent systems.

I would like to note that all of the aforementioned discussions are based on the assumption that Moore's law will continue in the future for several chip generations. Meanwhile, there are many discussions in the community regarding the ultimate limits of the law with the continuous development of new technologies. From the machine intelligence design point of view, there are significant increasing interests in the community along the direction of using hardware technologies to develop large-scale integrated intelligent systems. For instance, the FACETS (Fast Analog Computing with Emergent Transient States; 2009) project aims to design VLSI neural circuits to emulate substantial fractions of the brain. Their recently designed "chip brain" can implement 200,000 neurons and 50 million synapses, which provides strong support of using analog VLSI technology to potentially design such large-scale and complex intelligent systems. The BioWall (2009) project is another major step toward developing bio-inspired electronic tissues capable of evolving, self-repairing, self-replicating, and learning based on reconfigurable FPGA technologies. The goal of the BioWall project is to develop truly bio-inspired hardware systems for machine intelligence, ranging from "phylogenetic systems, inspired by the evolution of biological species, through ontogenetic systems, inspired by the development and growth of multicellular organisms, to epigenetic systems, inspired by the adaptation of individuals to the environment." It was reported that prototypes ranging from 150 to 3,500 units have been realized and tested, which represents the computational power of about 3,500 FPGAs coupled with an I/O interface.

In closing, I would like to tell one last story regarding hardware design for machine intelligence. I went to the 2009 International Joint Conference on Neural Networks (IJCNN 2009) in Atlanta, Georgia, where I have had the opportunity to hear the latest development on *Memristor* (short for "memory resistor"). Briefly speaking, the concept of memristor was formulated back in 1971 by Dr. Leon Chua, in which he argued that memristor should be considered as the fourth fundamental circuit element based on the symmetry between the resistor, inductor, and capacitor (Chua, 1971). Very recently, Hewlett-Packard Labs announced that their team actually built a nanoscale switching memristor (Tour & He, 2008; Strukov, Snider, Stewart, & Williams, 2008). The exciting news for the machine intelligence community is that memristor could potentially significantly improve the hardware design capability to develop integrated electronic circuits that can mimic the complexity level of neural structures in the human brain. Furthermore, since memristor handles the current and voltage in a similar way to the synapses, that is to say, both of them can build up voltage to a threshold before firing and letting a current pass, it could provide a unique advantage of using memristor to potentially replicate neural information processing in the brain. Therefore, new technologies such as memristor and other emerging techniques could potentially provide us the desired hardware platform to bring such a level of brain-like general-purpose intelligence closer to reality, of course only if we know how to do it. As the understanding of natural intelligence and developing integrated self-adaptive systems to potentially replicate such a level of intelligence remains one of the greatest unsolved scientific and engineering challenges, I hope that the research presented in this book will contribute to this challenging, exciting, and rewarding field.

REFERENCES

Arden, W., Cogez, P., Graef, M., Ishiuchi, H., Osada, T., J. Moon, A. J. R., et al. (2005). International roadmap committee, international technology roadmap for semiconductors, executive summary.

Bayraktaroglu, I., Balkir, S., & Dundar, G. (1996). Annsis: A circuit level simulator for analog neural networks. *Turkish Symposium on Artificial Intelligence and Neural Networks*, pp. 305–310.

Bayraktaroglu, I., Ogrenci, S., Dundar, G., Balkir, S., & Alpaydin, E. (1997). Annsys: An analog neural network synthesis system. *Int. Conf. Neural Netw*., pp. 910–915.

BioWall project [Online], Available: http://lslwww.epfl.ch/biowall/. (2009).

Chua, L. (1971). Memristor-the missing circuit element. *IEEE Transactions on Circuit Theory*, *CT-18*(5), 507–519.

FACETS (fast analog computing with emergent transient states) project [Online], Available: http://facets.kip.uni-heidelberg.de/index.html. (2009).

Maly, W. (1996). The future of ic design, testing, and manufacturing. *IEEE Design and Test of Computers*, *13*(4), 8–91.

Mead, C. A. (1989a). Adaptive retina. In C. Mead & M. Ismail (Eds.), *Analog VLSI implementation of neural systems* (pp. 239–246). Norwell, MA: Kluwer Academic.

Mead, C. A. (1989b). *Analog VLSI and neural systems*. Reading, MA: Addison Wesley.

Mead, C. A. (1990). Neuromorphic electronic systems. *Proc. IEEE*, 78, 1629–1636.

Mead, C. A., & Ismael, M. (Eds.). (1989). *Analog VLSI implementation of neural systems*. Norwell, MA: Kluwer Academic.

Moore, G. E. (2009). Our revolution *[Online], Available: http://www.sia-online.org/galleries/default-file/Moore.pdf*.

Strukov, D. B., Snider, G. S., Stewart, D. R., & Williams, R. S. (2008). The missing memristor found. *Nature*, *453*, 80–83.

Tour, J. M., & He, T. (2008). Electronics: The fourth element. *Nature*, *453*, 42–43.

Vittoz, E. A. (1985). The design of high-performance analog circuits on digital CMOS chips. *IEEE J. Solid-State Circuits*, *20*(3), 657–665.

Vittoz, E. A. (1990a). Analog VLSI implementation of neural networks. *IEEE Int. Symp. Circuit and Systems*, 4, 2524–2527.

Vittoz, E. A. (1990b). Future of analog in the VLSI environment. *IEEE Int. Symp. Circuit and Systems*, 2, 1372–1375.

Vittoz, E. A. (1996). Biology inspired circuits. *IEEE Micro*., *16*(5), 10.

Vittoz, E. A. (1998). Analog VLSI for collective computation. *IEEE Int. Conf. Electronics, Circuits and Systems*, 2, 3–6.

LIST OF ABBREVIATIONS

AA	Arithmetic Average
ACT	Adaptive Conformal Transformation
AD	Action Dependent
AdaBoost	Adaptive Boosting
ADASYN	Adaptive Synthetic Sampling
ADP	Adaptive Dynamic Programming
AUC	Area Under Receiver Operating Characteristic Curve
Bagging	Bootstrap Aggregating
BAM	Bidirectional Associative Memory
BC	Borda Count
BDNN	Bayesian Decision-based Neural Network
BM	Boundary Movement
BP	Biased Penalties
BPTT	Backpropagation Through Time
BSVC	Binary Support Vector Classifier
CBA	Class–Boundary Alignment
CBO	Cluster-Based Oversampling
CFD	Coincident Failure Diversity
CSRN	Cellular Simultaneous Recurrent Neural Network
DDM	Distribution Distance Mapping
DHP	Dual Heuristic Dynamic Programming
DPE	Data Processing Element
DPN	Data Processing Network
EKF	Extended Kalman Filter
EM	Expectation-Maximization

Self-Adaptive Systems for Machine Intelligence, First Edition. Haibo He.

ENN	Edited Nearest Neighbor
ESN	End of Input Sequence Neuron
FC	Frequency of Character
fMRI	Functional Magnetic Resonance Imaging
FPGA	Field-Programmable Gate Array
FW	Frequency of Word
GA	Geometric Average
GD	Generalized Diversity
GDHP	Globalized Dual Heuristic Dynamic Programming
GP	Genetic Programming
GSM	Growing Semantic Map
GSVM-RU	Granular Support Vector Machines—Repetitive Undersampling
GSVMs	Granular Support Vector Machines
HANN	Hetero-Associative Neural Networks
HDP	Heuristic Dynamic Programming
HKME	Hybrid Kernel Machine Ensemble
INOUA	Input–Output Association
IOA	Input Only Association
IPE	Information Processing Element
IPN	Information Processing Network
IR	Input Register
JOUS-Boost	Over/Under-Sampling with Jittering
KBA	Kernel–Boundary Alignment
KL	Kullback–Leibler Distance
KNG	Kernel Neural Gas
KNN	K-Nearest Neighbor
KW	Kohavi–Wolpert Variance
LB	Lower Bound
LFN	Learning Flag Neuron
LN	Learning Neuron
LOO	Leave-One-Out
LSE	Least Square Error
LSTM	Long Short-Term Memory
LTM	Long-Term Memory
MANN	Multi-Associative Neural Network
Memristor	Memory Resistor
MLP	Multilayer Perceptron

MTS	Mahalanobis-Taguchi System
MUX	Multiplexer
MWDN	Multiple Winner Detection Neuron
NCL	Neighborhood Cleaning Rule
NLSV	Negative Local Support Vector
OFS	Orthogonal Forward Selection
OOA	Output-Only Association
OSS	One-Side Selection
PCA	Principal Component Analysis
PCN	Prediction Checking Neuron
PDP	Parallel Distributed Processing
PE	Processing Element
PMN	Prediction Matching Neuron
PN	Prediction Neuron
PR	Precision-Recall
PSO	Particle Swarm Optimization
PSVM	Proximal Support Vector Machine
RAM	Random Access Memory
RAMOBoost	Ranked Minority Oversampling in Boosting
RNN	Recurrent Neural Networks
ROC	Receiver Operating Characteristic
ROWLS	Regularized Orthogonal Weighted Least Square
RS	Ranked Subspace
RVM	Relevance Vector Machine
SALH	Simple Active Learning Heuristic
SCL	Statistics of Capital Letter
SCM	Support Cluster Machine
SDA	Stepwise Discriminate Analysis
SDC	SMOTE with Different Costs
SIFT	Scale Invariant Feature Transform
SLR	Short Latency Response
SMOTE	Synthetic Minority Oversampling Technique
STM	Short-Term Memory
SVC	Support Vector Classifier
SVM	Support Vector Machine
SWTA	Stiff WTA
TAF-SVM	Total Margin-based Adaptive Fuzzy SVM
TCF	Three Curve Fitting

TD	Temporal-Difference
TLRN	Time-Lagged Recurrent Neural Network
TP	Time Pointer
UB	Upper Bound
VC	Vapnik–Chervonenkis Dimension
VLSI	Very Large-Scale Integration
VSTM	Visual Short-Term Memory
WTA	Winner-Take-All

INDEX

Printed in the United States
By Bookmasters